Anglicanism: A Global Communion

Anglicanism

A Global Communion

EDITED BY
Andrew Wingate
Kevin Ward
Carrie Pemberton
Wilson Sitshebo

 CHURCH

CHURCH PUBLISHING INCORPORATED, NEW YORK

Library of Congress Cataloging-in-Publication Data
Anglicanism: a global communion/edited by Andrew Wingate [et al.]
    p. cm
    Includes bibliographical references.
    ISBN 0-89869-304-7 (pbk.)
    1. Anglican Communion. I. Wingate, Andrew
    BX5005.A55   1998   98-20897
    283—dc21   CIP

Church Publishing Incorporated
445 Fifth Avenue
New York NY 10016

5 4 3 2 1

Typeset by York House Typographic Ltd, London
Printed and bound in Great Britain by Biddles Ltd, Guildford and King's Lynn

Foreword by the
Archbishop of Canterbury

I am delighted to have this opportunity of commending this comprehensive survey of the life of the Anglican Communion, which has been compiled by the Centre for Anglican Communion Studies at the Selly Oak Colleges.

What is so inspiring is that it brings together a wide range of voices from every corner of the globe, many of them hitherto unknown to more than a few beyond their own regions, telling the stories of the Church which we all need to hear. The volume will be an enormously important resource to the Communion, not only in this year of the Lambeth Conference, but well beyond it into the new millennium.

What may seem extraordinary to some people is the extent to which the Churches of the Communion, in really quite a short time, have become so firmly rooted in their own cultures and peoples. Whilst we have to acknowledge that 100 years ago, there was some truth in the charge that world-wide Anglicanism was little more than the Church of England abroad, I know from my extensive travels around the world that it is no longer the case. We can truly claim to be an international communion, and when I visit the Church of Uganda, or the Anglican Church of Kenya or the Episcopal Church of Brazil, I know that I am visiting the peoples of those countries, who have found Christ through membership of their own Church, but who value the richness of belonging to a world-wide body who hold fundamental teachings and traditions in common. This collection of essays powerfully demonstrates that old adage of Anglicanism 'Unity in Diversity'.

This feature of Anglicanism is no accident. Nor is it some new discovery. It lies at the heart of the development of the Anglican tradition. From our very roots in the sixth century, with the arrival of St Augustine in Canterbury, and the need to develop a church with the existing British and Irish Christian traditions, 'ordered freedom' became the watchword. In Britain and, gradually, elsewhere as Anglicanism grew, we have encouraged a style of being church which has encouraged open discussion and argument, we have allowed a great deal of latitude in the practice of our faith whilst remaining confident in the fundamentals as contained in Scripture and the early Creeds and Councils. As it was said in an appreciation of William Temple:

> He welcomed disagreement because it is the difference of our thoughts
> which makes it worthwhile to pool them.

We have internalized dissent. We have allowed the battles, such as they have been, to be conducted within the Church, rather than exclude those with whom we disagree. Uncomfortable as that may be at times, I believe it has served us well.

Of course, it was during the Reformation that this genius of Anglicanism became institutionalized. Some historians try to claim that the Church of England is no more than the result of a personal and political whim of King Henry VIII. This is far from the truth. We all know well that the theological controversies which raged in the rest of Europe were alive in England as well, and many of the great figures of that era who ultimately remained loyal to Rome sought to bring about change in the Church, as well as those of a more radical bent, who in the end were able to advance in the row between King and Pope. Anglicans have always asserted that our Communion is Reformed and Catholic. At the Reformation nothing of credal importance was lost and many good traditions were retained. However those doctrines and customs which had been added by the medieval church were reformed in the light of Holy Scripture, the yardstick of Christian truth and belief.

Few within the Church today would dispute the fact that the interplay between the life of the Church and the life of the nation – wherever we live – is as inevitable as it is sensitive. It was that recognition which lay at the heart of the Elizabethan Settlement. Elizabeth I sought to unite her people under one monarch and one Church. In order to do that, she was pragmatic enough to recognise the need for flexibility, for diversity, and that, in the context of sixteenth-century England, is what the 39 Articles and the Book of Common Prayer (although the latter was not finalized in its present form until 1662) sought to do. Just as Pope Gregory advised Augustine to 'draw upon anything that will help you to bring the faith to others', so, in a mirror image of that extraordinary breadth of vision, Article XXIV states:

> It is not necessary that Traditions and Ceremonies be in all places one, or utterly alike; for at all times they have been divers, and may be changed according to the diversities of countries, times and men's manners.

That sense of 'living with difference' which has been fundamental to the Anglican traditions remains a powerful concept not just for the Church but for the world. So many of the contributions to this volume are written from contexts where people have resorted to violence and oppression to rid themselves of those with whom they disagree that we need to hold on to our vision firmly. It is not an excuse for laziness, however. God continues to challenge us to deepen our unity, to move onwards towards truth and peace – his truth, revealed in Jesus Christ, and the 'peace which passes all understanding'.

I hope all who read this valuable collection of essays will be renewed in their journey.

Contents

Section One: The Church in worship, spirituality and theology

SECTION TWO: The life of the Church

SECTION THREE: The Church in society

SECTION FOUR: Mission of the Church

SECTION FIVE: The Church and the future

Contributors

Riah Abu El-Assal is co-adjutor Bishop of Jerusalem.

Afe Adogame is a Nigerian priest completing PhD studies on the Aladura and Independent Churches of Nigeria, at Bayreuth University, Germany.

Georges Titre Ande is the Directeur of the Institut Supérieur Théologique Anglican in Bunia, Democratic Republic of the Congo. The ISThA is the provincial theological college and has recently gained accreditation from the government of the DRC.

Allan Anderson, Director of the Centre for New Religious Movements, Selly Oak Colleges, is a South African who was a member of a black-majority Pentecostal Church there.

J. Aruldoss is a Senior Lecturer at the American College, Madurai, South India.

Brigalia Bam is General Secretary of the South African Council of Churches.

Harcourt Blackett is a Roman Catholic priest from the Caribbean, at present Lecturer in Ecumenism and Mission at Mindolo Institute, Zambia.

Joyce Carlson is a lay member of the Church of Canada with First Nation connections.

Richard Carter is Chaplain, the Melanesian Brotherhood, Honiara, Solomon Islands.

Christabel Chamarette is a former member of the Anglican Social Responsibilities Commission in Australia. She is a psychologist, spending ten years working in prisons, and an environmentalist. A senator for the Green Party 1991–96, she has also worked in Bangladesh.

Russell Chandran, formerly Principal of the United Theological College, Bangalore, is now retired.

Diane Clutterbuck is a Methodist deaconess, formerly Overseas Service Secretary of the Methodist Church Overseas Division.

Esla Crawford is Diocesan President of the Mothers' Union, Trinidad and Tobago.

Pervez Deen is a Senior Lecturer in English at St John's College, Agra.

Reena Deen also lectures in Agra.

Andrew Deuchar is the Archbishop of Canterbury's Secretary for Anglican Communion Affairs.

Esther de Waal is a Church historian. In recent years, she has specialized in the study and practice of Benedictine, Celtic and other areas of spirituality.

Griphus Gakuru, ordained in the Church of Uganda, is now working as a priest in Birmingham Diocese, UK, having gained his PhD in Old Testament studies at Cambridge University.

Glynne Gordon-Carter is Jamaican. She worked as Principal of an Anglican secondary comprehensive school in Trinidad. For the past ten years she has been employed by the Church of England General Synod as Secretary to the Committee for Minority Ethnic Anglican Concerns.

Martin Heath is Mission Personnel Secretary, USPG, with a long association with South Asia.

John Hind is Bishop of Gibraltar in the Diocese of Europe.

Paula Hollingsworth is an Anglican priest, Tutor at Crowther Hall and on the staff of an inner-city parish in Birmingham. She was formerly a CMS Mission Partner in Uganda.

Martha Johnston Horne has been Dean and President of the Protestant Episcopal Theological Seminary in Alexandra, Virginia, since 1994. She is an ordained priest, a wife, and the mother of two sons.

Penny Jamieson is Bishop of Dunedin, New Zealand: the first woman diocesan bishop.

Amos Kasibante is a priest from Uganda, formerly Tutor at the (then) College of the Ascension. He is now a Lecturer at St Michael's College, Llandaff.

John L. Kater is Professor of Ministry Development at the Church Divinity School of the Pacific, Berkeley, California, having previously worked in Montreal, New York and Panama Dioceses.

James Keetile is a parish priest in the Diocese of Kimberley and Kuruman, South Africa.

Rosemary Kinyanjui is a Provincial Worker for the Mothers' Union in Kenya.

Samuel Isamu Koshiishi is ordained in and Acting General Secretary of Nippon Sei Ko Kai.

Una Kroll is an Anglican solitary in life vows. She lives in a small border town between Wales and England, and is a priest in the Church in Wales.

Kwok Pui-lan is Professor of Theology, Episcopal Divinity School, Cambridge, Massachusetts, USA. She is author of *Chinese Women and Christianity 1860–1927* and *Discovering the Bible in the Non-Biblical World*.

Aasuly Lande, Professor of Mission at Lund University, previously lectured at Selly Oak.

Barbara Lawes is World-Wide Projects Officer, Mothers' Union.

Harold T. Lewis is Rector of Calvary Episcopal Church, Pittsburgh, USA. He was formerly Executive Director of the Office of Black Ministries, Episcopal Church in the USA.

Gordon Light is Principal Secretary to the Primate of Canada. He was formerly Dean of St Paul's Cathedral, Cariboo, Province of British Columbia, and Ecumenical Officer, City of Winnipeg, Diocese of Rupert's Land.

Julie Lipp-Nathaniel is a Tutor at the United College of the Ascension, Selly Oak, and an ordained pastor of the Church of South India.

Lesley Orr Macdonald MA BD PhD is a feminist historian, theologian and activist, based at New College, University of Edinburgh. She is a member of the (Presbyterian) Church of Scotland, and of the ecumenical Iona Community. Lesley is currently involved in a range of ecumenical and international initiatives/networks in response to the global crisis of violence against women.

Jaci Maraschin is a priest of the Episcopal Church of Brazil and Professor of Religion, Methodist University São Paulo. A musician and author, he is a member of ARCIC and the WCC Faith and Order Commission.

Edward Saw Marks, a layman from the Church in Myanmar (Burma), now working in Singapore, was previously Director of Communications in the Diocese of Rangoon.

James Minchin is an Australian priest, working in Melbourne, and also a trained musician. He has worked in Singapore and England.

Philip Mokuku recently retired from 20 years as Bishop of Lesotho.

Esther M. Mombo, a graduate of St Paul's United Theological College, Limuru, Kenya, is at present undertaking PhD research into the Quaker mission in Kenya at Edinburgh University. She was formerly lecturer at St Paul's Theological College, Kapsabet, Diocese of Eldoret, Church of the Province of Kenya.

Enid Morgan, an ordained priest of the Church in Wales, is Director of the Board of Mission, Welsh-speaking.

Robert Mumbi is a parish priest from Zambia who has contributed to the Jubilee 2000 campaign in Britain.

Beatrice Musindi, an Anglican lay person from Bugisu, eastern Uganda, is now living in Newport, Wales, bringing up her family.

Tim Naish, an Anglican priest and CMS Mission Partner, who worked in what was then Zaire, is now a Lecturer at Mukono Theological College, Uganda.

Michael Nazir-Ali is Bishop of Rochester. He was previously General Secretary of CMS and former Bishop of Raiwind, Pakistan.

Bruno Ndriamahafahana has been Youth Officer for the Anglican Church in Madagascar for many years.

Njongonkulu Ndungane is Archbishop of Cape Town. He was previously Bishop of Kimberley and Kuruman.

Las Newman is Caribbean Regional Secretary, International Fellowship of Evangelical Students and Lecturer at the Jamaica Theological Seminary.

Livingstone Ngewu is Lecturer and Chaplain at the University of Transkei. He was formerly Visiting Fellow at the College of the Ascension.

Marc Nikkel is a priest from the USA who worked for many years with the Episcopal Church of the Sudan, sponsored jointly by the Episcopal Church in the USA and CMS.

Edith Njoki Njiiri is an Anglican priest in the Diocese of Kirinyaga, Church of the Province of Kenya.

Martha Matshidiso Nkoane was raised in Alexandria township, near Johannesburg, and is a primary health trainer in West Rand. A member of the Anglican Women's Fellowship, she writes on health, AIDS care delivery and environmental issues.

Clavéra B. Ntukamazima is President of the Mothers' Union in Bujumbura, Burundi.

Ken Okeke, a Nigerian priest, is West Africa Secretary of the Church Mission Society.

Cyril Okorocha, a priest from Nigeria, works as a staff member of the ACC, responsible for evangelism.

Helena Oliver de Wallis, an Argentinian, studied anthropology at Córdoba University, and works among the Mataco Indian communities of northern Argentina, living there with her anthropologist husband.

Akin Omoyajowo is a Nigerian priest completing PhD studies on the Aladura and Independent Churches of Nigeria at Bayreuth University, Germany.

Eddie Ong is a parish priest and Archdeacon in the Diocese of West Malaysia.

Luke Pato is Principal of the College of the Transfiguration, Grahamstown, South Africa. He is a former Tutor at the College of the Ascension.

Jayasiri Peiris is an Anglican priest and theological teacher from Sri Lanka.

Carrie Pemberton is an NSM curate in Ely Diocese, a freelance writer, researcher and mother of exuberant children. She was on the staff of ISThA, Bunia, Congo and has recently completed a doctorate at Cambridge University on the emergence of African Women's Theologies.

M. Louise Pirouet has worked in higher education in Uganda and in Cambridge, UK. She has been actively involved with issues of refugees in East Africa and Sudan and, in Britain, on matters related to asylum.

John Pobee belongs to the Church in Ghana and has been Director of the theological education programme at the World Council of Churches for many years.

Michael Poon is vicar of St Mark's Church and Principal of a school in Macau, where he serves on the Government Education Committee. He is also Head of Doctrinal Studies Department, Minghua Theological College, Hong Kong.

Kripaveni Prakasha Rao, ordained in the Church of South India, formerly worked in the Government Social Welfare Department.

Victor Premasagar, formerly Principal of the Andhra Christian Theological College, Bishop of Medak, and Moderator of the Church of South India, is now retired.

Peter Price was General Secretary, USPG, at the time of the writing of his chapter. He is now Bishop of Kingston, Southwark Diocese.

Mano Ramalshah is Bishop of Peshawar, north-west Pakistan. He worked for CMS in Britain and Pakistan through USPG.

Tiki Raumati is a Maori Anglican priest who trained at St John's College, Auckland. He has held both Maori and Pakeha (European) appointments.

Christina Rees is a writer and broadcaster and member of the General Synod. She is also Chair of National WATCH (Women and the Church), a forum for promoting women's ministry in the Church of England.

Israel Selvanayagam, a lecturer at Wesley College, Bristol, was previously on the staff of Tamil Nadu Theological Seminary for many years.

Nellie Siba is a Mother's Union worker in Ysabel, upholding MU objectives in the Diocese, providing speakers on health, agriculture, sanitation, nutrition, etc. She leads Bible study for those who can and do not read.

Wilson Sitshebo is an Anglican priest, and Tutor at the United College of the Ascension. He was born in Zimbabwe, and formerly Warden of Bishop Gaul Theological College, Harare. He is currently working on a PhD with Birmingham University on African views on death.

Fannie Storr, who retired recently as Health Officer at USPG, has vast experience in this field throughout the Communion.

Oswald Swartz is Diocesan Secretary and parish priest in the Diocese of Kimberley and Kuruman.

Sally Thompson is a social scientist and Secretary to the Family Network of the Anglican Communion.

Louise Vincer was assistant to Barbara Lawes at the Mothers' Union until recently, when she began training for the priesthood at Westcott House, Cambridge.

Hellen Wangusa is a Provincial Worker for the Mothers' Union in Uganda.

Kevin Ward served for 15 years as a CMS Mission Partner in Uganda (1975–90) and was ordained a priest of the Church of Uganda. More recently he has been a parish priest in Halifax in Wakefield Diocese, UK, and now lectures in African religious studies at Leeds University, UK.

Emma Wild is a CMS Mission Partner working in the Boga region of the Democratic Republic of the Congo, involved in theological education and developmental work for men and women.

Trevor Williams, a member of the Church of Ireland, is leader of the Corrymeela Community in Northern Ireland.

Andrew Wingate is an Anglican priest. He has been a Lecturer at Tamil Nadu Theological Seminary, South India. On return to Britain, he became

Principal, West Midlands Ministerial Training Course, Queen's College, and is currently Principal, United College of the Ascension.

Diana Witts is General Secretary of the Church Mission Society. Her long period of mission service was in Africa.

Jeremiah Guen Seok Yang was the first Korean Anglican to gain a British PhD, and is a Lecturer at Sungkonghoe University, Seoul.

Introduction

The Centre for Anglican Communion Studies (CEFACS) was established by USPG and CMS at the College of the Ascension and Crowther Hall in Selly Oak, Birmingham, in 1992, with the active encouragement of the Anglican Consultative Council. Using the facilities already available, and inspired by the earlier example of St Augustine's, Canterbury, the project aims to bring together Anglicans from around the Communion to reflect on the history of Anglicanism and, more especially, on the contemporary issues that have emerged from the many contexts of Anglican Provinces and dioceses, with a focus on mission, ministry, ecumenism and inculturation. Within any one academic year members of the seminar programme come from, on average, fifteen Provinces, and this represents therefore rather a special, if not unique, opportunity for such sustained encounter.

What has been apparent from the beginning is the paucity of books which represent the breadth of the Communion with which we are in day-to-day contact. Most of the easily available books – and there are many good ones – though they may have the word 'Anglican' in their titles, are, in fact, written about the Church of England or the Episcopal Church in the USA, and their authors tend to come from those Provinces. Books from other Provinces are there, of course, but are not easily available outside those Provinces and do not provide a breadth of cover. Moreover, work in the Centre and Selly Oak has brought us into contact with a whole range of potential writers, many of whom have been with us in Birmingham. As one of the two Directors of CEFACS, Andrew Wingate had the idea of bringing such writers together to provide a volume of essays that would show to fellow-Anglicans and ecumenical friends the breadth of experience and reflection taking place throughout the worldwide Communion. The approach of the Lambeth Conference of 1998, when worldwide Anglicanism will be more to the fore than ever before, seemed a suitable occasion to work towards.

We make no apology for having as many as four editors. Much work has been involved and, between us, we have a wide range of backgrounds and experience. The first four contributions are one from each of us, and have not been categorized as others are. It is important to say at the outset that we do not claim that our authors are 'representative' of each Province included. It has been emphasized to the authors that they are to write as individuals. The range of subjects is also very wide and can only be covered by one or two essays from different parts of the world. The end result is a kaleidoscope of essays, giving over all, we hope, a glimpse of the richness of life within the Anglican Communion and of the kind of reflection that is going on.

Editing has been for length and clarity. But the various styles of communication have been left and are faithful to content. One or two Provinces are not represented; this is not by design, but because those asked from that place have not returned their essays. Most essays are written by natives of the Province or diocese and, where overseas persons are writing, it is only when they have direct and extensive experience in the places concerned. Even within more than 70 essays, it is clearly impossible to provide 'balance' on each subject. But we do hope that, even where readers disagree with an author, they may value reading a reflection coming from a new situation or perspective. Essays are also mainly short, to keep within a reasonable total length. Again we hope they will stimulate thought and the possibility of further reading, rather than appear lacking because they do not give all the answers. Short bibliographies are appended to many of the essays. These are necessarily short, but we hope will give interested readers somewhere to look if they wish to go further. We hope the book may be a resource for such reflection around the Communion. The book provides an opportunity for new writers, and we hope that they will be encouraged to write more in the future. The vast majority of the essays have been especially written for this book. The one or two exceptions where pieces have been composed for other occasions are acknowledged, and have been edited to suit the purposes of this book.

We are conscious that essays are almost all in English. We have included one short piece in French as a sign of good intent, and an earnest that future books from the Communion should allow for contributions in various languages.

There are no essays from older parts of the Communion on standard subjects which can be found in other books. The small number of essays appearing from these countries, including the Church of England, are on particular cultural issues within those Churches. The essays are divided into sections; this is to make the book manageable, but we are also aware that many of the essays could be in more than one section. Church, society, mission are bound to overlap in content. There is an appropriate element of history in many of the essays, but the emphasis, we hope, is largely on the present and the future.

We are very grateful to the Archbishop of Canterbury, not only for encouraging contributions, but also for the foreword and afterword to the book. Thanks are due to Joan Marks, Principal's Assistant at the United College of the Ascension, and Secretary of CEFACS, for her key role in enabling the editors, in following up writers on our behalf, and in holding together the editing of this complex book. We are indebted to Gillian Paterson, Editor at Cassell, for her personal enthusiasm for the project.

We hope that readers, wherever they come from in the world, will find inspiration from the essays and feel that global Anglicanism has an important contribution to make to the worldwide Church, as it witnesses to our common Lord, Jesus Christ, as we enter the next century.

Andrew Wingate
Kevin Ward
Carrie Pemberton
Wilson Sitshebo

Salvation and other faiths – an Anglican perspective

edited by Andrew Wingate

(This is part of the chapter 'Christ and world faiths' from the Doctrine Commission of the Church of England's Report *The Mystery of Salvation* (London: Church House Publishing, 1995). The chapter is more than 40 pages long and too long to reproduce in full. These passages are republished with copyright permission: readers are encouraged to look at the whole chapter and, indeed, the whole report. Andrew Wingate was Inter-Faith Consultant to the Commission and drafted the chapter, which was then, after full consideration and amendment, agreed by the thirteen members, who represent a wide theological spectrum within the Church of England. These extracts are offered for consideration by readers from the wider Anglican Communion who were not represented in the writing of the book. Sections on experience, the Bible and history have of necessity been omitted, but they are clearly integral to the argument, for a church where doctrine is based on the balance between Scripture, tradition and reason.)

Theological perspectives

The common assertions we are able to make are based upon our understanding of God's love, spirit, and word, and their pivotal expression in the cross and resurrection of Jesus Christ.

God's love is unconditional, beyond restriction, and for all and not only for some. The guarantee that God is love is shown by the ministry of Jesus. As women and men experienced this ministry and linked it with the person of Jesus, this conclusion about the nature of God was affirmed. That love cannot be narrower than a love which includes tax-gatherers and sinners, penitent thieves and quarrelling disciples. These are the very people whom 'religion' excluded. Is it to include these, but not the good Hindu or Muslim? – or indeed the bad Hindu or Muslim, who throw themselves on the mercy of God, as they experience this?

It is also love related to justice and holiness. God does not save against these aspects of his nature (1 John, 'God is light, and in him there is no darkness at all'). Such love and justice are at the very heart of the concept of the Kingdom of God. It is an insight of those doing theological reflection on experience outside Europe, that has shown us how salvation unrelated to liberation and participation in a just society, means little to the struggling majority of the world who live in grinding poverty. Every religion needs to take this into account, whenever it drifts towards spiritualising the centres of its faith. Such spiritualising has left many Hindus as outcastes, untouchables, now 'Dalits' by their own naming. So, too, there are terrible examples like the acceptance of slavery for so long within the Christian tradition.

Secondly, there is the concept of the Spirit. We posit an essential continuity between the Spirit moving over the waters at creation, and being experienced by prophets and rulers in the Old Testament, and then becoming publicly displayed in the person of Jesus Christ, through his baptism and then through his church. Some may say the Spirit moved more widely before Christ's time, afterwards the Spirit is confined to the church. We do not say that. Certainly, the character of the Spirit is now revealed by Christ. St Paul writes of the Spirit of Christ, the Holy Spirit, the Spirit, the Spirit of God, but he appears to mean the same personal reality. The last Doctrine Commission report, *We Believe in the Holy Spirit*, argues for the view that the Spirit is not confined to the church, however named or described.

The Spirit's fruits are listed in Galatians 5 as love, joy, peace, patience, kindness, goodness, trustfulness, gentleness and self-control. These are some of the fruits of the Spirit seen in the life of Christ. He is the criterion for adjudging whether the Spirit is present in any context or situation or person. So our judging that the spirit may be found outside the church is not an arbitrary one, nor does it mean the Spirit can be found all and everywhere. But those who display such fruits amongst those of other faiths and indeed none, we believe, are amongst those who have responded to the spirit of God, and there is evidence that God is savingly at work in them, and will bring his work to fulfilment.

[I here give examples from Hindu, Muslim, Buddhist and Jewish background, of people who have represented that spirit to me.] We would affirm that such people live as they do, through the grace of God, and through his Spirit. However, as we look around our world, we can give many contrary examples from people of all faiths and none, who show that they do not live by that spirit, whatever they profess with their lips. We need not rehearse such: for example, the list of places of religious conflict is endless at any one time. Mahatma Gandhi rightly said that it is those who want to save religion who so often destroy it. Again our judgment is not arbitrary, it is by the Spirit of Christ.

Thirdly, there is the concept of the Logos, the Word of God, the cosmic Christ, without whom was not anything made that was made. The possibility of life, meaning eternal life, is there within all human beings, through the Logos. This cosmic Christology is reflected in John 1,

Colossians 1 and Hebrews 1, three major writers of the New Testament. To have a Christ centred understanding of salvation does not mean that we need to be confined to what happened to Jesus of Nazareth in the first century AD.

God is creator of all through his word and spirit. God wills all to be saved that he has created. This can only happen through that same Word and Spirit. The word is made flesh in Christ, and so we are given a criterion for where that same word is present elsewhere. It is the poor, the lost, the little ones who are given as examples. The Spirit can be seen specifically in the church, and in the nature of this body of Christ, both corporately and through its members. But the Spirit also blows where the Spirit wills. The Church extraordinarily is to include, not just Jews and Greeks, but those beyond the pale, barbarians and Scythians. God is surely not confined after the birth of Christ, and Pentecost, any more than he was before. The Spirit is the one who points to the future, as he leads us to all truth, beyond what we can bear now. That will not be contrary to the teachings of Christ (John 16.12–15). But it will build on them. Maybe people of other faiths and indeed of no religious faith, will teach us more than we yet know ourselves, as we interact with them, and discover new things together.

Fourthly, there is the distinctive understanding of God as Trinity, which should be at the centre of any inter-faith reflection. As Gavin D'Costa puts it, 'Without Jesus, we cannot speak of God, but that speaking is never completely exhausted in history, for the Spirit constantly and in surprising ways calls us into a deeper understanding of God in Christ' (D'Costa, p. 19). He writes of a 'Trinitarian Christology', which reconciles the exclusivist emphasis on the particularity of Christ and the pluralist emphasis on God's universal activity in history. The instruction to love our neighbour opens us to people of the world religions.

The recent book by Clark H. Pinnock, written to persuade his fellow-evangelicals to hold open attitudes towards questions of salvation, writes of the Logos as connecting Jesus of Nazareth to the whole world and guarding the Incarnation from becoming a limiting principle, and the Spirit as the overflow of God's love, 'active in human cultures and even within the religions of humanity'. Referring to the breadth of this activity of the spirit, he then comes back to the Trinity, 'The doctrine of the Trinity means that God, far from being difficult to locate in the world, can be encountered everywhere in it. One needs to take pains and be very adept at hiding *not* to encounter God' (Pinnock, p. 104). He ends by quoting the well-known hymn by Frederick Faber, 'There's a wideness in God's mercy'.

Where then does the cross and resurrection come into the picture? Here the challenge is different in connection with people of other faiths only in one particular way. Even as we think of Christians, we are required to say how this apparently obscure event in the past is connected with our salvation today. Hence the various theories of the atonement. The particular difficulty with people of other faiths is that they do not express a particular faith in Christ or that they may explicitly deny the central and saving importance of the cross. We have to explain our belief that 'Christ died for all' relates to them.

What saves is not the cross itself, but God. God alone saves, and that is his mission. God saves as Trinity, Father, Son and Spirit, all save, and none saves without the others. He wills to save all people, as he created them all. All fall short of his will for them, and so all need his forgiveness and acceptance. Salvation is not something that can ultimately be earned, but comes as sheer gift, as happened to those surprised people in Matthew 25. The cross and resurrection are God's gift to us. They both reveal and save. They reveal the love of God because of the nature of who is on the cross. And they change human history because here we believe is uniquely revealed the depth of God's love for us. Here also, in whatever language it is consequently phrased, something decisively occurs which makes a decisive difference to human destiny, indeed to the whole of creation. Salvation is opened up to the whole world by the cross. For some, this leads to a direct response to that love, as they become witnesses to it as members of the Body of Christ, the Church. But the death and resurrection remain objectively the proclamation of the ultimate victory of good over evil; in sacrificial language, they show the seriousness of human sin, and the degree to which God will go to show a way beyond it. He does something once and for all, on the cross. As such, what is revealed is so, regardless of whether anyone believes it or not. What is revealed is not the narrowness of God's action, but the sheer breadth of it, as Christ gives his life as a ransom for many (and this is an inclusive, not exclusive word).

In the past, much of the discussion about salvation has rested on the cross alone. But as we focus our attention on eschatology, we become centred also on the resurrection of Christ, and its relationship to our future destiny. Inter-faith dialogue brings out sharply the differences between the Christian understanding here, and that of other faiths. The resurrection of Christ is not an optional addition to any discussion about salvation – it is at the core of Christian understanding – and that is why Paul says that if it did not happen, then we are of all people, the most to be pitied. Is it to be an exclusive rising, though it was an inclusive creation and fall in Adam? And what are to be the criteria for judgment? They are about attitude, whether there has been an awareness of grace, and a sense of unworthiness and need for forgiveness; and along with this our lives can be judged by what has flowed from that response to grace.

The question of salvation is not only about whether we have responded to the Christian message, if we have been lucky enough to be born into it, or to have heard it clearly as we grew up or in later life. For there is forgiveness at the heart of God, which is the very centre of the Christian message, and most specifically proclaimed on the cross, in Christ's words in St Luke, 'Father, forgive them, for they know not what they do'. The prayer is that those who crucified Christ should be forgiven; are not the humble and good followers of another faith to be the recipients of the same prayer? Christian assurance about salvation can go along with a deep hope that others may be included in God's saving purpose both now and finally. We can never say that someone is not saved.

A Hindu was in an Indian jail because he had killed a relative in a family fight. He attended the Eucharist held there each month, at first out of curiosity. But then he began to receive unconsecrated host which was given to Hindus, as is done for catechumens in the Orthodox Church. One day he asked if he could join the Christians and share the cup. When asked why he wanted this so much, he said that since coming to the service, he had realised for the first time that he was guilty of sin, not just that he had made a mistake. He longed now for forgiveness and acceptance by God. He was told that he received this by the absolution pronounced each time. He said 'That is not enough. Unless I can kneel shoulder to shoulder with the priest, and receive from the same cup, I may know with my head that I am forgiven by God, but I cannot feel it!' As a Hindu, he had seen where the centre of the Eucharist and cross lies, in its being 'for the forgiveness of sins'.

An example has come to our attention of a Muslim who, contrary to all doctrinal orthodoxy, as a young student in Palestine and reflecting on the suffering following the Gulf War, wrote 'Every day they crucify him, every day they hang him'.

People under persecution so often seem to identify with the crucified Christ, of whatever faith they are. One of the Indian newspaper headlines, reporting the news that Gandhi had been assassinated, wrote 'Gandhi meets his Calvary'. A Jewish example in similar vein comes in the novel *My Name Is Asher Lev*, by Chaim Potok. The novel turns on the quest of an orthodox Jew who is an artist to express the pain of being a Jew in the modern world. To the horror of his community, he chooses to paint crucifixion scenes.

All finally focuses on what flows from our doctrine of God. As we have seen, it is God alone who saves, and God saves only according to, and not against his nature. At the centre of our Christian faith is the belief that God is love. This is revealed through Christ's birth, his teaching, his ministry, his death and his resurrection. That love is expressed memorably in a parable like the prodigal son, where the father goes out in love to receive back the child who has wilfully wasted the chances he had been given.

Conclusion

It is incompatible with the essential Christian affirmation that God is love, to say that God brings millions into the world to damn them; such is incompatible with the essential Christian assertion of God as love. Such a God also longs for all to come into relationship with him, and this is his purpose in creation. When he chooses certain peoples, such as Israel, or certain persons such as the prophets or apostles, he chooses them not for exclusive privilege or salvation, but for a purpose in the expression of God's self-revelation and showing of his saving love for all.

In practice, all religions are open to grave distortion, as Barth rightly asserts. The history of religions, including the Christian religion, reveals this graphically, as does the present map of conflict in our world. This is so corporately, between individuals, and within persons. It is by the criterion of Christ, his life, teaching, cross and resurrection, that all faiths, including Christianity, are judged and/or affirmed. As a fact there are conflicting truth claims made by religions. As Christians, we cannot agree with Muslims, for example, in saying Christ did not die on the cross, or with Hindus, in accepting reincarnation.

In terms of ultimate salvation the decision is entirely God's. As Christians we cast ourselves on the mercy of God as revealed in Christ, assured that God will receive those who respond to him in faith. Trusting in his just and merciful treatment of ourselves, so we are able to trust that God will act in the same just and loving way towards all his children, including those of other faiths. Ultimately, we believe, and this is why we are Christians, that it is through Jesus Christ that God will reconcile all things to himself. How that will come about, we can only be agnostic about, whether it is through some real but unconscious response to the Christ within them now, or whether it is in response to some eschatological revelation, or by some other means.

Meanwhile, we live in a world of many faiths, and it is our very Christian calling that leads us to feel humility and respect before the transparent goodness of many within other religious traditions (and indeed, many of no overt religious faith). We do assert that God can and does work in people of other religions, and indeed, within other religions, and that this is by his Spirit. Such is an essential basis for genuine dialogue with them. We do assert that God has not only worked through the peoples of the Middle-East, but that he did intend, for example, some significant experience of his presence in the Indian Sub-Continent in the centuries before Christ, and indeed amongst many of those who follow the so called 'primal religions'. This is to be expected, since God created the potential for a religious sense

9

in all human beings, and this is indicated in the diverse and widespread phenomena of the religions of humanity.

We can see empirically that people are enabled to live better lives through loyally following other faiths, and this must mean that God is at work in these faiths, even if it cannot determine the question of whether those faiths have value for ultimate salvation or not. God can and does encounter people graciously outside the Christian religion, making it possible for them to come into relationship with himself, and to receive his gifts. Several of us would also affirm from personal experience, the authenticity, as we would judge it by the above criteria, of the lives, but also the spirituality, of particular people coming from other faith traditions. We can be ready to affirm this without prejudging the issue of salvation, Lambeth 1988, 'People sometimes fear that to affirm the presence of any encounter with God outside Christianity is to imply that any truth to be found there may in its own right be "saving truth". We wish to affirm that the only "truth" which has saving power is God' (Report, *The Truth Shall Make You Free* (Church House, 1988), p. 95).

But we would also sensitively but firmly assert that fullness of relationship with God is possible only in Jesus Christ, who is the definitive revelation of God. For many this may happen only in an eschatological dimension (cf. 1 Corinthians 15.22–28). But it is from this assertion that comes the imperative, expressed throughout the New Testament, of the universal mission of the church, to proclaim the Gospel to all nations. A Pakistani Christian woman working in London, reflecting on what she sees as the reticence that people in Britain have about witnessing to people of other faiths, and comparing it with the difficult context in which she lives, reflects, 'If we love our neighbours, it is our duty, out of that love, to tell them about the sacrifice Christ has made for them. Otherwise we are keeping them in the dark, forgetting our mission of love and the sharing of good news. And that love will make us work at finding the language that will be understandable by them.' An Indian Christian woman, working in a British city amongst people of various faiths, echoes this, 'Our mission is to show people life in its fullness as experienced in Christ. Standing by our Muslim brothers and sisters, as they fight for a better deal in education, health and recreation, standing by them when they face racism, that is part of the Christian mission of love.'

Hence, Lambeth 1988, 'We are called to proclaim God's love and forgiveness by word and deed. We must use every means available to spread the message of salvation. Our proclamation must be sensitive to the culture and beliefs of others. Nevertheless Christ calls all people to turn from evil and all that hurts or enslaves, and to receive the fullness of life that he alone can give' (Report, p. 30). Unfortunately, as we well know, the church often gets in the way of such a proclamation, 'Christ is not the property of us

Christians, and if we rejoice when the Holy Spirit opens men's eyes to His glory, we must at that moment remember how often the church has blinded them, and pray that we may be not once more a stumbling block' (Taylor, p. 196). But, as John Taylor also points out, the Holy Spirit, which has been at work in all ages and cultures, often breaks through, not by evolution, but revolution, with the experiences of awakening and disclosure that the Spirit gives in encounters between Christians and people of other living faith.

Lakshman Wikramansinghe, the former Bishop of Kurunagala, Sri Lanka, died prematurely, as he gave his ministry to struggling to hold people of different races and faiths together, on his troubled island. In the Lambeth Inter-Faith Lecture of 1979, in similar vein to the quotations above, he said 'Now we see the goal of dialogue but darkly. In the realised realm of truth and righteousness, recorded in the last chapters of the Book of Revelation, we shall see face to face. The servants of God shall see him, who is the Source, Guide and Goal of all that is, and adore. The riches of other streams of salvation will be drawn into that realm by the Divine Light that illumines and attracts. What is now hidden will be revealed. Until then, we follow the path open to us in this era, and seek to have foretaste of what mankind in its fullness can be. Then togetherness will enrich uniqueness, and uniqueness will illuminate togetherness. To that final dawn may the Father of all lead us.'

So there is a plurality of ways people are being made whole in the here and now, these are ways the Spirit of God is working. And there is an expectation in the future, that, while people may have the freedom to reject the salvation that is available to all, through God as Trinity, God will save ultimately those who are willing to be saved, by their penitence and acceptance of the love which stretches out to them, in the way that it meets them in their lives and within their traditions. There is only one way, but that way is one that is without barbed wire or boundary fences, so that all may join this way. If we think of salvation in the broadest sense as encompassing all that heals and enhances human life, then clearly aspects of salvation are available in many ways, not only explicitly through Jesus Christ. In the ultimate sense, salvation is defined by having Jesus Christ as its source and goal. This pluralism and this exclusivism are reconciled, not in some form of inclusivism (in the usual sense) but eschatologically. To recognise the life, death and resurrection of Jesus as 'constitutive' of salvation as well as revelatory, as Christians do, is to anticipate that he will prove to be the definitive focus of salvation in its fully comprehensive meaning. It may be, too, that our understanding of Christ will itself be enhanced when people of other faiths are gathered in.

The task is to proclaim by word and to display in action, that God has created a world that is good, and that we are responsible for that creation;

that the kingdom of God, a kingdom of justice and peace, has already begun in Christ, and that we can be assured of its future consummation through him; and that the gift and assurance of salvation and eternal life is available now, and the mark of this life is love. We deny the fullness of that love if we deny the truth and goodness which Christ, as Logos, and God by the Spirit, can also inspire in those of other faiths and none. But we believe that God has chosen to provide the fullest revelation of himself in Christ, and the fullest revelation of his love for all humanity in the cross and resurrection. Hence we naturally pray that God will bring all people, including those of other faiths, to explicit faith in Christ and membership of his church. This is not because we believe they cannot be saved without this – but because this is the truest and fullest expression of his love, and we long for them to share it – as St John puts it, 'I am come that you may have life, and have it abundantly'.

Further reading

Recent books on this subject are seemingly without end. Some books referred to in this chapter are:

Alan Race, *Christians and Religious Pluralism* (SCM, 1983).
Stanley Samartha, *One Christ, Many Religions* (Orbis, 1991).
Gavin D'Costa, 'Christ, the Trinity and religious plurality' in *Christian Uniqueness Reconsidered* (Orbis, 1990).
Andrew Wingate, *Encounter in the Spirit* (2nd edn; WCC, 1991).
H. Pinnock Clark, *A Wideness in God's Mercy* (Zondervan, 1992).
J. V. Taylor, *The Go-Between God* (SCM, 1972).

To be noted, excellent on Anglican missionaries,
K. Cracknell, *Justice, Courtesy and Love: Theologians and Missionaries Encountering World Religions, 1846–1914* (Epworth, 1995).

See also works by Kenneth Cragg, Roger Hooker, Christopher Lamb, Marcus Braybrooke, Philip Lewis, Colin Chapman, Norman Anderson, Hugh Goddard, David Thomas, Dan O'Connor and others for recent work by English Anglicans, to which the scope of this article is limited. It is to be noted that for most of these, as well as for the author of this article, their primary exposure to this field was overseas, and this led them to reflect theologically on the context within Britain.

The development of Anglicanism as a global communion

Kevin Ward

President Yoweri Museveni of Uganda (who happens to be an Anglican) was interviewed at the time of the Edinburgh Commonwealth Conference in October 1997. Asked about the role of Britain and the English language in the new Commonwealth, he replied with a parable: 'When we were fighting in the bush, the regime in power got arms from abroad. Our job as guerrillas was simply to wait and grab those arms. Similarly, you came to our countries and we captured your language. Here I am speaking to you in your own tribal language.'

The Anglican communion faces similar challenges in relation to culture, language and ownership. The term 'Anglican' seems to signify particularity, locating the communion in a particular part of the British Isles, and in a particular time: the era of global expansion, imperial domination and colonial settlement. This age came to an end, rapidly and irrevocably, in the mid-twentieth century. Yet, the Anglican communion not only survives but expands with great momentum and vigour. Some parts of the communion prefer to designate themselves by the more theological, or at least ecclesiological, term 'episcopal'. But that too could be deemed overly particular, privileging one aspect of Christian faith – apostolic oversight – over many other equally worthy and important elements. Neither being 'English' nor being 'episcopal' is at all an adequate description of the worldwide Anglican Communion. Many have indeed 'captured' the faith and appropriated it according to their own needs and perspectives. It is a communion which can address the English in their own 'tribal' language, but exists in a rich variety of local vernaculars.

In 1997 the Church of England celebrated the fourteenth centenary of the arrival from Rome of St Augustine to Canterbury, and the establishment of a Church among the English. But as Bede made abundantly clear in his *Ecclesiastical History of the English People* (*gentis Anglorum*), the Church of England also acknowledged a non-English heritage in the great Celtic tradition. Throughout the Middle Ages, the term *ecclesia anglicana* was simply a description of that part of the Catholic Church situated in England; the idea that Anglicanism could or should expand worldwide would have seemed a contradiction in terms. The Church is universal, but it always exists in particular societies. The Reformers did not in any way want to constrict that vision. Rather, they looked for a renewal of the whole Church based on a rediscovery of the Gospel. Yet one consequence of the Reformation was a further fracturing of the one body of Christ, to add to earlier schisms between Orthodox East and Catholic West. Nevertheless the Anglican reformers retained a lively sense of belonging to an inter-national movement which was by no means narrowly parochial. The recovery of an understanding of grace, the justification of the sinner by faith, the faithful preaching of the Word of God and the proper ministering of the Sacraments (Article 19) – these were God's priceless gifts which were being restored to the Church of Christ, far and wide, in a movement of the Spirit which knew no racial or national barriers. Yet part of that recovery consisted in a new sense of a local, even a 'national', identity, an affirmation not only of political but of cultural and spiritual worth for the various communities inhabiting this Earth. The English Bible and Archbishop Cranmer's Book of Common Prayer sprang from a sense that God's revelation could and should be made accessible to all. Moreover all Christians, and not only a clerical caste, were called to discipleship. This sense of the autonomy and 'ownership' was expressed in Article 34 of the Thirty-Nine Articles: 'Every particular or national Church hath authority to ordain, change, and abolish, ceremonies or rites of the Church ordained only by man's authority, so that all things be done to edifying.' This has become an important charter for the subsequent expansion of the Anglican Communion.

The Church of England (in this it was typical of all 'national' Churches, Protestant and Catholic, in Europe at that time) was established by the ruler (the so-called 'godly magistrate') and all subjects were required to be members: it was the Church of the whole nation. The next three centuries in Britain was to be the steady erosion of that idea of 'one Church, one king, one nation', as the right to religious liberty and dissent from the established Church was asserted and conceded. An early concern for local communities which were not English came in translating the Bible and Prayer Book into the Welsh language. Representing a dominant culture, Anglicanism has often been seen as an agent of cultural imperialism. This was even more the case in Ireland. The first Anglican Church to have an identity separate from the Church of England was the Church of Ireland, until 1867 the established Church of that land and affirming its continuity with the ancient Church of St Patrick and St Kevin. But by the seventeenth century it had become clear that the Reformation could claim the allegiance of only a small minority of Irish people, for whom Roman Catholicism was a badge of religious and national identity.

Scotland was different – since it was an independent country, the Reformation took its own course there, and attempts after the Union of the

Crowns in 1603 to bring the Church of Scotland into conformity with the English Church led to civil war. In 1690 the established Church of Scotland was finally confirmed as Presbyterian, with different traditions of worship, theology and polity from the established Church to the south. The Great Britain which emerged after the 1707 Act of Union, and which spread its influence throughout the world in the next two centuries, was a state with two different established Churches. The later reluctance of British colonial officials simply to endorse the Church of England as the 'state' Church in other parts of the world may have something to do with this state of affairs, strengthened by later concepts of religious toleration and even-handedness, as well as considerations of administrative expediency, particularly in areas with large Muslim or Hindu, or other non-Christian, majorities. In fact, it was in Scotland itself that the first dissenting form of Anglicanism emerged after 1690: the Scottish Episcopal Church was the first Anglican Church to exist as a small minority without state support (indeed in the first part of the eighteenth century with active state harassment).

The Church of England had meanwhile crossed the Atlantic – but it had an official position in only a minority of the American colonies settled by English migrants. Several attempts were made in the eighteenth century to provide bishops for these American colonies, but they were frustrated, somewhat to the relief of many American episcopalians, who were very sensitive that a number of their sister colonies had been established precisely to escape the 'oppression of prelates'. This was an episcopal Church without bishops. It was only in 1783 that, in the newly independent United States of America, Samuel Seabury was consecrated as first bishop – by Scottish bishops, to avoid the problems (for both the British government and the USA) of receiving episcopal mandate from the British crown, which would have been necessary had the ordination happened in England.

The Church of England slowly began to take seriously its missionary obligation overseas, with the creation in 1698 of the Society for Promoting Christian Knowledge (SPCK), and in 1701 the Society for the Propagation of the Gospel in Foreign Parts (SPG). SPG's charter mentioned two tasks: to minister to English people living overseas, and to evangelize the non-Christian people who were subject to the British crown. John and Charles Wesley went out to America under SPG auspices. In the Caribbean (supported by the creation, in 1714, of the Codrington Missionary Training College, Barbados) SPG endeavoured to reach the enslaved peoples of African descent, but they made slow progress in the face of the indifference or hostility of the plantation owners (one factor in the subsequent expansion of the Methodist and Baptist Churches in these islands). State control of the Church of England often gave it an inflexibility and ponderous character. At the end of the eighteenth century, the Church failed to contain the great Methodist awakening within its life and structure. The Church also failed to be as responsive as it should have been to mission overseas. The important work undertaken by SPG and SPCK in Tamil Nadu, South India was largely undertaken by royal Danish patronage and German Pietist missionary personnel, inspired by the vision and commitment of Count Zinzendorf and the Moravians. In the nineteenth century the Basel Mission was to continue to have a close relationship with Anglican missions, supplying them with a stream of missionary personnel at a time when it was difficult, largely because of structural problems within the Church of England, to recruit English clergy.

William Carey, the Baptist missionary to Serampore in North India, raised the profile of mission in England at the end of the eighteenth century. Evangelicals in the Church of England, especially prominent lay people such as William Wilberforce, became deeply involved in the humanitarian movement for the abolition of the slave trade. This led in 1799 to the formation of the Church Missionary Society for Africa and the East, explicitly evangelical, explicitly a Church of England voluntary society. The loosening of social and commercial restrictions in a fast-industrializing Britain was accompanied by a sense that this was the decisive time to free the Gospel from all that constrained it, so that the good news could be preached to the whole of humanity. Abolition provided the opportunity for British reparation to the peoples of Africa. The most dynamic missionaries in West Africa were the freed slaves and Creoles of Sierra Leone, including Samuel Adjai Crowther, in 1864 to become the first African Anglican bishop. CMS also campaigned vigorously for the East India Company to abandon its opposition to missionary activity among the Indian population – in this they were aided by evangelical chaplains employed by the company itself, such as Henry Martyn, whose co-worker Abdul Masih became the first Indian priest in Anglican orders. In New Zealand, whole communities of the Maori people responded to the Gospel brought by CMS missionaries, who saw themselves as protectors of native peoples against the corrosive forces of European settlement. Missionaries helped to broker the treaty between the British colonial power and Maori chiefs in 1841 – but they were not able ultimately to prevent the decline of the population in the face of white intrusion. Missionaries, here as elsewhere, occupied an ambiguous position – often deeply critical of the values of Western society, they nevertheless served as the major transmitter of those very values, along with their specific religious message.

It was the intention of CMS to work in areas of the world which were not under British control (partly so as not to compete with SPG). But in the nineteenth century Empire tended to catch up with the missionaries (in some, though by no means all, cases with the active encouragement of missionaries advocating an expansionist policy). The major areas where

SPG and CMS worked remaining outside British control were Japan and China; and in those parts of the Ottoman Empire where they were able to get a precarious foothold. At the end of the nineteenth century the Episcopal Church of the United States also began to be involved in missionary work, almost entirely outside British spheres of influence or control: Japan and China, the Philippines, and South America – all areas where they had an increasing commercial or diplomatic interest. Australian and New Zealand Anglicans also developed an interest in mission work, both in their part of the world and further afield.

Many of the early nineteenth-century evangelicals looked to the mission movement as a vehicle for the transformation of the structures of the Church of England itself. It was, however, to be the Oxford Movement, the Catholic revival from the 1830s, which achieved a redefinition of the episcopal office, so that it could better serve the growing worldwide Church. In England, bishops had come to be seen pre-eminently as servants of the Crown, and there was much difficulty in imagining how bishops could function, even be legally appointed, if they were to serve outside British dominions. Bishop Samuel Wilberforce (the son of the great abolitionist, but influenced by the Anglo-Catholic movement) was inspired by the appointment of 'missionary' bishops in the Episcopal Church in the USA. He argued that a young and fit missionary bishop, setting forth into heathen lands, unencumbered by the pomp and circumstance which inevitably weighed down an establishment bishop, was the epitome of what apostolic ministry and missionary work was all about. Such a bishop, successor to the apostles, carried with him *in nuce* an already existing Church, into which converts were to be incorporated. This ideal strongly influenced the UMCA (The Universities' Mission to Central Africa), founded in 1856 in the wake of the interest which David Livingstone had aroused. Equally important in developing the structures of Anglicanism was Bishop George Augustus Selwyn, who established synodical government and a constitution for the Church in New Zealand, independent of the state connection. A further impetus in this direction came from the calling of the first Lambeth Conference in 1867. The quarrel between Bishop Robert Gray of Cape Town and William Colenso, Bishop of Natal, which provoked the Conference was part of an ongoing struggle between a secularizing State and a Church conscious of its spiritual independence. It also involved crucial issues about the nature of belief and the limits of doubt and critical enquiry, especially in relation to the Bible. But, however problematic Colenso was for episcopal colleagues, in South Africa he is a figure of great importance, both for his defence of black African rights against an encroaching imperial power, and in his sympathetic understanding of the dynamics of African social life, for example in his discussion on polygamy.

In constructing the Church worldwide in the nineteenth century, there were two very basic structural problems which Anglicanism has had to come to terms with. One was the fact that the sections in the Church of England which were most enthusiastic for mission tended to be decisively committed to the Evangelical or Catholic parties, at a time of increasing factionalism and rancour. This often resulted in Churches in the mission field gravitating to one end of the Anglican spectrum, rather than incorporating the diversity of Anglican theology, spirituality and practice. The other major problem was the presence of conflicting interests between Churches which were largely 'colonial' – in which the concerns of settlers of British origins dominated; and the 'mission' Churches, in which the needs of indigenous people were, or should have been, paramount. Where both colonial and mission interests existed side by side the development of the constitutional life of the Church could often be fraught – in Jamaica, New Zealand, Ceylon (the famous disputes between Bishop Coplestone and missionaries), South Africa, and, in the twentieth century, in Rhodesia and Kenya. Even in areas which did not have to confront the conflicting aspirations of these two groups, the whole climate, in the high noon of British imperialism, was inimical to the development of local responsibility and initiative. The 'effortless' superiority of whites, their efficiency and judgement, the need to run complex institutions such as schools and seminaries and hospitals, all put an emphasis on the idea that native Churches were in 'leading strings', firmly under the direction of their missionary nannies. These combined with evolutionary theories of racial difference, which invariably disadvantaged native peoples. The theories of Henry Venn (the great Secretary of CMS 1841–72) about 'euthanasia of the mission', and the fostering of self-governing, self-propagating and self-financing Churches, were re-interpreted in a tortuously gradualist and restrictive way, or forgotten altogether.

The even more radical ideas of Roland Allen (arising out of his experience as an SPG missionary in China around 1900), concerning the spontaneous expansion of the Church, tended to be dismissed as good theory but impractical. Crowther, consecrated in 1864, was the only African diocesan bishop for nearly a century. Despite the tremendous growth of the Church in Uganda, a Church of martyrs and evangelistic zeal, no Ugandan bishop was appointed until 1949. It was only in the 1960s (and in areas where white rule persisted, even later) that hierarchies became African. It was hardly different in India. The first Indian bishop was consecrated only in 1912: Vedanayagam Samuel Azariah of Dornakal. Again, it was only after independence in 1947 that there was any substantial move towards a predominantly Indian episcopate. Azariah's moving speech at the Edinburgh Missionary Conference of 1910 still resonates: 'Through all the ages to come the Indian Church will rise up in gratitude to attest the heroism and self-denying labours of the missionary body. You have given your goods to feed the poor; you have given your bodies to be burned; we also ask for *love*. Give us *friends*' (Gibbs, 1972, p. 335).

There were, of course, missionaries whose ethos and spirit stood out against these mentalities: James Long of Calcutta in the nineteenth century, whose campaigning for the oppressed jute workers landed him in gaol; Charlie Andrews, the friend of Gandhi, Arthur Shearly Cripps in Rhodesia, Archdeacon Owen in Kenya; Michael Scott in Namibia, Trevor Huddleston in South Africa. These men were all engaged in one way or another in a critique of colonialism. In their own very different ways, in the Uganda of the 1930s, Mabel Ensor and Joe Church, in their search for spiritual revival, affirmed the radical equality of black and white, undermining the 'veranda Christianity' which (quite literally) refused to invite people in, keeping them waiting outside the missionary bungalow: a powerful symbol of the failure of love about which Bishop Azariah spoke.

But in understanding the dynamics of mission one should not dwell primarily on the limitations of the 'transmitters' but on the ways the Gospel was understood and internalized. Vernacular translation of the Bible (always a co-operative venture between missionary and native speakers) was of inestimable value in affirming oppressed or marginalized peoples, in promoting the rediscovery of the traditional cultural values – Samuel Johnson's great history of his own Yoruba people in Nigeria and Sir Apollo Kaggwa's similar work for Buganda in East Africa, are just two examples from Africa. Moreover, for the vast majority of people, the Gospel did not come to them from a white missionary, but from one of their own sons or daughters, in their own language and culture. Worship and song were overwhelmingly vernacular – it may have been translations of Cranmer's liturgy and Victorian hymns at first, but even these became incarnated into the local culture in ways which are difficult to comprehend from the outside. Then there began a deeper inculturation of the Gospel into the local society – the Tamil lyrics of South India, or the intensely communal ethos of the *Balokole* (The Saved People), a revival movement which has its origins in the Anglican Church in Uganda and Rwanda but which has had a profound impact on many other denominations throughout East Africa; a movement fully grounded in evangelical theology, but with a spirituality and praxis drawn from deep African wells. The movement of peoples into the episcopal Churches of contemporary Sudan or Congo are even less dependent on the ancient Anglican forms of worship. And overwhelmingly such Churches are not the result of formal mission work, least of all from Europe, but a response to deep spiritual yearnings, in conditions of war and economic disruption.

The contribution of women to this expansion is crucial. Though in many parts of the world the men had the first opportunity to hear and respond to the Gospel, almost everywhere it was the women who became the mainstay of the life of the church. The wives of missionaries, their daughters, single women missionaries, professed members of religious communities – they were important both in the extension of missionary work, and in the broadening of women's opportunities at home. Women missionaries often worked strenuously to uplift the condition of women in the societies where they worked. Christianity has empowered women in numerous ways, and the work of the Mothers' Union continues to be of great importance, though at the same time the prevailing 'Christian' values have often resulted in a narrowing of horizons. Increasingly women are transcending the invisibility to which they have too often been confined. Most countries have a story to tell of their struggle for recognition as catechists and evangelists. The ordination of Li Tim Oi as the first woman priest in 1944 was a milestone in the development of the Anglican Communion. Churches in Asia, America, Australasia and Africa began to ordain women before the Church of England took that decision.

What gives Anglicanism its unity? It is not the legacy of empire, nor the use of English (though in many parts of the world English is increasingly used in worship, especially in urban settings, and its influence in the formal theological education of clergy is unlikely to decrease in the near future). The Lambeth Quadrilateral of 1888 talked of four basic issues for reunion with other Churches: the Scriptures, the Creeds, the two dominical sacraments, the historic episcopate 'locally adapted to the varying needs of the nations'. In addition a specific Anglican identity has been fostered through the use of the Book of Common Prayer, an adherence of some sort to the faith as expressed in the Thirty-Nine Articles, and an acknowledgement of the role of the Archbishop of Canterbury. Increasingly these have to be regarded with great flexibility, not because it should be necessary to disown them – and they remain indelibly part of the Anglican tradition, but because it is important not to define things too narrowly. It was right in 1947, at the creation of the Church of South India, for Indian Anglicans to allow their Anglican identity to be absorbed into a new wider ecumenism. Similar union negotiations in Africa, at least in colonial times, were often aborted not so much because Africans are less ecumenically orientated than Indians, but because they often seemed more about reinforcing missionary control than about allowing the local Church to express itself. Indeed, one of the reasons why Africans have often been anxious to retain their Anglican identity is that they have felt it safeguards a comprehensive and flexible approach to local culture, while still standing for Gospel values. But Anglicans cannot rest on their laurels in this regard – the worldwide movement of pentecostalism can be as little managed or minimized by a staid and brittle institutional clericalism as could the Methodist movement of the eighteenth century. The flaunting of a self-satisfied Anglican identity can all too easily appear as Anglican imperialism to other Christians. Episcopacy is also, in many parts of the Anglican Communion, as complex an issue as it was in the early nineteenth century for England. How can it be called to account, made more democratic, less susceptible to factional or 'tribal' manipulation, or the aggrandizement of individual power? Another complex legacy of British patronage is the tendency to accept an establishment mentality, even if unofficial and informal – though there are also outstanding examples of heroic resistance to brutal regimes: the martyrdom of Archbishop Janani Luwum of Uganda; or the joyful defiance of Archbishop Desmond Tutu, not only in opposing apartheid but, as chair of the Justice and Reconciliation Commission, in facilitating the process by which post-apartheid South Africa can go forward in truth and honesty about its past.

It has been said that the 'centre' of the Anglican Communion has, at the end of the twentieth century, decisively shifted to the south and particularly to Africa, where the Anglican Churches are large and growing and young, and Anglicans often enjoy a high profile in state and society (though, even in Africa, Anglicanism is just one fairly small Church). But it is probably wrong to think in terms of centre and periphery, or to concentrate on numerical growth or decline. Throughout the world, small minority Anglican Churches exist in a variety of contexts alongside other forms of Christianity and other faiths. Tiny communities survive and witness in a society dominated by a religious or secular world view which is not Christian. During shorter or longer periods, Anglican Churches, big and small, survive and witness during repressive regimes. Anglican Churches, especially in the North but by no means only there, struggle to relate the faith to a secular society. There are Churches (freely as in India, or by necessity as in China) whose Anglican identity has been merged into a more embracing Christian fellowship. There are others whose situation makes it important to assert a specifically Anglican identity. Ultimately the future of the Communion does not depend on any careful locating of precise boundaries, but on the willingness to support each other, with love, prayer, human exchange and practical aid, as each engages in its task of worship, witness and action, to the honour of God, Creator, Word and Spirit.

Bibliography

M. E. Gibbs, *The Anglican Church in India 1600–1970* (ISPCK, 1972).
Adrian Hastings, *The Church in Africa 1450–1950* (Cambridge, 1994).
Elizabeth Isichei, *A History of Christianity in Africa* (SPCK, 1995).
W. M. Jacobs, *The Making of the Anglican Church Worldwide* (SPCK, 1997).
William Sachs, *The Transformation of Anglicanism: From State Church to Global Communion* (Cambridge, 1993).

Five years in: where are women in the Church of England?

Carrie Pemberton and Christina Rees

A personal perspective – Carrie Pemberton

On 28 May 1994 I stood with the other women under the Octagon of Ely Cathedral. Many of us came with some bruised memories but hearts full of hope and thankfulness to a God who had been faithful to the prayers of many thousands across the Anglican Communion. As the ordinal charge was pronounced over us, and the hands of commission touched my head, I felt the presence of Isingoma and Mugisa, colleagues and friends from the Congo, children from my time teaching in Tamil Nadu, the murdered Archbishop of Uganda, Janani Luwum, a family friend, my own children, my husband, so many in the crowd of witnesses who urged me forward, and had sustained me in this pilgrimage.

This was one of the outcomes of the vote of General Synod in November 1992. But further developments have been impeded by other obstacles. I wonder, for instance, whether the presence of the two integrities has inhibited the creativity with which the Church has welcomed its ordained women. As a married woman with children, my call to ministry could mean part-time work or a job share. This is a culturally accepted way of millions of English mothers juggling the worlds of work and home. While the two integrities remain in place, what price the full integration of women, as ministers, fellow workers and sisters within the Church? On what terms are women to be incorporated into a traditionally male work-place? The welcome on that score has been somewhat muted.

By the summer of 1996, one-third of ordained women, the majority in the supposed 'prime of life', were receiving no stipend while being actively deployed as 'assistant curates'. No data have yet been published on how many of these women are wanting stipendiary employment but cannot receive it due to either reluctance by diocesan bishop, parishes, their starting age, or the inappropriateness of the terms and conditions of parochial opportunities offered. Has the church been slowed down in its adjustment to women priests because it cannot respond in unison? Is there not an element of entrenchment necessarily built in to the continued presence of 'flying bishops' and 'opt-out clauses'?

When a PCC member of a neighbouring parish tells me that my priestly ministry is unacceptable to them but 'it's nothing personal, only . . . ', and the 'only' is my gender outlawed by a clause deployed to resist equality, what am I to think? In the parable of the Prodigal Son the reluctance of the elder brother was not allowed by their Father to stop the household's enjoyment of a banquet. Might not sisters returning from exile hope for the same determination to celebrate women's gifts in their common home? (Luke 15.31.)

A resounding 'yes' – Christina Rees

On 11 November 1992, the General Synod of the Church of England voted to allow women to be ordained to the priesthood. The vote was passed by at least a two-thirds majority in each of the three Houses, with the highest majority, three-quarters, in the House of Bishops.

Surveys of wider popular opinion around the time of the vote showed an even greater acceptance of women priests. In its own peculiar and pains-taking way, the Church of England had taken the huge, historical step already taken by so many other Provinces in the Anglican Communion.

Within two years nearly 1,500 women had been ordained to the priesthood, all of them formerly deacons, with a few priests from other Anglican Churches. Currently, there are over 2,000 women priests in the Church of England, which means that more than one in ten of the clergy are women. These women occupy a variety of posts, including incumbent, chaplain, rural dean, residentiary canon and vice-provost. There is still only one female Archdeacon and no female Deans. Almost half of these women are in full-time stipendiary work.

The women have been overwhelmingly welcomed and accepted by their congregations and communities. Stories abound of women and men return-ing to the Church because of the ministry of a woman priest. Lay people speak of women's different styles of leadership, with an emphasis on collaboration and less on maintaining a formal hierarchy. Overall, people consider that it was a decision long overdue.

However, not everyone was happy at the time of the vote, and there remains just under a third of the Church who are opposed to women priests. In the last five years around 400 clergy out of a total of 10,000 left the Church because of women priests and, of those, a tenth have already returned. The fear of a split or of a large exodus to Rome has proved unfounded. Nevertheless, particular problems do exist, both for women priests and for those opposed to them.

The Act of Synod

In November 1993 an Act of Synod was passed with further safeguards and provisions for the opponents of women priests. Although not a legal measure, an Act of Synod carries considerable moral force.

The Act made provision for up to three special bishops, consecrated to meet the pastoral needs of those unable to accept the ministry of women. These bishops would be available across the country to give extended episcopal oversight to those who requested their care.

At the time of the debate on the Act, voices were raised by supporters as well as by opponents of women priests warning that such an arrangement would create more problems than it would solve. The Revd Martin Flatman, who had made it clear that he was going to leave the Church over the issue of women priests and become a Roman Catholic, nevertheless raised the question of unity. He said in his speech to the General Synod:

> ... when we debated (the ordination of women) those who were against ... because they wanted unity. The whole principle was unity. So for the Church of England that remains to legislate for a sort of strange disunity within itself does not make sense to me. If I were going to stay, I would have to stay loyally in communion with my bishop. I would not want to be ... manoeuvred into some kind of ghetto. (Report of Proceedings General Synod, November 1993)

The Revd Joy Carroll, a deacon at the time, also spoke strongly against the Act:

> It seems to me that to endorse this Act of Synod is to endorse a theology of the episcopate that is at best nonsense and at worst offensive. What I am voting against is inconsistency and bad theology, for fear that the Church may find herself bent so far backwards that she might fall over. (Report of Proceedings General Synod, November 1993)

Canon Philip Crowe was possibly the most outspoken opponent of the Act of Synod. Like some of the other speakers, he warned that the Act would be 'deeply subversive of episcopacy', and that passing it would only serve to institutionalize schism. On a practical as well as a spiritual level, there would be increased discrimination against women. By passing the Act, Crowe said, the Synod would be stating

> that within the Church of England there are two legitimate views about the ordination of women. One says that when you are legally and canonically ordained you are a priest in the Church of God, and the other says when you are legally and canonically ordained in the Church of God you are not a priest. . . . we hedge about the ordination of women with qualification and ambiguity. I think that is a dreadful thing to do to the women. (Report of Proceedings General Synod, November 1993)

In the end, the Act was passed with a large majority. Synod trusted the Bishops, who had brought the Act before Synod, and wanted to show good will towards those opposed to women priests. Also, the hope was that no diocese would become a 'no go' area for women priests, even if a diocesan bishop were to be against.

The current situation

Five years after the original Measure was passed, four years after the Act of Synod and three years after the first ordinations of women priests, where are women in the Church today?

On one level, women priests are becoming more fully integrated into the Church, and increasingly accepted as the norm. On another level, in the working out of the Act of Synod, the problems are developing and deepening.

A theory created for *extended* episcopal oversight has, in practice, begun to provide *alternative* episcopal oversight. The authority and ministry of women priests are being undermined, as are the authority and ministry of diocesan bishops. A new, competing system of authority has grown up in the Church, and the Church is beginning to realize the price of the unity offered by the Act.

The Revd Dr Judith Maltby from Corpus Christi College, Oxford, sees in the outworking of the Act the precedent for alternative hierarchies in the Church, and a serious threat to Anglican comprehensiveness:

> It is the single hierarchy and mutual acceptance of orders which has enabled comprehensiveness. The historic understanding and working out of comprehensiveness in our Church has never, until the Act of Synod, included the creation of alternative succession of orders or sacramental validity. (Quoted in an unpublished paper reporting on a Windsor Consultation, 22–24 September 1997)

While the Church moves slowly but steadily closer to appointing women bishops, a step which will most likely be taken within the next eight to ten years, it will first have to resolve the issue of alternative episcopal authority.

At some point the Church will have to decide whether or not it heard God correctly in 1992, when it voted overwhelmingly to go forward with ordaining women to the priesthood. The subsequent Act of Synod, which gives the two contradictory positions on women's ordination equal 'integrity', must ultimately come to an end. Not only does the present position discriminate against women and compromise the ministry and mission of the Church: theologically, philosophically and ecclesiologically, it doesn't make sense.

How African Anglicans deal with death, funerals and bereavement

Wilson T. Sitshebo

Most African Christians in Zimbabwe deal with death, funerals and bereavement at two levels, namely, the African traditional and the denominational levels. These two levels represent the parallelism that exists in the people's lives. The African traditional level helps to maintain the cultural community relationships which extend beyond death, while the denominational affiliation maintains the Christian relationships which are mostly interdenominational, that is, if an Anglican dies, other Christians share the concern as if it were a member of their denomination and vice versa. This is not surprising because African traditional religion and Christianity have historically developed as parallel and rival religions. Perhaps it is also a reflection of 'the lack of "fit" between Christian theology and African life'[1] attributable to the absence of mutual dialogue between the missionary and the African convert. These two had fundamental cultural and traditional differences which strongly contributed to and shaped their understanding of life and the world. The absence of dialogue meant that each had to retain what it thought was significant, so the parallel development was characterized by suspicion.

In death, funerals and bereavement the missionary saw the African convert as overemphasizing the role and significance of these rites, while on the other hand the African convert perceived the missionary as desecrating and underemphasizing this vital area of life. Acknowledging that religion has a strong influence on both the attitudes and the practices of its adherents, we can begin to appreciate why there is parallelism. In the Zimbabwean context where African traditional religion and Christianity coexist as essential religions with essential roles in the lives of the people, this parallelism offers communities and individuals symbolic structures for the understanding of these life changes. Professor Bhebe, a Zimbabwean historian, calls them 'pluralists', that is, those who at once hold fast to their old way of life (African traditional religion) and embrace the new faith (Christianity).[2] This pluralist position adequately shows that though many Africans become Christians they still cling to their traditional beliefs and so there are the two levels of dealing with death, funerals and bereavement.

We should understand the traditional world views that form the background and basis for dealing with these life changes. They are entrenched into the African child's psyche, with variations, from birth. They help in the shaping of the individual's personhood (*ubuntu*), while giving life and the world some values. African traditional world views acknowledge three actively interrelated worlds: the world of the living, the world of the departed, the spirit world. All these worlds make one unit under God's direct control and influence each other's activities. The physical world, planet Earth, is the world of the living. The land of the departed, entered into through death, is believed to resemble the world of the living, so 'as a whole, life beyond death is a copy of what it is in this world'.[3] Though its location is problematic, for the Shona and Ndebele, at least, it is around the homes of the human beings. Graves are the linking points, therefore their significance in the relationship between the worlds and their inhabitants. The respective inhabitants – that is, the living, the departed and the spirits – are under God's direct control and influence. Together they make the human community complete. There is a hierarchy reflecting society, with God at the top followed by the spirits, then the living. The dead are a vital link between the living and the spirit world. Let us now explore how they deal with the individual stages of death, funerals and bereavement within this framework.

Death

The first way in which death is dealt with is to share it. Once it occurs, there is weeping and wailing mostly by the women in the home or village concerned. This peculiar wailing informs whoever hears it that something has happened. As Dickson rightly observes, 'death affects the whole community', and those who hear the cry leave whatever they are doing and head in its direction. There they will find out who has died, and related details. They extend their hands in condolence to others already attending, saying *nangalezo* (sad news), a procedure repeated by subsequent arrivals. Other women including relatives of the deceased join the weeping as they approach the home.

The family elders assemble to discuss the distribution of news of this death to relatives and friends far and near. They quickly send someone to the priest to advise him of the death of an Anglican. The expectation is that the priest will come over and say some prayers and make arrangements for further sessions. They also send word to local leaders or ministers of other denominations with the expectation that they will be present at certain times and hold prayers as a sign of Christian solidarity. When the elders feel they have exhausted the list of all people to be advised of the death they adjourn and make themselves available to those who will still be arriving.

Secondly they deal with death as a phenomenon 'that does not sever the bond between the living and the dead'. They believe that it is the gateway to the other world and the beginning of the journey to the world of the departed. Mbiti captures it very vividly when he says 'death transposes the music of life from one key to another switching it from the rhythm of the physical to the spiritual world'.[4] So whatever happens the deceased continues to be a member of the family. It is with this understanding that we comprehend words used to relate death as conveying the idea of moving from one place to another. Expressions such as *usitshiyile* (has left us), *uhambile* (has gone) are implicit. This notion of movement associated with death also finds expression in Anglicanism, e.g. 'Eternal rest grant them O Lord'. The sentence 'X has passed away' often cited in relation to death has a clear movement message. When one moves from one place to another, that does not sever bonds; this is also true of death.

Thirdly, there is a sense in which death is dealt with as fear, thus making it both ambiguous and paradoxical, that is, natural and unnatural. This stage involves the emotions. Death is considered natural when one looks at human life as a whole and appreciates the developments therein. As Mbiti has perceptively noted: human life follows also another rhythm which knows neither end nor radical alteration; this is the rhythm of birth, initiation, marriage, procreation, old age, death and entry into the company of the departed.[5]

Though for the African Anglican the rhythm of life is a reality, fear is a factor, hence the ambivalence. The first part of the rhythm up to old age is acceptable, but when it comes to death the picture changes. 'After a serious and long illness or senile age ... people may talk of a timely death. Here they see death as a natural process, as something inevitable and expected.'[6] Words such as *usephumule* (has rested) or *ubengenzani* (what else could they do?) convey a sense in which death has to be accepted as the only natural option. Otherwise death 'is a disrupting, suspicious phenomenon, unnatural, shocking and dreadful'.[7] It separates the living from their loved ones and 'existence in relationship' is dented. For most people therefore, 'no one should die. Man should live forever. Death is not natural. Even a very old person should never die and life is only removed by an offended *mudzimu* (ancestral spirit).'[8] However, for the African Anglican life is only removed by God, so there is the need for prayer support.

The funeral

They deal with the funeral as with any other event, reflecting social stratification more evidently; that is, men and women have very distinct roles. It is a very significant last rite characterized by solemnity, feelings of loss and high emotions. Perhaps this reflects the pain of disposing the physical part (corpse) of the loved one. Elderly close relatives of the deceased prepare the corpse for interment. If this were done at the undertaker's, the elderly relatives would still have a role to play. They take all items used while preparing the corpse for burial to the grave where they bury them also 'so that what killed them should not kill us'.[9] This is also done with the blankets, clothes, mats and utensils which the deceased used prior to death, if illness preceded death.

Early in the morning on the day of the funeral, the family representative undertakes the grave-marking ceremony. This ceremony is important in retrospect: (a) no one builds a house in the village without having the family elder's approval, (b) the grave links the living and the dead. So marking the grave means that the deceased is still a member of the family, and through the ceremony this grave is the official link. After this, most of the men present will do the rest of the digging. Characteristic of most African events is that people should be fed; so while the digging is going on, another group of elderly men slaughter a beast for this purpose. The skin of this beast is used as either a mat to line the floor of the grave or a blanket to wrap the coffin.

There are set times for burying the dead, early morning and late afternoon; all the people engage in their various duties knowing which of the two is applicable. When all preparations are over and people are ready for the interment the elders and close relatives of the deceased have their private consultation and commendation indoors where they do *isintu* (the African style). When they take out the corpse, people sweep the room or hut where it has lain and the dirt is taken to the grave so that they also inter it with the deceased.

The main reason for this is first to remove the smell from the hut (room) and secondly drive away the infection and the magic powers that have caused the death. The fear of death and suffering comes first in people's minds and consequently this rite is a very important one.[10]

From here onwards the Anglican affiliation is honoured. The priest blesses the grave and assumes control of the burial process as per the relevant rite. Selected relatives and friends will help lower the coffin into the grave at the appropriate time. The priest commends the dead and throws some soil into the grave. Close relatives and friends take turns saying 'Hamba kuhle usikhonzele (Go in peace and plead for us) . . . as they throw into the grave a handful of soil on the coffin or corpse as a way of bidding farewell'.[11] It is important that the funeral is done well and 'the body must be buried with every sign of respect and regard, and heed must be paid to the grave'.[12] This is to make sure that they do not anger the ancestors. A clear demonstration of parallelism!

After the burial all are expected to make their way to the home through designated entry points where dishes of water mixed with herbs are strategically placed for them to wash their hands at least. This is to make sure that the grits of soil stuck in their fingernails drop into the water, so they do not transport this death to their own homes. The herbs in the water serve as a disinfectant. As they enter the home, they are asked to sit so that they can be given food which will have been prepared while the burial was going on. In keeping with communal unity, this feeding process marks the conclusion of the funeral.

Bereavement

They deal with this at the African traditional level. The Church is occasionally reluctantly involved. The communal support system is vividly at work in dealing with bereavement. It is the community which attempts to address bereavement from all possible angles, such as the physical, the psychological and the spiritual. They give some people the role of personal counsellors and attendants to the grieving relatives. They make sure that the grieving persons are given food and taken care of. An ongoing engagement is that of making the grieving come to terms with the reality. This has to be done in stages; society plays a role in effecting this through small ceremonies and rites while the counsellor helps by talking about it. In all this the place and significance of prayer cannot be overemphasized; though it is done as a separate thing.

On the day after the burial the relatives of the deceased are brought together to mark the beginning of the mourning period. In some places their heads are shaven and they are given pieces of black cloth which they wear over their shirt or coat sleeves for up to a year. This outward sign of mourning also identifies them with the bereavement. The widow or widows are given black dresses to wear for the same reasons. They are not supposed to stitch the dress up should it start tearing away; if they do, it is believed that they will always be victims of death. Society overall is considerate towards these people because it understands the symbolism. During this whole time no joyful celebrations can take place in the home, e.g. no marriage ceremonies would be entertained.

One week after the burial the ceremony of the cleansing of the tools takes place in the home. These are the dirty tools left here by the diggers who were very tired. This ceremony has a twofold purpose, to clean these tools and to console the bereaved. The bereaved are encouraged to think positively about their plight because death does not end life. Should one be overcome by emotions and burst into tears or even break down, they are not frowned at. This is considered a healthy way of dealing with the reality. Prayers continue to be held as an ongoing support.

The length of the mourning period for family and relatives is about a year. On the African traditional religious side yet another ceremony, *umbuyiso* or *kurova guva*, marks the end of the mourning period, which is the calling back home of the spirit of the dead person. The usual times of having this and other related ceremonies are Zimbabwean winter and spring (April to September) before the rains. Bourdillon, a renowned Zimbabwean sociologist, notes that these rites from death to *umbuyiso*

> are divided into three main stages: a rite of disassociation in which the person departs from the community and from his/her old status, some- times symbolised as death: a rite of separation, in which the person is cut off from the community for a while and learns his/her new role: and a rite of regeneration, in which the person is accepted back into the commu- nity in his /her new status.[13]

The African Anglicans have adopted a memorial service known as 'the unveiling of the tombstone'. This observance is modelled on the African traditional religious observance of *umbuyiso*, the only difference being that prayers of thanksgiving for the life of the deceased are offered, sometimes punctuated by private family observances. One is tempted to submit that Bourdillon's observation is equally valid for the African Anglicans. This is probably an attempt at indigenization, which still has a long way to go. It is important to note that the parallelism which featured in the other rites continues right to the end.

Conclusion

Noting the parallelism that characterized the marking and observances of these rites, Anglicanism in Zimbabwe seems (a) more concerned with its ceremonials and rituals than the people, and (b) not to take its *African* context seriously, so it replicates the mistakes of nineteenth-century foreign missionaries. This situation needs reversing so that the people, their history and experiences of God become the focus. Understanding the people in this way leads ideally to a discovery of how God's hand moves in it. The inward-looking tendency of the Church might be challenged when it understands that God's revelation is addressed to all. Inculturization as a theological engagement would highlight the significance of culture for theological development, thus giving individuals and their existence proper attention, which is not so right now.

The Anglican Church in Zimbabwe needs to reflect its Africanness seriously if it is to be relevant. This brief study of how African Anglicans deal with death, funerals and bereavement suggests a need for serious inculturization. On the other hand, the parallelism that accompanies the observance of these rites is a plea for adequate anthropologic-socio-theological dialogue. Inculturization would help to bring all these loose threads together by presenting the culture of the people and the faith of the Church as equally valuable and not parallel.

The setting in which the three last rites are dealt with is deliberately rural. This is because most of these rites are rooted there. The few dealt with in the urban areas still reflect this rural flavour, which they symbolize. For most people the rural areas are *home* while the urban residence is *house*. Ceremonies and rituals are held at home. It is probably because of this that many people expressed a

> preference to be buried in their traditional homes: if the latter were not possible and they had to be buried in town, wished for a sod of earth to be taken from their graves to their home for the ritual ceremony and later kurova guva (calling home the spirit of the deceased) to be performed in their village, where their spirits would be able to live amongst their kin.[14]

Notes

1 O. Imasogie, *Guidelines for Christian Theology in Africa* (Worthing: Africa Christian Press, 1983), p. 12.

2 N. Bhebe, *Christianity and African Traditional Religion in Western Zimbabwe 1859–1923* (London: Longman Group Ltd, 1979), p. 115.

3 J. S. Mbiti, *New Testament Eschatology in an African Background* (Oxford: Oxford University Press, 1971), p. 157.
4 Ibid., p. 131.
5 Ibid., p. 13.
6 C. S. Banana, *Come and Share* (Gweru: Mambo Press, 1991), p. 27.
7 Ibid., p. 27.
8 J. J. Seymour, 'The changing trends of the Shona family in Zimbabwe – how the Church can help' (doctoral thesis, SLSA, Harare, 1990), p. 19.
9 W. Bozongwana, *Ndebele Religion and Customs* (Gweru: Mambo Press, 1983), p. 29.
10 Ibid., p. 28.
11 Ibid., p. 28.
12 M. Gelfand, *Shona Religion* (Cape Town: Juta & Co. Ltd, 1962), p. 120.
13 M. F. C. Bourdillon, *Religion and Society* (Gweru: Mambo Press, 1990), p. 21.
14 M. Gelfand, *African Crucible* (Cape Town: Juta & Co. Ltd, 1968), p. 20.

Further reading

T. Adeyemo, *Salvation in African Tradition* (Kenya: Evangelical Publishing House, 1979).
C. S. Banana, *Come and Share* (Gweru: Mambo Press, 1991).
K. Bediako, *Theology and Identity* (Oxford: Regnum Books, 1992).
N. Bhebe, *Christianity and African Traditional Religion in Western Zimbabwe 1859–1923* (London: Longman Group Ltd, 1979).
M. F. C. Bourdillon, *Religion and Society* (Gweru: Mambo Press, 1990).
W. Bozongwana, *Ndebele Religion and Customs* (Gweru: Mambo Press, 1983).
K. A. Dickson, *Theology in Africa* (London: Darton, Longman & Todd Ltd, 1984).
M. Gelfand, *Shona Religion* (Cape Town: Juta & Co. Ltd, 1962).
O. Imasogie, *Guidelines for Christian Theology in Africa* (Worthing: African Christian Press, 1983).
J. S. Mbiti, *New Testament Eschatology in an African Background* (Oxford: Oxford University Press, 1971).
J. S. Mbiti, *An Introduction to African Religion* (London: Heinemann, 1975).
J. S. Mbiti, *African Religions and Philosophy* (Oxford: Heinemann, 1990).

Section One

The Church in worship, spirituality and theology

African Anglicans and/or Pentecostals

Why so many African Anglicans become Pentecostals
or combine their Anglicanism with Pentecostalism

Allan Anderson

African Pentecostalism

The editors of this publication have confirmed what I had long suspected:
that Anglicans in Africa, like members of many other Western-mission
founded Churches, are becoming Pentecostals. Some are leaving the Anglican Communion, but many others remain committed Anglicans while
practising a pentecostal form of Christianity. Those that do not, tend to
practise their traditional Anglicanism side by side with participation in
pre-Christian African religious practices. In addition to this, there are
within Anglicanism in Africa several examples of pentecostal influence or
at least of manifestations of pentecostal phenomena, such as in the Iviyo
LoFakazi bakaKristu of Bishop Alpheus Zulu (Hayes, 1990), the East
African Revival Movement and the more recent charismatic renewal
movement which has profoundly affected Anglicanism in South Africa, for
example. The Pentecostal and Charismatic renewal movements are concerned primarily with the experience of Holy Spirit baptism, accompanied
by gifts of the Holy Spirit, especially (but not always) speaking in tongues,
prophecy and healing. The term 'pentecostal' is taken from the Day of
Pentecost experience of Acts 2.4, probably the distinguishing 'proof text' of
Pentecostalism, when believers in Jerusalem were 'all filled with the Holy

Spirit, and began to speak in other tongues as the Spirit gave them utterance'. This experience of being 'filled' or 'baptized' with the Holy Spirit is that which distinguishes pentecostal Christians (in their own view) from others (Anderson, 1992, p. 2). My use of the term 'pentecostal' is intentionally more inclusive than the Western use of the word (Hollenweger, 1972, pp. 149, 151). That enormous branch of African-initiated Christianity which we call 'African Pentecostalism' (Anderson, 1992, pp. 2–6) raises some serious questions for us to face. The remarkable growth of African pentecostal Churches and the corresponding decline in membership among mission-founded Churches, including Anglican ones, surely means that there must be something in African Pentecostalism's mission methods from which we can learn in our ongoing task of proclaiming the Gospel in Africa.

African Pentecostalism is essentially of *African* origin with roots in a marginalized and underprivileged society struggling to find dignity and identity. It expanded initially among oppressed African people who were neglected, misunderstood, and deprived of anything but token leadership by their white ecclesiastical 'masters'. But fundamentally, it was the ability of African Pentecostalism to adapt to and fulfil African *religious* aspirations that was its main strength. We need to define what precisely these needs were, and whether the same needs are being met by the church in its mission today. And to what extent have African pentecostal Churches contextualized and indigenized Christianity in Africa? Daneel (1989, p. 54) speaks of the 'spontaneous indigenisation of Christianity' in these Churches, and Harold Turner (1979, p. 209) suggests that they offer solutions to problems that exist in *all* of Christianity with 'a series of extensive, long-term, unplanned, spontaneous, and fully authentic experiments from which [the Church] may secure answers to some of its most difficult questions'. One of these questions concerns the widespread use of ritual symbolism, also found in Anglicanism and other older Churches. Which symbols are borrowed from Western Christianity and which from traditional religion and culture – and just *why* are these symbols retained while others are discarded or even rejected? To give some examples, why is there a general preference for adult baptism by immersion, for an abundance of symbolic liturgy (such as the sacramental use of water) and for episcopal leadership? Why is traditional divination rejected, and why has the prophet so effectively replaced the diviner? Why do many Pentecostals reject the ancestor cult while some adopt a certain ambivalence towards it and others accommodate it? These questions in turn raise further questions concerning the problem of continuity and discontinuity, the intercultural communication of the Christian gospel, and the encounter between Christianity and another living religion. Of great importance to the proclamation of the gospel in Africa is the pneumatological emphasis given by these Churches to their mission to meet felt needs in Africa (Anderson, 1991). Turner (1979, p. 210) observes that it is these Churches 'who help us to see the overriding African concern for spiritual power from a mighty God to overcome all enemies and evils that threaten human life and vitality, hence their extensive ministry of mental and physical healing. This is rather different from the Western preoccupation with atonement for sin and forgiveness of guilt.'

African Pentecostal spirituality

Pentecostalism has grown in the past thirty years to such an extent that it has become *the* major force to be reckoned with in world Christianity, now with 497 million, surpassing 'Anglicans' and 'Protestants' combined in sheer numbers (Barrett, 1997, p. 25). This growth in much of the world has largely been at the expense of mission Churches like the Anglicans, and calls into serious question the relevance of these Churches as we approach the next millennium. It is already a fact that more people in many parts of Africa belong to Churches which originated in African initiatives than to those Churches which originated in European and North American missions. In South Africa, for example, over the past 31 years the percentage of the total population of people belonging to the older 'mission Churches' more than halved from 70 per cent in 1960 to 33 per cent in 1991, according to official government statistics. This factor alone raises disturbing questions about the content and relevance of theological training and the curricula of most theological colleges, seminaries and university faculties in Africa. In most of these institutions African-initiated Churches in general and Pentecostalism in particular hardly even feature. In countries such as South Africa, Zimbabwe, Ghana or Nigeria, African Pentecostals are rapidly becoming their most significant expression of Christianity.

It is necessary to appreciate the unique contribution of the Pentecostals in the early years of this century to a multitude of African-initiated Churches (AICs), and their common historical, cultural, theological and ecclesiastical roots (Anderson, 1991, pp. 26–9; 1992, pp. 20–32). The pentecostal AICs have in turn made their own distinct contribution to African theology, to the extent that they have developed along quite different lines from the more Western Churches. A study of these Churches is in its essence a study of what happens when Pentecostalism encounters the traditional spirituality of Africa, and what African people, when left to themselves, do with pentecostal pneumatology. Walter Hollenweger (1986, pp. 5–6) considers the growth of Pentecostalism in the Third World to have taken place not because of adherence to a particular pentecostal doctrine, but because of its roots in the spirituality of nineteenth-century

African American slave religion. The main features of this spirituality were an oral liturgy, a narrative theology and witness, the maximum participation of the whole community in worship and service, the inclusion of visions and dreams into public worship, and an understanding of the relationship between the body and the mind manifested by healing through prayer. There are many movements throughout the world, like most of the thousands of AICs which are phenomenologically 'pentecostal' movements, where the features outlined by Hollenweger have persisted, and which have developed a form of Christianity quite different from Western Pentecostalism.

Africans have found in Pentecostalism a 'place to feel at home' (Welbourn and Ogot, 1966). African Pentecostalism has Africanized Christian liturgy in a free and spontaneous way that does not betray its essential Christian character, and has liberated it from the foreignness of European forms. This sympathetic approach to African life and culture, with its fears and uncertainties and world of spirits and magic, has been a major reason for the attraction of these Churches for people still oriented to the traditional thought world. This is accentuated in African urban areas, where rapid urbanization and industrialization have thrown many people into a strange, impersonal, and insecure world, where they are left groping for a sense of belonging. African Pentecostals, with their firm commitment to a cohesive community and their offer of full participation to all, provide substantially for this universal human need. For this reason, among others, they grow even faster in an urban environment than they do in a rural one. Pentecostalism's roots in the African-based slave religion of the United States, and the genesis of the movement in the black-led Azusa Street revival in a Los Angeles ghetto, together with Pentecostalism's emphasis on 'freedom in the Spirit' which rendered it inherently flexible in different cultural and social contexts, made the transplanting of its central tenets in Africa more easily assimilated. Harvey Cox (1996, p. 259) observes that 'the great strength of the pentecostal impulse' lies in 'its power to combine, its aptitude for the language, the music, the cultural artefacts, the religious tropes . . . of the setting in which it lives'.

African Pentecostals are among the most committed churchgoers. They have experienced the living Christ through the power of the Holy Spirit; they have been healed from sickness and delivered from many problems related to the African thought world; and their lives have been radically changed as a result. This conversion, or 'born-again' experience as the Pentecostals call it, has so transformed them that they do not generally have much need for traditional religious practices, as this conversion represents a radical break with the past. They are sometimes aggressive evangelists, adding members to their churches at a rapid rate. They proclaim a holistic salvation that embraces the whole person, includes an entire healing, and is

Allan Anderson

significantly different from the 'salvation of the soul' which was so often proclaimed by Western missions. Pentecostalism fills a basic human need for satisfaction in all of life, and not just the 'spiritual' part of it. In Africa it seems to adapt to traditional African ways more easily than most other types of Christianity do. It offers solutions to basic human problems, especially healing from sickness and deliverance from a seemingly malevolent and capricious spirit world. Above all, it offers a mighty baptism of God's power which enables a person to overcome the threatening world of unpredictable ancestors, spiteful sorcerers and inherently dangerous witchcraft. This all seems to present a new and vigorous Christianity which offers help to all of life's problems. The 'spirituality' of Pentecostalism is in fact a new and holistic approach to Christianity which appeals more adequately to the African world than the older Christianity has done; and in many respects it is also more satisfying than the traditional religion has been. Furthermore, African Pentecostalism is more meaningful precisely because it has continued some religious expressions which are also truly African.

Pentecostalism as it has been incarnated in Africa is a dynamic, constantly adapting, and vigorously growing phenomenon that is fast becoming one of the major manifestations of Christianity in the world. The one who would wish better to understand Christianity in Africa must reckon with the fact that the Pentecostal church movements are already becoming its most substantial expression. We ignore this at our peril.

Challenges for Anglican missions

If the African Pentecostals are gaining in strength at the expense of Anglicans and other Western-mission-founded Churches, then what are the implications of this for mission in Africa? This essay raises important questions about the relevance of the faith and life of the mission-founded Churches in Africa. If their teachings and practices are perceived by people as powerless to meet everyday 'this-worldly' felt needs (and sometimes 'other-worldly' needs too), then how can they continue with 'business as usual' in the face of such obvious shortcomings? Anglicans are therefore challenged with the need seriously to rethink their mission strategy in Africa. We may pontificate about the need to engage in ecumenical comity arrangements and to desist from 'sheep-stealing'; but if the sheep are not receiving satisfying food, they will seek greener pastures. If the Anglicans are to be on the cutting edge of missions in Africa they will have to address and remedy these shortcomings or else continue to minister to an ever-decreasing membership who are content to practise their Christianity side-by-side with African traditional religion or, even worse, who have succumbed to a secular society and no longer practise Christianity at all.

38

African Pentecostalism provides what Turner (1979, p. 19) called 'a salvaging or rescue function' in relation to the older Churches, by 'preventing dissatisfied members from reverting to paganism by providing a recognizably Christian and easily available alternative spiritual home'. Anglicanism continues to lose members to African Pentecostal Churches, although many Pentecostal Church members today are second- or third-generation Christians. Daneel (1987, p. 26) puts the challenge in another way: 'the "historical churches" can form a vivid picture of the value, mistakes and limitations of their own missionary policy in the past'. He says that the AICs demonstrate 'the foreignness to the African context of the sober, rationalistic, often dualistically spiritualized approach of Western Christianity'.

African spirituality, as Turner (1979, p. 195) points out, 'concerns the whole man, and therefore the healing of his sicknesses and the prosperity of his family and affairs'. This African holism, a concern for the whole of life and not just the 'spiritual' part of it, is to a great extent a biblical holism, and a dimension that the Church needs to rediscover in its mission to the world. At the same time, we must ask ourselves questions about the content of our message. If there is indeed good news in the gospel of Jesus Christ, if we believe that there is 'no other name' by which humankind can be saved, and if we believe in the ability of God through his Spirit to liberate people from every conceivable kind of human problem, whether physical, emotional, mental, social, personal, or any other – then our mission is both to proclaim and to practise this good news. Our mission includes of necessity both the *proclamation* of the gospel and the *demonstration* of its power. The gospel we proclaim involves a message of an all-inclusive salvation from evil in all of its forms as encountered by African people, and the power of this gospel is demonstrated when African people perceive our message to actually work, in bringing deliverance to the whole of life as they experience it. God's salvation must also be seen in different manifestations of his abiding presence through his Spirit, divine revelations which assure that 'God is there' to help us in every area of need. The African Pentecostals urge us to reconsider seriously the effectiveness, the content and the relevancy of our mission in Africa. We must be humble enough to learn from the example of African Pentecostalism, which makes full use of African opportunities to proclaim the gospel. Whether at a night vigil, where the whole community has gathered to comfort and be comforted, or during a Church conference celebration of the Eucharist, we see African Pentecostals using these and many other occasions to zealously evangelize, resulting in the growth of the Church. We must continue both by word and deed the mission of Christ to the world.

Joyce Carlson

Further reading

Allan Anderson (1991) *MOYA: The Holy Spirit in an African Context* (Pretoria: Unisa Press).

Allan Anderson (1992) *BAZALWANE: African Pentecostals in South Africa* (Pretoria: Unisa Press).

David B. Barrett (1997) 'Annual statistical table on global mission: 1997', *International Bulletin of Missionary Research*, 21:1.

Harvey Cox (1996) *Fire from Heaven: The Rise of Pentecostal Spirituality and the Reshaping of Religion in the Twenty-first Century* (London: Cassell).

M. L. Daneel (1987) *Quest for Belonging* (Gweru, Zimbabwe: Mambo).

M. L. Daneel (1989) *Christian Theology of Africa*. Study guide 1 for MSB301-F (Pretoria: University of South Africa).

Stephen Hayes (1990) *Black Charismatic Anglicans: The Iviyo loFakazi bakaKristu and Its Relations with Other Renewal Movements* (Pretoria: University of South Africa).

Walter J. Hollenweger (1972) *The Pentecostals* (London: SCM).

Walter J. Hollenweger (1986) 'After twenty years' research on Pentecostalism', *International Review of Mission*, LXXV/297.

H. W. Turner (1979) *Religious Innovation in Africa* (Boston: G. K. Hall).

F. B. Welbourn and B. A. Ogot (1966) *A Place to Feel at Home* (London: Oxford University Press).

First Nations spirituality and the Anglican Church in Canada

Joyce Carlson

Early contact between First Nations and Europeans

'In the beginning was the Word, and the Word was with God. . . . ' So began ninety-year-old Sarah Simon of the Gwich'in First Nation relating the first words of the first Anglican missionary to her people in Canada's north in the mid-1800s. Sarah's grandmother, a little girl at the time of his arrival, scampered and crawled among the legs of the crowd to reach a point where she could see and hear him, ' . . . a little short man with a nice little blue coat and a little straw hat. He had a cane and was carrying something. It was really queer . . . '[1]

The missionary brought out his 'talking paper' and told the people of God's love from the Gospel of John. And the people heard and understood. The Gwich'in live along 'The Great River', called the Mackenzie by Europeans. The northernmost tribe of the Dene First Nation, they adapted in this land over thousands of years. An intimate knowledge of plant life and animals which they harvested for their survival was essential.

The people understood because their knowledge was transmitted through story. Keepers of stories were elders, the most respected people in the community. Sarah's mother had died when she was two and so she was raised by her grandmother, an elder who relied upon young Sarah to guide her. Elders had well-trained minds; their stories revealed the truth of their own experience. They were open to this God: 'All the elders loved those words – we all memorized them.'

The Anglican missionary had been introduced by the Native wife of a Hudson's Bay trader. In Canada's northwest, people say: 'The Hudson's Bay were here before Christ.' This company was formed in 1670 by King Charles II of England, anxious to assert British sovereignty in the area, and to trade for rich furs much in demand for fashionable clothing. By royal charter Charles established the Company of Adventurers of England trading into Hudson Bay. The 'Adventurers' were eighteen of his most influential subjects. The charter granted the right to trade in all lands draining into Hudson Bay, an area covering almost a million and a half square miles and called Rupert's Land after the King's cousin, Prince Rupert.

'Many tender ties' formed between traders and First Nations women, which made survival possible for traders who would have had an extremely difficult time without their First Nations wives in this extremely harsh climate. Of traders Sarah said ' . . . the poor men must have been lonesome. There was no one to talk to, and their food was different. So finally, some of them married Native women. The girls didn't like white older men. They ran away from them . . . ' Sarah's grandmother married after her older sister, frightened, refused. 'Take the younger one', her mother said.

Early Anglican missions

While official company policy was to be impartial, traders favoured the Anglican Church with allegiance to the Queen over Oblate priests with allegiance to the Pope. The Native wife of the local trader prepared the people for the Anglican missionary telling them 'a real man' was coming to tell them about 'the true God' – and then translated. The next missionary, of mixed race ancestry from the Hudson Bay Colony at Red River, married a young woman from his confirmation class. She helped him learn the language and translate the Bible – and she had many relatives. The missionary lived among the people for over 40 years, travelling from camp to camp. Much loved, he taught the people to read and write. Women particularly responded to the liberating words of Christ.

When trade was no longer as profitable, the Hudson's Bay Company negotiated with the Canadian government who opened lands for settlement. 'The Bay' received generous grants of prime lands in newly-formed provinces, while retaining a monopoly on small trading posts across the north where trapping remained viable. The government entered into 'Treaties' with First Nations who felt forced to relinquish their lands because of mass starvation and deaths from diseases to which they had no immunity.

The end of a way of life

The policy of the Canadian government was to 'assimilate' First Nations. This included forced removal of their children to attend residential schools. The Church, trusted by communities, was involved in administering residential schools. The schools caused a deep alienation of children from their parents and way of life. Racism, negative experiences of education, and a different world view made employment outside communities difficult.

Marginalization of indigenous and tribal peoples continues. This injustice cries out to be addressed. Churches attempt to work in solidarity and partnership – but there seems a gap in our understanding. This gap continues to exist because we have not yet taken into serious account the 'stories', the faith experience of First Nations. Whatever one might feel about the methods used to bring the gospel, indigenous peoples the world over have embraced it. Statistics indicate that in the worldwide Communion, only 4 per cent of Anglicans are now in the Church of England.

Spiritual connecting points in the sharing of story

First Nations elders have taught me so much. I saw the liberating words of Christ through the eyes of women in a hunting culture where their lives could be at risk. Through an elder in a matrilineal culture of the northwest coast, the depth of the patriarchal structure of the Church was revealed in ways I hadn't comprehended. From an elder whose home was near mine, I saw my own world with new eyes. With delightful and entertaining stories of the habits of creatures, of plants, he invited me to know my own world in a more intimate way. There are eleven different cultural groupings of

First Nations in Canada, and many differences. What all have in common is a world view which celebrates relationships between human beings and the created world revealed through 'story'.

Following the apology to Native peoples by the United Church of Canada in 1986, elders and leaders across Canada spontaneously and with gratitude wanted to share something of themselves. And what did they share? Their stories, their faith experience. For hundreds of years, they had been seen as the 'recipients'. They were not seen as 'gifted' people, as having anything to offer of value. What does it feel like when one is treated as though one has nothing to 'offer'? They were finally able to give, and the stories overflowed from their hearts.

Unravelling colonial understandings

Some of my ancestors were traders who had married First Nations women and had their children baptized by Anglican missionaries. In Anglican archives, First Nations wives of traders were referred to only as 'Indian wife'.

When I met Sarah, I understood her to be one of nameless ones. The incredible long summer light didn't begin to match the inner light she carried. She spent her life travelling across the vast territories of the north together with her husband preaching the love of God in the midst of the breakdown of her culture. She delivered babies, handed out medicines, and consoled her people. Two of the three children born to her died of childhood disease. She adopted and raised seven others. When she began to share her experience, the true history of this country came to life.

In negation of the Native, we negated the 'Sarahs' of our ancestry. Our families aligned themselves with Europeans, encouraging children to take advantage of education which was British. I had memorized Wordsworth's 'Daffodils' by heart. Years later when I lived in Britain I wept when I saw daffodils bursting through the earth in spring. I suddenly understood how he must have felt. The writers I loved had profoundly affected the development of Anglican spirituality and faith in England. Their literature was deeply connected to their 'place', but didn't connect with mine. I love that literature – but how wrong to be separated from the stories of my own place. The discrepancy of 'place' created an alienation difficult to describe until I was able to integrate the variety of stories – and celebrate stories of other cultures and continents. This is so enriching to the landscape of my soul.

Secular society sometimes seems more progressive than the Church. This area was re-named *Manitoba* from the Cree *Manitou-bah*, meaning 'voice of the Great Spirit', while the neighbouring province became *Saskatchewan*, meaning 'fast flowing waters', when land rights were transferred from the Hudson's Bay Company to the Canadian government. The Anglican Church, however, retained Rupert's Land for the local diocese as well as the Ecclesiastical Province which includes ten dioceses. Rupert's Land is the largest Ecclesiastical Province in Canada, and the place where most First Nations continue to live. Shall we continue to uphold Prince Rupert, the man who guided the Hudson's Bay Company to becoming one of the most powerful in the empire while playing a large role in the destruction of the way of life of a whole people?

The Church has made great strides in working in solidarity with First Nations, but we must incorporate some of their understandings in worship and liturgy, thereby affirming their gifts, and opening ourselves to new truths. It may take considerable debate to work out a balance and transmit the truths of the faith within our own context, but it is absolutely necessary. If we don't, we fail to see the light in the eyes of Sarah – and the many Sarahs throughout the worldwide Anglican Communion.

Precisely because the Anglican Communion transcends countries and cultures it is in a position to have a profound political impact on relationships between cultures and countries if we are able to 'connect' meaningfully. We must examine and transcend our colonial past, and create space to work in new ways together so that all our understandings are enlarged. The 'sharing of story' is critical to bring 'healing' to our aching 'creation' and balance and wholeness, speaking to the heart, as well as the head.

> White Rock
> I come to you the rock of wisdom
> Reveal to me the meaning of my being.
> Make me a wise and brave leader
> Or show me a way to cure our sickness.
> And may I
> Even as I grow weak from hunger
> Be ready to give thanks
> For the water that whispers.
> Be patient –
> Send my vision o rock:
> Release me from this temptation.
> Take my spirit to the unknown world of wisdom;
> So, as I return, I can prove
> I am a true son
> With a heritage of being brave
> Steady and unmoving as you are
> Unchanging with the moving of time

Thank you white rock
For letting me to be what I am – an Indian.

As we welcome the gifts, the stories, of First Nations members of our communion we may be empowered to speak with more relevance in our current world crisis. At a World Council of Churches address in São Paulo, Brazil, First Nations leader Stan McKay stated: 'In its urgency to bring some justice to the poor, the church in Brazil has seen the need to say, "If we follow the gospel of Christ, we must help the poor become powerful . . ." But what they have not dealt with is what our elders have taught us from the beginning.'

Note

1   Sylvia Van Kirk, *Many Tender Ties: Women in Fur-Trade Society in Western Canada, 1670–1870* (Winnipeg: Watson and Dwyer Publishers, 1980).

Where God still walks in the garden

Religious orders and the development of the Anglican Church in the South Pacific

Richard A. Carter

It is 5.30 in the morning. A bell made from a gas cylinder is rung. In the darkness over 100 young men aged between 18 and 35 wake up, get up from their mats and prepare for prayer. In the chapel they kneel in silence. The sun is rising and light streams through the window above the altar. The parrots arrive and bounce on the blossom outside. First Office begins and the whole community bursts into a rich roar of song. This is Tabalia, on the island of Guadalcanal in the Solomon Islands. It is the headquarters of the Melanesian Brotherhood, reckoned to be the largest male religious community in the Anglican Communion. The community works in the Solomon Islands, Papua New Guinea, Fiji, Vanuatu, and Palawan in the Philippines. It numbers more than 250 brothers under vows and more than 150 novices in training.

Anyone who has visited the Church of Melanesia in the Solomon Islands cannot fail to have noticed that religious life is flourishing. Today, when many religious communities are finding it hard to attract young vocations, the contrast in Melanesia is remarkable. There are four Anglican religious communities working in the Solomon Islands: the Melanesian Brotherhood, the Sisters of Melanesia, the Society of St Francis and the Sisters of the Church. All these communities are living under the vows of poverty, chastity and obedience and all these communities are full of young people, with far more applications than they are able to accept. This is partly because the religious communities provide education and opportunities which will take young people beyond their home village or island, but there is more to it than that. Those who seek to join one of the religious communities know that it is not an easy option: it will involve discipline, motivation and self-sacrifice.

The fact is that many have been inspired by the life of other brothers and sisters and the stories they have heard about these communities. Each village will talk with pride about any relative who has joined. These young people have a grace which is unmistakable. They are greatly respected and yet have a simplicity and humility that reaches the hearts of all age groups. Their life has a spontaneity and joy very close to the song of the beatitudes. People sense that this is what the Christian Church should be like. These are the real evangelists: the good news people. This is not paper evangelism, this is not about lists, aims and procedures, budgets, modules, offices, committees and endless administration or 'super evangelists' and experts flown in from overseas. This is real evangelism that goes on largely unsung, unfinanced, undocumented. The evangelists walk the roads with bare feet and no money. These are evangelists whom the people can welcome into their own homes like returning sons or daughters, who will share whatever food there is and who will sleep on a mat and help hoe the garden, catch the fish or repair the roof. These are the evangelists who will come whenever they are called to pray for the sick, solve a village dispute or calm down a husband who is drunk. And when they visit your home they bring a sense of goodness; the sense that something better is possible. Goodness is reciprocal. Even the poorest family can become their host. 'There's food here, brother, come and eat.' These brothers and sisters will feast and famine with the community.

The Melanesian Brotherhood was founded by a remarkable man named Ini Kopuria, a Solomon Islander, on the island of Guadalcanal in 1900. After being educated at the Anglican Church schools at Pamua and later Norfolk Island, he joined the British Protectorate's native armed police force. But in 1924, when he was recovering in hospital from an injury to his leg, he received an experience of Christ which was to change his life. He believed that Christ spoke to him and told him that he was not doing the work that

Christ wanted him to do. He began to realize God was calling him to start a community of native Solomon Island men who would take the Gospel of Christ to all who had not received it. Much of the population of the Solomon Islands lived on remote islands, villages high up in the hills and bush or coastal villages with no easy access either by sea or by land. Ini Kopuria believed the Gospel was for all people and just as he had visited remote villages as a policeman now he would visit as a missionary. On St Simon and St Jude's Day, 28 October 1925, he made his promises renouncing possessions, marriage and freedom of action. He gave away all his property and a large area of his family's land to the Brotherhood. The following year the first six brothers joined him.

The purpose of the Brotherhood was evangelistic, 'to declare the way of Jesus Christ among the heathen', but as a Melanesian Kopuria evangelized in a Melanesian way. He sought not to draw the people away from their villages and communities but to take Christ to them. The coming of Christ should not go hand-in-hand with the invasion of a foreign culture and individualistic concept of personal salvation without consideration for one's own people. This was the kind of mission the first Bishop and martyr of Melanesia, John Coleridge Patteson, had envisioned. Fifty years before, he had written that his aim was not to make English Christians in white men's clothes but Melanesian Christians: 'The secret of these islands is to live together as equals. Let them know that you are not divided from them.'

The Melanesian Brotherhood did and continues to do just that. Arriving in often hostile villages they aimed to share the life of people in all things. There would be no forced conversion. It was not long before their reputation began to grow. These brothers were prepared to come and stay. They were not frightened of devils and ancestral spirits. Their prayers could drive away fear. People began to speak of their miracles of healing and the signs they had witnessed. The brothers, or 'Tasiu' as they became known in the Mota language, had mana and spiritual power. Many villages were converted by the brothers. Unfortunately, there were not always priests available to follow up this work of primary evangelism.

Today this community of the Melanesian Brotherhood is still very much loved and respected by the people. In a very real sense it belongs to them, to Melanesia. Ini Kopuria was a Melanesian of whom Melanesians are proud and in many of the villages throughout the Solomon Islands you will find men who have been brothers in their youth and now whose children have become brothers. They receive three years' training as a novice before they are selected by the brothers for admission. While brothers they must take a promise of poverty, chastity and obedience, but these are temporary vows which can be renewed. Kopuria believed that after five years' service a man should be free to return to his community and start a family if that was his

47

calling. Release from the community, after a valuable period of service, was not a thing of shame but to be celebrated at the feast day. Groups called the Companions were set up within each village. Their work was to support the Brotherhood through prayer and material support and to follow up the ministry of the brothers when the brothers moved on to the next village.

The Melanesian Brotherhood have established 27 households in all five provinces of the Solomon Islands. Most of them are small leaf-roofed working households built in the more remote missionary areas which will become the base for about four to six brothers for mission and touring. A lot of the brothers' work now involves secondary evangelism, helping to encourage and build up the faith of many who are still Christian but only in a very nominal way. These bare-footed evangelists will tour the remotest villages, lead Sunday Schools, youth groups and adult teaching, lead worship, and act dramas in the villages and be with the people in all the major events of their lives. Their households aim to become a parable of community life.

The Melanesian Brotherhood is the oldest community within the Church of Melanesia and also the largest, yet each of the other religious communities shares in much of the same ministry while having its own charisma and gifts to offer. The Sisters of Melanesia were founded by a woman from Guadalcanal, Nesta Tiboe, in 1979. In 1967 Nesta received a vision in which she realized that Melanesian women were also called to serve God 'without fear, shame and doubt'. Nesta is a brave and determined woman and, though facing much male opposition at first, established a community of women on the same lines as the Melanesian Brotherhood. The community now numbers 30 professed sisters, with no lack of vocations. The sisters' community is marked by its joy and simplicity of lifestyle. Although it has been more difficult for young women to tour the villages, they now have an active outreach programme, a disciplined and devout prayer life and a very deserved reputation for help and hospitality.

The ministry of the Sisters of the Church was extended to Melanesia in 1970, one hundred years after their foundation. Mother Emily, the English-woman who began the order, was a woman of tireless energy whose vision combined both adoration and action; both are very much in evidence in the Solomon Islands today. Their households have become sanctuaries for mothers and their children escaping domestic violence, and the sisters are frequently called upon to protect women and children from drunk and violent partners. Recently the sisters have both uncovered and addressed the problem of street children in Honiara, at one point providing accommodation for nine under-ten-year-olds whom they had found living on the streets and fending for themselves. The Sisters have opened the eyes of many people and by their example have encouraged the Church to become more socially aware. They have also won the respect of many people by showing the wonderful potential and gifts women have to offer within the Church.

The Society of St Francis Pacific Island Province is also growing more quickly than any other within their order. It is an ecologically aware community, as one would expect, and, in a country where the rain forests are being devastated, their friaries at Hautabu and Little Portion are a refreshing alternative with their tree-planting, chickens, organic farm and cattle. Many of the Franciscan households are to be found in the towns. The urban problems are growing and all the religious communities are increasingly called upon to minister to these needs. The modern 'heathen' are often more difficult to convert for their world is no longer related to the world of the spirit but to the modern gods of materialism.

At their best the religious communities are living the Gospel in a very direct way and that is their major contribution to the Church. By living such a radical alternative to the values to which modern society has become addicted, they open up to others the hope and the possibilities of the kingdom of which Christ spoke. A kingdom which quietly grows without self-publicity, like a seed taking root in its rich native soil; a kingdom where the lost ones are welcomed with joy; a kingdom which, once experienced, is so precious that we long to be part of it. People recognize in the life of the religious communities the presence of Christ. They know that that is what the Church should be – if only it were possible – and humbly these brothers and sisters say to us 'it can be like this; live the Gospel and you too will see'.

An old man has died near the village of Vila. He was a lonely man who had arrived from the weather coast on the other side of the island with no family with him. The village were suspicious of him and the children frightened. High grass was growing around his home and he never seemed to eat or wash. For some reason or problem he had been rejected by the community and now the Melanesian brothers were his only visitors. When he was found dead in the grass by his house no one would touch him. He had been sick: perhaps they would get sick too. They called two novices who carried him back to his home, washed and cleaned his body and prepared him for burial wrapped in a bed sheet. In the evening more Melanesian brothers and novices arrived and prayed and sang around his body through the night. The villagers, no longer afraid, came and joined them. In the morning the body of the old man was buried. A lonely death but one transformed and embraced by the love of God.

Tabalia is preparing for the Brotherhood feast day of St Simon and St Jude.

For two weeks people have been arriving from every part of the Solomon Islands to join the celebration. The brothers and novices have vacated their rooms and dormitories; these will be for their visitors and they themselves will sleep anywhere they can find – verandahs, sheds, even down at the piggery. More than five thousand people will arrive in time for the weekend of the feast day. The taps dry up. No one complains; water is carried half a mile from the river. No one is bossing, no one is shouting; there is an atmosphere of joy and celebration. The community is working together with a harmony that remains a mystery to the overseas guests. No one pays, no one is quite sure where it has all come from or who is feeding whom, but like the feeding of the five thousand again and again there is enough for everybody. It is the miracle of reciprocity.

Luluwai, the chief of Surapau village, is complaining. He has heard that some people want the Brotherhood's household on his land to move to a different place. 'If they want to move the brothers they'll have to cut my neck first', he says, 'I'll go back to my heathen ways and so will the whole village', he threatens. When the South Sea Evangelical missionaries came, they came only once and then went away. 'I don't want to join a Church which comes and runs away', says Luluwai. 'When the brothers came they stayed with us, they cast out the devils and ancestral spirits and built their household. We helped them. I gave them the land to build their house.' Luluwai says that before the brothers brought the Church there used to be much fear:

> If there was a problem, like you broke a custom, if you didn't sacrifice a pig, the devils would take revenge and kill one of his children or bring sickness. Now problems can be settled in the Church. We have forgiveness. This time we are not frightened to welcome strangers. Those devils and spirits from before have no power now.

A new bishop is being consecrated at Tulagi. The brothers are leading the worship. The 'Gloria' becomes a hymn of Melanesian praise. The brothers are wearing customary dress and as they sing they dance and the liturgy lives within the culture. They weave backwards and forwards in this powerful dance, with the carved frigate birds in their hands, circling and diving, and the whole chapel echoes with the sound of drums, rattles and the roaring harmony of their voices: it seems that even the stones on the ground will start to dance and sing.

A young novice, Manasseh Paulo, is dying from cancer in Honiara hospital. The doctor has told us he does not have long to live. I go to celebrate the Eucharist for him. He sits up with great effort and pain. 'No, it's all right', I say, 'you can lie down.' But he will not let me begin until he has properly prepared. 'I must wear my Melanesian Brotherhood medal', he says. They put it round his neck. His devotion is moving. We are all very quiet now. His father says 'After you are better we will take you home'. 'No', says Manasseh, 'my home is with the brothers now.'

Later he asks some of the brothers to buy a chicken for him at the market; 'tonight I want to have feast with all of you'. They have been sleeping on the hospital floor for many days at the foot of his bed. 'Don't forget the feast', he reminds them.

They go out to buy the chicken and to cook it. When they return Manasseh has died. But the divide between life and death does not seem so great: the feast they prepare on earth will be celebrated in heaven. And for Manasseh and many other brothers and sisters God is no stranger. For God is still walking in the garden.

Further reading

R. A. Carter (ed.), *Offices and Prayers of the Melanesian Brotherhood* (Honiara: Provincial Press, 1996).

Manfred Ernst, *Winds of Change: Rapidly Growing Religious Groups in the South Pacific* (Suva: Pacific Council of Churches, 1994).

Charles E. Fox, *Lord of the Southern Isles* (London: A. R. Mowbray, 1958).

Charles E. Fox, *Kakamora* (London: Hodder and Stoughton, 1962).

John Garrett, *Footsteps in the Sea: Christianity in Oceania to World War II* (Suva, Fiji: University of the South Pacific, 1992), especially ch. 13, 'Solomon Islands'.

John Gutch, *Martyr of the Islands: The Life and Death of John Coleridge Patteson* (London: Hodder and Stoughton, 1971).

David Hillard, *God's Gentlemen: A History of the Melanesian Mission 1849–1942* (Queensland: University of Queensland Press, 1978), especially ch. 8, 'Dreams and disenchantment', pp. 227–32.

Margaret Lycett, *Brothers: The Story of the Native Brotherhood of Melanesia* (London: SPCK, 1935).

Brian Macdonald-Milne, *Spearhead: The Story of the Melanesian Brotherhood* (Honiara: Provincial Press).

Alan R. Tippett, *Solomon Islands Christianity* (Pasadena, CA: William Carey Library, 1967).

Celtic spirituality: a contribution to the worldwide Anglican Communion?

Esther de Waal

The essential starting point for any appreciation of Celtic Christianity must begin with its geographical origins in Scotland, Ireland and the Isle of Man, and Wales, Cornwall and Brittany, of two linguistically inter-related groups in countries which lay on the fringes of the Roman Empire. Thus for purely historical and geographical reasons they escaped the social, economic and cultural influence of Rome. These Celtic peoples had no experience of cities or urban civilization; they lived close to the earth, bound by ties of kinship, aware of their relationship not only to one another but also to the elements, above all to stone, water and fire.

The Christianity that reached them in the fifth and sixth centuries came by way of missionary movements from the continent, highly influenced by the monastic and ascetic tradition of the desert. What we are watching here is what a leading Celtic scholar has called 'the interaction of original Celtic tribal and primal religion with the young Christianity'.[1] This gives Celtic Christianity particular significance for tribal indigenous peoples worldwide. Sharing Celtic litanies, creation celebrations, domestic prayers or protection blessings with Native American peoples in Oregon, with black South Africans in Johannesburg, or with ordinands' wives in Tanzania, for example, has been an extraordinary personal experience, for their immediate reaction has been that this speaks to them of what they instinctively know, and they feel themselves totally at home, finding much that is already familiar in their own traditions.

The sense of connectedness to the earth itself, to the rhythm of times and seasons, to the coming of dark and light, brings an awareness of the centrality of God the Creator. The eighth-century writer of the 'Deer's Cry', also commonly known as 'St Patrick's Breastplate',[2] evokes all the presences that met him with grace in the world of sense and of spirit.

> I arise today
> Through strength of heaven,
> Light of sun,
> Radiance of moon,
> Splendour of fire,
> Speed of lightning,

Swiftness of wind,
Depth of sea,
Stability of earth,
Firmness of rock.

Bishop John V. Taylor ends his book *The Primal Vision: Christian Presence Amid African Religion* by quoting this in full and commenting 'It sums up and contains all the spiritual awareness of the primal vision and lifts it into the fullness of Christ. Would that it were translated and sung in every tongue of Africa!'[3]

The *Altus Prosator*, the long seventh-century poem (attributed to St Columba), opens by describing God as 'the High Creator, the Unbegotten Ancient of Days, [who] was without origin of beginning, limitless'. The fifth stanza deals with the material order of creation, the world of nature which humankind is to 'rule by prophecy':

The Most High, planning the frame and harmony of the world, has made
heaven and earth, and fashioned the sea and the waters,
and also shoots of grass, the little trees of the woods,
the sun, the moon and the stars, fire and necessary
things, birds, fish and cattle, beasts and living creatures, and finally the
first-formed man, to rule with prophecy.[4]

There is much splendid early monastic creation poetry, such as the tenth-century *Saltair na rann*, or psalter of 150 verses, which opens with an account of the creation and which sees God as king physically engaged in the fashioning, shaping and forming of his world: 'King who hewed gloriously, with energy out of the very shapely primal stuff, the heavy round earth with foundations, length and breadth'.[5] But there are also creation celebrations in Celtic oral traditions, collected in Ireland and in Scotland at the end of the last century, by Douglas Hyde, whose *Religious Songs of Connacht* was re-issued by the Irish University Press in 1972, and by Alexander Carmichael, whose *Carmina Gadelica: Hymns and Incantations from the Highlands and Islands of Scotland* was originally published in six volumes from 1900 onwards, and re-issued recently by Floris Books. A mother would start the day in the western Scottish islands of the Outer Hebrides by asking her children to sing their morning song to God just as the birds were singing, 'giving glory to the God of the creatures for the repose of the night, for the light of the day, and for the joy of life ... giving glory to the great God of the creatures and the worlds', and telling them that humans should join in this song of common creation.[6]

The words of the twentieth-century Welsh poet Gwenallt remind us how much this is a tradition alive today. 'God has not forbidden us to love the world ... To love it with all the naked senses together. There is a shudder in our blood when we see the traces of his craftsman's hands upon the world.'[7] It is wrong, however, to see Celtic spirituality as creation-centred even though that is a claim that is commonly made. It is certainly creation-filled, but the cross remains at its heart. People who know fragility and pain in the history of their nations as well as in their personal lives have a strong sense of suffering and of the forces of darkness. But equally they had a sense of the triumph of the cross, of Christus Victor, a figure who has many of the attributes of the warrior hero who comes to set his people free from all that would enslave them, whether internally or externally. There is much superb writing on the subject of the cross, such as these lines from a tenth-century Welsh poem in which Christ is depicted as a conquering hero, and the text consciously imitates the language of the secular heroic tradition.

> I shall praise God, great triumph of his love,
> God who defended us, God who made us, God who saved us ...
> God who proved himself our liberation by his suffering ...
> Terrible grief, God defended us when he took on flesh.
> Through the cross, blood-stained came salvation to the world.[8]

When the eighth-century Irish monastic poet Blathmac described the scene of the crucifixion he wrote of the whole of creation suffering with Christ:

> The sun concealed its proper light; it lamented its lord. A swift cloud went across the blue sky, the great stormy sea roared.
> The whole world became dark, great trembling came on the earth; at the death of noble Jesus great rocks burst open.[9]

Death was accepted naturally as part of life in a world in which the yearly agricultural cycle spoke of dying and rebirth. The bed blessings of oral tradition, which ended the day for the crofters and their families, say quite simply:

> I lie in my bed
> As I would lie in the grave,
> Thine arm beneath my neck,
> Thou Son of Mary victorious.[10]

Celtic Christianity was above all monastic Christianity,[11] and all Christians took their ideals of prayer and asceticism from the monasteries. Unless this is recognized, the spirituality of the laity cannot be seen in its true perspective. Conversion, grief for sins, and penance are important and any attempt to make it a spirituality without tears does not do it justice. Litanies of confession and the whole penitential understanding are, however, far removed from any negative connotation of guilt. This is compunction, the sorrow that makes for joy, and the soul friend, the *anamchara*, who accompanies the journey is, like Christ himself, the physician bringing healing to the wounded.

Penance becomes private, not the shaming public act that it was in Europe at the time. Penance is the path to transformation and to glory. Monastic spirituality is essentially corporate, never personal or individual-istic but looking beyond self to others. The early monastic city owed much to the model of the ring forts of the secular rulers, with a succession of circles to include laity, artisans, families.[12] If people learn to pray in the monastic way they do not separate work from prayer, living from praying. This is precisely what we find in the spirituality of family and household in the oral tradition. They pray from the start of the day until its end, and they pray for one another. A woman as she kindles the fire each morning says:

> God, kindle Thou in my heart within
> A flame of love to my neighbour,
> To my foe, to my friend, to my kindred all.[13]

Hospitality is a traditional Celtic virtue. Monastic cities opened their arms to all; an old woman in the west coast of Ireland today can say:

> I would like to have the men of Heaven in my own house;
> With vats of good cheer
> Laid out for them.[14]

But this extends beyond human relationships to connectedness to the wild creatures, a reciprocal relationship, seen in the legends of the friendships between the saints and the birds and animals.[15] It also extends to the entire created order to include the angels and saints. The emphasis on the communion of saints, the closeness of the living and the dead, seemed entirely natural, and the saints holding converse with angels was a common feature of hagiography.[16] With little sense of linear time saints and angels were felt to be close at hand, and prayers for their help and support in the work of the household or farm were common. A simple milking blessing from the *Carmina Gadelica* addresses:

> teat of Mary
> teat of Brigit
> teat of Michael
> teat of God.[17]

A people who think of themselves in relationships will naturally find it easy to see the Godhead as three Persons in unity. The Trinity is completely natural in the Celtic world. The presence and protection of the triune God is claimed daily, for Father, Son and Spirit each has a role to play throughout life.[18]

But this corporate emphasis is combined with the eremitical, a recognition of the place of the solitary, whether in oneself or in society. Still today the place names Disserth, Dysart recall the places where hermits lived their lives of contemplative prayer – and produced some of the earliest nature poetry known in Europe. They saw the world with 'eyes washed clear by contemplation' and wrote of the beauty which surrounded them.[19] Poetry has always played a vital role in Celtic Christianity, and the use of the imagination, the role of symbol and image, central in the pre-Christian world, became important now to Christianity. This included skills in art, in metalwork and above all in illuminated manuscripts. The high crosses of Ireland, which date from the seventh century, and the simpler sculpted crosses of Wales, Cornwall and the Isle of Man remain unique among the artefacts of Europe, while the ninth-century *Book of Kells* is undoubtedly one of the greatest treasures of early medieval Europe.[20]

The fullness of the Christian faith of these first centuries led to evangelism. The *peregrini*, the wandering saints, left Ireland in their small coracles to carry the Word of God to Britain and to Europe.[21] One of the greatest, St Columbanus, reached Italy and founded the monastery of Bobbio. As he passed through Gaul and was challenged by the bishops, he replied 'Let Gaul, I beg, contain us side by side whom the Kingdom of Heaven shall contain'. Here we are given a statement of the ideal of unity and diversity. Rome always held a high place in their esteem[22] and it is wrong to speak, as is sometimes done, as though there were a separate and distinct 'Celtic Church'. Here we have the experience of a single, unified Church containing within itself distinctive tendencies and features, which, provided they are reclaimed with integrity, as this article has attempted to show, can contribute much that is significant for the worldwide Church in the coming millennium.

Notes and references

NB: This is intended to provide a full working bibliography. The works referred to are in print and easily available.

1 Oliver Davies, *Celtic Christianity in Early Medieval Wales: The Origins of the Welsh Spiritual Tradition* (Cardiff: University of Wales Press, 1996), p. 5.
2 See N. D. O'Donogue, 'St Patrick's Breastplate' in James P. Mackey (ed.), *An Introduction to Celtic Christianity* (Edinburgh: T. & T. Clark, 1989), pp. 45–64, which gives his own new translation.
3 John V. Taylor, *The Primal Vision: Christian Presence Amid African Religion* (London: SCM Press Ltd, 1963; 3rd impression 1972), pp. 195–6.
4 Thomas Owen Clancy and Gilbert Markus OP, *Iona: The Earliest Poetry of a Celtic Monastery* (Edinburgh: Edinburgh University Press, 1995), pp. 39–69.

5 For the full text see Esther de Waal, *A World Made Whole: Rediscovering the Celtic Tradition* (London: Fount, 1991), pp. 69–71. This appeared in America under the title *Every Earthly Blessing* (Michigan: Servant Publications, 1991), and was re-issued in England as *Celtic Light* (1996). The three chapters of the section 'The celebration of creation', pp. 67–101, quote much original material. For an academic discussion see Mary Low, *Celtic Christianity and Nature: Early Irish and Hebridean Traditions* (Edinburgh: Edinburgh University Press, 1996).

6 See Esther de Waal (ed.), *The Celtic Vision: Selections from the Carmina Gadelica* (London: Darton, Longman & Todd, 1988), pp. 5, 19–35.

7 A. M. Allchin, *God's Presence Makes the World: The Celtic Vision Through the Centuries in Wales* (London: Darton, Longman & Todd, 1997), pp. 88–151.

8 See Oliver Davies and Fiona Bowie, *Celtic Christian Spirituality: An Anthology of Medieval and Modern Sources* (London: SPCK, 1995), pp. 31–2.

9 A. M. Allchin and Esther de Waal (eds), *Threshold of Light: Prayers and Praises from the Celtic Tradition* (London: Darton, Longman & Todd, 1986), p. 30.

10 De Waal, *Celtic Vision*, p. 97.

11 Uinseann O Maidin OCR, *The Celtic Monk: Rules and Writings of Early Irish Monks* (Kalamazoo, Michigan: Cistercian Publications, 1996).

12 Lisa M. Bitel, *Isle of the Saints: Monastic Settlement and Christian Community in Early Ireland* (Ithaca and London: Cornell University Press, 1990).

13 De Waal, *Celtic Vision*, p. 74.

14 Quoted in *Threshold of Light*, p. 40.

15 Esther de Waal (ed.), *Beasts and Saints* (London: Darton, Longman & Todd, 1995).

16 It can be seen particularly in the life of St Columba. The best translation and commentary is Richard Sharpe, *Adomnan of Iona: Life of St Columba* (London: Penguin Books, 1995).

17 De Waal, *Celtic Vision*, p. 78.

18 I discuss this in *The Celtic Way of Prayer: The Recovery of the Religious Imagination* (London: Hodder & Stoughton, 1996), pp. 39–50; (New York: Doubleday, 1997), pp. 38–51.

19 See *The Celtic Way of Prayer* (London), pp. 86–103; (New York), pp. 94–115.

20 There are great numbers of specialized works. Henry Françoise, *Early Christian Irish Art* (Cork: Mercier Press, 1979) gives a useful overall survey. The most useful handbook to the Irish High Crosses is Hilary Richardson and John Scarry, *Early Irish Christian Art* (Cork: Mercier Press, 1990).

21 Douglas Dales, *Light to the Isles: Missionary Theology in Celtic and Anglo Saxon England* (Cambridge: The Lutterworth Press, 1997).

22 Eamonn O Carragain, *The City of Rome and the World of Bede* (Jarrow Lecture, 1994).

An Anglican's view of the Bible in an East African context

Griphus Gakuru

Uganda's Anglican spirituality has had an impact on Anglicanism in the rest of East Africa. This article explores Ugandan use of the Bible and tries to determine if there is in Uganda a specifically 'Anglican' or 'Church of Uganda' hermeneutical style.[1] I will then assess the impact of the Bible on the Church itself as well as on individuals.

The Church of Uganda's position on the Holy Scriptures: a double heritage

The Church of Uganda's position on Scripture derives from its double heritage of Anglicanism and traditional African culture. The Church of Uganda is traditionally Anglican and monolithic in its churchmanship, a Low Church tradition in which the Scripture occupies paramount status in the life of both the Church and individual Christians.[2] Uganda was evangelized by three Evangelical missionary groups: the Church Missionary Society (CMS), the Africa Inland Mission (AIM) and the Rwanda Mission (now Mid-Africa Ministry) who brought the country this heritage. Consequently the Church of Uganda does not recognize the Deutero-canonical books, which many call 'forbidden books'. It is apparent that elsewhere in the Anglican Communion these books are in liturgical use and this leaves many Ugandan Anglicans perplexed.

Coupled with the Anglican missionary heritage is the traditional African heritage regarding the authority of narrative (story and proverb). This led the Church to appropriate the Scriptures for guidance and for providing answers to or throwing light on existential questions.[3] Though traditional African narrative is oral, as opposed to Biblical narrative which is written, the two meet when the Bible is read out aloud. Thus the Scriptures are regarded as a deposit of authoritative and 'universally' recognized African-like sayings. The Bible has become 'their supreme paradigmatic history, through which they recognize new situations and even their actions'.[4] Graham Kings views this status of the Bible as 'proverbial'.[5] The authoritative, universal and timeless nature of the African proverbial narrative has been bested in the Bible, summoning all people to listen and obey.

The Scriptures in the private sphere

The Church of Uganda emphasizes the importance of reading the Bible in worship and private devotion. Every confirmed Christian is expected to read the Bible every day. The family is the most important context for the private reading of the Bible. The reading of the Bible in the private sphere makes its translation into the local vernacular imperative. Because Bibles can be very expensive and thus out of reach of the peasants and wage-earners, the Church has committed itself to helping the Uganda Bible Society to subsidize the price of Bibles. With the help of other donors as well, this has made the Bible accessible to all sections of people. For most families in the rural areas, the Bible is the only book on the shelf. Its presence in every Anglican's home and the absence of other literature makes it the most read book. Many homes read some portion once or twice a day; other people, who do not prefer the discipline of reading it at a fixed time, may pick it up for pleasure or as a pastime. This 'democratization' of the Bible has made it a reference in daily conversation.

The hermeneutical method used in the private reading of Scriptures can be loosely classified as *allegorical*, though sometimes the *proverbial* method is used. The allegorical method is one whereby it is assumed that most of what is written in the Holy Scriptures represents present-day situations, experiences and individuals. In this approach the word of God, which is believed to have intrinsic authority, becomes alive and extrinsically author-itative in a way today's Bible critic will not find it to be. This method also keeps the reading of the Bible simple and largely superficial. What the reader enters into is the world of the text itself, by-passing the historical-critical and literary-critical concerns. And while this approach to the Bible makes it readable to all, it is incapable of yielding answers to complex and urgent questions, such as issues of justice, peace and the integrity of creation.

The Scriptures in the public sphere

When it comes to the public sphere, the Scriptures play a slightly different role. Because the public domain is likely to be interpreted in terms of power relations in society, thus in political terms, there is greater urgency in the Church of Uganda for its ministers to apply more tools to the task of reading the Bible. There is thus an increasing awareness of the necessity of theological training and of careful and prayerful hermeneutics. Increasing attention is being paid to the importance of the people's life situation as the starting point of reading the Bible. This change of methodology from

Scripture to experience as the starting point is significant to the life of the Church and its action in society. In some cases it has demanded a re-reading of Scripture and a shifting of position on some issues. For instance, previously when allegorical hermeneutics was dominant, the Church was unable to adequately address issues of justice and human rights, poverty and war, disease and food shortage, education and public morality. The lack of a down-to earth hermeneutic, for example, made it impossible for the Church of Uganda to condemn Obote's reign of murder and terror in the early 1980s.[6] It also made the Church to lag behind in responding pastorally and sensitively to the AIDS epidemic. The original inter-pretation of HIV/AIDS was that God had visited the nation with chastisement for sexual immorality. Using the allegorical method, some Church leaders frequently quoted Deuteronomy 28.22a, 27–28.[7] Today, using experience as the starting point, HIV/AIDS is being looked at in a more comprehensive and non-condemnatory way. As a result, issues of justice, poverty, exploitation of women, relief for the orphans, etc. are being raised in connection with AIDS.

The Bible and the East African Revival

A consideration of the place of Scripture in the public life of Ugandan Anglicans will be incomplete without mentioning the use of the Bible within the Revival movement. The East African Revival is a term given to the great Anglican spiritual awakening which started in the 1930s with the Rwanda Mission (whose missionaries were composed of Ugandans and Europeans). Though originally not welcomed by the Church of Uganda,[8] the Revival has by and large taken centre stage in Ugandan Anglican spirituality. What makes Ugandan Anglicanism unique is this Revival ingredient which has influenced the Anglican mode of talking about God and reading the Scriptures.

It has been mentioned above that the Church of Uganda expects its members to read the Bible in their homes every day. To many non-Revival Anglicans this amounts to difficult or impossible discipline. It is among the members of the Revival, whose numbers are increasing, that this expectation is met. Most Revival families read the Bible twice a day. The practice of memorizing Scripture and quoting it as occasion demands is a typical Revival feature.

The public reading of Scripture at Revival meetings

Whether it is a small local meeting as the one described above (called a fellowship meeting) or a large regional monthly or annual gathering called a convention, the Scriptures are at the heart of it. At the larger gatherings a theme is chosen in the form of a verse or phrase from the Bible. If one verse is the theme, the text from which it is taken becomes the Bible reading for the day. A series of speakers talk about the verse or text, blending their personal encounter with the text together with constant exhortations to those present to be open to a similar encounter. In this way Scripture and personal story reinforce each other. This synergistic relationship of Scripture to personal story bridges the gap between the text and the present and also lends tremendous authority to the speaker's testimony.

The Revival and the use of the Bible in mission

The Church of Uganda's engagement in mission has been associated with Revival Christianity because it is mainly the Revival Anglicans who have spearheaded mission and evangelism. Though due importance is given to the provision of material things to the needy as an aspect of mission, the proclamation of forgiveness through the atoning death of Jesus Christ and of new life through his resurrection is the key feature of mission. The impact of this approach to the Bible in mission has been significant, especially during the Decade of Evangelism. The number of 'conversions' has increased dramatically, particularly among the under-50s age groups, and various areas of public life have been changed as an increasing number of Revival members have taken up positions of responsibility in government, the civil service, trade and industry and the military forces.

Conclusion

The Ugandan way of reading Holy Scripture is not static but dynamic. Thus, for instance, the emergence of a more existentialist approach to reading the Scriptures in the public domain should be seen in this light. There is a great need to support and maintain the democratization of the Bible by keeping it accessible to all. There is also a need to train more theologians to enable the Church to cope with the demands of the new way of reading the Scriptures where human experience is the interpretative starting point.

Griphus Gakuru

Notes

1 'Church of Uganda' is the official name of the Anglican Church in Uganda.
2 Holy Communion, though highly regarded, is only occasional. In worship the sermon is the liturgical climax.
3 This way of using Scripture is Africa-wide, and has been identified by J. D. Y. Peel in the reports of African CMS missionaries from West Africa. See Peel, 'For who hath despised the day of small things? Missionary narrative and historical anthropology' (1993), pp. 14–17 (unpublished paper).
4 To use the words of Peel, op. cit., p. 14.
5 In J. Stott *et al.*, *The Anglican Communion and Scripture* (Oxford: Regnum/EFAC, 1996), pp. 135–43.
6 For comparison and context, see K. Ward, 'The Church of Uganda amidst conflict' in H. B. Hansen and M. Twaddle (eds), *Religion and Politics in East Africa* (London, etc.: James Curry, 1995), pp. 72–105, especially pp. 87–98. Only three prominent voices were heard during this period: Bishops Festo Kivengere (see A. Coomes, *Festo Kivengere: A Biography* (Eastbourne: Monarch, 1994), p. 423), Misaeri Kauma and Yokana Mukasa.
7 Incidentally, the disease symptoms listed in these verses are some of the symptoms of full-blown AIDS: wasting away, persistent fever, inflammation, boils, tumours, persistent itching of the skin, confusion of mind (due to an attack of *Candida* fungus on the brain), and death.
8 The first Revival theological students were expelled from Bishop Tucker College in 1941. See K. Ward, '"Obedient rebels" – the relationship between the early Balokole and the Church of Uganda: the Mukono crisis of 1941', *Journal of Religion in Africa* (1988).

Further reading

The Book of Common Prayer (1662) (Cambridge: Cambridge University Press, 1968), p. 613.
J. Church, *An Account of Revival in East Africa* (revised edn; London: ACP, 1973).
J. Church, *Quest of the Highest* (Exeter: Paternoster, 1981).
A. Coomes, *Festo Kivengere: A Biography* (Eastbourne: Monarch, 1994).
H. B. Hansen and M. Twaddle (eds), *Religion and Politics in East Africa* (London, etc.: James Curry, 1995).
J. D. Y. Peel, 'For who hath despised the day of small things? Missionary narrative and historical anthropology' (unpublished paper, 1993).
J. Stott *et al.*, *The Anglican Communion and Scripture* (Oxford: Regnum/EFAC, 1996).
K. Ward, '"Obedient rebels" – the relationship between the early Balokole and the Church of Uganda: the Mukono crisis of 1941', *Journal of Religion in Africa* (1988).

Inclusivity, language and worship

Kwok Pui-lan

In worship we invoke God's presence, confess our sin, cry to God for help, offer thanksgiving for our blessings, and bless God's name. Since corporate worship is one of the most significant aspects of Anglican tradition, it is critical that we pay attention to the images, metaphors, concepts, and language used in worship. The very words used to describe God shape our understanding of God and who we are as a faith community.

In the past several decades, the issue of inclusive language has been raised by Christian women from many parts of the world. They have pointed out that language constitutes our reality, influences our thinking, shapes our behaviour, and defines social relationships. A predominantly masculine portrayal of the divine alienates many women because their experiences are not reflected in worship and in religious imagination. The images of God as father, lord, and king can be used to rationalize a patriarchal social structure that is based on domination and submission. These images of God, found throughout the Book of Common Prayer, exclude women and other marginalized groups because of race, class, colonialism, and sexual orientation. Furthermore, an anthropocentric understanding of Christianity denies that other earth creatures reflect God's glory and participate in the cosmic symphony to praise God. This chapter discusses various forms of exclusion and their implications for the language of Anglican worship.

Gender and inclusive language

Sexism in religious language is particularly acute in the Anglican tradition because of the specific characteristics of the English language. Masculine nouns and pronouns have been used to refer to God, and 'men' has been used generically to refer to humanity. When the Bible was translated into English, the feminine and neuter terms in the original Hebrew and Greek were invariably rendered into the masculine form. Liturgical formulae, such as 'in the name of the Father, Son and the Holy Spirit', reinforce an androcentric notion of the divine.

The issue of gender inclusivity in religious language has created much controversy in the English-speaking world. The prophetic voices of feminist theologians and women in the pews have led to certain liturgical reforms. In the United States, for example, the National Council of

Churches has published an *Inclusive Language Lectionary* (1983–85). The New Revised Standard Version of the Bible was published in 1989 to correct the inherent bias of the English language toward the masculine gender. Within the Episcopal Church, USA, the issue of inclusive language was addressed in the language of Rite Two in the Book of Common Prayer and in its Psalter adopted in 1979. The Standing Liturgical Commission has also paid attention to the power and promise of language in worship.[1]

The issue of sexism and religious language has not received much attention in the Two-Thirds World. There are several reasons for this. First, many Christian women and men believe that other issues, such as poverty, survival, neo-colonialism, safe drinking water, militarism, and sex-tourism, have primacy over the change of religious language. Second, the structures of languages in many Two-Thirds countries are quite different from those of the Indo-European languages. For example, the Chinese language, spoken by more than one billion people (more than twice the number of English-speakers), has different pronouns for God, male, and female. The Chinese generic term for human being – *ren* – is an inclusive term which can be both male and female. Third, in the religiously pluralistic contexts of the Two-Thirds World, there are both male and female images and metaphors for the divine.

But gender inclusivity is not an issue for middle-class, native English-speaking Christian women in the Western world alone. The whole Anglican Communion should pay attention to it because English is still widely used in Anglican worship in many parts of the world. In fact, some of these Churches are still using the Prayer Book of 1662, brought by missionaries during the colonial period. When the Book of Common Prayer, the Bible, and the Anglican hymnody were translated into different languages, the masculine metaphors for God remained. In some cases, these masculine metaphors were further reinforced by other androcentric biases in indigenous languages and concepts of the divine. For example, even though the Chinese language does not use the male pronoun for God, Catholic missionaries have translated the term 'God' as 'Lord of heaven', and mainline Protestant missionaries rendered it as 'the king above'. Such translations are still used in the Chinese Churches. Gender inclusivity, therefore, is a valid issue for Churches in the whole Anglican Communion.[2]

Some Christian Churches have begun to use gender-inclusive liturgical formulae, such as 'God the Creator, Redeemer, and Sustainer'. Others have included explicit female referents in addressing God, such as 'God as father and mother' and 'God of Abraham, Sarah, and Hagar'. Some women have also found female metaphors of God, including Goddess, Mother, Sister, and Grandmother, as iconoclastic and helpful to challenge deep-seated androcentric conditioning. Pronouns 'he' and 'she' have been used to refer to God.[3] Many of these liturgical renewals have been initiated by Euro-American women. Women in other parts of the Anglican Communion should be encouraged to contribute to reshaping God-language in worship and community life.

Race, class, colonialism, and inclusive language

The first Book of Common Prayer (1549), known as the First Prayer Book of Edward VI, emerged during strong national consciousness and the ecclesiastical politics of the English Reformation. The Book of Common Prayer contains prayers for the English monarch and reflects cultural heritages of the Church of England. When the British became a colonial power, the Book of Common Prayer was brought to the colonies as a prized possession of the colonizers and the English Church.

The Book of Common Prayer is a cornerstone of Anglican tradition and defines the shape of its liturgy. One of the most acute issues facing the Anglican Communion is how to maintain Anglican identity, while respecting plurality and diversity within the Anglican Communion. Today, the majority of Anglicans are people from the Two-Thirds World, who are not of English or European descent. Ethnocentrism and Christian imperialism undergirded the oppressive system of colonialism, and some of the language of the prayers for mission in Morning Prayer easily convey a feeling of superiority: 'Grant that people everywhere may seek after you and find you; bring the nations into your fold.'[4] Popular hymns, such as 'At the name of Jesus every knee shall bow', disregard the religious sensitivity of people of other faiths. Furthermore, the images of God as 'the King eternal' (Collect for the renewal of life), a 'great King above all gods' (*Venite*), and the 'heavenly King' (*Gloria in excelsis*) can be used to provide religious sanction for kingship on earth. The image of the kingdom of God, ambivalently linked with the domination of the Roman Empire since the time of Constantine, can be used to justify the supremacy of the British Empire.

The colonization process begun in Europe was closely related to the assumption that the white race was superior to all other races. The Book of Common Prayer is full of imageries of light and darkness, some of which can be traced back to the biblical tradition. God is imagined as the eternal light chasing away darkness, which is taken to be the symbol for danger, ignorance, or death: 'Be our light in the darkness, O Lord' (Collect for aid against perils), 'O send out thy light and thy truth' (Introductory sentence, Morning Prayer), 'O God, the King eternal, whose light divides the day from night and turns the shadow of death into the morning' (Collect for renewal of life). The glorification of light and the denigration of darkness in the Bible and in our common prayers both marginalizes dark-skinned people and creates false racial stereotypes.

The issue of inclusive language in worship concerns more than masculine imageries and pronouns, the glorification of light over darkness, and the privileging of the experiences of the middle class. It also brings into sharp focus the question of whose culture, imagination, and experiences are excluded or completely left out. Anglican churches are very small in the Asian countries because many Asian people find the liturgy foreign to their experiences. In Africa where the Anglican churches are growing fastest, some churches have revised the Prayer Book, incorporating indigenous elements into the liturgy. A critical issue facing the Anglican Church in the post-colonial era is how the Book of Common Prayer can be enriched by the cultural diversity of the Anglican Communion.

Homosexuality and inclusive language

The Anglican Church's response to the diversity of human sexuality will be a controversial topic discussed at the Lambeth Conference. In some parts of the Anglican Communion, lesbian and gay people have challenged the heterosexist practices of the Churches. The Episcopal Church, USA has been debating the ordination of gay men and lesbians to the priesthood for some time and there is no common consensus.

Much has been said concerning whether the Bible supports or condemns homosexuality. Proponents on both sides have drawn from the Christian tradition to support their claims. While some have argued that the Christian Church has always condemned homosexuality, historian John Boswell has clearly demonstrated that gay and lesbian people were treated differently in various periods of the Christian Church. The Church had been tolerant of gay men and lesbians until the medieval period, and blessing of same-sex unions was practised throughout Europe.[5]

Heterosexual Christians have seldom reflected on how the language used in the Bible and worship has been based on heterosexual experiences. The creation of Adam and Eve in the book of Genesis has been interpreted as the union of man and woman. Hosea uses the images of a husband and his adulterous wife to portray the relationship between God and unfaithful Israel. Renita Weems has challenged the male privilege implicit in the use of marriage metaphor in the prophets.[6] In the New Testament, Christ has been depicted as the bridegroom in the Gospels. In the Household Code in Ephesians, the relationship between Christ and the Church is portrayed as similar to that between husband and wife (Eph 5.22–24). The Book of

Revelation uses the image of the bride adorned for her husband to depict the new Jerusalem (Rev 21.2).

The language of the Book of Common Prayer and the creeds presupposes the image of a holy family: Father, Son, and the Blessed Mary. The repeated usage of these images in our liturgy suggests that the 'normal' family is a nuclear family, while excluding other forms of family life. Marriage between a man and a woman is considered a sacrament, and the liturgy reinforces heterosexist biases: 'The bond and covenant of marriage was established by God in creation. ... It signifies to us the mystery of the union between Christ and his Church.' At the same time, the Church does not allow for same-sex marriage and is reluctant to bless same-sex unions.

The word 'worship' means 'to make worthy' or 'to respect'. The teachings of the Church and our liturgy have made lesbian and gay people feel shameful, worthless, and guilt-ridden. A truly inclusive Church should embrace people of diverse sexual orientations, and our liturgical imagination should be broadened to reflect the spectrum of human sexual expressions.

Ecology and inclusive language

Much of the religious language used in Anglican worship is anthropomorphic. God is referred to as lord, king, and father; and Jesus as lord, saviour, and redeemer. The anthropocentric images and metaphors in Christianity have been criticized as elevating human beings above all creation, thus contributing to the ecological disaster. Brian Wren, a noted hymn-writer, has proposed other expansive metaphors for God in our ecological age: maker of rainbows, spinner of chaos, midwife of changes, God of hovering wings, and energy of love.[7]

In Anglican liturgy, the Morning Prayer has 'A Song of Creation'. In some forms of the prayers of the people, prayers for the good earth and thanksgivings for fruits of the earth are included. However, much of the liturgy needs to be changed to affirm that human beings are an integral part of creation, all beings are interrelated, and God is immanent in creation. The New Zealand Prayer Book is a noteworthy attempt to cultivate an ecological sensibility. The introduction to the Prayer Book says: 'There has been an increasing awareness of the delicate ecological balance within our country, interdependent with others.' The Prayer Book is bilingual, with English and Maori side by side. Maori and other Pacific people have profound reverence for the earth and nature. The Prayer Book contains several forms of Eucharistic liturgy. The form 'Thanksgiving for Creation and Redemption' includes a 'Benedicite Aotearoa', which illustrates beautifully the ecological vision of the New Zealanders:

O give thanks to our God who is good:
whose love endures for ever.
You sun and moon, you stars of the southern sky:
give to our God your thanks and praise.
Sunrise and sunset, night and day:
give to our God your thanks and praise.
All mountains and valleys, grassland and scree,
glacier, avalanche, mist and snow:
give to our God your thanks and praise.
You kauri and pine, rata and kowhai, mosses and ferns:
give to our God your thanks and praise.
Dolphins and kahawai, sealion and crab,
coral, anemone, pipi and shrimp:
give to our God your thanks and praise.
Rabbits and cattle, moths and dogs,
kiwi and sparrow and tui and hawk:
give to our God your thanks and praise.
You Maori and Pakeha, women and men,
all who inhabit the long white cloud:
give to our God your thanks and praise.
All you saints and martyrs of the South Pacific:
give to our God your thanks and praise.

I hope other Churches of the Anglican Communion can also create liturgical expressions that embrace their land, flora and fauna, and people.

Notes

1 See R. A. Bennett, 'The power and promise of language in worship: inclusive language guidelines for the Church' in *The Occasional Papers of the Standing Liturgical Commission*, Collection 1 (New York: The Church Hymnal Corporation, 1987), p. 50.
2 See G. A. Ng, 'Inclusive language in Asian North American Churches: non-issue or null curriculum', *Journal of Asian and Asian American Theology*, 2:1 (1997), pp. 21–36.
3 Marjorie Procter-Smith has developed several guidelines in constructing emancipatory God-language: see *In Her Own Rite: Constructing Feminist Liturgical Tradition* (Nashville: Abingdon, 1990), pp. 111–14.
4 Unless specified, quotations are from the Book of Common Prayer of the Episcopal Church, USA (New York: The Church Hymnal Corporation, 1977).
5 J. Boswell, *Christianity, Social Tolerance, and Homosexuality: Gay People in Western Europe from the Beginning of the Christian Era to the Fourteenth Century* (Chicago: University of Chicago Press, 1980) and *Same-Sex Unions in Premodern Europe* (New York: Villard Books, 1994).

6   R. J. Weems, *Battered Love: Marriage, Sex, and Violence in the Hebrew Prophets* (Minneapolis: Fortress, 1995), pp. 27–30.
7   B. Wren, *What Language Shall I Borrow? God-Talk in Worship: A Male Response to Feminist Theology* (New York: Crossroads, 1991), pp. 140, 146, 147.

Anglican Christianity and communication of the Gospel through the arts in Myanmar

Edward Saw Marks

It was one of those pleasant winter evenings in the month of December in 1993. People from this village, which lies on the bank of the Ayeyarwaddy (Irrawaddy) river, had started gathering into the open space of the village football field. Nearly throughout the whole day, the loudspeaker hanging on top of a tree at the corner of the field had been playing songs, music and an audio drama with a biblical message.

Villagers from this area, who were mostly farmers, had been winding up their harvesting these days and were very eager to relax, have fun and enjoy entertainment, which seldom came their way.

The incessant playing of the loudspeaker had informed them that there would be a special programme that night at the open space. This is one of those many villages that have no daily newspaper. There is no telephone and not even the electricity reaches there. But almost everybody in the village knew that a Christian group from the city had arrived the previous day and they were expecting the group would put on an interesting programme at the village.

Even though most of the villagers might not have heard about Christ, they somehow knew that Christmas was approaching at that time. This is a special time for Christians. Usually, they expect a treat from their Christian friends during this season. They expect a heartfelt welcome to their beautifully decorated homes, and that they will be treated with delicious food and gifts.

The mist had started to rise in the field as the sun slowly went down. Young children and the elderly people began to gather. They began to lay out the mats and rugs in front of the makeshift stage. The children were making sure that their parents, brothers and sisters who would turn up late, because of their work, would surely get a place to sit in the audience.

This Christian group from the city was the evangelizing tour group from the Anglican Church. To stay for three days at the village was part of their Ayeyarwaddy delta new mission area campaign trip. The group was made up of clergymen and laymen ministry leaders.

The programme began with music and songs. Testimonies and sharings of the Good News were given and were followed by the showing of videos with biblical themes. Short talks and sharings at video breaks evaluated the previous show and made clarifications of the message.

That night the programme that drew the most attention was the showing of a Christmas video which was produced in the same setting of the villagers. The story was based on the incarnation and the reconciliation. The audience were totally engrossed in the show and it could be seen that they could totally identify themselves with the characters from the video. The children could be seen with wide, unblinking eyes and the older ones nodding their heads.

One thing was peculiar about these people. They would not go back home until the first light of dawn appeared. They would patiently sit and watch throughout the whole night. When they came they had prepared to stay until sunrise. They brought foodstuffs and drinks along with them. Some even brought along blankets. If they got very tired, they would lie down and go to sleep at the same spot where they sat. If the programme finished halfway in the night, they would be very annoyed. They could not go back home in the dark.

That particular night, about three hundred people who gathered there heard the Good News. Most of them came to understand more about Christmas, Christ and Christianity. John 3.16 was conveyed through all the media used that night.

Home visitations, fellowships, interactions and Bible discussions followed in the next two days, before the group left for the next village. The follow-up would be in the hands of the area catechist.

The population of Burma (Myanmar) is estimated at about 43.1 million (1994) of whom about 75 per cent live in rural villages.

'To the people of Burma (Myanmar) a festival or fair of any kind means a "pwe". It is a time to gather the entire family and go to watch a marvellous mixture of dance, music, comedy and recreation of epic drama.'[1]

Since the days of the Myanmar kingdom, *zat pwe* or performing arts were very popular among the royals as well as their subjects. These *zat pwe* are the ultimate mélange of music, dance and dramatics. Traditionally the main part of these performances is based on the stories of the 'Jataka', tales of the

Buddha's prior incarnations. Watching these performances younger generations will learn their moral values while the older generations will
refresh their beliefs.

Up to this modern day Myanmar people, especially rural villagers, are
very fond of watching *zat pwe*. This is the medium that is very effective to
convey the message to the majority of people in Myanmar.

As in the performing arts, the Jataka have also taken up a very strong
foothold in the field of Myanmar traditional paintings. This can be seen as
early as the era of the Bagan dynasty. During this era, Buddhist pagodas
and temples were built with murals or paintings on the inside walls. The
famous Myanmar writer Zaw Gyi noted that 'one can say that Buddhism
was spread and stayed very strong during the era of Bagan because of the
important role played by the paintings of that era'.[2]

Up to this day paintings still play an important role in spreading the
message of Buddhism. Almost at every corridor at Buddhist temples and
pagodas one can find paintings of the Jataka tales and Buddhist teachings.
These paintings are done in the Myanmar traditional style and the people
feel at home reading the message out of these paintings.

P. Solomon Raj, the Christian artist of India, once said 'In my country
we Christians are a minority, and so we find that we must preach the Gospel
and convey our faith to our Hindu brothers through the medium of art,
which appeals to the eye and the ear'.[3]

In Myanmar rural villages sticking posters and pictures on the walls of
their home is a very common practice. Usually they will put up the pictures
of movie artists, pictures of models promoting consumer goods, wall-sheet
papers of pop music bands and the covers of used calendars of previous
years.

In most houses of villagers, common room walls are covered with these
pictures partly as decorations and partly for the purpose of patching up a
hole in the wall.

When friends or relatives pay visits, guests and hosts will sit on a mat in
the common room and chat. The conversation will go from the purpose of
the visit, present-day business, sociopolitical affairs and religious matters.
Discussions also go on about posters and pictures hanging on the walls.

The Church has been printing Church calendars every year and the
distribution was done up to the remote places of the country. These
calendars have the front cover printed full-page full-colour with paintings
of biblical themes. These calendar covers will usually end up on the walls of
villagers' houses. They will be viewed and discussed about the theme and
will hang there till old enough to go into rags.

In the near future the world will have 'the interactive TV' which
television, telephones and computers meld into, and which will let the

viewers order movies or pizzas, E-mail the kids' teachers, shop or browse the Internet.[4]

Myanmar is opening up to the outside world. But because of the values, the concepts and limitations of the resources, the old traditional ways of communications will still be going strong as before.

The indigenization of the Anglican Church is vital at this moment. If we look back to the history of the Church and the growth of its ministry in today's situations, we must be aware of its context and the increasing significance of local cultural expression of the Christian message.

The first clergy to work in Burma were not 'missionaries' in the usual sense, but Army Chaplains, who came with Sir Archibald Campbell's army in 1825.

The Church of England, through the SPG, first took up the work after the Second Burmese War in 1852.[5] (Purser)

The foreign missionaries had to leave the country for good in 1965–66. From that day onwards the Church is under the indigenous leaders.

Myanmar is a country very rich in tradition, art and culture. Conveying the message of the Gospel, we must use the most effective tools in communicating with the people.

I would like to conclude with G. R. Singh's words: 'Christian artists face this challenge of translating or interpreting the Gospel with its life and soul. Their communication is built on understanding and participation in the Gospel. Here art can become one of the effective forms of witness to the divine merely in Christ.'[6]

Notes

1 Wilhelm Klein, *Inside Guides: Burma (Myanmar)* (Apa Publications, 1996), pp. 27–93.
2 Zaw Gyi, 'The nature of paintings during the era of Bagan dynasty' in *Shu Ma Wa: Paintings During Bagan Era* (Rangoon [Yangon], July 1951).
3 P. Solomon Raj in *Image: Christian Communication, Christian Art in Asia* (18 December 1983) (Publication of Asian Christian Art Association), p. 2.
4 C. R. Purser, MA, 'The history of the Church in Burma' in *The SPG Handbooks – Burma* (Westminster, London SW1).
5 Ibid.
6 G. R. Singh, 'A theology of art' in *Image* (18 December 1983).

Death has come to reveal the faith

Spirituality in the Episcopal Church of the Sudan amidst civil conflict

Marc Nikkel

Largely hidden in one of the earth's most brutalized war zones, the Episcopal Church of the Sudan (ECS) continues to survive. Indeed, it not only survives but flourishes, often revealing a remarkable spiritual dynamism. Our title comprises the first line of a song, composed early in the present, most ruinous phase of Sudan's civil war. Wrestling with death and upheaval, the young Church has given expression to diverse and vital spiritual visions.

> 1: Death has come to reveal the faith.[1]
> It has begun with us, and it will end with us.
> O you who fear death, do not fear death.
> It only means that one will disappear from the earth.
> Who is there who can save his life and leave death aside?
> We who live in the world, we are mere sojourners upon the earth,
> As the Lord has said: 'Let us serve the truth.'
> Upon the earth there is no man we can call our 'father'.
> We abide together equally in unity as brothers.
> God did not create us to be the slaves of mere mortals like ourselves.
> This cannot happen upon the earth! . . .

> 4. Let us encourage our hearts in the hope of God
> who once breathed the breath of life into the human body.[2]
> His ears are open to prayers; the Creator of humankind is watching;
> He reigns from his high place, seeing the souls of those who die.
> Turn your ears to us: upon whom else can we call?
> Is it not you alone, O God? Let us be branches of your son.
> Jesus will come with the final word of judgement,
> Bringing glory to the earth, peace and the truth of faith.

Sudan's Episcopal community had hardly been born before civil conflict, erupting with national independence, threatened to eradicate it. Apart from a single decade, war has ravaged land and people since 1955. In 1964 all foreign missionaries, including the last remnants of the Church Missionary Society (CMS), were expelled by the Islamic regime. Two Sudanese

Marc Nikkel

bishops and 44 ordained pastors were left to care for beleaguered Episcopal communities, many scattered through the forests of Southern Sudan and in exile in neighbouring countries. Yet, it has been this very isolation, this reliance on indigenous initiative and resources, that has given rise to distinctive and confident visions of the Spirit. Out of its obscurity and isolation this Church has, during the 1980s and 1990s, often been described as the fastest growing Church in the Anglican Communion.

Superficially, the ECS might appear a replica of nineteenth-century British low churchmanship, with its reliance on vernacular translations of the 1662 Book of Common Prayer, its lengthy processions of white-clad members of the Mothers' Union, the clergy in their all-important dog collars, draped with surplice and stole. Unlike in other parts of Africa there has been little impulse to create 'independent Churches' in defiance of the missionary heritage. Far from deprecating pioneer missionaries, the Sudanese are more likely to embrace them as spiritual ancestors and saints, sources of stability. Listen, and it becomes apparent that, in virtually every vernacular Episcopal community – Avokaya, Azande, Baka, Bari, Jieng, Juur, Kakwa, Kuku, Mandari, Moru, Nuba, Nuer – this Anglican tradition has been richly embellished with vernacular song and extemporaneous prayer, with dance, and biblical interpretation that preserves the African soul incarnate, even amid upheaval and exile. In the ECS the bones of Cranmer's Morning Prayer may be enfleshed for three hours and more. Contrary to expectation, the residual Anglican scaffolding has served more to protect and hallow Sudanese identities than to suppress them.

Well represented in this article are examples from the ECS among the Jieng,[3] largest of Sudan's ethnic groups, among whom the Church's growth has been rapid and unprecedented. Striking for its fervent, culturally rooted strains of theology, ritual and symbolism, it is but one of numerous 'spiritualities' now evolving. Yet, the 'confederation of tribal Churches' that has arisen from the vernacular missions of the CMS holds numerous challenges. Its very diversity and richness is a facet of fragmentation exacerbated by war, a formidable challenge to the future cohesiveness, integration and shared vision of the Province.

Today it is the youth and the women, the widows and children of war, who are frequently in the vanguard. Articulate women are among the most effective evangelists, preachers and church planters. The youth, too, are valiant warriors of the spirit. Vulnerable, having narrow scope for education, many express but one confidence, as in a line from a popular Arabic chorus:

You are here today, but tomorrow you'll be here no more.
Our only hope is Jesus Christ, so receive him now.[4]

The vision of God born in the Sudanese context is, at once, severe, imminent and compassionate. In Sudan no OT passage is better known than Isaiah 18, a chapter that an influential English version unfortunately labels 'God's judgement on Sudan'. Survivors recall how they've seen the corpses of their kinfolk, 'left to the mountain birds of prey and to the wild animals' (v. 6). Isaiah's prophecies of annihilation and hope are fulfilled today. It is not uncommon to see women kneeling, folding themselves down into the ground, hands extended, palms open, beginning their prayers with extemporaneous confession, as does an unschooled widow:

> We thank you, the Trinity, our God, on this day and through the days before us. God of evil people, God of mercy: You are the God of bad people, and we have become very bad. There is nothing like us among all the things you have created, even among all the animals in the forest. Now I have taken the place of animals. My house is where the vulture sleeps ... Be merciful to me, O God, for I am the worst among all my sisters. I am a woman who has not given birth properly. O God of Glory, if you have visited me, O Lord of hosts, come upon me with your entire heart. I am so sick, O God, and I am unable to pray. I am hungry; I am naked.[5]

If there is divine judgement there is also the redemption of an 'open-hearted' God. Christians encourage themselves with the phrase 'God has not forgotten us!', 'God has not abandoned or discarded us!'

OT images of exile and exodus, of divine protection and leading, are as pervasive as those of judgement. In the Dioceses of Yei and Kajo-Keji, where the ECS has long been established, touched by currents of the East African Revival, visions of Exodus merge with contemporary pilgrimage. In 1990, as the SPLA planned an attack on the government garrison at Yei, Bishop Seme Solomona (ECS, Diocese of Yei) and Father Peter Dada (Vicar-General of the Catholic Diocese of Yei) were encouraged to evacuate their people. Departing by night for fear of government attack, the churchmen, in a convoy of some 100 vehicles under SPLA guidance, accompanied the masses southward toward Kaya. The settlement on the Ugandan border soon became a burgeoning community in exile, home to some 30,000, in which the two Churches were essential to all aspects of life. By 1993, however, Kaya itself came under threat and the two leaders determined to lead their throngs further southward, across the Ugandan border. In the midst of the rainy season, suffering from cold and exposure, Koboko became the new encampment. As has become custom in exile, churches were constructed first, taking precedence over houses. Gradually stability grew, but by 1996 the pilgrimage veered back toward Sudan. As insecurity increased in Northern Uganda the fortunes of the SPLA shifted, resulting in the recapture of Kaya. Yei itself came under SPLA control for first time. Among Christians grounded in the Bible, exodus and 'wilderness journey' became bywords. As an estimated 80,000 souls trekked homeward a 'faithful people' acknowledged their 'faithful God' whose divine presence accompanied them throughout their sojourn.[6]

Often it has been from the visions of new converts at the heart of the war zone that fresh symbols of conciliation and transformation arise. Young Philip Makuei saw an overwhelming image of Christ crucified, a brilliance that would not leave him, waking or sleeping. As a craftsman, he searched for metal he could work, and found the malleable alloy of a gas tank inside the carcass of a MIG jet bomber. The Libyan aircraft had been used in bombing raids across the war zone and crashed in 1988, near Philip's village of Jalé. From this metal Philip fashioned a pectoral cross. The crucifixes he creates combine silhouettes of four MIG bombers, their nose tips colliding, to form a cross. Time and again, during this war, the most brutal tools of destruction and death are transformed into images of life.

Similar is the massive Church of Zion, near the old cattle camp of Pakeo in Upper Nile Province, probably the largest mud and thatch construction in Sudan. Built in 1992, each aspect of its cruciform design was conceived in dreams. According to one widely embraced vision, four peoples, long in conflict with each other – the Jieng, Nuer, Murlé and Mandari – will enter, one through each of its four doors, there to be reconciled. The ancient cruciform pattern, first introduced by Anglican missionaries, plants the hope that Sudanese will find a place of conciliation within the cross of Christ.

Across Nilotic regions long, hand-held crosses made of wood, metal and ivory bristle over church gatherings, declaring the presence of a compassionate God, and the radical transformation of spiritual allegiances. Crosses are fashioned from the razed sacred posts and trees that once stood at the heart of sacrificial shrines. Sacred spears, long the symbols of Nilotic religion, have evolved into finely carved crosses to serve as 'swords of the Spirit' against unseen powers. Newly-converted diviners remake their wands and fly whisks, long used to invoke ancestral divinities, to declare the glory of the crucified.

In Northern Sudan, as well, the Spirit moves in unanticipated quarters. Waves of war have, since the mid-1980s, pushed over two million people of African descent northward where, as oppressed minorities, often near starvation, many find solidarity within the Church. Extraordinarily, this exodus has replanted Christian communities in regions such as Dongola where none have existed since the decline of Christian Nubia over five centuries ago. Even when war ends, however, many will not return south. The presence of the displaced has unalterably transformed the face of Northern Sudan, and Muslim and Christian must learn to live together in an open society.

The intolerance and brutality of Khartoum's National Islamic Front, far from creating an Islamic state, has alienated many moderate Muslims, nudging some, particularly of the Nuba ethnic groups, into the embrace of Christ. Merging a passionate, new-found faith with strains of Islamic asceticism, the ecstatic experiences of these converts have created new engines of Christian evangelization. If Islamic regimes of the 1960s tried to uproot Christianity by edict, later Muslim governments cannot deny that the ECS and its sister Churches have become an incontrovertible part of Sudanese life.

It is impossible, then, to speak of a single 'spirituality' of the Episcopal Church of the Sudan, but of diverse expressions unified in a synthesis of suffering and celebration. Whether on the battle front, or in desolate displacement camps, believers experience the numinous, healing, recreating presence of God. An impoverished, often ill-administered Church continually reveals its capacity to hold onto life, to build and rebuild through waves of devastation. Far from being acquiescent and depressive, it is, in many contexts, celebratory, evangelistic, and charismatic. Though God's action may be conceived in OT terms of judgement, he is unreservedly the God of salvation revealed in the One who has passed through death and now abides among his people. The diversity of this Church is both its strength and its weakness, its hidden wealth, and its fragmentation. We close with an acclamation from one of Sudan's most popular vernacular hymns:

Let us give thanks. Let us give thanks to the Lord in the day of devastation; and in the day of contentment.
Jesus has bound the world round with the pure light of the word of his Father.
When we beseech the Lord and unite our hearts and have hope, then the evil power has no strength. God has not forgotten us.
Evil is departing and holiness is advancing, these are the things that shake the earth.[7]

Notes

1 This song of four verses was composed in the Jieng Tuich dialect by Mary Alueel Garang from Upper Nile Province, and translated by the author. Deriving from a lineage of composers in the vernacular musical idiom, Mary was a new convert and had only begun to learn to read when she composed this song.
2 The term here translated 'breath of life' is the Jieng word *wei*, which missionaries often used to translate 'soul', 'inner life' or 'spirit', but might better be defined as 'life force' or 'dynamism'. Like the Greek *pneuma* and Hebrew *ruach*, it is linked to concepts of 'breath', and so recurs in verse 4.
3 The Jieng are more commonly known as 'Dinka' to the outside world, but

John S. Pobee

Jieng is the name by which this Nilotic people know themselves, and by which many would prefer to be known.

4 From a new chorus in colloquial Arabic, popular in Equatoria Province. Colloquial Arabic gives voice to prayer and an outpouring of choruses that serve to unify communities in urban centres, but may lack the subtle richness and profundity of vernacular language.

5 The worlds of Rebecca Lueth Wël, Mothers' Union leader for the Diocese of Bor, at Loboni Displacement Camp, Southern Sudan, 23 September 1994. Translated from Jieng by Revd Akurdit Ngong and the author.

6 For a fuller description, see Andrew C. Wheeler, 'Church growth in southern Sudan, 1983–1996, a survey of present understanding' in *Experiences in Evangelisation* (Nairobi: Pauline Press, soon to be published).

7 Verse one of six in a song composed by Mary Alueel Garang among the displaced at Pagere just after fleeing the fall of Torit in June 1992, repeatedly sung to welcome the Archbishop of Canterbury in Southern Sudan (New Year 1993).

Further reading

Stuart A. Brown (ed.), *Seeing an Open Society: Inter-Faith Relations and Dialogue in Sudan Today* (Faith in Sudan Series, no. 2; Nairobi: Pauline Publications Africa, 1997).

Brian de Saram, *Nile Harvest* (privately published in England, 1992).

Marc Nikkel, 'The origins and development of Christianity among the Dinka of Sudan with special reference to the songs of Dinka Christians' (unpublished doctoral thesis, University of Edinburgh, 1993).

G. Vantini, *Christianity in the Sudan* (Bologna, 1981).

Andrew C. Wheeler (ed.), *Land of Promise: Church Growth in the Sudan at War* (Faith in Sudan Series, no. 1; Nairobi: Pauline Publications Africa, Oct. 1997).

An African Anglican's view of salvation

John S. Pobee

There is not one African; there are many Africans. The adjective African refers to a vast continent, indeed, the second largest, in which are located diverse and different peoples, cultures, temperament and hundreds, if not thousands, of languages. The Church of the Province of Southern Africa, for example, does its mission and ministry in the context of plurality of Africans and has to proclaim the gospel to these several diverse and different expressions of *homo Africanus*. I am hereby pleading caution against an oft-heard expression: *'the* African'. In terms of communication, we need to get onto the wavelength of these many and diverse Africans so as to grip them for Christ, 'our only Mediator and Advocate' as Christians affirm.

To be an African and Anglican implies a potential contradiction and inconsistency. The word 'Anglican' signals a certain 'tribalization' of the faith; for that word in origin means English. Anglicanism, whatever else it is, is the English culturing of the 'one holy, catholic and apostolic Church'. Thus to be an African Anglican is in many ways to be trapped in an English captivity. The spirituality, the worship, the reading of scriptures, etc. bear the heavy marks of Englishness which are not exactly on *homo Africanus's* wavelength. The implication is that there is no salvation outside the English cultural expression of the one holy, catholic and apostolic Church. Hence some of the insistence on taking English names as a symbol of a change or conversion and, conversely, the calls in Africa for indigenization, inculturalization, accommodation, adaptation, incarnation, *skenosis*, etc.

The world of politics also offers salvation. Kwame Nkrumah, doyen of African nationalism in the 1950s and 1960s, articulated that yearning for political salvation when he said 'Seek ye first the political kingdom and all other things shall be added unto you'.[1] Of course, we also know how, after political freedom, corruption in diverse forms and sizes reduced the promising land of freedom to penury and suffering and pain. Some of Nkrumah's lieutenants were avid and 'faithful' churchgoers; some of them were serious Anglicans. They had little difficulty with the way things were going under Nkrumah. This Ghanaian case helps to focus the issue in a way: first, how does the particular/political/economic offer of salvation relate to the offer of salvation proclaimed by the life of religious people? The second issue is that salvation can never be a *fait accompli*; it is a process. It is an ongoing struggle against ever-threatening forces of evil and destruction like corruption.

In the family of Christians stand the African initiatives in Christianity. They too preach salvation but with a very striking slant. Many are attracted to them, indeed from our Anglican family too, because they desire health and wholeness. A catechist of the Musama Disco Christo Church asked in a homily: 'We are all in this Church because we have found healing here. But for this Church the great majority of us here assembled would not be alive today. This is the reason why we are here; is that not so?' C. G. Baeta, a distinguished Ghanaian Evangelical Presbyterian pastor and ecumenist, who did research on MDCC, records: 'To that question came from the congregation an answer, a unanimous and most decided Yes.'[2] Salvation that does not include health and wholeness cannot be satisfying for Africans. Yes, Anglicans have Church clinics and hospitals, but it is not the same as the demonstration of the Spirit's power to heal by a particular spiritual person.

Similarly, Africans in their pluriformity come to Anglicanism not as empty shells to be filled with information about salvation; they come with some knowledge, some experience, some expectations, some yearnings for the transcendent, for salvation, etc. They deceive themselves who think Africans can just divest themselves of their heritage and culture.

The New Testament, the Charter of the Christian Church, insists that the work of the Church is to proclaim the cross of Jesus Christ, and the power is salvation in Jesus's name. The message of the cross is foolishness to those who are perishing, but to us who are being saved it is the power of God (1 Cor 1.18; cf. 1.21). Anglicans, like other Christians, proclaim salvation through the death and resurrection of Jesus Christ. The fourth Gospel puts it another way: 'These (the record of the deeds and words of Jesus) are written so that you may come to believe that Jesus is the Messiah, the Son of God, and that through believing you may have life in his name' (John 20.31). One hardly needs to state that life is the fourth Gospel's language for salvation through Jesus Christ.

Even if the theme of salvation is the common patrimony of all Christians, the expressions of it will be different. Just as a Jewish expression of salvation is different from a Hellenistic expression, so too even within the one communion, we can expect different ways of expressing the theme of salvation. Uniformity of expression is not the true test of belonging to one family.

Secondly, the Anglican Consultative Council and the Lambeth Conference represent but two expressions of the one communion. The basic meaning of the Greek and Latin words translated as communion is participation. It is participation in the triune God. There is communion because together we participate in God, Father, Son and Holy Spirit. Participation is the salvation we proclaim. Left to ourselves we are not working to participate in God. But in God's grace, not by our own efforts nor in our own right, God offers us and takes us into communion with God-self. That is the ultimate salvation. To that extent, salvation is an unmerited favour of God. Starting from such an understanding of salvation, worship becomes a crucial element of the experience of salvation. Worship is a way of appropriating the offer of salvation by God through Jesus Christ.

There is another element of communion – it has a horizontal dimension, which we may call fellowship. Because we have the vertical reference to the triune God, we share fellowship with others who have the same reference point. So, different as an African may be from the Caucasian or Asian or Pacific Islander, we are together in that one body of Christ, sharing God's grace of salvation. There is a sense in which the horizontal expression of the communion is an expression in the life of society of the vertical communion. Holding together the vertical and horizontal communions is on the road to the furtherance of salvation. Salvation may not be summed up in only worship, the vertical aspect of communion; it requires also the horizontal. That is why apartheid in South Africa and genocide in Rwanda and Burundi have been an affront to salvation in its fullness and, therefore, of communion.

As an African, communion–community has a particular note. The prototypical community is the family which consists of the living, the dead (the living dead, ancestors) and those yet-to-be-born. For an African Anglican I am as much concerned with my own salvation as with that of the family or wider community. The salvation of my generation is intimately connected with those who have gone before and those yet-to-be-born. As an African I am dissatisfied with only my salvation. I am happier if it embraces my ancestors and descendants.

It hardly needs arguing that the language of the first century AD has to be interpreted and translated into today's African's world-view, if it is to speak and grip them. Literalistic interpretations will not do. And we need to remember that every translation involves interpretation. Paul's letters use four images to describe the message of salvation: redemption, reconciliation, sacrifice and justification and new birth. How may these images be interpreted into the African idiom so that Africans too may hear the word of God in their own language? There has to be an inter-cultural interpretation. Mission must be the perspective from which the interpretation is done. This is important for two reasons: first, scriptures of the earliest community took shape and were preserved in the context of the mission of the Church; second, the goal of interpretation is so to communicate God's word as to win people over to God through Christ.

I want to examine two images of the word 'mission'. One is that of going out to the ends of the world (Matt 28.19). The other is a gathering-in represented by the language of harvest so common in the teaching of Jesus.[3] The language of gathering-in used of mission is consistent with our self-understanding as communion.

There are two more aspects of the issue of scripture. Its use is not a one-way street. It speaks to us. But also we question scripture even in its message of salvation. The story of the pain and death and poverty of African situations is putting a question to the biblical message of salvation as good news. Is it really good news when people are being pummelled both at home and internationally, not always through their own fault?

The second is the culture of pluralism which is our African story, more so because in several places of Africa – e.g. the Gambia, Guinea, etc. – Churches are a tiny minority in a sea of Muslims. We need to remember Judaism, Islam and Christianity are together The Religions of The Book – we have common and similar roots. It is one reason why I earlier suggested taking a model of mission as a gathering-in. It is also the reason why we need

John S. Pobee

ecumenism as the perspective for our Bible reading and for being the Church. The culture of pluralism requires us to recognize that truth is spoken by many voices. So the only viable way forward is dialogue between the African situation and the biblical message. The call and life of salvation is nurtured and sustained by scriptures, read, marked and inwardly digested.

Anglicans are committed to tradition. Tradition is not some solid rock from the dead past. Tradition is understanding the complexity of the past so as to secure the future. It is something dynamic, a stream of how the Churches in the light of scripture tried to speak to the challenges of their world and time. As such it is a helpful instrument for coping with our situations.

Anglicans are serious about the first five centuries of Christian history and tradition. We can learn from tradition but not be trapped in it. The operative test is whether the tradition is able to renew people for Christ's sake.

Reason is the third hall-mark of Anglicanism. The Johannine affirmation that 'the word (Reason) became flesh' commits us to rationality. For that reason I am unhappy with the fundamentalist reading of scripture concerning salvation.

All too often the message of salvation has been laid out in institutional terms, i.e. in terms of the Church, the sacraments, etc. We have often spoken as if salvation is impossible or not realizable outside the Church. Cyprian of Carthage (d. 258) left us the statement 'extra ecclesiam nulla salus est', i.e. outside the Church there is no salvation. He formulated his piece of theology in the context of the controversy over the large numbers who lapsed from the faith during the persecution of the emperor Decius in 249. The Church, he said, is the body of Christ and will share in the victory of its head, Christ. He continues 'No one can have God as Father who does not have the Church as mother'. Thus salvation was locked into the institution of the Church. This tradition of the Church from an African Church Father sees salvation in terms of Church and sacrament and in very exclusivist terms. It is not healthy to see salvation in primarily institutional, ecclesial and sacramental terms. We need to pierce through the institution to the Communion with God which the Almighty has been offering peoples created in God's image.

Anglicans in Africa still live in the style of Cyprian in spite of all the ecumenical developments such as *Baptism, Eucharist and Ministry*.[4] The discerning observer can agree that there are signs of God's hand and saving activity outside the Church. There are many outside the Church who are feeling after God that they may find God and do not feel attracted to the Church partly because the Church does not make them welcome and feel at home. When we consider the complicity of Churches and Church people in some of the most heinous crimes against humanity and society, who are we to limit salvation to the Church and to call the Church alone the arc of salvation? Let us heed the stricture of Jesus: 'The tax collectors and the prostitutes are going into the Kingdom of God ahead of you' (Matt 21.31). Persons in leadership positions may take heed of what Paul writes to the Corinthians: 'I punish my body and enslave it, so that after proclaiming to others I myself should not be disqualified' (1 Cor 9.21). Salvation is never a *fait accompli*; it is a process, a pilgrimage and the reward is God's gift to give, not our right. This last point is worth stressing because African Christianity as a whole has a tendency to emphasize the Old Testament because of the affinity between the Semitic culture and some African cultures. As a result it constantly runs the risk of legalism.

One lesson I take from the earliest Christian community is that it was a worshipping community; its life and identity were marked by worship. Worship was a way of being in tune with the salvation wrought in and by Jesus Christ. The stylized picture of the Acts of the Apostles was that they spent much time in the temple and synagogues, kept the hours of prayer, praised God, broke bread (Acts 2.42 – 3.1). Some of the worship life was sacramental, i.e. baptism and Eucharist.

The worship in some ways was a drama of their beliefs, especially of salvation through the death and resurrection of Jesus Christ (1 Cor 10.16–22, 11.23–32). In a simple way the drama of baptism communicated the dying of Jesus and his rising (Col 2.11–15). The Eucharistic celebration dramatically portrayed and taught the salvation from the cross. Art became a mode of instruction and inculcation of the word of salvation. African Churches have a lot to learn from this. Many in African churches are non-literate and do not understand technical theological language. Drama, art, liturgy, worship are appropriate and effective ways of communicating the gospel of salvation. But if it is to communicate, it must be in the language and symbol of *homo Africanus*.

Symbols and images are crucial for communicating the message of salvation because 'they speak to humans existentially and find an echo in the inarticulate depths of their psyches. Symbols transform the horizons of human life, integrate the perception of reality, alter the scale of values, reorient one's loyalties, attachments and aspirations in a manner far exceeding the powers of abstract conceptual thought.'[5] Many of the faithful in Africa may 'not know book' but are being renewed, put on the way of salvation through worship.

Of course, there is the warning to be added that the ritual alone does not do the trick. It is not a formula to be applied like 'Hey presto!' and salvation is achieved. There is always the danger of treating worship as a magic formula. Indeed, the distinction between religion and magic is only a thin wall. John Chrysostom (*c.* 347–407) spoke of two altars, one within the sanctuary, the other outside in the public square. This was his way of saying

Christian worship in the Church is inseparable from committed engagement in society and culture. The liturgy that transpires inside a church building – prayers, songs, chants, creeds, proclamation of the word, the Eucharist and baptism – are important but not the whole thing. Beyond and outside the worship building there is a task of redeeming all life to God. Ion Bria, an Orthodox theologian, calls this the 'liturgy after the liturgy'.[6] In the liturgy, in mission, in witness, in engagement with life's struggles in society and culture we strain at the salvation on offer through Christ and in Christ's name. Paul the apostle expresses similar sentiments when he appeals to the community of believers in Rome (Rom 12.1–2). The Gospel of salvation starts with a sense of the gracious and gratuitous gift of God through Jesus Christ and brings with it an obligation to go out and live it. Hence it concerns the reconciliation of Hutu and Tutsi in Rwanda–Burundi, Black and White in South Africa, and Arab and Negroid in Sudan, the Ewe and the Akan in Ghana, Konkomba and Dagomba in northern Ghana, etc. It concerns justice for women; it concerns a just, participatory and sustainable society. Only then can the message of salvation be the *cantus firmus* of our living as persons committed to Jesus, Lord and Christ in Africa and elsewhere.

Notes

1 J. S. Pobee, *Kwame Nkrumah and the Churches in Ghana 1949–1966* (Accra: Asempa, 1988), pp. 118ff.
2 C. G. Baeta, *Prophetism in Ghana* (London: SCM, 1963), p. 54.
3 See Teresa Okure, 'Mission as gathering in: a key in the search of a new hermeneutic for mission', ch. V in J. S. Pobee (ed.), *In Search of Renewed Biblical Hermeneutics for Mission* (forthcoming).
4 *Baptism, Eucharist and Ministry*, Faith and Order Paper no. 111 (Geneva: WCC, 1982).
5 Avery Dulles, *Models of the Church* (expanded edition: New York, Doubleday, 1974), pp. 20–1.
6 Ion Bria, *The Liturgy after the Liturgy* (Geneva: WCC, 1996).

Anglican spirituality and worship among the Maori people

Tiki Raumati

To understand the effects of Anglican spirituality upon Maoridom one needs to know a little of the Anglican Church history in Aotearoa/New Zealand. Anglicanism was not known in the early birth of Christianity in Aotearoa. The Maori were more interested in agriculture than religion, but because kindness and *aroha*/love were shown by the early Pakeha missionaries, the Maori responded in like manner. The missionaries learned the Maori language very quickly and took advantage of Maori spirituality by infiltrating Maori understanding of God, their creator.

Christianity brought a new way, in particular to the Maori of Taranaki. 'Glory to God in the Highest and peace and goodwill to all men.' Te Whiti O Rongo Mai left these words to his people to practise in life and to never forget. When the land wars broke out the religious walked out and the constabulary walked in. These atrocities have never been brought to justice, so the Church, or Christianity, which was introduced by the Pakeha, could not be trusted. 'You tell us to close our eyes and bow our heads in prayer and when we lift up our heads and open our eyes, our land has disappeared.' Te Whiti forbade his people to learn to read or write, for fear of losing their land at the stroke of a pen.

The early missionaries got in and mastered the Maori language by translating the 1662 Prayer Book and the Holy Bible. Let me say at this juncture, by preserving the Maori language in writing, the early missionaries had a vision of Maori Anglicanism and not Pakeha Anglicanism, although there was a time Maori was forbidden to be spoken. There were those who wanted little black English people, for the Maori to lose his identity completely – a monument was built on One Tree Hill, Auckland, to a dying race.

In 1814, Marsden established the Maori Church, and 43 years later, in 1857, Bishop Selwyn wrote his constitution, calling it an evidence of growth and maturity in the New Zealand Church. The Anglican Church somehow blundered along with no Maori whatsoever included in the Constitution of the Church. By 1928, the Rt Revd F. A. Bennett was made suffragan of the Diocese of Waiapu and Bishop of Aotearoa and so were the Rt Revd W. N. Panapa and Rt Revd M. A. Bennett. For 50 years, the

Maori were not given their freedom, but were under the control of an 1857 Constitution.

There is now a new Constitution, which the Church of Aotearoa/New Zealand is handling and coping with, although some would like to turn the clock back. Within the Church of Aotearoa/New Zealand we have three *Tikanga* (*tikanga* literally means 'my way'), Tikanga Maori, Tikanga Pakeha, Tikanga Pacifica. No Tikanga is to dominate the other, but to seek a consensus and come to an amicable agreement for the good of the Church of Aotearoa/New Zealand and the Pacific.

There is very little written by our early Maori priests on Maori spirituality, maybe because they were so indoctrinated by the missionaries and teachers of the faith to give away anything that held them of their past. Some tribes were forbidden to build their meeting houses with carvings, for it was seen by the missionaries as a form of worshipping idols. There were those clergy who would not have anything to do with anything of a spiritual nature in Maoridom.

Thus we of this era are clinging on to what little is known and trying to put down on paper what can be gleaned from whatever source is available. The Anglican Church has come to realize that you will not get to the depth and inner being of Maoridom, or its spirituality, unless you let it be. There has been a great turn around in the Anglican Church of Aotearoa. Its theologians realize that the Church is a growing and alive organism, living and vibrant. That if it is to endorse its catholicity then it must take into account every part of it, irrespective of its size or people, otherwise they just vote with their feet, and some have done so.

Faith-healing was rampant in the 1920s and 1930s and not all of it was good. There were many who claimed the gift of healing. Wiremu T. Ratana began its ministry at that time and had many Maori followers. It is still the largest indigenous religious organization in Aotearoa/New Zealand. Many so-called faith healers got in on the act to the extent that they started to tell their clients what to take as medicine, and what to do, to their detriment. Thus a law was passed by the government that those who practised faith-healing had to stop. Today some Christian bodies practise faith-healing.

Today, we have a Prayer Book which tries to bring together all Tikangas, as shown very clearly by the different language and some services that were not in the 1662 Prayer Book, although there was a separate translation of that Prayer Book into Maori which was revered and loved. In the New Zealand Prayer Book 1989, nearly all services contain the Maori language both in diglot and in Maori alone. Every church in the land using the Prayer Book, when doing any service we are reminded that we belong to one another and it tells us that we have something new to add to the spirituality of our nation. *Pai marire.*

Section Two

Life of the Church

Anglicanism in Jerusalem

Riah Abu El-Assal

History

The genesis of Anglicanism in the Middle East was in the middle of the nineteenth century, and springs from a desire to establish a 'Protestant' presence in the primary city of Christendom, the mother city of our faith – Jerusalem. The two major Protestant powers of the time, Britain and Prussia, initiated a joint endeavour by establishing a Bishopric in Jerusalem. In 1841, Michael Solomon Alexander was named the first Bishop. Alexander had many qualifications for this joint venture: born in Germany, he was a convert to Christianity and an Anglican priest. Being a former Jewish Rabbi, Bishop Alexander, a member of CMJ (Church Mission among the Jews), had as his aim the conversion of Jewry in Palestine.

The beginning did not relate much to the indigenous Arabs and Christians of this land. However, the second Bishop, Samuel Gobat, expanded the ministry of the Church, especially in educational terms, and directed mission in an indigenous direction. He was the first to build schools for local people. He ordained the first three Arab priests.

Bishop George Blyth (1887–1914) was responsible for the building of the Cathedral church of St George in Jerusalem. During his episcopate, a further step was taken towards the indigenization of the Church: the Palestine Native Church Council was founded in 1905. The CMS (Church Mission Society) gained the upper hand in the Council, at least in financial terms. But, in 1976, the Church moved toward a new provincial structure with the installation of Bishop Faik Ibrahim Haddad as the Anglican Bishop in Jerusalem. Thus, the Church achieved total independence on Epiphany 1976, the day of the installation.

Haddad's successor, Bishop Samir Kafity, currently the Bishop in Jerusalem, and formerly the President-bishop of the Province, once stated that 'Anglicanism is at its best when it is an integral part of the local environment'. He has achieved some major targets in the history of the diocese and the Province, strengthening ecumenical relations with other sister-Churches and serving as President of the Middle East Council of Churches. He still has one more year in office, and will be suceeded as thirteenth Bishop in Jerusalem in September 1998 by his coadjutor, Bishop Riah.

Expectations, fears and hopes

The Easter Orthodox Icon of the Annunciation shows Mary being greeted by the Angel as she walks towards the well of water. In this icon, Mary, whose womb became God's throne, represents the Church, perceived as a pilgrim 'walking' Church. She walks towards the well of life: her God. In this very way I view the history of the Anglican Church in Jerusalem and the Middle East. It has been walking, travelling and roaming this land of the Holy One as a pilgrim, walking in life, seeking integration with the people and the culture. For, as the Church walks God-ward, she also walks towards the people, with them, and through them in order to achieve her eternal goal: God. The way towards that goal is hard, painful and arduous. Like Mary, the Church has to walk the Via Dolorosa with her God, in order to attain victory and triumph, and shine forth to all people.

Our Church stems from the people, and she has taken upon her the responsibility to explain the Palestinian plea and make it manifest to all, especially in the West. This little tiny Church knows that her Lord and God started His ministry in Nazareth, proclaiming liberty and freedom for humanity, calling for justice to all. Already from the beginning, the Church with her leaders has been examining ways to illustrate the message of Christ in the spirit of openness, gentleness, and love, so that people in the West may be conscious of our existence and our history. In fact, our Church has been known for its advocacy of peace, preaching a Justice based on truth and peace for both Palestinians and Israelis.

This peace-making task is one of the major targets that the Church aims at and hopes for its success. However, the challenges of the Church are numerous. The threatened situation of Christians in the Holy Land is our biggest concern. This situation is not due solely to the Israeli occupation and harassment of local people. There is an exodus of Christians, not only from the Holy Land but from Turkey, Lebanon, Iraq, and Egypt. The possible extinction of Christianity in the Middle East is a matter of concern to the Church everywhere, as would be a similar threat in any part of the world. The disappearance of indigenous Christian communities from their land is a big loss, given the historical – and sentimental – ties of Christianity in this land. The loss would be sad, especially of our ancient communities, with their cultural traditions; it is an impoverishment of the human community. Christians will not stay, simply for the sake of staying. They will stay, if they can not only survive, but also make a reasonable life for themselves and their children. Accordingly, the Church locally believes that it must create a viable economic and political basis for such continued existence. This would be worthwhile. Such a step certainly could move our Church from the only-receiving end to the giving end, giving to all those in need in Palestine and abroad.

Alongside this particular need, one must take into consideration our relations with the contemporary world faiths, especially those monotheistic religions existing and living in Palestine: Judaism and Islam. As Bishop I always put an emphasis on the importance for the small Christian communities of practical co-operation with Palestinian Muslims, and the need to stress what the two faiths have in common. Christians, though, should not ignore their distinctive understanding of God and his purpose in Creation and Redemption. God in Christ calls the whole human race into unity given by the Holy Spirit; and witness to that faith in our land is bound up with the quest for reconciliation and unity among Christians themselves here in Jerusalem, Bethlehem, Nazareth and everywhere. I believe therefore, that 'Unity first' should be taken seriously in the Church. Alongside this goes the dialogue with our Muslim sisters and brothers, and with our Jewish neighbours. In fact, the Church is only at the beginning of a new relationship with other religions; and our final understanding must be that dialogue ought to replace hostile rivalry. One should also stress the importance of distinguishing Jews and Judaism from Israelis and the State of Israel.

For Christians, Justice is inseparable from God's forgiveness and reconciling love. These three together make up the basis for the kingdom of God. This kingdom becomes in the New Testament a reality in human life through the suffering and death of the word of God become human in Jesus.

To conclude, one may realize that Peace is vital as a prerequisite for the comfort and flourishing of all people in our land, Muslims, Christians and Jews. Unless there is peace, there is no hope for a better situation of living, or even security. The future of a Jewish homeland depends largely on the recovery of the dignity of the downtrodden Palestinians. Future regional and even world peace would depend on the establishment of a lasting peace in the region.

It is one of the great anomalies of recent Church history that while Christians throughout the world have engaged energetically in favour of the oppressed in all kinds of areas, there has been almost total silence on the persistent abuse of human rights by the successive governments of Israel.

The road to a settlement based on justice and peace for all the people of the region is sure to guarantee a more significant Christian presence throughout the Diocese of Jerusalem, which covers Palestine, Israel, Jordan, Lebanon and Syria, this place which in a particular way is his land, the Holy Land. The risk for peace must be taken by all sides, that Jerusalem may once again be 'a vision of peace' for all people.

Anglicanism and the Aladura Churches in Nigeria

Afe Adogame and Akin Omoyajowo

Introduction

The earliest missionary efforts in what became known as Nigeria was in the sixteenth and seventeenth centuries when Spanish Capuchin Fathers arrived at Warri in 1515, and Portuguese Augustinian monks from São Tomé entered Benin in 1570. This early attempt at sowing the seed of Christianity left very faint and scanty footprints in these areas. With the re-Christianization in the mid-nineteenth century, a remarkable impact was witnessed from then onwards. This latter enterprise commenced through the pioneering efforts of Methodism and Anglicanism respectively. The planting of Anglicanism in Nigeria was actually initiated and nurtured by the Church Missionary Society (CMS) missionaries in 1842. What began with a lone missionary has grown today into a virile and self-determining province of about sixty dioceses with membership conservatively put at several millions.

From the mid-1920s onwards, an initiative in making Christianity a religion in which Nigerians 'feel at home' or which they 'perceive as their own' was experienced. One way of describing some of these movements which emerged and become prominent in western Nigeria is as Aladura Churches. *Aladura* derives from Yoruba *al adua* (the praying people/owners of prayer). They are so called from their penchant and proclivity for prayer, healing, prophecy, visions and dreams, and the prominence of other charismatic gifts and activities. They are also often led by a charismatic figure. The churches that fall under this umbrella include the Christ Apostolic Church (CAC), Cherubim and Seraphim (C&S), Church of the Lord – Aladura (CLA), Celestial Church of Christ (CCC), Evangelical Church of Yahweh (ECY) and their various appendages and splinter formations. In spite of the affinities among the Aladura group of Churches, it is important to note that each has its own religious dynamic. One distinguishing feature is easily noticeable in their histories of emergence as well as differences in specific doctrines and details of ritual acts and performance.

This chapter explores the relationship between Anglicanism and the Aladura Churches as two brands of Christianity that have become well-established in Nigeria. The pre- and post-independence era will be examined in order to see whether and in what ways both Christian traditions have influenced or shaped one another in their polity, world-views and ritual structures. We suggest how the strengthening of already existing ecumenical dispositions or the forging of a more profound ecumenical spirit will become meaningful and resilient in the emerging global religious and socio-political dispensation. The import of such ecumenical initiatives between and beyond both traditions in such a culturally plural-istic entity as Nigeria cannot be over-emphasized.

It is expedient to examine Aladura pattern of emergence in order fully to understand the 'polemic exchanges' between them and the Anglican Church. The pattern of emergence of the Aladura Churches can be categorized into two levels. The first refers to those which emerged as *egbe adura* (prayer groups) within the Anglican tradition, but soon severed and established themselves as 'independent'. Churches which fall under this category include the CAC, C&S and CLA. For instance, the Diamond Stone Society of the Anglican Church metamorphosed through a complex process into CAC in the early 1930s. Under the second level are movements born independently without any links with the Anglican Church. The genesis of such groups depended largely on the initiative of a prophetic/charismatic figure. An example of such a movement is the CCC founded through S. B. J. Oschoffa in 1947. Though it had its emergence in Porto Novo (Daho-mey), it was in Nigeria that its most profound impact has been witnessed.

A feature that runs through both categories is that former members of the Anglican Church form a noticeable percentage of their nucleus mem-bership. Aladura Churches also serve as a form of attraction to some members from the Anglican Church as soon as they start to expand and proliferate. It is therefore within these contexts that the examination of the inter-connections between Anglicanism and Aladura becomes more understandable. Peel (1968, p. 205) has shown through an earlier survey of the Aladura Churches in the 1960s that 63 per cent and 66 per cent of converts into CAC and C&S branches in Ibadan were from the Anglican Church alone.

Anglicanism and Aladura in pre-independent Nigeria

Before a consideration of the relationship between the two brands of Christianity in the immediate era prior to Nigeria's independence, we may perhaps ask what factors informed the polemical attitudes. The Aladura Churches accuse Anglican members of practising ambivalent Christianity, idolatry and a faith too dressed in foreign (Western) garb in their polity and liturgical content. They claim that their *raison d'être* was to 'cleanse or purify the world, including the established churches of spiritual bankruptcy'. The Anglican Church, on the other hand, criticizes the Aladura Churches for having too close a rapport with the Yoruba cultural matrix, syncretism, and what they perceive as an indiscriminate use of charismatic gifts.

With the religious, political and socio-cultural circumstances surrounding the emergence of the C&S in 1925, CLA and CAC in 1930 from within the Anglican mainstream, it is clear that the relationship between the Anglican Church and the severing groups in the pre-independence era was both genial and antipathetic. The nucleus of these movements started as prayer bands/fellowship groups within the Anglican Church. They were warmly accepted as full-fledged associations within the Church. As active members, they participated in all church activities and programmes aside from holding their own prayer meetings and extra Bible study discussions. Another feature of such meetings was the exhibition of charismatic gifts of prophecy, visions and dreams which were not given equal prominence in the Anglican mainstream. Central to the activities of the prayer groups was the awareness for a more ingrained African Christian spirituality, and their repugnance for the spiritual ambivalence of fellow members in the Anglican Church who secretly patronize traditional medicine men and diviners for their existential problems. It was these concerns that partly culminated in the eventual emergence of new indigenous Churches such as the Aladura type.

The Anglican authorities became gradually uncomfortable and sceptical of the new initiatives of these groups. Their attitude towards the 'prayer groups' began to change when they noticed these charismatic experiences, what they called 'irregularities' and 'innovations', being introduced into the doctrine and rituals of the Church. Such members and their activities were immediately condemned as unscriptural. For instance, due to such allegations, Ositelu was summoned on 2 February 1926 before the Church authorities to defend himself against the charges of introducing irregularities or innovations in the Church (Turner, 1967). When he could not successfully convince the authorities, he was suspended and later dismissed from the Anglican Church on 19 April of the same year.

Shortly after the planting of the first CCC parish in Makoko-Lagos in 1951 the new movement began to gain popularity through healing miracles witnessed during their services. It was claimed that Oschoffa healed an insane woman soon after he arrived in Lagos. The news of this healing miracle spread around the Lagos area within a short time. Such a development made the established Churches uncomfortable, as several of their members became attracted to this new group. This probably explains why a number of clergymen from various Churches (including the Anglican Church) invited Oschoffa to a meeting at a hall in Yaba-Lagos (CCC Constitution, 1980, p. 14). The meeting was aimed at allaying their fears, suspicion and scepticism about the new group which was attracting wide publicity. Through other miracles which followed this meeting, many members of the Anglican Church and other mainline Churches got converted into the growing group.

The colonial situation further made the relationship between the Aladura Church during their formative years and the Anglican Church far from cordial. In the earlier years of Anglicanism in Nigeria, there existed a somewhat intimate relationship between the colonial government and leaders of the Church who were mostly white missionaries. Such a connection no doubt favoured the Anglican Church to the detriment of the emerging indigenous Churches. As far as the Aladura Churches were concerned, such a cordial relationship of the Anglican Church with the colonial government, the foreignness of their polity and liturgical tradition was insufferable.

There was also the cold and spiteful posture often shown by the colonial administration towards the Aladura Churches. For instance, Omoyajowo (1978, p. 97) highlighted the impression of a colonial officer (Captain Ross, the Resident at Oyo) about the indigenous Churches when he wrote in 1930 that 'they are not recognized Christian missions and they should be regarded as enemies'. The colonial governments were also apprehensive of the danger which such groups might pose to constituted authority if they became 'well established' and 'strong'. Such an attitude influenced the Nigerian elite to a large extent and they treated these Churches with contempt during their formative years. 'They preferred the more socially dignifying, and more sophistication-conscious mission-connected churches to the spiritually-oriented Aladura Churches which were almost exclusively patronized by the poor, the illiterate, and the sick' (Omoyajowo, 1978, p. 98).

Anglicanism and Aladura in post-independent Nigeria: the birth of ecumenical initiatives

By 1960 when Nigeria attained its political independence, the administration of the Anglican Church in Nigeria had already fallen exclusively on local Bishops and clergy. Consequently, a recognizable change in the disposition of the Anglican Church to the Aladura Churches became more evident, just as the 'gulf' between them started to dwindle. What emerged was a shift from animosity, antipathy towards sympathetic inquiry and empathetic understanding (Turner, 1978, p. 45). A Report of the Christian Council of Nigeria (CCN) in 1960 on *Christian Responsibility in an Independent Nigeria* drove this point home when it noted that:

> ... the praying bands which began within the Lagos churches have almost separated themselves from them. It has to be recognized that these groups (Aladura) have arisen out of dissatisfaction with the life of the Church (or its lack of life) ... There is cause to examine ourselves to see whether the full and joyous life that marked the early Church is present in our congregations, whether we show the same sensitivity to the influence of the Holy Spirit, and an equal dependence on prayer ... (p. 103)

The Anglican Church among other mainline Churches gradually became more and more objective in their estimation of the Aladura. Such a changing tide had been reciprocated by an increasing ecumenical appetite on the part of the Aladura Churches. The CCN Report (1960) further struck the ecumenical chord when it asserted that 'the challenge to be one with Christ and to take Christ with us into all walks of life is an eternal one' (p. 9). By the year of independence, some Aladura Churches had demonstrated their thirst for ecumenism by applying for membership in both national and international ecumenical councils. Though the process was not as smooth, as some applications were rejected at the start of the decade, yet they were later granted membership. The C&S made early attempts to apply for membership into the CCN in 1960. Rejecting two applications, the then General Secretary of the CCN, Revd W. S. Wood, called on the Aladura Churches to get united first before forwarding further applications (Omoyajowo, 1978, p. 102). To date, the Aladura Churches have been conspicuously absent from the CCN umbrella. However, both Anglican and most Aladura Churches belong to the Christian Association of Nigeria (CAN), All African Conference of Churches (AACC) and the World Council of Churches (WCC).

A remarkable precedent towards ecumenism was laid in 1962 when the Christian Churches in Lagos initiated and sponsored a week-long revival service and extended invitations to all Christian organizations. This kind of intra-religious event has continued to be repeated in Nigeria till present times. Another level of mutual interdependence between Anglicanism and the Aladura Churches is evident in the various services performed for each other's members. Aladura prophet-healers have turned 'spiritual consultants' and their churches as 'spiritual clinics' and 'out-patients ward' for some members of the Anglican Church who sought panacea for their existential problems outside their own Church. Though the tendency is for many of them to patronize the Aladura Churches secretly, the conversion stories of some members lend credence to the fact that Aladura Churches were portrayed as 'problem-solving Churches'.

Emphasis on prayer and praying groups are now becoming a prominent feature of the Anglican Churches. Musical instruments (traditional and modern) coupled with dancing and clapping are also freely used to put life into their worship services. Omoyajowo's clarion call to the Church of Nigeria (Anglican Communion) in his capacity as the then serving General Secretary of the Church no doubt underscores the Anglican recognition of the rate of proliferation, and the successful mission stories of Aladura Churches. He remarked:

> The time has come when the very rich cultural heritage of Nigeria should be reflected in our worship. Thanks to the African Independent churches for bringing us to this awareness. The (Anglican) liturgical committees should work hard and give us liturgies that are relevant and meaningful to Africans. (Omoyajowo, 1994, p. 283)

He concludes that the (Anglican) Church must co-operate with other Churches to redeem Nigerian society and make their impact felt in all spheres of human endeavour in the nation (p. 286).

Education and effective Church administrative machinery

Prior to the take-over of mission schools by the Nigerian government, the Aladura have educated most of their children through the Anglican schools and Bible colleges. Some had been brought up in the Anglican tradition before joining an Aladura group. For instance, Josiah Ositelu was a schoolteacher and a former catechist in the Anglican Church before establishing the CLA. At the inception of other Aladura movements, the 'self-trained' Aladura leaders have relied largely on the resources of the Holy Spirit rather than any forms of Western theological education. For instance, Oschoffa throughout his lifetime did not see the necessity for a CCC seminary, as he was often quoted as saying that 'God saw all the educated people but left them to choose me, an illiterate'. The Anglican emphasis on education, right from its inception in Nigeria, has no doubt influenced the Aladura in colonial and post-colonial era as they started to build their own schools, colleges, seminaries and thus also make provision for ministerial training.

A profound upsurge has been reckoned in the quality and quantity of ministerial and members' education in the Aladura fold, while the number of Bible schools and theological seminaries is on the increase. Aladura Churches have also established some kind of loose relationships by way of affiliation with or sponsorship by an older Christian body from within or overseas (Turner, 1978, p. 46). Aladura youths are in some cases sponsored abroad for more theological training. For instance, Adejobi of the CLA (as Deputy Head) was trained at the Glasgow Bible Training Institute between 1961 and 1963.

Over the years, Aladura members have relied on Anglican Church bookshops and journals for Christian literature. Today, most of the Aladura Churches now have their own bookshops, magazines, journals and other Christian literature. Brooks (1994, p. 35), Omoyajowo (1978, p. 109) and Peel (1968, p. 151) have shown respectively how the Aladura hymn repertory and vestments have been drawn largely from the Anglican Church. The Aladura have been influenced by Western patterns and structures in such areas as their polity. Some concepts and terminologies have been retained even though much change may have occurred in substance and actual praxis.

Inter-relationships and the implications for the Christian Church

The impact of the ecumenical initiatives and other inter-connections, whether official or informal, between Anglicanism and the Aladura Churches may be viewed as a double-edged sword. On the one hand, the Christian Church in Nigeria needs to be increasingly awake to its responsibility in meeting the challenge of new conditions and institutions. Co-operation and accommodation is required not only to spread the gospel but to guide Christians as they grapple with problems of Christian citizenship, intra- and inter-faith relationships. Christian denominations such as the Anglican and the Aladura Churches, which had hitherto existed as separate 'islands', must now strengthen ecumenical ties and regard one another at least as fellow labourers, if not yet as fellow brethren in God's vineyard.

The benefits of recognition by the world Christian community, of a wider experience and broader outlook, are sufficiently obvious (Turner, 1978, p. 45). The very attempts at greater unity and ecumenism may generate inherent problems likely to result in new schisms. But, even though it is likely to be weakened by divisive trends, the efforts at more co-operation and understanding will prove invaluable for Christianity in such a pluralistic context as Nigeria.

Further reading

E. A. Ayandele, 'The Aladura among the Yoruba: a challenge to the "Orthodox" Churches' in Ogbu Kalu (ed.), *Christianity in West Africa: The Nigerian Story* (Ibadan: Daystar, 1978).

C. Brooks, 'In search of an indigenous African hymnody: the Aladura Churches among the Yoruba', *Black Sacred Music* 8 (Fall 1994), pp. 30–42.

Celestial Church of Christ Constitution (Nigeria Diocese) (published by the Board of Trustees for The Pastor-in-Council, 1980).

Christian Responsibility in an Independent Nigeria (a report of the Christian Council of Nigeria, 1961).

J. A. Omoyajowo, 'The Aladura Churches in Nigeria since Independence' in E. Fasholé-Luke *et al.*, *Christianity in Independent Africa* (Bloomington and London: Indiana University Press, 1978), pp. 96–110.

J. A. Omoyajowo, *Cherubim and Seraphim: The History of an African Independent Church* (New York: NOK, 1982).

J. A. Omoyajowo (ed.), *The Anglican Church in Nigeria (1842–1992)* (Lagos: Macmillan, 1994).

J. A. Omoyajowo (ed.), *Makers of the Church in Nigeria 1842–1947* (Lagos: CSS, 1995).

J. D. Y. Peel, *Aladura: A Religious Movement Among the Yoruba* (London: Oxford University Press, 1968).

H. W. Turner, *African Independent Church*, vols I and II (London: Oxford University Press, 1967).

H. W. Turner, 'Patterns of ministry and structure within Independent Churches' in E. Fasholé-Luke *et al.*, *Christianity in Independent Africa* (Bloomington and London: Indiana University Press, 1978), pp. 44–58.

H. W. Turner, *Religious Innovation in Africa* (Massachusetts: G. K. Hall & Co., 1979).

L'Eglise Anglicane du Congo: une province francophone

Georges Titre Ande

Titre Ande writes of the significant growth of the Church despite its isolation from the centres of Anglican life, its great poverty, the challenges to its unity posed by its expansion and the influence of traditional religions and the need for better training for both men and women, laity and clergy.

L'Eglise de l'Angleterre au Congo est installée surtout grâce au chef Paulo Tabaro II (17ᵉ roi de la dynastie de Boga), parti voir le chef Kasagama de Toro, Ouganda, pour que cette région soit sous la juridiction britannique. Le contact avec les enseignements sur la nouvelle foi a permis à Tabaro de demander des évangélistes pour qu'ils viennent propager ces enseignements à Boga. Ainsi sont venus Petro et Sedulaka, suivis d'Apolo Kivebulaya. Effectivement, ils ont réussi débuter l'Eglise Anglicane à Boga.

Elle compte maintenant six diocèses dont celui de Kindu vient d'être inaugurée le 26 août 1997 par l'Archevèque Njojo Byankya. En mai 1996, elle a célébré ses cent ans d'existence, mais une vingtaine d'années de son épanouissement seulement suite à la crise qui a assombri son histoire pendant près de quatre-vingt ans.

Son développement matériel

Les écoles, les hôpitaux et les bureaux des diocèses de la Province de l'Eglise Anglicane du Congo (PEAC) sont mal équipés. Dans les institutions bibliques il n'existe pas de bibliothèque et de professeurs qualifiés en nombre suffisant. Les chapelles, quant elles, sont en pisé, sauf dans de grands centres. En plus, les serviteurs de Dieu et leurs fidèles sont victimes de la pauvreté provoquée par le gouvernement de Mobutu. Cependant, les membres de la Province de l'Eglise Anglicane du Congo ont pris conscience de l'état actuel des choses et voudraient bien l'améliorer.

En plus, dans le cadre de partenariat, serait-ce souhaitable que la PEAC bénéficie de la sympathie et de la solidarité de la Communion Anglicane à travers ses organes: traduire en français les documents importants en anglais pour équiper les institutions de formation biblique et théologique et aussi financer la formation des cadres autochtones capables d'assurer à l'Eglise son indépendance socio-économique afin de manger avec la sueur de son front.

Sans doute, c'est possible que la PEAC soit victime de son identité francophone. Ce qui concorde avec l'avis de la Conférence Internationale sur l'Anglicanisme d'expression française, tenue à Limuru, Kenya, du 12 au 17 mars 1996, no. 3 de ses résolutions:

> L'inventaire des ressources théologiques, humaines, spirituelles, matérielles, a permis de constater un très grand déséquilibre entre le monde anglican d'expression anglaise et celui d'expression française. Les membres de la Conférence souhaitent que se renforce un partenariat juste et soutenu en vue de parvenir à un équilibre afin que le monde anglican d'expression française puisse mieux s'acquitter de sa mission d'évangelisation.

C'est dire que la Communion Anglicane devrait servir de pot contenant tous les anglicans et que ses organes servent de trait d'union entre tous les membres au lieu de faire de l'anglophonie le 'poumon' de l'anglicanisme. Ceci nuancerait la différence trop visible existant entre les anglicans francophones et anglophones en Afrique.

Son enseignement doctrinal

Or l'Eglise, lors de son extension très rapide depuis 1972, a connu des problèmes d'ordre doctrinal et structurel:

- L'incorporation hâtive et impulsive en son sein des 'membres' des autres 'communautés chrétiennes et sectaires'. La conséquence en est que, dans la PEAC, les uns doutent, par exemple, de pédobaptême et de l'efficacité de baptême par aspersion, d'autres pensent que les oeuvres priment sur la foi pur le salut.
- La confrontation des religions traditionnelles. Beaucoup de gens continuent à croire que les esprits des ancêtres sont en action et peuvent influencer leur vie quotidienne et ont une confiance de plus en plus croissante aux 'wafamu', les guérisseurs indépendants et prestigitateurs. Faut-il aussi parler même de la 'résurrection' des religions traditionnelles du Congo. Ces croyances remettent parfois en cause certains attributs de Dieu comme l'omnipotence, la fidélité et la compassion de la vie pratique de chaque jour.

Dans la religion de Kindu, chez les 'warega', il existe une divinité appelée 'Kimbrikiti' qui, à cause de ses exploits, a gagné la confiance de la population de la place. Il est pris pour le 'père' de la morale. Il a tout un

Georges Titre Ande

groupe de gens à son service dans un village au milieu de la forêt, très éloigné des habitations. Un vrai 'murega' doit y passer par l'initiation de quelques mois avant qu'il soit considéré comme un homme digne de la société. Tant les chrétiens que les païens y passent jusqu'aujourd'hui de peur d'être puni car sa punition est directe et immédiate. Voilà un défi pour l'Eglise.

Du ministère des femmes

La femme, depuis longtemps, se voyait infériorisée par la tradition congolaise. L'Eglise Anglicane du Congo reconnaît la diversité des dons dans l'Eglise et est convaincue qu'ils ne sont pas accordés par l'Esprit Saint selon les sexes. Ainsi les femmes peuvent exercer les différents ministères dans l'Eglise. Surtout que la notion d'une 'femme-prêtre' n'est pas nouvelle aux Congolais car elle existait déjà dans plusieurs traditions congolaises.

Son avenir

La présentation de la PEAC nous a révélé que l'Eglise est en train de se tailler un chemin dans le roc. Elle a le problème de son développement matériel, mais aussi elle est appelée à enseigner de plus ses adeptes. Ceci en comptant sur ses propres efforts, mais aussi sur ceux de ses partenaires de la Communion Anglicane. Ainsi, elle pourra réaliser son devise: évangélisation, enseignement et oeuvres sociales.

Translation

The Church of England in the Congo was founded by Chief Paulo Tabaro II (seventeenth king of the Boga dynasty), following contact with Chief Kasagama of Toro, Uganda, who hoped that this region would come under British jurisdiction. His contact with the teachings of the new religion enabled Tabaro to invite evangelists to come and spread the faith at Boga. In response Petro and Sedulaka came, followed by Apolo Kivebulaya. They were successful in founding the Anglican Church at Boga.

This church now has six dioceses, of which the newest is Kindu, which was inaugurated on 26 August 1997 by Archbishop Njojo Byankya. In May 1996 the Church celebrated its centenary, but in fact it had only been flourishing for about twenty years, as a crisis had overshadowed it for nearly eighty.

Its material situation

The schools, hospitals and Provincial offices of the Anglican Church of the Congo (PEAC) are poorly equipped. In the theological colleges there are no libraries and there is a shortage of qualified staff. The churches themselves are made of clay, except in large towns. The ministers and the people share the poverty brought upon their country by the Mobutu government. But they are well aware of the situation and prepared to take all possible steps to improve it.

In the context of the partnership of the Anglican Communion, the PEAC deserves the sympathy and support of the Anglican Communion and its institutions, in translating the important documents into French, in equipping its theological colleges and supporting the training of local workers so that the Church can achieve socio-economic independence by the sweat of its brow.

There is no doubt that the PEAC is disadvantaged by its French-speaking identity. This was established at the International Conference of French-speaking Anglicanism, held at Limuru, Kenya from 12 to 17 March 1996, in Resolution no. 3.

> Our inventory of theological, human, intellectual and material resources has shown a very large imbalance between English-speaking and French-speaking Anglicanism. The Conference members recommend that a fair partnership be set up and maintained, which can lead to a more balanced allocation of resources, enabling French-speaking Anglicanism to carry out more effectively its evangelistic mission.

This means that the Anglican Communion must function in a way which includes all Anglicans, and that its institutions must unite all the members, rather than make speaking English the heart of Anglicanism. This would blend the colours which are at present too distinct, between French-speaking and English-speaking Anglicans in Africa.

Issues of belief

The very rapid growth of the Church since 1972 has faced doctrinal and structural problems.

- The hasty and impulsive welcoming of members from other 'Christian communities and sects' has led to a situation in which, within the PEAC, some doubt infant baptism and the efficacy of baptism by sprinkling, while others believe that works, rather then faith, are essential to salvation.

101

● The confrontation with traditional religions. Many people continue to believe that the spirits of ancestors are active and can influence daily life; there is an ever-growing trust in 'wafamu' – the independent wonder-working healers. It is also worth pointing to the renaissance of the traditional religions of the Congo. Such beliefs contradict certain attributes of God such as omnipotence.

In the Kindu religion, among the 'warega', there is a divinity called 'Kimbrikiti' who by his exploits has won the allegiance of the population of the area. He is regarded as the moral 'father' of the people. He commands a large group of ministers who live in a village in the middle of the forest, far from all other towns and villages. A true 'murega' must go through an initiation of several months here, if he is to be considered a true citizen. Even today Christians as well as pagans are going through this initiation for fear of reprisals, for the punishment of this divinity is direct and sudden. This is a challenge for the Church.

The ministry of women

Women have for a long time been seen as inferior by Congolese tradition. The Anglican Church of the Congo recognizes the diversity of gifts within the Church and is convinced that they not are distributed by the Spirit on grounds of gender distinction. Thus women exercise various ministries in the Church. The priesthood of women is not new to the Congolese, as it did exist in various Congolese traditions.

The future

The account which PEAC has given of itself shows a Church which is forging a path through hard rock. It faces the problem of material poverty, but it is also called to teach its members. This is to be achieved through its own efforts, but also though the efforts of its partners in the Anglican Communion. Thus it can fulfil its mission: evangelization, teaching and social concern.

Jubilee – a call to renew the Church of South India after 50 years

J. Russell Chandran

Introduction

The inauguration of the Church of South India on 27 September 1947 was hailed by Churches all over the world as the most significant event of the Church Union Movement. In 1997, the Church celebrates the Golden Jubilee of that event. It is also significant that the year coincides with the Golden Jubilee year of the nation's political independence.

Jubilee in the Bible

According to Leviticus 25.8–31 every fiftieth year is to be declared as the jubilee year. The jubilee year is a year of emancipation and restoration, proclaimed by the blast of the trumpet throughout the land. During the year the fields were to be kept untilled, slaves were to be set free, lands and houses that had been sold were to revert to their former owners or their heirs, debts were to be cancelled.

Though it is doubtful whether in practice such a jubilee was ever celebrated, it had come to be regarded as an integral part of the vision for the future, the vision of the fulfilment of God's righteousness. It is the jubilee year which the prophet Isaiah had in mind when he spoke of 'the year of the Lord's favour' in his messianic vision (Isa 61.2). Jesus quoted this in his Nazareth manifesto (Luke 4.29).

The CSI jubilee

When we celebrate the Golden Jubilee of the Church of South India the main thrust should be a message of liberation and renewal.

J. Russell Chandran

Renewal of the ordained ministry

In the practice of the ordained ministry wrong traditions have developed and the people as well as the ministers are to be liberated from the mistakes of the past. The problem is not peculiar to the CSI but experienced in other Churches too.

Paul in 1 Corinthians 12 and Ephesians 4 has listed a number of ministries, namely, apostles, prophets, evangelists, pastors, teachers, miracle workers, healers, speakers in tongues, leaders, suggesting the manifoldness of the ministry. In Ephesians 4.12 the purpose of giving to the Church the gift of the manifold ministries is 'to equip the saints for the work of ministry, to build up the body of Christ'. The ministry belongs to the whole people of God, not just to the ordained ministers.

The ministry is essentially the ministry of Jesus Christ, made known through his earthly ministry, and to be continued by the Church, the community of Christ's disciples. It cannot be fulfilled by any single form of ministry, or by any single individual or group. It is also important to remember that the ministry is not a static structure. New situations keep arising and in response the Church has to develop new ministries. For example the Church has been guided to develop several special ministries to deal with different problems or issues such as the outbreak of AIDS, refugees, migrant workers.

The tradition of the three-fold ministry of bishops, presbyters and deacons is to be understood as a structure for interpreting the manifold ministries, witnessing to and expressing the totality of the ministry of Christ. The bishop symbolizes the unity of the Church called to bring unity for humankind. The ministry of the presbyter is essentially for the proclamation of the gospel, through the preaching and teaching ministry. The ministry of deacons needs reinstatement as the ministry of justice and service, following that of Jesus Christ. It is unfortunate that in almost all Churches the diaconate is held as a subordinate ministry, a stepping stone to becoming presbyters.

In the Indian context, it is good to avoid the word 'priest'. The minister needs to be liberated and protected from the poojari concept which has vitiated the practice of the ministry. (The Hindu priest, known as 'poojari', is above all the conductor of rituals, and his task is to do that in a pure fashion.) In the New Testament the term priest is applied only to Jesus Christ and to the Church as the whole people of God, and never to any section of the ministry. Hindu gods can only be approached through the priestly caste, in the popular view. The New Testament shows that there is only one mediator, Jesus Christ, and that through him we have direct access to God in the Spirit.

The ministry also needs to be freed from wrong concepts of and attitudes to authority and power, to be *authoritative* rather than *authoritarian*. Secular concepts have vitiated this difference. The servant image of the Church witnessing to the Servant Lord, Jesus Christ, needs restoration. Particularly the bishop's office has been associated with wrong exercise of power and authority. Certainly the dignity of the office has to be maintained and due respect has to be given to the bishops and other ordained ministers. But it is inappropriate for the ordained ministry to be associated with the exercise of magisterial authority as in secular life. The authority of bishops, presbyters and deacons is subject to the authority in Christ, who took the image of a servant and submitted himself to be crucified. It is the role of the ordained ministry to draw attention to Christ's authority and to enable people to submit to his authority, always remembering that the risen Lord was also the crucified Lord.

One of the problems in the CSI has been that bishops and presbyters have been so much involved in the administration of the different service institutions, educational, medical and others, that they do not have sufficient time for the ministries for which they have been ordained. The institutions also suffer because the ordained persons do not necessarily have the knowledge and expertise needed for the institutions.

BEM (*Baptism, Eucharist and Ministry*), the document unanimously adopted by the Faith and Order Commission of the World Council of Churches in 1982, interprets the concept of episcopal succession not as a guarantee for the continuity and unity of the Church, but as a sign of these things. The same distinction is valid for interpreting ordination and consecration. The receiving of the laying on of hands by presbyters and bishops is no guarantee for receiving the gifts needed for the ministry. It is a sign of the gifts and, therefore, implies a mandate to be aware constantly of the gifts God gives through the Holy Spirit for the exercise of the ministry.

According to the Constitution of the CSI the basic functions of the bishop are general pastoral oversight of all members of the diocese, leadership in evangelization, teaching, worship and ordination. It is the duty of the bishops, individually as well as collectively, to see that the members are nurtured in the true faith of the Church. Equally important is the bishop's role in checking that those who lead the people in worship are adequately prepared for giving the congregations the benefit of the richness of the different traditions of worship that have come into the CSI through the union.

Renewal of mission policy

Liberation from wrong missionary policy is also an important objective. The earlier missionary policy of requiring converts to give up all that belonged to the former faith has resulted in the cultural, religious and spiritual impoverishment of the Indian Christians. We have been alienated from the national heritage. The charge sometimes made by the Hindu nationalist critics that Indian Christians are a denationalized community is not altogether baseless.

The Revised English Bible renders the word translated 'fulfil' as 'complete'. Both in the Old Testament and in the New Testament we have the vision of the riches of the nations being brought to enrich the worship of God (Isa 60.11; Rev 21.26). The riches or wealth of nations cannot be interpreted merely as material wealth. What the nations bring is whatever is true, beautiful and good in their culture and in their religious and spiritual heritage. God is the source of all that is true, beautiful and good everywhere. What we abandon through the acceptance of the Gospel of Jesus Christ is only whatever is sin and evil. This is particularly true of the scriptures and festivals of the different Asian religions, which should be part of our Christian education.

We can learn from the balanced attitude taken towards Gentile converts at the Jerusalem Council in Acts 15. Converts were told that there was no intention to lay any great burden upon them. They were only asked to abstain 'from meat that has been offered to idols, from blood, from anything that has been strangled, and from fornication' (Acts 15.29).

Only that which was discerned as evil or culturally objectionable needed to be given up. In India some of the great converts such as Brahmobandhav Upadhyaya and Manilal Parekh wanted to call themselves Hindu Christians. They held that they continued to be culturally Hindus while accepting the discipleship of Christ.

The traditional Christian response to the multifaith context in India was determined by policies adopted by Western missions, considered normative. The missionaries did not just convert our ancestors to the Christian faith, but made them Roman Catholics, Lutherans, Anglicans, Methodists, Baptists, Presbyterians, Pentecostalists, etc. The divisions which had occurred in the West were transplanted into India as well. The freedom to develop the pattern of faith and practice implied in the decision of the Jerusalem Council was completely forgotten or abandoned.

The consequence of this policy has been disastrous for the Church's mission. In India only less than 3 per cent of the large population have become Christian. Many who would have wanted to acknowledge faith in Christ were prevented from doing so because of the requirement that they renounce all aspects of Hindu, Buddhist, Jain, Islamic or other faith before becoming Christian. If they had been told that Christ came to fulfil and not to destroy, and so they could believe in Christ without ceasing to belong to their own community, many would have come forward to confess their faith in Christ. Such would call for a new and radical ecclesiology, recognizing a multi-faith community as a form of the Body of Christ.

The celebration of the Golden Jubilee should be an occasion for the Church to critically review its mission policy and to make a bold step to announce a more aggressive evangelistic approach to make Jesus Christ known to every one, to invite all to be disciples of Christ and at the same time to tell every one that Jesus Christ does not require them to renounce anything in their religious faith and practice which they hold as precious, as true, beautiful and good. Equally important is our willingness to be enriched by what is true, beautiful and good in other faiths.

Liberation from evil

In adopting a missionary policy to deal with new converts, the first Jerusalem Council did insist on the converts adopting a new quality of life, renouncing certain practices as above. We need to bear in mind that the Indian Churches did not insist that renouncing earlier faiths meant renouncing some evil traditions such as caste discrimination and male domination. Today we need to include among the evils to be renounced any form of caste discrimination, sexism and involvement in any form of corruption. We also need to ask whether there is any justification for maintaining caste identity within the fellowship of the Church.

Another serious evil in India is communalism, based on religious or caste exclusivism. This has been particularly so since the demolition of the Babri Masjid in December 1992, and the violent consequences of that. This has resulted in several organizations working for the strengthening of secular democracy and communal harmony. The Churches should not remain simply as spectators, but should exercise a ministry of reconciliation among people of different faiths.

Liberation from bondage to status quo

We have become used to belonging to the CSI and are not receptive to the ways in which the Holy Spirit may be guiding us towards further unities. But in 1947 the CSI was described as a Church-in-via, a Pilgrim Church.

At the very first meeting of the Synod following the inauguration it was decided to explore the widening of the oneness of the Church by union with other Churches. An invitation was sent to all the non-Roman Catholic Churches for negotiations for union. A proposal was made for the CSI and the Lutheran Churches to come together as the Church of Christ in South India. There were a complexity of factors which prevented action. One of the factors was the failure to explore new models of unity.

Soon after the formation of the Church of North India steps were initiated to implement an earlier commitment for the CSI and the CNI to come together to form the Church of India. This led to the formation of the Joint Council of the CNI–CSI and the Mar Thoma Church. This was meant to bring a new model of *conciliar* unity, going beyond the older concept of *organic* unity represented by the CSI and CNI models.

Name is important for the recognition of identity. While the CSI and the CNI have been willing to adopt a common name, the Mar Thoma Church has expressed some reservations. Even after clarifying that the adoption of a common name does not in any way affect the autonomy of the Churches the MTC has not been willing to move forward to accept a common name.

No particular model of unity can be made the norm for unity for all time and for all places. Organic unity, for some, has been associated with 'a kind of static uniformity and organizational merger'. Others see in it 'a loss of identity that deserves to be preserved'. The members of the CSI need to be helped to realize that they are now not just members of the CSI but of a larger fellowship symbolized and expressed by the Joint Council of CNI–CSI–MTC. Our prayer at all our liturgical worship is not only for the Moderator of the CSI, but also for the Moderator of the CNI and the Metropolitan of the Mar Thoma Church, and this is not mere ritual. And having arrived at the Joint Council we also need to be open, in obedience to the Holy Spirit, to moving forward to union with other Churches as well, such as the Methodists, Baptists, Lutherans and others.

Socio-political unity

The jubilee year stands for a periodic, once-in-50-years, restructuring and liberation of the social, political and economic life of the people. The jubilee year renewal, therefore, is not just for the renewal of the Church but also for the renewal of the nation. This is particularly relevant in our situation because this year we also celebrate the Golden Jubilee of our national independence.

The jubilee year liberation for our nation calls for identifying the different structures of oppression from which people suffer. Our independence in 1947 was liberation from colonial rule. It did not bring liberation to a vast section of people living in poverty, unemployment, caste oppression, etc. Even today about 40 per cent of the people, i.e. about 400 million, live below the poverty line. Women suffer especially at all levels. The Dalit situation, now coming under the WCC programme for indigenous peoples, along with Aborigines in Australia, Maoris in New Zealand and others, is explored in another chapter (below, pp. 294–300). It is important to realize that the situation of oppression people experience in India was not brought about only by Western colonialism, but was also the consequence of the Aryan conquest and the imposition of Brahmin domination. The celebration of the jubilee year of the CSI as well as of the nation is an occasion for identifying all oppressive structures and mobilizing people for struggle against those structures, through specific programmes for liberation.

Note

This chapter is edited from an article in *South India Churchman* (March 1997).

Further reading

Sam and Lily Amirtham (eds), *Greater Peace, Deeper Fellowship, Fuller Life* (Madras: CSI Synod Centre, 1997).

M. Gibbard, *Unity Is Not Enough* (London: Mowbray, 1963).

Herbert Hoefer (ed.), *Debate on Mission* (Madras: Gurukul, 1979). Issues from the Indian context.

Indian Church History Association, *History of Christianity in India* (Bangalore: St Peter's Seminary, 1982 onwards), esp. H. Grate (vol. 4, part 2) on Tamil Nadu in the nineteenth and twentieth centuries.

R. Paul (ed.), *Renewal and Advance* (Madras: CLS, 1963).

R. Paul, *Ecumenism in Action* (Madras: CLS, 1972).

The role of the Archbishop of Canterbury within the Anglican Communion

Andrew Deuchar

On a recent visit to New Zealand, the Archbishop of Canterbury was treated to a wonderful welcome from the people of the Polynesian Islands who are, of course, an integral part of the Province of Aotearoa, New Zealand and Polynesia. The whole ceremony was a great outpouring of energy, beauty, respect and love for a person who, in their terms, is a great leader. Of course, this is an honour which is given to the Archbishop not so much as an individual – although Dr Carey, as his predecessors, is deeply respected – but for the symbolic importance of his office to Anglicans and indeed to many other Christians across the world.

After the ceremony, which had contained important ritual welcomes, the whale's tooth, which had been used during one part of the ceremony, was given to the Archbishop. This is an honour of the highest order, and I understand it needed Government permission for this to happen. As Bishop Bryce passed it to me for safekeeping, he emphasized how important it was that this gift should be prominently displayed by Lambeth Palace, because future visitors from Polynesia would immediately know that they were at home.

Those visitors from other parts of the Anglican Communion do, I believe, very quickly feel at home when they visit Lambeth, despite its apparent grandeur and associations with both ecclesiastical and political history of the United Kingdom. Over several years now, there has been a growing sense, particularly in the main chapel and the crypt chapel, of the Palace becoming a focal point for the Communion. It is a different focus from the grandeur of Canterbury Cathedral, with that beautiful compass rose symbol in the nave. This is a very personal focus, emphasizing that relationships between people are at the heart of what it is to be a Communion.

The crypt chapel at Lambeth is a holy place. You sense the prayer of centuries as you sit under the fine vaulted ceiling and contemplate the broken plaster from hundreds of years ago, imagining the thousands who must have passed in and out of the doors. But the sense of the numinous comes not simply from great age or history. It comes also because it is prayed in today, every day; and it comes too because that prayer is surrounded not only by 800 years of history but also by symbols of today's Church all over the world – an altar from Sabah, a fresco given to Archbishop Ramsey by Pope Paul VI, a wonderful ebony statue of Virgin and Child from Tanzania, a crucifix from Mozambique. I have celebrated the Eucharist in there with a young group of pilgrims from Australia, I have discussed the problems of the Holy Land with Palestinian students, I have planned an international pilgrimage to mark the 1,400th Anniversary of St Augustine's arrival and the death of St Columba, I have taken wealthy, powerful American visitors there. All are moved to silence by the place, and almost universally sense a homecoming.

To know one's roots, and to appreciate the significance of those roots for one's life as in any other area of life is important: the crypt chapel at Lambeth connects with people in a quite extraordinary way, not because it is in England (although to deny the Englishness in our roots would be to pretend something other than is the case) but rather because it focuses in a very powerful way a common international foundation of prayer, and 'our

Archbishop' symbolizes a common prayer-life for the Communion in a tangible and personal way.

Now, I suspect that this represents a significant part of why the Archbishop of Canterbury remains an important icon for the Anglican Communion. As has been explained on numerous occasions, ours is a Communion which is bound together primarily because we wish to be bound together. We recognize in our common tradition a way of expressing our faith that has at its heart generosity and openness combined with a clear commitment to our Gospel foundations. It has enabled Anglicanism to adapt through history and as it has spread into different cultures around the world. Today we find Anglicans alive and well, often in quite small numbers, in contexts which might at first appear quite incongruous and unexpected – in Iran, for instance, and in many of the predominantly Roman Catholic countries of South America. In such places membership of a Communion which encourages flexibility and adaptability while at the same time offering people a clear identity is deeply appreciated.

The Anglican Communion has no confession of faith; it has no common code of canon law nor yet any sort of institutional hierarchy designed to impose discipline on its members. Its spiritual leader has no jurisdiction beyond his own Province, and the other instruments of unity, the Lambeth Conference, the ACC and the meeting of Primates, have no power to impose, only to consult and advise.

Such openness and freedom leads on to the potential for considerable frustration and misunderstanding, especially among the ecumenical partners. It has certainly led on occasion to messy situations, which have more than raised eyebrows either in other Churches, or in Anglican Provinces elsewhere. The Porvoo agreement between the Lutheran Churches of the Nordic–Baltic region and the Anglican Churches of Britain and Ireland is a case in point. Protracted negotiations produced agreement to proceed to full communion, and this has now happened. It is a cause for celebration, but it has left some Anglican Provinces feeling isolated from that whole process.

Another example might be in the area of issues of personal morality, which have such a high profile these days. They are approached in widely differing ways in different cultures, and the Anglican Church in some areas of the world is perceived by others to be moving faster to change 'traditional' discipline and teaching than can be handled elsewhere. This creates a tense situation in which the extent of freedom and flexibility is disputed. Indeed, in recent months we have heard calls for clear statements on some 'fundamental' issues which should define more clearly an Anglican position. To take this step would be a major development of the Anglican way, but many people are calling for a greater commitment to the idea of interdependence between Provinces, with less focus on autonomy. The

Andrew Deuchar

Virginia Report of the Inter-Anglican Theological and Doctrinal Commission, which will be one of the key documents discussed at the Lambeth Conference, raised this directly:

> The world-wide Anglican assemblies are consultative not legislative. There is a question to be asked whether this is satisfactory if the Anglican Communion is to be held together in hard times as well as good. Indeed there is a question as to whether effective communion, at all levels, does not require appropriate instruments with due safeguards, not only for legislation, but also for oversight. (The Virginia Report, para. 5.20)

It would not be appropriate to try to gainsay Lambeth by commenting on where these developments might go, but it is significant that, in the absence of such decision-making within the structures which exist, there is a clearly discernible growth in expectation that the Archbishop of Canterbury, whose primacy of honour is universally respected, and who, as I argued at the beginning, has an iconic role for the Communion, will use his undoubted moral authority to make authoritative statements on issues of the moment. Such statements could not, of course, be binding, nor I suspect would the Communion as a whole allow them to be!

The structures and tradition of the Office of the Archbishop of Canterbury simply do not allow for that sort of role. Indeed, were they to do so, the traditional role would be compromised and the office would almost inevitably become a focus of disunity. It could be valuable to make a brief comparison at this point with the papacy. The Pope has, of course, always been the 'Spiritual Leader' of the Roman Catholic Church, but that role is inevitably perceived differently within that Church since he has jurisdiction in every diocese and has the authority to make binding decisions and statements. That implies a rather different understanding of the term 'spiritual leadership'.

> For the Roman Pontiff, by reason of his office as Vicar of Christ and as pastor of the entire Church, has full, supreme and universal power over the whole Church, a power which he can always exercise freely. (Vatican Council II, *Lumen Gentium*, para. 22: ed. A. Flannery OP (Dublin: Dominican Publications))

It is a concept of oversight which would be entirely foreign to traditional Anglicanism, and I suspect few would accept changes which seemed to move us in that direction. Indeed, when we observe the role which Pope John Paul II has developed in his twenty-year pontificate, it must raise these questions in a particularly sharp way. In him we have seen a truly charismatic leader who has through his extraordinary personality engaged the world – and not just the Catholic world – in a conversation about the things of God which could hardly have been imagined in previous occupants of the Holy See. Yet in the same man we have seen an authoritarianism and a determination to control the direction of the Church which has faced the Roman Catholic Church with questions at least as sharp as those which the Anglican Communion, with its 'laid-back' structures, is having to face.

The question is, is there a middle position to be found? Is it possible to be the symbol of unity which, despite the many questions relating to the Archbishop which are beginning to be explored now – do we need him, must he be English, wouldn't an elected President be better, etc. – he still is, and also to practise some more formal role as a mouthpiece for the Communion? Can an Archbishop of Canterbury be both an intimate symbol of our communion together in Christ and also a figure of authority and discipline?

I have now travelled with the Archbishop of Canterbury to many parts of the world. The reception he receives, whether in Sudan, the United States or New Zealand, is uniformly enthusiastic, even if occasionally there is a nervousness about what he might do or say. He does not generally attract the sort of crowd size that Pope John Paul does, although around 100,000 in Juba, Sudan was an extraordinary experience. But my experience suggests that the Archbishop's accessibility, his willingness to meet people, not just shake hands, to sit and discuss at length current issues with young people, with journalists or with presidents is more valuable and more appreciated. For those who come into contact with him, that is a memorable experience and I believe it is an icon of how the Anglican Communion should be. To develop a role for the Archbishop of Canterbury which entails him in making more authoritative statements will remove him from the people, as he becomes surrounded by advisers, and speaks only from prepared texts.

When surrounded recently by hundreds of people in Auckland Cathedral, pressing in from all sides to catch a word with the Archbishop, who was thoroughly enjoying himself, an admiring journalist asked me 'Are you his bodyguard?' (Consistently, my colleague and I were referred to as Archbishop's minders.) I was glad to be able to say no, that we travel as a party of four, and we rarely have any extra security. That is the image of the Archbishop of Canterbury that I am happy to continue to promote. The structures of Communion, and of authority within the Communion, must continue to develop as its member Provinces require, but the Anglican Communion is primarily about people on a pilgrimage of faith, and I hope that its figurehead will be allowed to remain among them, a leader certainly, an inspiration and encouragement, I hope, but a fellow pilgrim still.

Why have an Anglican Church on mainland Europe?

John Hind

Why not? Anglicans in every continent are members of a recognizable communion of Churches. There must be some reason for their existence, and why should mainland Europe be different?

In most parts of the world Anglican Churches enjoy no special position, have no special responsibilities and privileges. The 'established' nature of the Church of England is very much the exception. Indeed, even the Church of England lacks today the almost exclusive position of dominance (whether in law or level of practice) which characterizes some Churches in other countries, whether Catholic, Protestant or Orthodox, which enjoy a remotely analogous form of legal relationship with their respective states. Despite its status 'as by law established', and many historic links to society at every level, the Church of England today, in the pluralism of modern Britain, has to behave in many respects as an equal partner with the Roman Catholic and Free Churches.

As a consequence, English Anglicans are having to face the questions of confessional identity which other Anglicans have long confronted. 'Why an Anglican Church?' is increasingly becoming a question throughout the world, not just on mainland Europe. It is as we learn to answer this question and discover what is distinctive about the Anglican tradition, that the role of Anglicanism on mainland Europe becomes clearer.

It is appropriate to begin with a description of the present situation of the Anglican presence on mainland Europe. There are four jurisdictions, whose different histories reflect something of the diversity of the Anglican Communion.

The present Diocese (of Gibraltar) in Europe was formed in 1980 by the extension of the Diocese of Gibraltar to include the Fulham jurisdiction (North and Central Europe) of the Bishop of London. It now has about 200 congregations in more than 30 countries, stretching from Russia to Morocco and the Canary Islands and from Norway to Malta. It thus covers the entire European mainland (including dependent islands and Malta), and has a presence in Africa and Asia as well. The Diocese has a complicated relationship with the Church of England to which for most purposes it is 'deemed to belong' and has the Archbishop of Canterbury as its Metropolitan.

The Convocation of American Churches in Europe is under the juris-diction of the Presiding Bishop of ECUSA. The Convocation is centred in Paris, where the Bishop-in-Charge has his seat; it has eight parishes in Belgium, France, Germany, Italy and Switzerland.

In the Iberian peninsula there are two small indigenous Churches, the Spanish Episcopal Reformed Church and the Lusitanian Church. The origins of both Churches lie in the Roman Catholic Church, and some have seen their path as analogous to that of the Old Catholic Churches. Their associations with Anglicanism go back to their origins in the nineteenth century, but it is only since 1980 that they have been extra-provincial members of the Anglican Communion. The Archbishop of Canterbury is the Metropolitan of both the Iberian Churches.

Any description of mainland European Anglicanism must also take account of the Churches of the Old Catholic and Porvoo Communions with which Anglicans are in communion. There are thus a number of countries in northern and western Europe where parallel Anglican jurisdictions coexist or where one or more Anglican jurisdictions coexist with another episcopal Church 'in communion'.

European Anglicanism thus represents three different inheritances, that of the English national and 'Established' polity, that of self-governing Episcopalianism and that of a nineteenth-century reform movement within Iberian Roman Catholicism. It is expatriate and indigenous, multi-ethnic and polyglot. It is also a minority Church, and, except in Spain and Portugal, a 'guest'.

This description remains largely true despite increasing numbers of local nationals in many congregations, and, in the case of some chaplaincies of the Diocese, a history dating from the sixteenth and seventeenth centuries. In addition there are other ancient episcopal Churches which, albeit not Anglican, share many elements of a common heritage and with whom intimate ecclesial relationships exist.

The purpose of this chapter is not, however, to describe the history or present status of Anglican Churches on mainland Europe but to say something about their *raison d'être*. Perhaps the expression should be *raisons d'être*, since, as my opening paragraphs make clear, the different Churches have different backgrounds and characteristics.

The worldwide Anglican Communion experiences a tension between aspirations to be a local and to be a confessional Church. The tension is not unique to Anglicans of course, being shared by the Roman Catholic Church, the Orthodox Churches, Nordic Lutherans and some Reformed Churches, all of whom are in some places deeply-rooted 'national' Churches, but who are elsewhere diaspora, minority, expatriate or 'guest' communities. In these latter circumstances it is more important for Churches to identify where they stand, and what they stand for. Some may define themselves primarily in ethnic, linguistic or nationalist terms; others may prefer to stress some particular doctrine or doctrinal emphasis as their distinguishing mark.

Many, but of course not all, members of the Church of England do not have any particular sense of 'being Anglican'; they simply think of themselves as Christians who are English. Other Anglicans do not generally have this option (although there are of course some parts of the English-speaking world where Anglicanism is particularly associated with a particular social class). For them other reasons are necessary, and, except in the case of strictly diaspora chaplaincies serving short-term expatriates, there is a need to identify what it is about Anglicanism which justifies its separate denominational identity.

Christian history does not suggest an easy resolution of this dilemma for Anglicans as a whole and particularly on mainland Europe. It is however a matter which has to be addressed, not only for the purposes of this chapter, but especially for the future of European Anglicanism.

Until quite recently it was relatively easy to distinguish generally between the constituencies served by the different jurisdictions. The Spanish and Portuguese Churches were entirely indigenous and local-language-speaking (albeit with close links to the Church of Ireland and Churches in both South and North America); the Convocation of American Churches in Europe and the Diocese in Europe were both largely expatriate and English-speaking, and in the main served Americans and Britons (including other Commonwealth citizens) respectively. At the same time, many members of congregations were non-Anglicans, who were attracted by English-language ministry and worship.

These distinctions have broken down markedly in the past half-century. It is now clear that Church of England and American Episcopalian congregations are generally indistinguishable, and now serve, in addition to their historic constituencies, many other expatriates for whom English is a more accessible means of communication than the local language. At the same time many congregations in both English-speaking jurisdictions have seen a small but steadily increasing adhesion of local nationals and are also facing the pastoral questions about which language to use, especially in Sunday Schools, where many children of mixed parentage have at best a limited facility in English. Meanwhile in Spain and Portugal the local Churches are beginning English-language ministry and similar pastoral pressures are beginning to impinge on a number of the chaplaincies of the Diocese.

European Anglicanism is currently a kaleidoscope of world Christianity and both now and in the future must serve a variety of different needs. Congregational members may be short- or long-term expatriates or local nationals; they may be English-speakers, whether as a first or second language, or Anglicans from a different linguistic background; they might equally be people of a different confessional identity. Although not all this diversity is represented in every congregation, it is true of the continent as a whole and challenges all four jurisdictions to evolve a clearer ecclesiology and sense of their own answer or answers to the question posed in the title of this chapter.

It has often been claimed that Anglicans have no doctrine of their own but simply the faith of the undivided Church. This claim has had a rather shorter history than some of its proponents would like, and it has worn increasingly thin in recent years. Indeed, some writers have argued compellingly that even to make such a non-confessional claim is to make a confessional claim. It is in short the dilemma of self-confessedly 'non-denominational' Churches the world over.

Nevertheless, it is one thing to accept that Anglicanism no less than other denominations has a confessional identity, but it is a different and more difficult task to show simply and clearly what it is. This is partly due to the internal diversity of most Anglican Churches, but this can be no excuse since most mainstream Churches demonstrate in practice a similarly wide diversity even when their official formularies deny it. Indeed, it could be argued that what is characteristic of Anglicanism is often the unrealistic claim itself, and that one of the reasons why Anglicans often find their internal unity a problem is the lack of a clear identity which could set confessional boundaries, boundaries which could themselves enable and even encourage appropriate diversity within them.

It is not within the scope of this chapter to attempt the difficult task of describing the confessional identity of Anglicanism. It is, however, important to identify certain general features before considering what contribution Anglicans have to make to the map of Christian Europe.

Every faith community has to find a balance between the various components of religious life and practice. Whether or not it is due to the rather pragmatic English temperament to which much contemporary Anglicanism owes its ultimate origins, there appears to be a general Anglican reluctance to isolate different elements from one another. Thus they have characteristically sought to balance scripture, tradition and reason in their understanding of authority in the Church; the living authority of Christ in his Church is seen in the faithful witness of all the baptized as well as in the ordered authority of the ministry; synodical government affirms the episcopal governance of the Church but associates the whole church in the exercise of oversight ('Bishop-in-synod').

This cluster of characteristics is sometimes described as 'dispersed authority'. It is a rather unhappy expression, easily misunderstood, but it should be seen as a positive option for the various ways in which God leads his people, rather than, as is sometimes claimed, a recipe for no authority.

The Anglican instinct is not to give doctrinal precision or juridical norms a priority over the actual lived life of the Christian community. The role of the Authorized Version (the 'King James' version) of the Bible and the liturgical tradition of the Book of Common Prayer have shaped the devotional and moral life of the Church over several centuries. This vernacular pattern has given every worshipper direct access to the written tradition and helped form the individual conscience as well as the official teaching of the Church. *'Lex orandi, lex credendi'* and, we might add, *'lex agendi'*.

Against this background it is easy to see why Anglicanism can appear so diverse. It also helps explain why some issues, such as the ordination of women, have proved so traumatic. Held together more by a common family inheritance and pattern of worship, and by a doctrinal and moral theological method, than by tight confessional formulae or structures of authority, Anglicans lack clear criteria for developments in doctrine and practice. There is a tendency in fact to find it easier to cope with diversity in the expression of doctrine than in matters of Church order. The ordination of women is proving a particularly interesting test of Anglican method. Although in recent ecumenical dialogues Anglicans have frequently stressed the necessity of a single interchangeable ministry as one of the marks of full visible unity, they have had to devise some more tolerant mechanisms in relation to their own internal life.

Finally, in this brief sketch of Anglican identity relevant to the situation on mainland Europe, it is important to observe that the Churches of the Anglican Communion assert that they are part (and only part) of the one, holy, catholic and apostolic Church. Few if any Anglicans would make exclusive claims for their inheritance, and their gratitude for the distinctive elements in their own tradition leads them to see those elements as their own contribution to the wholeness of the Church.

This leads naturally to one of the most sensitive aspects of the present situation. In no part of the continent is an Anglican Church the 'Church of the nation', and, at the same time, as we have seen, the idea of European Anglicans as being entirely expatriate has never been the whole story and is now becoming outdated everywhere. It follows that some different rationale is to be sought. Although, because of their varied backgrounds, the four jurisdictions have different perspectives on how it is to be lived out in the modern Europe, they are agreed that there is a recognizable Anglican confessional identity, albeit not as precisely defined as that of some other denominations.

The present writer considers that there are four main areas in which Anglicans have a particular contribution to make during the next few years.

The first is to witness to the distinctive proportion of faith referred to earlier, and to share it widely for the renewal of the Church. The second is to share with the other Churches of mainland Europe in God's own mission to the continent at a time of great change and soul-searching. Third, to contribute to the ecumenical quest by relating as closely as possible to the other Churches, and giving more practical expression to existing ecumenical agreements. Fourth, to minister to expatriates in Europe from all over the world, and especially to support those working in the European institutions and in the worlds of international trade and diplomacy.

The ecumenical dimension to this is clear. Proselytism is rightly an acutely sensitive issue, and the policy of the Diocese in Europe remains as it always has been: to refrain from any words or actions which overtly or covertly seek to persuade members of other Churches to become Anglicans. The Church must never be defined by linguistic or ethnic restrictions, however, and in an increasingly secularized Europe it is to be expected that a number of local nationals in many countries will come to faith through Anglican parishes, and may well freely choose to make their home there.

A further ecumenical dimension concerns the presence of Anglican Churches in countries where there is another Church in communion. Already tentative steps are being taken to involve Old Catholic and 'Porvoo' bishops in oversight of Anglican congregations, and this, together with moves to draw the four Anglican jurisdictions together, should significantly change the shape of mainland European Anglicanism in the near future.

Further reading

R. Coleman (ed.), *Resolutions of the Twelve Lambeth Conferences 1867–1988* (Anglican Book Centre, 1992).

D. L. Edwards, *Christians in a New Europe* (London: Collins, 1990).

General Synod of the Church of England, Debate on European Institutions, *Report of Proceedings*, vol. 21, no. 2 (July 1990), pp. 649–72.

General Synod of the Church of England, Debate on Church Involvement in Mainland Europe, *Report of Proceedings*, vol. 25, no. 3 (Winter 1994), pp. 867–90.

A. Wessells, *Europe: Was It Ever Christian?* (London: SCM, 1994).

Youth Exchanges

Opportunities for young people to experience the Anglican Communion

Paula Hollingsworth

We were far from the main road, far, we thought, from the nearest village, when we had the puncture – a group of Zambian and British youth, piled into a Mothers' Union minibus broken down in the heart of the Diocese of Central Zambia. We had a spare wheel, but the jack proved hopelessly inadequate for the job. Then three young men appeared at the side of the road, seemingly out of nowhere. They summed up our plight in a moment, disappeared and returned a few minutes later carrying a log – a beautifully shaped and perfectly symmetrical log. It was just the right size to wedge under our minibus to enable the wheel to be changed. I remember thinking at the time how remarkable it was that such a log should just be lying around. Not being mechanically minded, I wandered off while the work was being done, and spotted a sign further up the road. 'Church of God. Pastor F. Ngwe' was written on a piece of bark, stuck on a tree; I realized I was beside a church. There was no roof. The walls, shoulder-high, were made of wattle and daub, the pews were branches, held off the ground by V-shaped supports, cut from branches. There were stronger supports at the front for the altar ... but where was the altar? It took me some time to realize. It was underneath our minibus.

For all of us in that minibus, that incident has remained very significant as a picture of the calling of the Church to serve people in the world, for the Church to be ready to respond to people's needs. I see Youth Exchanges as serving a small, but very important, part of the need of the worldwide Church.

Meeting a visitor from Birmingham Diocese's Link with Malawi recently at Gatwick Airport, I learned that this was his second visit to this country – twelve years before, he had come as part of a visit with other young people. As he has talked I have seen how significant that visit has been as part of his leadership development, and I know from first-hand experience that he plays an important role in welcoming visitors from other parts of the world to his Diocese, and in helping them to have a meaningful visit.

At a church meeting a few years ago a woman rushed up to me, hugged me and said 'Thank you for my daughter! She went to Zambia with you as a girl. Now she is a young woman.'

I write this article as someone who has been involved as a leader of five groups of young people who have visited other parts of the Anglican Communion (dioceses in Kenya, Uganda, Israel/Palestine, Zambia and Malawi); I have met a number of such groups of young people from different parts of the world visiting the UK, and I am at the moment very actively involved preparing for a visit of young people from Malawi to Birmingham next Easter. I write as someone who believes passionately in the importance of such visits not only for the young people involved, but also for the dioceses that host them – and I want to share that enthusiasm with as many people as possible!

One of the parts of the Bible that I find the most fascinating is the account in the Book of Acts of the early Church wrestling with cross-cultural issues. We see how, in Acts 10, Peter learns to understand that God has no favourites, but we also see how much Peter himself has to change before he can accept the Gentile Cornelius as his brother. Then in Acts 15 there is the dilemma of the Church in Jerusalem about whether or not Gentile believers need to be circumcised. The new Church, rooted as it was in Judaism, had to learn to engage with the culture of its new followers.

In all our countries there are changes. As our cultures change, how will our Churches engage with new issues and relate to people in new ways? The younger generation in our countries will face even greater changes than the older generation have already faced. How will they, the leaders of tomorrow, be prepared?

Youth Exchange programmes give young people the opportunity to move outside their own cultural context, to see the world through different eyes, to meet with Christians whose culture is different and whose Church may operate in a different way from their own. As young people, they go at a very formative time in their lives. Through the group reflections what is learned is always applied to people's home context. Some Youth Exchange participants may well go on and become future Church and community leaders; others will be faithful members of their churches in the villages, towns and cities of our dioceses – but all of them should carry with them and build on their experience for the rest of their lives.

There is no set formula for such visits. Some are set up through Mission Societies, some through Companion Diocesan Links, some through personal contacts. Some involve just a one-way visit, some a visit each way, some an ongoing programme of visits. Some are visits between Anglican groups, others are more ecumenical. Some visits evolve and develop. For example a group of young people from Bath and Wells Diocese visited Zambia, their Diocesan Link, in 1993; now a two-way exchange is happening involving the Methodist and Anglican Churches from the Bath and Wells area, and the United Church and the Anglican Church of Zambia.

What such visits share in common is that it is the receiving Church who plan and carry out the programme (obviously with consultation with the visiting group), but the visiting young people come as a group, so that there are also people from their own culture with whom they can reflect and share. As part of that group there will be one or two people, who already have some cross-cultural experience themselves, who will take a leadership role within the group when needed. The size of group varies; between eight and twelve people works well from my experience, but the nature of the visit (and the funds available!) may well determine the size of the group. The term 'youth' is understood differently in different countries. In my experience groups have often been aged between 18 and 30 – the group members need to be young enough to be flexible, adaptable and open to new ideas but mature enough to be able to reflect on and apply what they are learning to their home situation.

The emphasis of such a visit, I believe, is in the word 'experience' – indeed many visits or programmes include the word 'experience' in their titles. The visit is not a work camp or a mission or a holiday (which may need to be made clear to all concerned at the outset) – though all those elements could form part of the programme. The aim is to meet young people, and to experience something of the reality of what it means to be a Christian in their country. In Nablus, in the Occupied West Bank (as it was when we visited), we stayed with young people and their families, we heard about their experiences under curfew, we listened as they shared their dilemma over whether to stay in their country or to take up opportunities many of them had to leave. We were humbled by the decision many had made to stay to keep the tiny Christian presence alive in the Holy Land. A group of young people from Nigeria recently visited Liverpool Diocese in the UK. They experienced at first hand the lack of young people in many churches there and how isolated young Christian people can feel – but then they went to Greenbelt, camping with 20,000 other young people at a Christian Arts Festival, and so they began to explore the role of the Church in the spiritual quest of the many British youth. A group from Britain spent eight days on a very rural Zambian mission station. Initially the group was enchanted by the quiet and the geographical setting, but nearer the end one girl confessed she would now be glad to get back to a town – but now she understood much more the reality of the lives of those who lived in remote areas.

Through experiences of sharing one another's lives deep friendships are often built up across the cultures, and prejudices and false conceptions overcome. What often emerges is much more common ground than people expected. 'The young people here are facing almost all the same issues that we face in our churches at home', one of the group in Zambia said to me in tones of deep surprise, quite early on in our visit, 'I don't know whether that makes me feel really pleased or really disappointed.' Tensions between youth and church leadership, between young people and older people, different styles of worship, the pull of Pentecostal Churches – all these are reflected in many parts of our Anglican Communion, and as these common issues are recognized there can be much opportunity for discussion, learning from each other's experiences and ways of doing things and prayer together.

Other experiences may be new: it may be a first experience of being in a country where Christianity is the major religion, or a first experience of Christianity being a very minor religion; it may be a first experience of the reality of living under the economic regime of a Structural Adjustment Programme; or of living in a materialistic and secular society. These first experiences take place in a context of a group of young people from two different cultures learning together. So if there is real opportunity in the programme for spending time with people (and so not trying to visit and see everything and everyone), for discussion, and some time for the visiting group to reflect on their own what they are learning, there is tremendous potential in such a visit for people to grow enormously in their under-standing of God, of his Church and of his world – and that is true both for the visiting group and for the youth whom they meet and share with in the dioceses they visit, and for the many others in the dioceses, of all ages, who will meet them more briefly; and those in their home diocese with whom they will share what they have learned.

Two other important contributions which the Youth Exchange pro-gramme offers to the Anglican Communion are that it offers young people a real experience of partnership across the Anglican Communion, and that it raises the profile of young people.

Mission Societies, some Companion Links and other organizations run other experience programmes with similar aims and objectives to Youth Exchanges. For example the Root Group Programme run by USPG and MCOD (the Methodist Church Overseas Division) offers a group cross-cultural experience in Britain. Participants are young adults coming from different parts of the world. After an initial period of training together they go in small groups to work alongside inner city churches in multi-cultural areas. Many mission societies, such as CMS, MAM (Mid-Africa Mission) and SAMS (South American Missionary Society), offer 6–18-month experi-ence visits to young adults; other programmes, such as the Experience Exchange Programme offered by CMS and MCOD, extend those opportun-ities also to people over 30. An increasing number of opportunities are available for individual Christians in the Anglican Communion to make

extended visits to other parts of the Communion to study and share in
church life – with good preparation, opportunities for reflection during the
visit and de-briefing on return home, such visits can be of great value.

Partnership for World Mission has produced a set of Guidelines for Good
Practice from the experience of some people who have been involved in the
visits to and from the UK. There is more detail on some of the practical
arrangements. In particular the need for adequate preparation and de-
briefing of the group is emphasized.

There is no formal programme. Youth Exchanges happen ad hoc where
there are links between dioceses. The financial constraints of some dioceses
mean that exchanges to countries a long distance away can only happen if
one diocese contributes most of the funding. However, apart from the cost
of the group travelling, the costs of a youth exchange programme are
relatively small, especially if the group stay in people's homes. Could more
exchanges happen between countries that are closer together?

In Malawi last summer, my group from Birmingham Diocese met a
young British girl who was travelling with her rucksack around Africa.
After we had heard of some adventures she asked us what we were doing in
Malawi and we explained about the youth exchange. 'You mean', she asked
wistfully, 'you stay with Malawian people? In their homes?' We assured her
that we did. 'Oh!' was her reply, 'Lucky you!' Lucky us, indeed.

Alternative patterns for ministry: North and Central America

John L. Kater Jr

The emergence of alternative patterns of ministry in North America

When the conclusion of the War of Independence led Anglicans in the
newly-established United States to form their own Protestant Episcopal
Church, they acknowledged their indebtedness to the Church of England
for 'her first foundation and a long continuance of nursing care and
protection'. But they also affirmed that the Church's discipline 'may be

altered, abridged, enlarged, amended, or otherwise disposed of, as may seem most convenient for the edification of the people, "according to the various exigency of times and occasions" '.[1]

One might say that the framers of that first American Prayer Book were simply offering an apologia for a reality that had already occurred; for the conditions under which Anglican Christianity took root on American soil were so radically different from those of England that the emergence of alternative forms of ministry was inevitable. Nearly two centuries without a resident bishop; vast expanses of frontier; hostile populations whose religious allegiance, if any, was to Rome or Geneva or the Quakers; Native peoples not always ready to accept the 'civilizing' efforts of Anglican missionaries; and ongoing claims by France and Spain to substantial portions of the continent – all these and other, often complex, factors assured that the patterns of ministry which evolved in the Americas would be something new in Anglicanism.

The structures of ministry which crossed the Atlantic with the first Anglican missionaries reached the Americas as part of a purpose broader than simple evangelism. They were conceived as one of the means by which English control would be extended to territories and people far distant from the setting in which Anglican Christianity had emerged and flourished.

The records of the early efforts of those early missionaries who accompanied the westward expansion of the English-speaking settlers in Canada and the United States amply demonstrate their belief that one of the fruits of the Gospel would be the ordering of a chaotic frontier society. To that end they sought to establish parishes, schools, hospitals and the role of the Anglican parson and bishop as sources of order and stability – in short, to do things as they had always been done.

As early as the mid-nineteenth century, a few North American Anglicans were warning that the form in which their Church practised its faith made it ill-equipped for its new settings. Episcopal clergy were often unable or unwilling to address the masses of people who were populating the wilderness, sometimes preferring to focus their efforts among the small minority they considered most likely to respond to their ministry. The structured dignity of the Book of Common Prayer held little appeal for people accustomed to the rough-and-ready evangelical religion of the frontier. Anglican efforts at evangelizing the Native peoples were often ill-conceived and lacking in respect for the traditions of the First Nations whom they encountered in the great expanses of the West.

The story of the expansion of Anglicanism in western North America bears testimony to the patient and faithful work of many clergy and lay leaders who understood that 'new occasions teach new duties', and set out to find more appropriate ways of carrying out the Church's ministry. In particular, the broad expanses of unchurched territory provided ample opportunity for dedicated women workers whose service might have been rejected or ignored in the East but found a ready, if often paternalistic, welcome from bishops and clergy in the mission fields of the West.[2]

It was in the Episcopal Church's Diocese of Alaska that the most dramatic changes in the Church's patterns of ministry first occurred. Bishop William J. Gordon, consecrated bishop of the territory often called 'America's last frontier' in 1948, became convinced that clergy prepared in the traditional way were often ill-prepared for ministry among Alaska's large Native population. Indeed, their presence often challenged the position of the elders, traditional spiritual leaders of the Native peoples. Gordon knew that a classical theological education was highly irrelevant in the settings of the Native villages of Alaska, nor did his diocese have the financial resources to pay for traditionally-educated clergy. He became convinced that with minimal training, Native elders could be ordained as 'local priests' and provide day-to-day ministry for their people under the supervision of the bishop and regional authorities.

Bishop Gordon's insights mirrored the pioneering work of Roland Allen, an English missionary active in China early in the twentieth century. Allen challenged Christians to follow St Paul in adapting ministry to local cultures rather than attempting to replicate traditional patterns. Nearly a hundred years later, his ideas have contributed widely to the emergence of alternate forms of ministry throughout the Americas.[3]

In the period following World War II, a number of other experimental programmes designed to make the Church's ministry more effective emerged in the Episcopal Church. Teams of clergy influenced by the nineteenth-century urban missions in the Church of England and by the worker-priest movement in Europe began attempting to make the Episcopal Church a significant influence in poor inner-city neighbourhoods. The National Town–Country Institute, based at Roanridge, Missouri, taught clergy who were the product of urban-oriented theological training how to function more effectively in non-urban settings.

The ecumenical climate of reform and experimentation signalled by the Second Vatican Council in the 1960s had effects among Anglicans as well. The Liturgical Movement, fostered in the Episcopal Church by Associated Parishes, was awakening among Episcopalians a new interest in, and understanding of, the Eucharist as the principal act of worship for Christians. At the same time, ecumenical scholarship was reclaiming an understanding of liturgy as truly the 'work of the people', rather than a performance undertaken by the clergy *on behalf of* an essentially passive congregation.

One of the primary effects of the Liturgical Movement on the emergence of new patterns of ministry was the perceived need for the ongoing presence of a priest able to celebrate the sacraments with a congregation on a regular basis. Bishop Gordon's experience in Alaska was studied and incorporated in a number of settings in the rural United States and Canada, nowhere more than in the Diocese of Nevada.

Bishop Wesley Frensdorff, Bishop of Nevada from 1972 to 1985, is credited with much of the theoretical and practical innovation which resulted in the emergence of important new alternative patterns of ministry. Under his leadership, the Diocese of Nevada developed a concept which it called 'total ministry'.[4]

Beginning with the desire to provide access to the sacraments to all its members, the diocese found itself being led to a new understanding of the nature of the Church as ministering community. In doing so, they became part of a much broader ecumenical rediscovery of the primary role of Baptism in constituting the whole Church as a ministering community.

In such a model of Christian identity, the sacrament of Baptism draws individuals into a community empowered by the Holy Spirit to perform all the functions necessary to the fullness of Christian life: worship, pastoral care, administration, evangelism. Within the broader body, each of the orders of specialized or ordained ministry – bishops, priests and deacons – has a distinctive role to play; but the purpose of ordained ministry is to facilitate the ministry of the whole Church, not to act in its place.

While the Diocese of Nevada provided leadership in the recovery of this ancient theology of Church and ministry, other individuals and dioceses, both in the United States and Canada, were moving in similar directions and in frequent dialogue with Nevada and its bishop. A decade after his work as Bishop of Nevada began, Frensdorff was instrumental in the calling of the Pacific Rim Conference held in honour of Roland Allen, which brought together representatives from the United States, Canada, Latin America and the Philippines to discuss how Allen's insights could help shape the future of ministry among Anglicans throughout the Pacific.

As the insights of pioneers like Allen, Gordon and Frensdorff spread among Anglicans in the Americas, some fundamental changes in common assumptions about the nature of Christian ministry began to emerge.

Bishop Stewart Zabriskie, Frensdorff's successor in Nevada, affirms that

total ministry moves away from a primary focus on the ministry of the ordained and includes the laity in the mutual work of ministry. There is *one* ministry in Christ and all baptized people – lay and ordained – participate in it according to the gifts given them.[5]

Thomas K. Ray, Bishop of Northern Michigan, another diocese in the Episcopal Church where concepts of total ministry have had great impact on the Church's life, describes the commissioning of the leadership team for one congregation where these principles have been put into practice in a congregation that numbers some thirty people.

The support team commissioned that day numbered thirteen, a third of the congregation. Of these thirteen who had prepared together for several years, three were locally-ordained priests and one a locally-ordained deacon. This congregation can now gather at any time on any day and have a full, lavish, nourishing sacramental life and spirituality . . .

> The Ministry Support Team of 13 adults pursued their study and formation collegially, rotating leadership and responsibilities. Throughout the process they were accompanied by a seminary-trained consultant. This team will provide support for the daily baptismal ministry of the members of the congregation, but they do not minister to the congregation.[6]

What the 'total ministry' pattern of ministry is attempting to accomplish is nothing less than a re-visioning of the traditional understanding of the Church's ministry. Frensdorff noted that the model of ministry focused on the professional clergy creates spiritual and economic dependency, underlines the contradiction between hierarchical and servant-based models of ministry, and results in what he called 'sacramental captivity' (the availability of the sacraments depends upon the presence of a highly-trained priest). Ministry is conceived entirely as a function of ordination.[7] But in the perspective of 'total ministry', ministry is the calling of the congregation, and leadership does not rest in the clergy but in the congregation's elected representatives. Clergy are called by their congregation, trained to minister in the context to which they belong, and exercise their functions to make the sacraments available to people who are themselves clear in their own call to ministry. Bishop Ray adds that deacons, priests and bishops serve to

> remind us, encourage us, affirm us in that . . . ministry that is already deeply embedded in our lives, hallowing our homes, workplaces, neighborhoods, community, and church, but rarely recognized, affirmed, and respected.[8]

Diaconate, priesthood and episcopate are in the end not restricted to a clerical caste within the Church, but describe modes by which *all* Christians live in the world.

In the Episcopal Church, a series of canonical changes beginning in the 1980s made it increasingly easier for dioceses to ordain clergy whose training reflected the specific context of their future work and whose ministry would be limited to one place or community, as well as to license laypeople for specific ministries customarily reserved for the clergy in the past.

Another innovative change in Episcopal Church structures with significant consequences for ministry began in 1979, with the establishment of the Navajoland Area Mission. Initially under the jurisdiction of the Diocese of Arizona (Bishop Frensdorff served as its bishop from 1983 to 1988), in 1990 Navajoland consecrated its first Navajo bishop, Steven Plummer. This diocese, which exercises jurisdiction over all Navajo people, transcends diocesan boundaries and allows all Navajo to benefit from ministry structured to their particular tribal context.

It would be a mistake to imply that such monumental changes in patterns of ministry have occurred without tension and conflict. Some consider the emergence of a community-based model of ministry to erode the special priestly identity that has shaped the clergy's sense of vocation. Congregations sometimes prefer the more passive role permitted them by the old patterns. Concerns about adequate and appropriate education are often raised as well. In dioceses where some clergy are seminary-trained while others are the products of locally-based formation, conflicts can and do arise.

But after several decades of intense theological debate and dozens of alternative models of ministry among Anglicans in both Canada and the United States, it is now clear that the recovery of the priority of Baptism in Christian identity has far-reaching consequences for how Christians live and work in the world. In particular, it has been re-claimed as the sacrament of *vocation* for all Christians.

Alternative patterns of ministry in Meso-America

Anglicanism in Meso-America can be traced to a variety of sources: English mission in Belize (British Honduras) and the Caribbean coast of Nicaragua, one facet of the British challenge to Spanish control of the region; support for American, British and West Indian expatriates engaged in commercial enterprises in Panama and Costa Rica; and, in the case of Mexico, an indigenous religious movement only later connected to Anglicanism. But ministry among Spanish-speaking Central Americans began in earnest only after a series of decisions taken in the 1950s and 1960s. Initially responsible to the Bishop and Diocese of Panama, a Diocese of Central America formed the focus of development until by 1992 each Central American republic had its own diocesan bishop and structure.

From the beginning, development of leadership for the new Churches was an important concern. While the Episcopal Church in Mexico had its own seminary, most Spanish-speaking dioceses outside the United States, which formed the Episcopal Church's Province IX, sent their candidates for ordination either to American seminaries or to the American-style

Seminario Episcopal del Caribe, located in San Juan, Puerto Rico. That seminary closed in 1967, when rising costs and a growing sense that ministry in Latin America demanded different models of training combined to bring it to an end.

Since that time, the dioceses of Central America have struggled to find alternative patterns of ministry and ministerial preparation. Those questions have, however, been part of a much broader attempt by Anglicans throughout Latin America to achieve autonomy. In their context, autonomy means the ability to develop their own liturgy, hermeneutic, styles of ministry, leadership and evangelism and to participate fully in their own societies without the burden of an identity too closely tied to that of the English-speaking Anglican community.

James Ottley, formerly Episcopal Bishop of his native Panama and currently Anglican Observer at the United Nations, has written that for Central Americans, 'the challenge that emerges is related to ministry in . . . a pluralistic, changing society'.[9] That challenge, Ottley affirms, is multi-faceted. There is the challenge of *power*: 'In a pluralistic society power can never be centralized; it must be shared.' There is the challenge of *stewardship*: 'I do not believe the world is coming to an end, but I do believe that God is calling us to react in love to the world, to creation, in order that the proper harmony might be observed as we deepen our relationship with one another and with God.' And there is the challenge of the *Church's structures*. Bishop Ottley points to the experience of the Diocese of Panama in affirming a number of new patterns for ministry:

1. Emphasis on the diocese rather than the congregation as the centre of mission;
2. The value of team ministry;
3. The importance of a ministry plan that will 'take into account the initiatives that come from "below", from the grassroots';
4. The priority of the poor as the locus of the Church's ministry;
5. The importance of community as the basis for ministry; and
6. A concept of the Church as 'a transforming agent of the structures of society'.[10]

We join in a common ministry, not parochialism or clericalism, but a ministry of the whole people of God. The church shows its awareness of the global village and our mission in Christ when it gives the laity their rightful place.

. . . [W]e are becoming more aware of who we are – the people of God. Clergy and laity, in a common ministry, develop new structures that make for better partnership as participants in Christ's mission, aware always of our mutual responsibility and interdependence in the Body of Christ and of our relationship with God's creation.[11]

In many of the dioceses of Central America, the Episcopal Church has embraced a concept of ministry that puts it squarely in the midst of the struggles still shaking the region. Each diocese has attempted to find ways to provide a contextual education for its ordained and lay leaders. A historic vote of the Episcopal Church's 1997 General Convention approved the formation of an autonomous Iglesia Anglicana de la Región Central de América (Anglican Church of the Central Region of America). This decision means that Central American Anglicans join the Anglican Church of Mexico, which achieved autonomy two years earlier, in claiming authority to create their own patterns of ministry that will respond more adequately to the cultures and realities they embrace.

Glenda McQueen, a lay leader in the Diocese of Panama, envisions great significance to the movement towards autonomy.

> Anglicanism finds itself immersed in this reality. ... If we make the decision to confront it, to suffer and weep, to accept that neither we nor history are the same, then change, that transformation of which we speak so much, will happen here in our Church. We will be watching the awakening of a new dawn, we will be the salt of our earth.[12]

Notes

1 The Book of Common Prayer (New York: Seabury, 1979), Preface, p. 9.
2 See, e.g., W. Kip, *The Early Days of My Episcopate* (New York: Whittaker, 1892); D. Tuttle, *Missionary to the Mountain West* (Salt Lake City: University of Utah Press, 1987); A. Hayes (ed.), *By Grace Co-Workers: Building the Anglican Diocese of Toronto 1780–1989* (Toronto: Anglican Book Centre, 1989); M. Donovan, *A Different Call: Women's Ministries in the Episcopal Church 1850–1920* (Wilton, CT: Morehouse-Barlow, 1986), especially ch. 9, 'Women as missionaries', pp. 123–45.
3 See D. Paton and C. Long (eds), *The Compulsion of the Spirit: A Roland Allen Reader* (Grand Rapids: Eerdmans, 1983).
4 J. Borgeson and L. Wilson (eds), *Reshaping Ministry: Essays in Memory of Wesley Frensdorff* (Arvada, CO: Jethro, 1990).
5 S. Zabriskie, *Total Ministry* (Washington: Alban, 1995), p. x.
6 T. Ray, 'The small Church: radical reformation and renewal of ministry', *Anglican Theological Review*, LXXVIII (1997), p. 625.
7 W. Frensdorff, 'Ministry and orders: a tangled skein' in Borgeson and Wilson (eds), op. cit., pp. 17–41.
8 Ray, op. cit., p. 622.
9 J. Ottley, 'The challenge of the present' in J. Kater (ed.), *The Challenges of the Past, the Challenges of the Future* (Berkeley: CDSP, 1994), p. 43.
10 Ottley, op. cit., pp. 43–55.
11 Ottley, op. cit., p. 53.
12 Glenda McQueen, 'Anglicans and the problematic situation of Latin America' in J. Kater (ed.), *We Are Anglicans: Essays on Latin American Anglicanism* (Panama City: Diocese of Panama, 1989).

Further reading

J. Borgeson and L. Wilson (eds), *Reshaping Ministry: Essays in Memory of Wesley Frensdorff* (Arvada, CO: Jethro, 1990).

A. Brooks (ed.), *Eclesiología: Presencia anglicana en la Región Central de América* (San José: DEI, 1990).

M. Donovan, *A Different Call: Women's Ministries in the Episcopal Church 1850–1920* (Wilton, CT: Morehouse-Barlow, 1986).

A. Hayes (ed.), *By Grace Co-Workers: Building the Anglican Diocese of Toronto 1780–1989* (Toronto: Anglican Book Centre, 1989).

J. Kater (ed.), *We Are Anglicans: Essays on Latin American Anglicanism* (Panama City: Diocese of Panama, 1989).

J. Kater (ed.), *The Challenges of the Past, the Challenges of the Future* (Berkeley: CDSP, 1994).

D. Paton and C. Long (eds), *The Compulsion of the Spirit: A Roland Allen Reader* (Grand Rapids: Eerdmans, 1983).

A. Rowthorn, *The Liberation of the Laity* (Wilton, CT: Morehouse-Barlow, 1986).

S. Zabriskie, *Total Ministry* (Washington: Alban, 1995).

The experience of African Americans within ECUSA and their contribution to the past, present and future

Harold T. Lewis

It is estimated that of the 2.5 million members of the Episcopal Church in the USA (ECUSA) approximately 5 per cent are black.[1] While found in virtually every one of the hundred or so dioceses in ECUSA, black Episcopalians are concentrated (as are Episcopalians in general) along the Eastern seaboard of the United States. The black presence in the Episcopal Church can be directly attributed to the missionary endeavours of the Society for the Propagation of the Gospel in Foreign Parts (SPG), founded in 1701 to provide overseas chaplaincies for Englishmen and to evangelize African slaves in North America and the Caribbean. Most black Episcopalians trace their membership in ECUSA to the efforts of the Society in the North American colonies, where slave chapels were established on cotton plantations throughout the South. But perhaps 40 per cent of black

Episcopalians have roots in the West Indies where SPG focused its attention on slaves who worked the sugar plantations. When West Indian immigrants, 'well trained by the Church of England, [and] possess[ing] a strong sense of the Anglican ethos',[2] came to the United States during the first half of this century, they typically found or founded Episcopal parishes. Indeed, the Caribbean migration of Anglicans accounted for the shift of the black Episcopal population from the Southern to the Northern states.[3]

To appreciate fully the role that blacks have played in the history of ECUSA, however, it should be pointed out that the Anglicanization of slaves in the colonies was at best conditional – that is, while purporting to dispense religion, the SPG 'accepted slavery as a vital factor in British prosperity' and 'secured legislation that would ensure that slaves' civil status would not be altered by baptism'.[4] Indeed, the Bishop of London, in response to a question raised by planters in Virginia in the early eighteenth century, gave his theological sanction to such a doctrine, when he wrote that 'the freedom which Christianity gives, is freedom from the bondage of sin and Satan, . . . but as to their outward condition, whatever that was before, whether bond or free, their being baptised, and becoming Christians, make no manner of change in it'.[5] One SPG missionary in South Carolina, obedient to his bishop's ruling, inserted a caveat in the order of service for the baptism of slaves:

> You desire in the presence of God and before this congregation that you do not ask for Holy Baptism out of any design to free yourself from the Duty and Obedience you owe to your master while you live, but *merely* for the good of your own souls, and to partake of the graces and blessings promised to the members of the Church of Jesus Christ.[6]

As late as 1846, Bishop Wilberforce of Oxford excoriated the Episcopal Church for its complicity in the slave trade, and suggested that the Church had failed in its mission:

> What witness, then, has as yet been borne by the Church in these slave-states against this almost universal sin? She raises no voice against the predominant evil; . . . and in practice she shares in it. The mildest and most conscientious of the bishops of the south are slave-holders themselves.[7]

Given the circumstances under which the Episcopal Church preached the Gospel to its black constituency, a situation in which, according to one historian, 'white Episcopalians exhibited a racism that prompted them to treat their black brethren as step-children separated from the main body of the flock',[8] it should come as no surprise that after the abolition of slavery at the end of the Civil War, black Episcopalians bolted *en masse* from the

133

Church of their baptism, and 'flocked to churches where they would be free from white domination'.[9]

A few black congregations had been established in the North before the Civil War. The first among these was St Thomas', Philadelphia, founded by Absalom Jones, the first black priest in the Episcopal Church. Absalom Jones and Richard Allen were lay Methodist preachers who worshipped with other free blacks in the gallery reserved for blacks at St George's Methodist Church in Philadelphia. Because their growing numbers resulted in an 'increase of white anxiety and resentment', the two men and their fellow black worshippers were ejected from St George's. Absalom Jones and his followers subsequently affiliated with the Episcopal Church and founded St Thomas', whereas Allen and his friends remained with the Methodist Church and eventually founded the African Methodist Episcopal Church, a black offshoot of Methodism. Since most African American Christians are spiritual sons and daughters of Allen,[10] Jones's decision served to place black Episcopalians in a decidedly small minority among black Americans. Because of this fact, black Episcopalians have had often to justify their membership in and allegiance to the Episcopal Church.

After the Civil War, a faithful remnant of black Episcopalians organized several congregations, especially in the South.[11] But the founding of these congregations was cause for less jubilation than it would seem. In case after case, their applications to be admitted as parishes with the rights and privileges of other parishes were summarily rejected because the same Southern Episcopalians who found it impossible to recognize those formerly in bondage as equal citizens under the law found it just as impossible to accord them equal privileges in the councils of the Church.

Nor was this a phenomenon peculiar to the South. When St Philip's, New York, applied for recognition by the Diocese of New York, the following objection was raised on the floor of convention:

> But this cannot prevent our seeing the fact that they are socially degraded, and are not regarded as proper associates for the class of persons who attend our convention. We object not to the color of their skin, but we question their possession of those qualities which would render their intercourse with members of a church convention useful, or agreeable, even to themselves. It is impossible, in the nature of things, that such opposites should commingle with any pleasure to either.[12]

In 1883, a canon was proposed at the General Convention that year which would have permanently disenfranchised African Americans in the Episcopal Church. It would give the bishop of each diocese the right to organize black communicants into separate, extra-diocesan missionary districts under their direct supervision. This would mean that blacks could not vote in diocesan conventions or elect deputies to the General Convention.

Further, any hopes of electing a bishop of colour would be forever dashed. To protest the proposed legislation, a group of black clergy, led by the Revd Alexander Crummell of Washington, organized the Conference of Church Workers Among Colored People (CCWACP). Through sympathetic friends on the floor of the General Convention, they succeeded in defeating the canon.[13] Having scored this victory, the CCWACP made it a practice to represent the interests of black Episcopalians at subsequent conventions.

The significance of the founding of the CCWACP cannot be overstated. While it was not the first such caucus in the history of the Church,[14] it was the most significant. It flourished until 1968, when it was succeeded by the Union of Black Episcopalians, itself founded in protest against the summary dismissal of a distinguished black clergyman, the Revd Tollie L. Caution, who was on the staff of the then Presiding Bishop.[15] The founding of the caucus signalled the fact that although discriminated against, marginalized, and disenfranchised, black Episcopalians have firmly believed that they had a right to be in the Episcopal Church. But this stance came at great cost. Black Episcopalians have been seen as suspect for choosing to belong to the Church of the 'oppressor'. Having affiliated themselves with the very white Christians by whom they had been mistreated, they have been accused of selling their spiritual birthright for a mess of pottage of rather dubious nutritional value. John Melville Burgess, the first black priest to become a diocesan bishop in the United States, recalled: 'I personally have experienced the ostracism of being a member of a minority religious group, having doubts cast upon the validity of my Christian faith and experience.'[16] Too, the axiom attributed to Booker T. Washington, 'if any black man is anything but a Methodist or a Baptist, someone has been tampering with his religion', betrays a belief that there is something incongruous about being black and Anglican.[17]

The question, therefore, as to why blacks have chosen to remain in the Episcopal Church has been raised, and the answer has consistently been a theological one, that they hold the church to be a catholic institution, that is 'a church for all people, ... a church that was pre-slavery and therefore pre-racism, [whose] formularies, practices and constitutions were divine and in place before racial equality'.[18] Recognizing that 'there are no racial prohibitions or exclusions in the national constitution, canons or by-laws',[19] black Episcopalians, when confronted with attitudes, policies, and behaviour that have attempted and, in many cases, succeeded in ostracizing them, have historically attributed such actions to the shortcomings of their perpetrators and not to the intrinsic nature of the institution. Moreover, black Episcopalians have consistently held the Church's feet to the fire, and reminded it when its actions have been inconsistent with the principles it has espoused. In so doing, black Episcopalians have called the Church to be true to its catholic principles even when it had abandoned them, or had run the risk of abandoning them:

> Throughout their history, [black Episcopalians] have impelled the church to define the extent of its catholicity. ... African American Episcopalians have challenged the definitions that the Episcopal Church has generally given, calling white Episcopalians to recognize that genuine catholic fellowship requires and demands *full* incorporation and *full* equality.[20]

This emphasis on the Church's catholicity is not an insignificant contribution to its life, given that the Episcopal Church claims through membership in the Anglican Communion to be part of the historic catholic Church; upholds the doctrine of apostolic succession, and maintains that 'Protestant' in its official title does not refer to 'Reformation-Protestant' but is intended to mean 'non-Papist'. Yet it remains, in the American scheme of things, a Protestant denomination, indeed the quintessential Protestant denomination. To most Americans, the first image conjured up by the acronym WASP (White Anglo-Saxon Protestant) is the Episcopalian. It is to this protestant context that black Episcopalians have historically provided a catholic corrective.

By whatever yardstick used, African Americans in the Episcopal Church, by dint of their steadfast determination, have made significant strides. Early in this century, the only black bishops in the US were styled 'suffragan bishops for colored work'.[21] Today, there are over a score of bishops, three of whom (Orris Walker, Long Island; Herbert Thompson, Southern Ohio; and Clarence Coleridge, Connecticut) head large dioceses. One of them, Herbert Thompson, was a candidate for the Primacy of the Episcopal Church at its 1997 General Convention, and indeed led on the first ballot. Barbara Harris, suffragan of Massachusetts, the first woman bishop in the Anglican Communion, is an African American. Long victims of a discriminatory deployment policy which relegated them to predominantly black congregations, black clergy now serve integrated parishes and diocesan staffs. At least four black priests serve as cathedral deans, including Nathan Baxter, of Washington National Cathedral. African American laypeople have also served the Church with distinction. The late Charles Lawrence was the first black president of the House of Deputies; Diane Marie Porter was senior executive for program and vice-president of the Domestic & Foreign Missionary Society. There are virtually no standing commissions or boards of the national Church which do not benefit from the expertise of black communicants.

But African Americans' most significant contributions to the life of the Episcopal Church have not always been in visible positions of authority and leadership. Rather it has been the valiant witness often made by the unsung heroes and heroines of the faith who have borne the burden in the heat of the day, who have exercised a ministry of moral suasion, of faithful example, often in the midst of adversity. This was especially true during the civil rights era, when 'the Episcopal Church was jolted from its complacency'.[22] The Church felt a need to react to the volatile situation in the nation's cities, lest it be seen to be out of step with the nation.[23] 'The Episcopal Church was forced by the course of events to recognize the existence of a deep-rooted racial prejudice in its midst.'[24] The incongruity between such practices and the principles for which the Church claimed that it stood became painfully obvious. The Episcopal Church, therefore, began to acknowledge what black Episcopalians had claimed for nearly two centuries – that there had long been a disparity between the Church's catholic claims and the unjust treatment of some of its members. During the civil rights era, blacks within the Episcopal Church were given more attention because American society at large was beginning to heed the warnings of the black community. The Episcopal Church, long a non-pro*phet* organization, began to atone for past injustices. One outward and visible sign of this phenomenon was the acquiescence on the part of Presiding Bishop John Allin (formerly Bishop of Mississippi) to the demands of the Union of Black Episcopalians upon his election in 1973.[25]

The peculiar gifts of black Episcopalians may well be summed up in a statement promulgated by black bishops in 1990:

> Our existence as Afro-Anglican members of the Community of Faith, in the One, Holy, Catholic and Apostolic Church, has always been marked by ambiguous conditions. We have confessed Jesus Christ as Lord and Savior, but our confession has not always been sufficient to accord us full acceptance among others who make a similar confession. Our Episcopal Church has not in itself been a shelter from the stormy blasts of racism, oppression, sexism. Our blackness has not always blessed us with a stronger sense of God's justice at the hands or in the faces of others more powerful than ourselves. Yet we have struggled to maintain our rights to fullness of life and human dignity in the face of countervailing circumstances. Through it all, God has been 'our help in ages past'. We remain convinced that God will continue to be 'our hope for years to come'.[26]

Notes

1 American Institute of Public Opinion, *Gallup Opinion Poll: Special Report on Religion* (1967).
2 J. H. Edwards, 'The Episcopal Church and the black man in the United States' (unpublished MS, Archives of the Episcopal Church, Austin, Texas).

Harold T. Lewis

3 For a full discussion of the phenomenon of Caribbean Anglicans in ECUSA, see Harold T. Lewis, *Yet With a Steady Beat: The African American Struggle for Recognition in the Episcopal Church* (Valley Forge, PA: Trinity Press International, 1996), esp. ch. 6: 'West Indian Anglicans: missionaries to black Episcopalians?'

4 J. C. Hayden, 'Afro-Anglican linkages, 1701–1900: Ethiopia shall soon stretch out her hands unto God' (a paper delivered at the first Conference on Afro-Anglicanism, Codrington College, Barbados, 1985), *Journal of Religious Thought*, vol. 44, no. 1 (1987), p. 25.

5 Bishop Gibson, 'To the Masters and Mistresses of English Families Abroad' (1723).

6 The Rev. Francis Le Jau, St. James', Goose Creek, So. Carolina, cited in Edgar L. Pennington, *Thomas Bray's Associates and Their Work Among Negroes* (Worcester, MA: American Antiquarian Society, 1939); italics mine.

7 Samuel Wilberforce, *A History of the Protestant Episcopal Church in America*, 2nd edn (London: Francis & John Rivington, 1846), pp. 426ff.

8 Willard Gatewood, *Aristocrats of Color: The Black Elite 1880–1920* (Bloomington: University of Indiana Press, 1990).

9 J. C. Hayden, 'After the war: the mission and growth of the Episcopal Church among blacks in the South, 1865–1877', *Historical Magazine of the Episcopal Church* (1972), pp. 4ff.

10 According to C. Eric Lincoln, 'seven major black denominations account for more than 80 per cent of black religious affiliation in the United States': *Black Church in the African American Experience* (Durham, NC: Duke University Press, 1993), p. xii.

11 In this connection, it is worthy of note that since sixteen of the 25 black priests ordained before the Civil War had been sent as missionaries to West Africa, especially Liberia, there were not sufficient clergy to serve these parishes, necessitating the importation of clergy from the West Indies, who had been trained at Codrington College, Barbados.

12 *Journal of the Convention of the Diocese of New York* (1846).

13 This proved in many ways to be a pyrrhic victory. Since the canon was defeated because it was not approved by the House of Bishops, the bishops retaliated by instituting in their respective dioceses practices which were not approved by the national Church. Their practices coincided with the introduction of 'Jim Crow' in the South, which institutionalized strict segregationist and separatist policies which characterized life in the Southern United States until the middle of the twentieth century.

14 The Convocation of the Protestant Episcopal Church for Promoting the Extension of the Church Among Colored People had been founded in 1856 by James Theodore Holly, rector of St Luke's, New Haven, who later became Bishop of Haiti and the first black bishop in the Episcopal Church. After the Freedman's Commission, an official agency of the Church, had failed in its efforts to evangelize blacks after the Civil War, black Episcopalians founded the Society for the Promotion of Church Work Among the Colored People.

15 'Negro Episcopal priests form union', *New York Times* (9 February 1968).

16 J. M. Burgess, sermon delivered at the Institution of the Very Revd Quinland R. Gordon as Dean of the Absalom Jones Theological Institute, Atlanta, Georgia, 11 April 1972 (Archives of the Episcopal Church, Austin, Texas).

17 Kortright Davis, an Afro-Anglican scholar from Antigua, put it this way:

138

To be British and Anglican goes as a hand in a glove, but to be Black and Anglican seems to require both explanation and adjustment. . . . Anglicanism, it is said, is cold, stiff, formal, hierarchical – it lacks the warmth, flexibility, informality and communality of Africanism. How can both be placed together in any harmonious and lasting way? Is it not a commonly accepted norm that blacks should be Baptists? ('Afro-Anglicanism and the Ecumenical imperative', *Linkage* (October 1986), p. 2)

18 J. C. Hayden, 'Black Episcopal preaching in the nineteenth century: intellect and will', *Journal of Religious Thought*, 39 (1982), p. 12.

19 M. Moran Weston, *Social Policy of the Episcopal Church in the Twentieth Century* (New York: Seabury Press, 1964).

20 Eleanor Harrison, '"One, holy, catholic and apostolic Church?" The African American struggle for incorporation in the Episcopal Church: a case study of St John's Church, Savannah, Georgia' (BA thesis, Princeton University), p. 64.

21 Two such bishops were consecrated, under a compromise plan in 1918: Edward Thomas Demby in Arkansas, and Henry Beard Delany in North Carolina. They had jurisdiction over 'colored work' in their respective and neighbouring dioceses. But the experiment ended with them.

22 John Booty, *The Episcopal Church in Crisis* (Cambridge, MA: Cowley Press, 1988), p. 55.

23 In this connection, it is worth mentioning that the Episcopal Church made decisive steps towards integration only after the landmark Supreme Court decision, *Brown v. Board of Education*, declared school segregation unconstitutional and illegal.

24 Booty, op. cit.

25 For a full discussion, see Lewis, *Yet With a Steady Beat*, especially ch. X, 'The Episcopal Church and the Civil Rights Movement'.

26 *'But We See Jesus': A Pastoral Letter from the Black Episcopal Bishops to Black Clergy and Laity in the Episcopal Church* (New York: Executive Council, 1990), p. 1.

Being Anglican in a pluralist society: a Canadian perspective

Gordon Light

Introduction

In March of 1997, I joined with the Primates of the Anglican Communion for our meeting in Jerusalem. We were housed only a few minutes walk from the old city, and there was opportunity to be caught up in the rich

Gordon Light

variety of life that teems in its narrow streets and alleys. The clothing worn is of almost every conceivable kind: Haredim in black trousers, white shirts, black hats; Palestinian women in long dresses and white head-covering, men in kaffiyehs; schoolgirls in European uniforms; teenagers in miniskirts and jeans; tourists in shorts and T-shirts; clergy of all sorts in distinctive dress. One easily gets a flavour from contemporary life in the old city of the truth of the Pentecost story that speaks of 'Parthians, Medes, Elamites ... ' gathered together. It seemed the whole world was in Jerusalem.

The whole world is also in Toronto. All that I saw in Jerusalem I can see in the streets and subways of the city in which I live. The only difference is that it is rare to see clergy of any stripe in costume, and the 'collar' is perhaps the strangest attire of all to passers-by. Toronto, like every large urban centre in Canada, is a gathering place for the world's cultures. My own shopping street is Polish at one end and Somali at the other.

Canada is a nation of immigrants. Even the indigenous peoples of this land, who can lay claim to thousands of years of history here, were originally immigrants. Not long ago, certainly within living memory, Canada was overwhelmingly European in its makeup. We spoke of the two founding cultures – French and British. In many ways, those roots still inform the political, legal, religious and economic life of our society. But increasingly, we are a pluralist society. The cultural ethos of the USA has been described as 'melting pot '; the phrase Canadians customarily use to characterize themselves is 'mosaic'. The first speaks of a society where everyone is expected to share in the same culture, language and under-standing; the second suggests a society of a complex and diverse composition. Bilingualism and multiculturalism did not just happen when we weren't noticing; they are Canadian social policy – a conscious option. In Canada, pluralism is a deliberate and considered choice.

Two faces of pluralism

A pluralist society incorporates many cultures which, for the most part, have found a way to live together. The key values making this possible are *equality* and *tolerance*. It is not just that every citizen is to enjoy equality, but every group, every culture, every religion. And if we allow for that, then we must intentionally create an atmosphere of tolerance and mutual respect. Canada has worked hard at this, and Canadians enjoy the benefits that flow from this tolerance. Officially, we 'stand on guard'[1] against racism, against sexism, against any group, ideology, faith or political stance that seeks to dominate. This is *not* to say that we have created a world where no social ills

140

exist; our history is replete with examples that shame us. But Canadian social policy is such that tolerance is very much the flag we wave.

On balance, it works. Our cities, for the most part, are safe places to live; we delight in a wide variety of ethnic festivals and foods. Even that most global of sports events, World Cup Football, which excites national passions, is played out in Canada with an amicable politeness. In 1994, when Italy and Brazil contested the World Cup, the Italian and Brazilian communities of Toronto paraded, partied and honked horns in victory salutes; it all was good fun and the rest of the nation cheered them on. Reginald Bibby, a sociologist at the University of Lethbridge, Alberta, author of extensive research into trends in both Canadian society and Canadian religious attitudes, says '[pluralism seems] to have been very beneficial to Canada. Many of the imbalances of the country's first one hundred years are being corrected. Individual behaviour and expression have been increasingly emancipated in all spheres of life.'[2]

I believe that most Canadians appreciate the variety of culture in our present society. Dr John Pobee, Director of Theological Education at the World Council of Churches, speaks with an African voice, but his words would find a home in many Canadian hearts: 'Pluralism is one of the issues of Africa. In my view, pluralism represents the beautiful mosaic of God's creation – plural cultures, diverse and different peoples and races, plurality of faith traditions, different gender ...'[3] This is very much the bright face of pluralism.

There is another face, as well. Bibby quotes a federal government employee who said pluralism means 'we are supposed to stay out of each other's way'. Bibby comments that this is 'hardly an inspiring national goal'! More than this, he argues that pluralism can become the tyranny of the mediocre. Tolerating everything can mean committing oneself to nothing. A society that proclaims that all points of view are of equal weight gives little impetus to search for truth. Indeed, Bibby claims that 'truth' is not in the 'pluralism dictionary'. Donald Posterski and Irwin Barker, who have also done considerable research into Canadian religious values, echo these sentiments: 'Canada's social structures have been built to accommodate a diversity of creeds and cultures. In the realm of beliefs, pluralism demands a multiplicity of belief ultimates – one as valid as the other. Life cannot be reduced to one set of truths ... Tolerance parades as the golden rule. The only view that is intolerable is the view that states there is only "one way".'[4]

In pluralist society, truth becomes relative – each person chooses his or her own 'truth'. Individual opinion, as long as it doesn't tread on someone else's opinion, is highly regarded. This may seem not a bad thing, but it has the effect of detaching us from one another. The goal becomes a search for an individual and personal good more than a seeking after the common good. To quote Bibby again: 'The Canadian emphasis on pluralism translates into freedom for individuals. But pluralism does not go on to indicate how individuals are brought back into community ... Friendships, marriages, family life, work ties, and local, national and global citizenship are among the potential casualties.'[5]

In spite of our claims to tolerance, we have become in some ways a less hospitable society, perhaps less a 'society' and more a collection of individuals and groups. The country came to a telling moment in 1995, when only the slightest majority of Québecers voted to remain in Canada. And that issue has not yet been decided – we are likely to see yet another referendum in Québec soon. Our most recent federal election revealed voting patterns heavily rooted in local biases. A generation ago, Canadians wondered if three political parties were one too many. Today, there are five (at least two based on support that is narrow and regional), and the question is no longer even debated. The common good – arguably the driving force of the early part of our nationhood, and of our foreign policy – is the leftover in the equation. The best for the whole of the populace, including the marginalized, is not lost to the public agenda, but is overwhelmed by group and personal interests. We seem to live out the truth of words of Allan Jones, Dean of Grace Church Cathedral, San Francisco. 'Pluralism introduced us to ways in which we can live comfortably with collective irresponsibility in the name of freedom. We have ended up nowhere with nothing to say to each other ... We are so busy fulfilling ourselves, pursuing happiness, that we miss each other. There is no meeting, no real confrontation, no genuine engagement. No living word connects us ...'[6]

We are very much in need of a 'living word' that can heal what is fragmented and connect what is becoming disconnected. That clearly is the mission and ministry of the Church. I have suggested a few of the strengths and weaknesses of a pluralist society, especially in its Canadian manifestation! What about being Anglican in this context?

Being Anglican: the gift of connecting

If we have a special gift to offer as Anglicans, it is the gift of connecting. The Anglican genius is the genius of relationship. We belong to a family as wide and as culturally diverse as the world itself. Within the life of our own Anglican Communion is a living experience of a plural world. We speak and encourage the language of diversity; we understand the tensions of living in a household of faith that is linguistically, theologically and culturally composite. There are, of course, voices among us arguing for greater uniformity within the Communion. But, by and large, we hold dear our ties that give us both a sense of belonging and a freedom to know (and make known) God in our particular contexts. In spite of vast differences, we have found both the will and the desire to stay together.

Desmond Tutu was right when he said that the most important thing Anglicans do is 'meet'. In our 'meeting' (whether the Anglican Consultative Council, Primates, Lambeth, youth or women's or liturgical networks, companion diocese relationships, as partners in a variety of ways, in the Anglican Cycle of Prayer), we are pressed to speak and listen to each other, to challenge, encourage and care for one another. We do this with confidence because of a shared vision of a Gospel grounded in the scriptures and sacraments, in creeds and ministry, in common prayer. Our confidence can at times be strained, but generally we trust one another. That is no small thing, and I believe it to be a true gift of God. The living Word who connects us is found in those living words and actions which keep us in touch with each other. Our much-trumpeted and rightly prized 'diversity' finds its home in a deep unity in Christ. It is a unity cultivated in and by our frequent 'meeting'.

Without overstating the case, I would claim that we have gained wisdom about ministering in a pluralist society simply by encountering it for some time within our relationships in the Communion. We learn about bridging distances between cultures, about the nature of community, about justice, about letting the Gospel find a home in different ways according to local custom. We do not fear pluralism and we can attest to its benefits. Let me cite examples from our own Canadian Church experience.

Our connections with francophone Anglicanism from Africa to Haiti have grown steadily over the years. In Canada, there is a small but significant francophone Anglican community. Their life is helped by these wider relationships, and I would like to think that those provinces are given a stronger voice by their connection with us. But more than just 'church', our wider affiliations help us to relate more easily with non-church groups locally. Most of our dioceses, for example, have agreements with the Canadian Government Immigration Department to enable parishes to support refugees from all over the world. Because of our worldwide associations, our use of the Anglican Cycle of Prayer, church people are among Canadian groups countering the xenophobic, anti-refugee pressures in our society. The pluralism of international Anglicanism reinforces our commitment to openness and hospitality in Canada.

Pluralism, because it detaches us from one another, presses the Church to make real its commitment to healthy community. In an increasingly individualistic society, we discover that people are hungering for community. There are modest, but real, signs that we are finding ways to invite and welcome the alienated into parishes where they find acceptance. I think of an experience in a congregation in St Catharine's, Ontario, recently. The parish is located in an area which would once have been described as 'blue-collar and working-class', but, with the demise of manufacturing, is now characterized by high unemployment. I knew little about the parish and its outward appearance was not promising. But the experience was unexpectedly dramatic – the highest proportion of children and young people I have seen in a long time, and a service in which the young people had real visibility and audibility. When I asked the rector about the young people, his answer was 'If you came next week, you'd see the other half. A large percentage of these kids are from single-parent families and spend every second weekend with the other parent.' I learned from parish council that the parish is growing because of word of mouth advertising that says 'this is a place where you are going to be welcome, not because you've always been an Anglican, but because you need the place, and it is a place where you will find actual help in the raising of your children'.

The principle is what I call 'low hurdle entry'. Need alone qualifies a person for entrance. Once entered, there are not only resources for you, but also an integration within the community which leads to further commitment, learning and involvement. Part of the gift of ministry in a pluralistic society is the willingness to dare in God's name, to refuse to let tradition alone govern action, but to let the life to which the tradition testifies bubble up and find new paths. This parish and others like it are finding ways to connect that are fresh and life-giving. This may be the direction in which we will increasingly find ourselves moving – not just for survival, but for the sake of the Gospel.

I think, too, of a recent experience in Vancouver, Canada's doorway on the Pacific Rim. Asian immigration has dramatically changed the face of Vancouver. Within the Church, many parishes whose make-up had been largely white and Anglo-Saxon discovered their neighbourhoods and their churches undergoing some remarkable transformation in the past decade. The Diocese of New Westminster sponsors a ministry called 'Kaleidoscope' which works intentionally at cross-cultural relationships. I observed teams of ordained and lay persons from ten or so congregations exploring the fears and possibilities facing them. There was a sense of growing confidence in the promise of new life. Timidity was being replaced by the joy of making connections across cultural boundaries. In providing this ministry, the Church not only helps create new life in congregations, it also enables congregations to become communities of witness against racism.

At the heart of this is an evangelical and catholic spirit: evangelical, as we proclaim and live out the truth of God's love for the world in Christ; catholic, as we embrace in Christ the cultures, the wounds and the joys that live side by side in a pluralist society. We are in a similar position to Paul in the Athens market place when he discovered the 'altar to the unknown

God'.[7] He saw it as a bridge between Gospel and culture – a starting point for ministry. Although distressed that Athens was 'a city full of idols', Paul had the grace to find a point of contact within a society every bit as pluralist as ours, and enter into dialogue. Posterski and Barker, in spite of their criticism of pluralism, make this comment: 'Because pluralism makes room for the people of God to live alongside those who hold other views, it is a friend of the faith. Good churches will help people figure out how to live with the increasing diversity in society without losing their integrity and without hiding their faith.'[8] Anglicans are blessed with many of the tools for that task.

Conclusion

At the outset I described my experience of the old city of Jerusalem, and of my sense of the immediacy of the Pentecost story. Pentecost is the story of the Spirit of God entering into the world's plurality. The evidence of the tongues is testimony to communication in the multi-racial, multi-cultural world which God our Creator has entrusted to us. The Spirit, in forming the Church, gave us a plural identity, an ability to be ourselves for and with others. Being Anglican in a pluralist society is to let that truth inhabit our many varied contexts, so the gospel can be the living Word that connects us.

Notes

1 'O Canada, we stand on guard for thee': national anthem of Canada, stanza 1, final line.
2 Reginald Bibby, *Mosaic Madness* (Toronto: Stoddart Publishing Co., 1990), p. 89.
3 John Pobee in *International Review of Mission* (April 1990).
4 Donald C. Posterski and Irwin Barker, *Where's a Good Church?* (Winfield, BC: Wood Lake Books, 1993), p. 111.
5 Bibby, op. cit., pp. 96, 97.
6 Alan Jones, *Passion for Pilgrimage* (San Francisco: HarperCollins, 1988), pp. 7–10.
7 Acts 17.16–34.
8 Posterski and Barker, op. cit., p. 112.

Anglicans in the non-English world of South America

Jaci Maraschin

South America is a huge continent, of which Brazil is the largest country in size and population (150 million). Whereas most countries have Spanish as the official language, in Brazil it is Portuguese. In some places indigenous peoples still keep their own language like Quechua and Aymara in Bolivia and Peru, and Guarani in Paraguay and Brazil. English is spoken in Guyana and in Surinam, and French in French Guiana. But this represents a small minority. Indigenous people still keep their own religious practices. There are, especially in Brazil, large groups of Candomblé, an African cult brought by slaves, using Yoruba as their liturgical language. Ethnic groups, like the Germans, brought with them their own forms of religion: Lutheran, Orthodox, Baptist, Jewish. The missionary revival of the last century is responsible for the presence of almost all types of mainstream Protestantism. Anglicans arrived at the beginning of the last century as chaplains to English-speaking officials of British commercial companies. They had no intention of evangelizing – they saw South America as a Catholic, and therefore Christian, continent.

But at the end of the nineteenth century the Protestant Episcopal Church in the United States did begin missionary activity, specifically directed at the local populations, many of whom they considered either 'pagan' or 'idolatrous'. In some countries, like Argentina, the presence of the Church of England was more conspicuous than in others. In Brazil the missionaries presented themselves simply as evangelical preachers, whose chief mission was to preach the 'pure Gospel' against popular Roman Catholic practices. It took some time for the Brazilian Episcopal Church to discover its roots and ethos. It is really only at the end of this century that the Anglican Church in South America has become a recognizable reality in our different countries. Moreover, it has to face important challenges: the social, political and economic situation of our societies; the growing of the Pentecostal movement especially in Chile and Brazil; the question of inculturation; and the ecumenical movement.

I would say that the social, political and economic situation of our societies is the scenery where we live and struggle. This is, of course, linked to ethics and power. We are a society divided among classes. The poor are each time poorer and the rich, richer. Peasants and indigenous tribes live on the verge of misery. In Brazil, for instance, the Government boasts that it has won the battle against inflation but never admits the cost: unemployment and illiteracy for many. Public health and public education are not priorities. There is corruption and robbery in many levels of our public administration, without right judgement and accountability. The minimum salary in Brazil is only the equivalent of US$100, in a country where the wages of the rich are incalculable. We witness nowadays the struggle going on between the landless crowd and the traditional land owners with situations near a civil war. The Government has been always on the side of the powerful. The movement of the landless people is frequently blocked by the police or by the Army. In the big cities, besides transport chaos and filth in the parks and streets, there are crowds of homeless adults and children, generating criminals of all kinds. This dreadful situation creates a favourable climate for the use of drugs, the practice of prostitution and the elimination of human beings.

Many Christians have found in the Theology of Liberation a suitable way to help the Churches to face the social, political and economic situation in which we live. Anglicans are asking how they can use the tools of Theology of Liberation in order to fulfil their mission. This is a non-English world, and our concerns should also be local, indigenous and, therefore, non-English. Theology of Liberation starts from a new way of reading the Scriptures. The Gospel gives answers to the real situation where real people are living. People are invited to read the Bible afresh and to listen to what God is telling them to do in their own situation. In order to discern 'the signs of the times' Christians have to understand the process which generates injustice and misery. This presupposes that the preaching of the Church can be related to the social, political and economic levels of society. In doing this we are being the Church in the place where we live.

The Pentecostal Movement in South America has been called 'the refuge of the masses'. In a situation of despair a religion stressing religious experience and mystical ecstacy has been for many people this place of refuge. The Pentecostal experience has been present not only in the traditional Pentecostal Churches but in many other mainstream Churches – Roman Catholic, Presbyterian, Methodist – with the name of Charismatic Movement. Anglicans too are tempted to become 'pentecostal', attracted by the results the Movement shows in other Churches steady growth, generous giving and spiritual personal development. It seems to me, however, that Anglicans should resist this temptation for at least two basic reasons: the Pentecostals do their job better than we could be able to do it (it is their nature); in the second place, we Anglicans have a special mission in South America that nobody else could be able to perform if we abandon it. It becomes a question of faithfulness to our ethos and to the mission we have received from God.

147

Jaci Maraschin

At the 1988 Lambeth Conference there was a Buckingham Palace garden party. A member of the Royal Family asked me if I were a Roman Catholic priest and was astonished to hear that I was an Anglican priest and that there were Anglicans in Brazil. But are we merely a 'translated Church', trying hard to imitate what normally goes on in London or Canterbury as if we were ashamed to be an Anglican in the non-English world of South America? Has Anglicanism sufficient force and creativity to allow Christians of non-English background to profess the faith according to the Anglican ethos? This brings into our discussion the relationship between Gospel and culture. The great achievement of Augustine of Canterbury was to create, with his Roman monks, a new kind of Christianity in the British Isles. The Church of England developed its own forms of life and worship and became a distinctive part of the One, Holy, Catholic and Apostolic Church. At the time of the Reformation it was not transformed into a mere 'protestant' Church. The English Church had very strong roots in tradition and the Gospel to be what it always intended to be: the Church of the English people. South American culture is very different from British culture. It has its own features. Our countries have particular traditions and ways of being. How can an English Church became a South American Church?

Let me point out some of the differences of ethos. I am aware that it is risky to generalize. The English ethos is much more on the side of intellectualism whereas the South American ethos tends to exalt feelings and the expression of emotions. This results in a different experience of our bodies. While the English temper tends to be phlegmatic, the South American goes to the extremes of externalization. English persons hardly touch each other. South Americans are always embracing, touching and kissing friends and acquaintances. Our festivals are colourful and the music is hot and rhythmic. Our bodies carry in the skin our erotic experiences, through swaying movement. Our climate sustains a life in the open air. These differences appear in the way we live, work, love and worship God. As I understand, the English spirit appreciates order and tradition. We are not so aware of tradition, and we tend towards disorder! 'South American Time' is not 'English Time': we are always late ... Comparisons are not always fair. They tend to exaggerate. I know, for sure, that my English friends are able to cry and to laugh. On the other side, South Americans may not always show what they are feeling. But such comparisons do help us to understand why an Anglican Church in a non-English world should be different from the Church in England.

I think that Churches express what they are through their liturgies. This is what we do when we get together and the way we get together is the way we are. Fundamental to liturgical expression of worship is the Eucharist and baptism, reading the Scriptures and praying and singing. The history

148

of the Liturgy shows the influence of a great diversity of cultures through the ages and the spaces in its forms and contents. The Book of Common Prayer was and is an instrument for helping this life of worship in the Anglican Communion. It has become a symbol of our liturgical life and the best expression of the manner we believe. *Lex orandi, lex credendi* has always been an Anglican understanding of our faith and of our ethos. The Book of Common Prayer has had many translations and revisions in many different parts of the world. In South America, however, we have tended to be too content with mere translation. But translations are not the answer to the quest for inculturation. Translation can be a transitory procedure but never a definitive one. We face the paradoxical situation of being non-English but still deeply dependent on the English Liturgy.

Some inculturation, however, is happening in South America, through the creation of local liturgical music and art, as a result of a serious engagement with Liberation Theology, our own cultural roots, and the Ecumenical Movement. It is true that Anglicans in South America have been reluctant to accept this musical movement. Notwithstanding, we have achieved quite a remarkable collection of songs for worship. I have notice that in Paraguay and Bolivia people are used to singing the Psalms with local rhythms accompanied with local stringed instruments. Anglicans in this non-English world can now offer to the wider Anglican Communion their own contribution to the enrichment of our worship and of our life.

I will give some examples of what is happening in the Brazilian Province of the Anglican Communion because this is the place where I live and minister. There is a fundamental difference between our songs and *Hymns Ancient and Modern*. Although the themes are similar, the style is different. There is a heavy influence of Liberation Theology in our songs. A good example is the re-reading of Psalm 126, the liberation from captivity experienced by the People of God. In our actual situation in South America that liberation is still a promise. So we learn to sing in our own way: 'The God our Lord will lead us out of desolation; it is going to seem we're dreaming; then will our mouths be filled with exaltation. In joy, forever, will we sing. God will in the future appear as a gracious Lord; it is going to seem we're dreaming; then, joyfully we'll see the Kingdom near and the fulfilment of his freedom.'[1] This poem is set to what we call in Brazil 'marcha rancho'. It is a very popular rhythm very easy to be sung by our congregations. Another example is a Brazilian song with the theme of the Magnificat. In this poem Our Lady sits before a rose. She receives the Angel and meditates alone on his message. The poem stresses the powerful hand of God that scatters the proud, casts down the mighty from their thrones, and lifts up the lowly. She feels, in her secret maternity, the conception of an understanding which will give birth to the utmost freedom.[2] Our

Jaci Maraschin

Eucharistic songs are linked with the fruits of the earth and with the promise of a life of plenty and equality. So, we ask God to transform the grain which still lies under the earth, not only into his most sacred body but also into food for the poor of our continent. The wine is not only the blood of Jesus, but also the sign of a life, joyful and meaningful.[3] Among our local rhythms it is worth mentioning the use of samba, samba cancão, modinha, choro, marcha, marcha rancho, xaxado, baião and bossa nova. This kind of music is not suitable for either piano or organ. It requires guitars, drums, flutes and percussion. In South America there has been experience among other Churches of local music and poetry. Many will recall the beautiful *Missa Creolla* from Argentina and the *Missa da Terra sem Males* from Brazil. In our own Anglican Province we are singing Brazilian samba for the Kyrie, Gloria, Sanctus and Agnus Dei.

What is the perspective for the future? Anglicans in the non-English world of South America have a special mission which consists in the following: (a) to transcend the stage of translation in order to recreate the Prayer Book according to the signs of our time and place, keeping in mind, of course, the long and living tradition of the Universal Church; (b) to develop a local theological thinking related to the social, political and economic situation in which we live (for this Theology of Liberation can be of great help); (c) to express our bodily culture in our worship through gestures, dances and songs; (d) to work together with our fellow Christians of other Churches with the help of the ecumenical movement; (e) to be in dialogue with the Provinces of the Anglican Communion for consultation, mutual strengthening and co-operation; (f) to develop forms of art for all levels of church life including vestments, architecture, symbols, music and literature; and (g) to experience mission as a joyful enterprise related to the beauty of the Kingdom of God.

Notes

1 J. Maraschin (ed.), *Celebration of Life* (Salvador, Bahia, Brazil, 1992), song no. 11.
2 J. Maraschin, *Ofício divino das comunidades* (São Paulo, Brazil: Paulus, 1994), song no. 204.
3 *Celebration of Life*, song no. 16.

Australia – the last of lands

James Minchin

As a university student on a working holiday in Papua New Guinea, a junior priest ministering in Singapore, a pilgrim traversing the Asian region, and above all an Oxford college chaplain in the 1970s, the writer encountered little interest in Australia beyond its quaint fauna and love of sport.

Today things Australian are taken more seriously. The wonderful but painful story of our indigenous peoples and their sacred homeland is at last getting through to the rest of the nation and the world. Even so, the 'tyranny of distance' may still incline foreigners to ask 'Can anything good come out of Australia?'

This essay is primarily a partisan and critical reading of the role of the Anglican and other churches in Australia. But in detecting signs of God's Spirit at work it invites the reader also to revisit the question non-rhetorically.

Australia as of 1998

Australia is a nation of 18 million people, 90 per cent of them in or near cities hugging the coastline of a vast island continent the size of mainland USA – not to forget Tasmania! Bracketed by the Indian and Pacific oceans, Australia sports abundant wealth and vivid contrasts of climate and terrain. Three-quarters of the population is locally born, including 2 per cent indigenes (the total of 25 per cent born outside Australia is of course a large proportion). For 81 per cent English is the sole language spoken at home. By now, only about 40 per cent is pure Anglo-Celt: Australia's racial and cultural spectrum has been enriched by immigration, principally from Southern Europe, the Middle East, Southeast Asia and the Pacific, and by miscegenation.

A paradise on earth ... Yet so much of it God has disposed to be inhospitable. Aboriginal tribes eked out a fallible co-existence with it for millennia. 'White' settlement proposed to conquer it, sometimes constructively, sometimes brutally. Periodically the powers that be have lashed out at assorted groups whose differentness displeased them: 'blacks' (indigenes and Melanesian indentured labourers); Irish Catholics; republicans; communists; Jews; Muslims; Southern European or Indo-Chinese

James Minchin

immigrants. And for most of two hundred years jingoism and the slogans of the 'lucky country' have covered the good, the bad and the ugly of an aggressively macho culture.

Australia gained nationhood in 1901, a model of prosperity and democratic reform. A century later, prosperity and democracy have survived war and depression, but face even more testing times. Globalization is over-riding local structures and traditions; the speed of change produces a loss of nerve and direction.

As of 1998, many thoughtful, godfearing citizens believe that the day of reckoning draws near for sins not yet repented of, and, in many cases, still being committed. Fealty to Mammon has again proved incompatible with obedience to God. The harmony of neighbours, men and women, drawing out their uniqueness through co-operation – imaging, if faintly, the Triune God – is assailed by social Darwinism. The instinctive or deliberate emulation of Jesus Christ's work articulating God's purposes in human flesh has been usurped by a competitive individualism.

Moreover, in the Asia–Pacific region as elsewhere, rapid change has triggered economic and environmental turbulence, highlighting a dearth of resilient values and inspiring leaders dedicated to the common good.

For a Christian socialist like the writer, the reductionist right-wing ideas espoused by the current crop of 'conservative' political leaders and advisers create nothing but division. National compacts are being undone or inherited problems exacerbated. All is justified in the service of economic growth or of making Australians feel comfortable. Reaching consensus about core issues – e.g., a workable Australian republic; the proper mix of municipal, state and federal jurisdictions – is muddied by the Thatcherite device of picking the classes of individuals who deserve to prevail in squabbles over disputed claims or limited resources.

- The contradiction looms of deeming Aborigines and Torres Strait Islanders citizens while letting their loss of identity, children and land go unrepaired to appease greedy or racist grievances nursed by 'main-stream' sectional interests.
- Fear likewise is allowed to reinforce a harshness in immigration policy and implementation that defies Australia's treaty obligations.
- A 'fatalistic and Panglossian' embrace of globalization and 'borderless laissez-faire capitalism'[1] permits structural unemployment to persist, the social wage to deteriorate and income inequalities to be entrenched, a full-blooded industrial relations system and union movement to be leeched, physical infrastructure to be neglected, regressive or mal-distributive tax measures to be proposed, and health and social security recipients to be penalized.
- Shamefully low overseas aid levels are being further reduced.

152

- Ecological conservation is openly subordinated to economic growth, and made dependent on revenue raised from privatization.
- A recent review of tertiary education while mouthing the ideal of lifelong learning has capitulated in reality to market forces. There is inadequate monitoring of changes, such as in genetics, wrought by science and technology under the slewing and competitive pressure of commerce.
- The independence of civil services and judiciaries is under attack; as is the viability of nationally-owned and non-commercial public broadcasting.
- Ways are being explored of ending the compulsory voting which has, coupled with a preferential system, assisted Australia to preserve high levels of participation and fairness in electoral politics.

At present, the Governor-General, Sir William Deane, is the only public official willing to rise above party politics and plead for national unity based on justice. Christian agencies, commissions and synods provide a clearing-house for research and advocacy, but they are often compromised by being dependent on parsimonious government funding. Although a few church leaders have made the running on race relations or other specific issues, no social prophet of the calibre of Ernest Burgmann[2] looms on the horizon. Numbers of church members have joined with other people of goodwill in decrying 'spiritual wickedness in high places' or pressing for more fruitful alternatives. But by and large there is no powerful Christian voice. Perhaps there are just too many fronts on which vigilance and action are required. Or are there other reasons?

The Christian state of play in Australia

Christianity has been part and parcel of Australia's identity since 1788. Just over 70 per cent of the population still claims Christian affiliation (27 per cent Roman Catholic, 22 per cent Anglican, etc.). Between 15 per cent and 20 per cent of Australians attend Christian worship regularly – a rather higher ratio than in Europe or the United Kingdom (inoculated by the past against Christendom?), but lower than in the United States of America (where religion is a powerful if quasi-private factor).

Over the last ten years the Roman Catholic Church has supplanted the Anglican Church as the country's largest denomination – partly as a result of post-World War II immigration trends and of 'mixed' marriage policy.

Yet, apart from Pentecostal growth, active church membership appears to be in decline, rapidly among urban Roman Catholics, less spectacularly among Protestants – most of whose adherents have long been nominal but nowadays are less defined by Freemasonry and anti-Catholicism than by family or recreation! Congregations generally comprise a higher proportion of older women than does the population at large. Civil celebrants now conduct about half of all Australian weddings, and are called on more and more for other ceremonies. In 1996 18 per cent of males and 15 per cent of females professed no religion, while 9 per cent overall described inadequately or did not state their religion.

Anyone familiar with the Church's gathered life must be amazed that so many churchgoers have tolerated perfunctory or boring liturgy where neither wonder, stimulus nor camaraderie is in evidence. What profit is there in a fussy or shoddy performance of the essentials – Bible-reading, intercessory prayer, sacramental activity, singing, and the like – bespeaking scant respect for either the tradition, the congregation or its 'mission' context? Anglicanism in particular, if it snubs this three-fold respectfulness, lapses into formalism. Fortunately, there are many examples of Anglicans working with other Christians to provide inclusive and imaginative ceremonies when public prayer is most needed, for example, after the Port Arthur massacre in Tasmania in 1996; or, before the Gulf War, the inter-faith vigil in St Paul's Cathedral, Melbourne.

The Australian Council of Churches became the National Council of Churches in Australia in 1994, and now includes Roman Catholics. The ecumenical cause is alive but, because it works by consensus, is neither spectacular nor prophetic. The choice of Sydney for its headquarters is ironic, given the vehement anti-Romanism and anti-liberalism of leading Protestants there.

Much energy goes in presuming the Churches' decline and death. Some doomsayers gloat at the thought of having their attacks on institutional irrelevance vindicated. The media seize upon stories of clergy (sexual) misdemeanour or folly, of church conflict over faith, morals or polity, or of declining attendance, and predict the worst.

By contrast, there is little strategic planning, let alone allocation of resources, for personnel to be deployed for maximum impact on the centres and at the cutting edges of national life. What lies behind this failure?

On the one hand, church communities still dot the length and breadth of the land. Their membership is drawn from almost all parts of Australian society. There are obvious exceptions: the majority of teenagers and young adults, left-wing or green groups, and sizeable minorities adhering to other beliefs. Yet even people such as these are within easy reach of concerned Christian relatives or neighbours.

On the other hand, there is hardly ever a united Christian front. The introduction of 'God-talk' can intensify rather than defuse the arguments over the issues of the day. When running their organizations or prescribing personal ethics, Church leaders may opt for an amoral 'technical' approach, believing that faith cannot conjure with modernity. There is little evidence in practice that Christians' attitudes towards sexual relations, contraception, abortion and divorce differ very much from anyone else's.

The Anglican Church of Australia

'C of E' is still how Australian Anglicans and their Church are most commonly known. Yet General Synod initiated the change to 'Anglican Church of Australia' in 1981. Why does the old moniker persist?

Firstly, the whole kit and caboodle of English Anglicanism was transported to Australia. 'Ownership' of it, let alone adaptation of it to Australian circumstances, has been patchy. For example, the problems of the rural Church – distances to be travelled, dwindling population and resources in recessionary times, reluctance of clergy to work ecumenically, and so on – have led some to suggest that all but five country dioceses may go to the wall.

Of course none of today's bishops and synods parrot imperial shibboleths. Nor, to many Australians' surprise, is the Australian Church governed by the British monarch. To be sure, its Constitution commits it to the fundamental declarations of biblical faith and catholic order and to the ruling principles of its mother Church, enshrined in the Book of Common Prayer and the Thirty-Nine Articles of Religion. Indeed, under pressure from the leading lights of Sydney, the Anglican world's largest and most comprehensively Evangelical diocese, it deliberately set out to be more conservative and resistant to alteration than the Church of England had been.

However, since the mid-1980s, the legitimate plurality which Anglican formularies acknowledge has reappeared, being exceeded or denied depending on one's point of view. The 1992 Canon which enabled those dioceses that wished to ordain women to the priesthood to do so signalled a shift in 'political' power away from Sydney. The diocese's zealous Calvinist/ Brethren group – godly congregations promulgating salvation by right doctrine under the watchful eye of their elders – has sought unremitting redress: appealing to ecclesiastical and secular jurisdictions, and employing techniques which range from legal and procedural nitpicking to feral unilateralism.[3]

In reality Anglicans have known – in the biblical sense – every kind of liturgical and theological position. Although the Church's mission and belief have suffered thereby a loss of clarity that affronts some and stimulates others, the consequences in Australia have been mitigated by the apartheid of distance and history. 'Churchmanship' battles, certainly between and often within dioceses, not only perpetuate divergent styles of ritual and doctrine but are associated with very different ways of doing contextual mission. What is enjoined in one parish or diocese may be forbidden or overlooked in the next. Behind professions of loyalty to episcopal governance and Anglican tradition there flourish lawlessness in worship and tendentiousness in preaching and teaching.

Despite residual pretensions to be the paramount and 'proper' Church of this English-speaking nation, Australian Anglicanism has developed its own ethos.

It is, like the nation, a federation, and is made up of 23 dioceses and five Provinces based on the mainland States. Clericalism is rife, although there is nothing uniquely Australian about that. No other church has so exalted the vocation of priesthood, fusing sacerdotal, didactic, pastoral, conciliatory and representative roles in one 'parson', who has the cure of every soul within parish boundaries. Here is an invitation to sanctity – and heroic failure, whether in a far-flung multiple-centre country parish or amid hectic and anonymous city life.

Over time, Anglican priesthood has had to be re-worked and 'humanized'. In the process there has been blessing – above all, from the accession of women – but also confusion. What is the right relationship between priest and household, other liturgical ministers, parishioners, vestry ('elders'), bishop and diocese, the mission of the people of God to the world?

How are clergy trained? Australia has nine theological/ministerial colleges still functioning, including the indigenous ecumenical Nungalinya College in Darwin. Some are Church-owned, some private, most are linked to ecumenical divinity schools, all operate on particular churchmanship frequencies, except Nungalinya. Ordinands nowadays must take extra programmes, such as clinical pastoral education or ministry specialization, on top of the core theological subjects. Strangely, they serve negligible apprenticeships in practical liturgics and apologetics, both of which are critical to marrying Christian tradition with contemporary human experience.

From colonial days the Australian Church has been devoutly episcopal. Our diocesan bishops may not always get their way; not all are inspiring leaders, pastors or teachers; but their office carries more weight than in England or Roman Catholic circles. The widely accepted perquisites of episcopate here – special clothing, jewellery, remuneration – are also puzzling, given the egalitarian bent not only of servant ministry but of Australian self-portrayal. Consecrations since 1984 of Aboriginal and Torres Strait Islander assistant bishops[4] beg major questions, which also go to current proposals for a Defence Forces diocese. If these cultural and sectional episcopates are legitimate, why not others? Why should they not have equivalence with a territorial diocesan? How about party episcopates?

Synods and standing committees or diocesan councils have also been central to Australian Anglicanism, some evolving into large assemblies (e.g., 1,100 for Melbourne Synod). From the outset, the hierarchy has had to depend on lay support and money much more starkly than where the Church is established. The most potent bodies in both categories belong to the Diocese of Sydney. The tamest used to be the General Synod: but over the 1990s the plethora of controversial matters only capable of being handled nationally has made for fiery clashes. In turn, the desire for conflict resolution and more nuanced debate has encouraged resort to non-adversarial procedures.

Whither from here?

Looked at in isolation, Australia may appear 'the last of lands'. If so, its churches are quite peripheral:

- to a nation preoccupied with economic questions, its public education religiously illiterate, its agenda dominated by commercial media with little time for antiquated institutions;
- to the churches of the 'North', long-standing purveyors of the Christian tradition;
- to the high-energy-and-growth churches of Asia and Africa, with their global missionary zeal and aggressive certitude;
- to Christians being persecuted or subjected to involuntary hardship.

Yet in the divine providence nothing is peripheral, everything is connected. What then might God make of white Australian Anglicans, mainly middle-class, reasonably intelligent, anxious about the future, conscious of God's hand not only on them but on their indigenous and non-Anglo-Celt brothers and sisters?

Like our nation, we are being forced to managed change better, neither to idolize nor to resist globalization. In doing so, the Church has two advantages:

1. We are already part of the worldwide Anglican Communion within a larger household of faith.
2. The Church lives under the promise that to let today's persona go will mean renewal tomorrow. We cannot insure against internal disarray or unbelief, intractable circumstances, or small-minded Australians. God alone will choose how and whether our Church survives. Letting go does not mean being complacent: that would be to offer the iconoclasts a field day. Once the essentials are secured, our Anglican charter enjoins versatility, allows movement and institution to co-

Church whether gathered or dispersed, and bids us engage with our neighbours in Jesus' name.

Fortunately, instances of our apostolic calling being renewed, affording us something to offer our compatriots and other parts of the Anglican Communion, are not hard to find:

- When the 1995 General Synod endorsed *A Prayer Book for Australia*, members set the seal, perhaps inadvertently, on flexibility. Herein is not *the* book, but *a* book of authorized liturgical resources, both patterns and texts – in fresh and inclusive language for common prayer. Each community may then draw on all available cultural resources and exponents – traditional and contemporary; Judaeo-Christian, from other religions or from secular sources, domestic or foreign[5] – to dress worship locally and increase the chorus of thanksgiving for all that God is doing in Jesus Christ. Clergy and laity alike have found new vitality and missionary impetus from lovingly prepared 'in-house' liturgies, rites of passage, and civic celebrations.
- The attempts of some Anglicans (as mentioned above) to reduce the Australian Church to a sect have had a two-fold effect, particularly in Sydney. By insisting that God's authentic Word can only be distilled from the Bible via the English Reformation through a select set of propositions, they discount all other godly ways of proclaiming and obeying Christ. But their proselytizing success also goads the rest of us to wrestle afresh with Scripture and formulary, ethical dilemma and political engagement, for we are members no less of a Body whose Head has freed us before God and one another.
- The effects of decline and scarcity can paralyse or dishearten. But in a self-consciously voluntary organization they can also improve scrutiny and problem-solving between and within parish and diocese on a two-way rather than top-down basis. Anglicans nationwide are becoming more attentive to structural matters such as:
  - deciding how much to rely on 'live' income as against endowments or investments, and whether strategic planning will require self-sufficiency or cross-subsidy;
  - complementing lean administration with appropriate paid or unpaid advisory ministry, and using central technology to alleviate local administrative burdens (specially for country dioceses);
  - merging and co-ordinating welfare agencies, or developing national school policies.

Perhaps having inhaled millennial vapours, today's Anglicans are demonstrating a vigour of inquiry and self-expression that is typically Australian and unamenable to central control. The voices of those formerly excluded from pleading their Christian status, homosexuals for example, are now being heard, and the old clichés of condemnation are being tested against the ethic of love rather than law. This process will be protracted, and may not even produce a satisfactory outcome: but at least it is occurring. Interpretation and application of the Scriptures (and related studies) is being democratized, with large numbers of lay people taking classes from teachers of international calibre. Provocative books on faith or ethics are best-sellers. The multicultural nature of Australia brings new opportunities for evangelism and ministry, and for partnerships that cross national boundaries and give another lease of life to the 'missionary' agencies.

Perhaps Anglicans' inherited reputation for being something of a Clayton's Church will make us strangely attractive to disaffected Christians from other backgrounds: Roman Catholics and Orthodox who want a sacramental community without a prefabricated morality or hidebound theology; Pentecostalists and conservative Protestants who want less dependence on subjective experience or theocratic teachers.

The capacity of Anglicans and other Christians to have obvious influence, let alone final say, going into the second century of Australia's nationhood, is unlikely to be great. Many church people have accepted the self-fulfilling prophecy that religion is irrelevant to the structures of education and governance in Australia, that the Church – not only the hierarchy, but the general membership – should keep right out of politics. But they must then find other ways in which Jesus' teaching can be brought to bear. And let no one underestimate the power of Christians' fidelity in their chosen occupation or their informal contribution to the well-being of society.

If the images of the Church, the company of disciples, that Jesus taught retain any impact on our thinking, they are a source of encouragement: salt, yeast, light on a lampstand. None requires large numbers or more than modest visibility: in fact smallness and dispersibility are positive benefits. All embody the unique perspective of people captured by a God who loves this world, and ever transcends its limits.

Notes

1   G. Barker in *Australian Financial Review* (3–4 January 1998).
2   A Christian socialist, constitutional monarchist, bushman and boxer, he was Anglican Bishop of Canberra and Goulburn 1934–61. See the biography of him: P. Hempenstall, *The Meddlesome Priest* (Sydney: Allen and Unwin, 1993).
3   At the time of writing, four instances were to the fore: (1) pressure for diaconal or lay eucharistic presidency; (2) Sydney Synod's 1997 resolution to abolish the use of the term 'priest' in favour of 'elder'; (3) Sydney's refusal to pay its

James Minchin

national dues, particularly to ecumenical or inter-Anglican causes; (4) the
establishing outside Sydney of Calvinist/Brethren congregations by Anglicans
of that persuasion from Sydney.
4   The Michaelmas 1997 consecration of a second Torres Strait Islander seems at
the time of writing to have precipitated a major schism.
5   The lyrics and music of Christian hymns, for example, have frequently drawn
on or borrowed from general religious or secular material in the public domain
at the time, while being sensitive to the consciences of believers and the wider
community alike. The writer's experience in editing and writing the English
texts for the Asian hymnal *Sound the Bamboo* was most instructive in this
regard.

Bibliography

Australian Catholic Bishops' Conference, *Commonwealth for the Common Good*
(Collins, 1992).
T. Blombery, *The Anglicans in Australia* (Canberra: AGPS, 1996).
A. Cadwallader (ed.), *Episcopacy* (Adelaide: ABCE, 1994).
J. Davis, *Australian Anglicans and Their Constitution* (Canberra: Acorn Press,
1993).
J. Harris, *One Blood: 200 Years of Aboriginal Encounter with Christianity: A Story of
Hope* (Albatross, 1990; Lion, 1990).
S. Judd and K. Cable, *Sydney Anglicans: A History of the Diocese* (Sydney: AIO,
1987).
P. Kalder (ed.), *Winds of Change: The Experience of Church in Changing Australia*
(Sydney: Anzea, 1994).
I. Loh, F. Leliciano and J. Minchin (eds), *Sound the Bamboo* (Manila: CCA, AILM,
1991).
M. Porter, *Land of the Spirit: The Australian Religious Experience* (Geneva: WCC,
1990).
M. Porter (ed.), *Melbourne Anglicans, 1847–1997* (Melbourne: JBCE, 1997).

'Anglicane? Qu'est-ce que c'est?'

An experience of francophone Anglicans

Tim Naish

Sunday morning, and I'm driving as I do each week far into a crowded maze of dusty huts and open drains, often nosing the car between them where no path, let alone road, seems to exist. Journey's end will be one or other of the six or seven small wattle-and-daub or mud-brick buildings that comprise the Anglican Church in Lubumbashi, chief city of the Diocese of Shaba, which occupies the south-eastern quarter of the huge country of Congo-Zaire. Deep in the heart of this or that poor area of the city, I have to admit I'm lost, though I've been here several times before, and I stop to ask the way to the Eglise Anglicane. 'Anglicane? Qu'est-ce que c'est? Vous êtes chrétiens? C'est une secte, ou quoi?'

This response is not untypical; it is scarcely surprising that very few should know of the Anglican Church in a city with scores of obscure 'denominations' with colourful names. What may surprise, and offend, some Anglicans in other parts of the Communion is that their own Church should be ranked with such groups – The African Episcopal Baptist Holiness Church of God and so on – which would meet in similar out-of-the-way surroundings across the city.

This chapter can only give a glimpse of one small corner of francophone Anglicanism – I am not qualified to write of others. Regrettably, even for Congo, I must make generalizations which will often not be valid in some specific cases among such a diverse minority. Yet that passer-by's question 'Anglicane? Qu'est-ce que c'est?' offers food for chewing. The Anglican Communion, today more than ever, finds it difficult to identify itself. What is it that holds it together, gives it definition? Francophone Anglicans are among those who prevent us from looking for identity in tempting directions, of which I want to mention four.

First, the response raises the issue of *power*. The Anglican Communion as a whole and in general is used to occupying an established position; its members would expect a passer-by to know at least what it meant, if not always where the nearest building was. Even though in most countries where it has some strength this 'establishment' is a matter of 'feel' and influence rather than of law, it has shaped the nature of our Church. We are accustomed to being listened to and respected. We are fond of seeing ourselves as the *via media* but perhaps, often unconsciously, that means

161

thinking of ourselves *at the centre*, not just as between Catholic and Protestant, but as being *significant*.

Yet there are those within our Communion, like my sisters and brothers in Shaba, who as Anglicans are insignificant within their contexts. Very often they are those who do not speak English. And just as they derive little power from *being* Anglican, because no one has heard of them, they tend to be excluded from power *within* Anglicanism, because they are little known there too, and unheard. Moreover they tend to be oppressed in most other areas of life too: economically, culturally, socially, politically. The multiplication of factors tending towards their marginalization makes it the more important that they are not forgotten. Without making a god of the oppressed I would argue that our Christian listening needs to be biased in favour of their voices, for they tend to be those which are unaccustomed to speech. When they summon the courage, all too often, because they are inept with the jargon or they lack sophistication, they are not heard and the next time their courage fails. So they are trapped forever at the margins. There is a Christian imperative to attend with greater care to those on the edges.

The existence of awkward minorities such as francophone Anglicans serves as a reminder that significance for followers of Christ is not found at the centre but on the margins, 'outside the camp'. The awkwardness is compounded by the diversity of the francophone part of the Communion – the fragmented geography of the Malagasy Republic, the African Great Lakes, Guinea in West Africa, French-speaking Canadians. A beginning has been made to attempt to co-ordinate these varied groups.

Two vignettes underline this precariousness. Since the Diocese of Shaba was inaugurated, the bishop has faced the challenge of a rival claimant who in a variety of ways, often involving the secular authorities, has made things difficult. The rival has styled himself 'Founder Archbishop of the Anglican Church'. Bishop Kolini had at one stage to go to court to show that he was the rightfully consecrated Anglican leader. It is only in a context where no one much has heard of this Church that such a dispute can be sustained.

Another, and more positively: I well remember sitting with thirty or so of the leading Anglicans in Lubumbashi in late 1988 in the outhouse of the bishop's home that served as the Diocesan Office. The bishop had borrowed a video recorder, and we watched together the main Eucharist of the Lambeth Conference 1988 in Canterbury Cathedral. The concentration, wonder, and questioning of people was intense. The sense of astonishment and pride that *this* was our Church, as well as the humble slum buildings that we were familiar with, was evident. They had a glimpse of something powerful; and yet they in their 'ignorance' remind us that it cannot be in such power that we find our identity as Anglicans.

The second tempting direction in which to seek Anglican self-identity is in *language*. The creation of the category of 'francophone Anglicans', a category defined linguistically, is itself symptomatic of this temptation. They are labelled thus because they don't 'fit'. This is intimately connected with power of course: it is partly their inability to speak English that deprives francophones within the Communion of power.

Yet here there is an irony: I write about Shaba as an example of francophone Anglicanism, yet probably the majority of Anglicans in our 'francophone' diocese could not conduct a proper conversation of any length in French! Thus, at the end of my Sunday morning drive, having found with relief the building with its board announcing that this is an Anglican church, and gone in to find a few rickety benches or piles of bricks, with a table at the front, after half an hour or so when some people had gathered, I would open my Zaire Prayer Book and conduct the whole service in Zaire-Swahili. Much of 'francophone' Anglicanism does not worship in French, just as much as 'anglophone' Anglicanism does not use English. Indeed even Swahili would be a second language for most worshippers, though in the city at least it would be for many the language of daily life. There is therefore a certain arrogance in labelling these people as francophone, a refusal of the majority within the Communion to see them as they are. Labels of course have to be used for convenience, but I suspect that many conspire with the inaccuracies that the labels promote.

When Zaire was suggested as a location for our service as mission partners, it was partly on the basis of our progress through French at school; yet its practical usefulness was minimal within the diocese, though it enabled me to participate a little in ecumenical teaching. Mission partners are few on the ground these days; during their heyday, the acquisition and use of local languages was, arguably, some of their best work (see Lamin Sanneh, *Translating the Message*). Perhaps some of the sensitivity that the better missionaries showed needs to be evident in the attitudes of Church leaders and all who relate across Provincial boundaries within the Communion today. No one can learn all the languages of Anglicanism, but English speakers should not abuse the luxury of having so many willing and able to use their language, by taking it for granted.

As I struggled in Swahili or French it was greatly encouraging when someone expressed their recognition that I was thinking in, or translating into, an unfamiliar tongue; when they gave me space and freedom to bumble my way through. Within our fellowship, from international conferences to chance individual meetings, let us give each other that space and freedom, and let those whose language is 'marginal' in the eyes of the majority be especially encouraged. Francophone and other non-English-speaking Anglicans within the Communion (there are even smaller minorities, like the Portuguese-speakers of Brazil, Mozambique, Angola, and Portugal itself) are a reminder to us all of the need for careful listening. Their insights may be worth waiting for.

One concrete sign of this marginalization is the paucity of Christian literature in French that is specifically useful for Anglicans. Of course there is a great deal of immensely profitable writing by Roman Catholics, and Protestant Evangelicals have been active in producing literature, much of great value. We relied on this for training in Shaba. Yet when we wanted to help people to learn about Anglican history or worship, or nurture them in Anglican traditions of faith and practice (putting aside for the moment the extent to which these exist), we had few resources. The nicely produced French translation of the American Book of Common Prayer of 1979 was of some help, but we had little else to put into people's hands. The market for any material produced for French-speaking Anglicans would be small and its distribution something of a nightmare; but economic considerations should not be allowed to dominate. Even then there would remain the challenge of adapting such materials to the diverse contexts of francophone Anglicanism.

While Anglicanism all over the world has rightly been involved in the process of translation into local vernaculars, it has usually done so from the basis of an unthinking anglocentrism. As vernacular Scriptures, liturgies, teaching aids have been produced, so also an elite has been taught and introduced to the English originals. This could not happen in francophone areas, for there are no French originals. Where Anglicans have got together across Provincial boundaries, English has been assumed.

And so to the third point – we cannot allow ourselves to find our communal identity in a *colonial cultural inheritance*. Once my Sunday morning service was warmed up, the singing would be a fascinating mixture: translations into Swahili (done by the Brethren!), sung with a swing and rhythm that only partly disguised the European origin of the tune, would be interspersed with local choruses that reverberated with the moving vitality for which Zairian music is famous.

I believe that any sensitive traveller in post-colonial Africa and Asia still observes, for better or worse, the legacy of the colonial occupant. And francophone colonialists have left a different legacy from the British. This is a subtle thing and hard to pin down. It ranges through clearly visible factors such as styles of architecture and the layout of towns and cities, through legal and administrative systems to the intangible finenesses of word and gesture, courtesy and communication. Doubtless some of these differences are on the wane, but often I have found them surprisingly enduring. Crossing the border from the former Belgian Congo into what was Northern Rhodesia, one misses the care given to cuisine, but is grateful for the improved road surface! And I would claim that the British characteristic that is often labelled 'reserve' is present in Zambia in a way that it is not in southern Zaire. The interplay between these colonial legacies, new national identities, tribal factors, and personal or family temperament is of course immensely complex in shaping culture, society and religion. Writers on Anglicanism can declare that it has long ago transcended its 'Englishness'. But I wonder how much lingering and unconscious regret there is at this. We need to transcend such nostalgia.

Fourth and last, it is tempting to locate Anglicanism in terms of *historical continuities*, usually done on the basis of a 'between-Catholic-and-Protestant' analysis. When I stood in church on Sunday, the people before me would have a wide range of religious backgrounds. There was an unlikely blend of ex-Roman Catholic and ex-Independent Pentecostal (many were both), together with, in one part of the city, a group that looked back to Anglo-Catholic roots in Zambia. All this in a diocese and Province supposed to be broadly within the 'low church CMS' tradition. There is need to hear and acknowledge the diversity of Anglican histories.

The story of the Diocese of Shaba is interesting. It began with small numbers of Bemba migrant workers in what was then Elisabethville. Being Zambian Anglicans, they were used to a High Anglican tradition, and at one stage in the 1950s a priest was travelling from Zambia once a month to preside at Mass. They took over a small but near building vacated by the Dutch Reformed Church. Then in the 1970s President Mobutu created a Protestant umbrella called the ECZ and decreed that all churches that did not officially register as members of the ECZ were illegal. Some independent, Pentecostal-style groups in Shaba, mostly with roots in the neighbouring Kasai province, applied to the nearest Anglican bishop, hundreds of miles away in Bukavu, to become Anglicans. To their surprise, not only were they accepted, but the Archdeacon was consecrated suffragan and sent to them. In the process of training and integration that followed, many – indeed most – of the Bemba remnants and the Independents left in dissatisfaction, but others were attracted. In the old Bemba Church, the leader was ordained, and insisted on facing east to celebrate. While in some respects, the Church that exists today might be described as 'between Catholic and Protestant', it is so in a way that is different from what the phrase might traditionally have meant. Such surprising histories as these, not uncommon in francophone areas, need to be taken into account before an 'Anglican identity' is affirmed.

Power, language, culture, history: thinking back to the Canterbury Cathedral Eucharist, such concepts were there richly embodied in architecture, liturgy, music, dress and much else. My Zairean colleagues were glad of them, keen to belong, not resentful. Yet in their relative powerlessness and linguistic awkwardness, with their cultural variance and strange history, these francophone Anglicans point to new paths and patterns developing, especially among those who appear to be on the margins of the Communion. They too have a place and need to be heard.

Anglican models for theological education in Southern Africa

Livingstone Lubabalo Ngewu and Luke Lungile Pato

Introduction

Models of theological education and training for the ordained ministry in the Church of the Province of Southern Africa (CPSA) have been, to a very large extent, influenced by socio-political considerations. Three phases have been identified in this process, namely, the pre-apartheid, the apartheid, and the post-apartheid eras.

The three phases

The pre-apartheid era

Not so long after the Christian faith was introduced in Southern Africa, some missionaries began to explore possibilities for theological education that would be suitable in their regions. Models that emerged at that time were influenced enormously by two trends. There were those missionaries who reckoned that their stay in the region would be transient. These missionaries equipped their indigenes with skills so that they could, in due course, take over the machinery of the Church. Others were content to provide a model that would make African Christians permanently dependent on the skills of the missionaries. Models of theological education during the pre-apartheid era were shaped by the aspirations of such theological educators. Consequently models of theological education in the Anglican Church in South Africa at this time varied from one diocese to another.

In 1876, the Provincial Synod of the CPSA passed a resolution that a theological college be established as soon as possible. Indeed, in 1877 St Cyprian's College in Bloemfontein was established. But this attempt soon dissipated as a result of the Basotho wars. Also, Bishop Webb, who was the master-mind behind the resolution of 1876, was translated to Grahams-town Diocese in 1883. He brought with him the vision of theological education. It was, however, not until in 1902 that a hostel was opened in Grahamstown for the reception of theological students specifically and exclusively for the training of 'Europeans' (Constitution of Canons of the CPSA up to 1992, Act X). Thus a theological college, named St Paul's, and established along uniracial lines, was opened.

The story of theological education took a different model elsewhere. In 1871 Henry Callaway, a missionary in Natal, came to the realization that among Africans, Christianity could best be propagated by Africans them-selves. It was not until 1878, and as a missionary of the Bishop of the Diocese of St John's Kaffraria, that Henry Callaway took students to board with him. In June 1879, the foundation stone of St Bede's theological training institution was laid 'for the purpose of training young natives and colonists as clergy and lay teachers' (Benham, 1896, p. 321). Unlike in the Diocese of Grahamstown, theological education and training in the Diocese of St John's was never planned to be divided along racial lines. It has to be noted, though, that the successors of Callaway tended to send their white ordination candidates to the institution that was established for the exclusive use of 'Europeans'. When St. Paul's became a Provincial college in 1910, the understanding was that it would continue to train only white ordination candidates. Thus after Callaway St Bede's had ceased to be a non-racial college because the dioceses were sending only black candidates. So even before the apartheid era, theological training in the CPSA was modelled along segregational lines.

The apartheid era

In 1948, more than a hundred years after the planting of Anglicanism in South Africa, a regime which separated the races of South Africa one from another came into existence. The apartheid policy of South Africa did not imply that the South African races were formerly integrated. They lived alongside each other, separated largely by class and economic factors as opposed to being a legalized system of racial division. Models of theological training in South Africa in the pre-apartheid era followed the same pattern. They were modelled not only on the aspirations of educators but also on the social orientations of theological educators and Church leaders, some of whom were loyal to the policy of apartheid. Thus if apartheid did anything for the Anglican Church, it was to affirm the status quo within the existing models of theological education and training in the CPSA. The model of training that would equip indigenous Christians with leadership skills was abandoned. There was, on the part of the Church and those leaders who favoured racially-segregated theological education and training, a solid reason to justify training candidates in racially-divided theological colleges because integration was illegal. There was another dimension added into this which was based on geographic considerations by some missionaries. In terms of the Group Areas Act, black people lived in black residential areas. To this they drew the inference that it made sense for blacks to minister to blacks, inasmuch as cross-racial visits were regulated. The overall conclusion drawn from this was: since blacks would be ministering exclusively to blacks, it made sense to train them in the theological colleges where only black ordination candidates were registered. During this period, there were a few notable leaders within the CPSA who decided to defy the law of the land. In 1960, the Bishops of Johannesburg and Kimberley and Kuruman, Ambrose Reeves and John Boys respectively, sent their black candidates to St Paul's College, thereby deliberately challenging not only the law of the country but the Constitution of the college to which such candidates were sent. However, the experience of the black candidates in a predominantly white institution was not always a pleasant one as they constantly were reminded by white students in conversations that they were interlopers.

During the early 1970s onwards, attempts were made to provide students with cross-racial and cultural experience by spending some time in each other's colleges on the student exchange programme. It was becoming explicitly clear that the Anglican Church could no longer support apartheid through either its structures or complicity. The CPSA gradually moved towards integration as well as amalgamation. Indeed in 1973 a black staff member, the Revd Zolile Mbali, was appointed to serve on the staff of St Paul's College. However, Mbali was a 'migrant labourer' in that he lived in a dilapidated house in the black township at Fingo village. It was not until 1985 that St Paul's College took on black students in large numbers. Although this was illegal in terms of the law of the land, St Paul's College did not seek the government's permission to do it. In addition to politics, economic factors also played a significant role influencing decisions to admit ordination candidates across colour lines.

The post-apartheid era

In 1990 there was a paradigm shift in the politics of South Africa which started a process of not only jettisoning but also annihilating apartheid legislation. That process had serious ramifications for the CPSA in general and models of theological education and training in particular. In the early 1990s the Bishops of the CPSA decided to amalgamate two theological colleges which had historically been uniracial, St Bede's and St Paul's theological colleges. The idea to amalgamate was influenced largely by the fact that leavers from these historically segregated institutions would be required to minister to non-racial congregations, at least in some parts of South Africa. This was to be the case even apart from the fact that the effect of the Group Areas Act made racial integration something of a pipe dream for the new South Africa. Visitors to the College of the Transfiguration and to the formerly exclusive white or black parishes are often surprised by the almost conspicuous absence of racial mix. In respect of the theological college, this reality was further complicated by the development of diocesan schemes of theological education and training. These have tended to diversify theological education as a whole, but it became a pressure point for residential institutions. However, these alternative diocesan training schemes have a potential to fulfil needs that residential colleges are not fulfilling and cannot fulfil.

Contemporary theological education and training models

The College of the Transfiguration

From its very inception the amalgamated theological college, the College of the Transfiguration in Grahamstown, committed itself to serve God and the Church and society as a proactive agency for change on issues on the Church's agenda such as evangelism, advocacy with the poor and the oppressed, the ministry of women, ministry of and to children and young people. It committed itself to include in its theological programmes an appreciation of the relevance of Africa in theological understanding, stewardship of the environment, and crises in the social relations of humankind. It is towards the fruition of these goals that the college strives. The overarching ministry of the college is, of course, reconciliation in a country that has been ravaged by racism, sexism and classism. The college's commitment to these ideals can only be complemented by the Church's commitment to the same ideals. The college takes seriously the contexts from which the candidates come and in which they will serve. Thus both in its theological orientation and liturgical worship and in the teaching and administrative staff composition, the college reflects the contexts in Southern Africa.

Continuing Ministerial Education (CME)

Within the CPSA there is a recognition that time spent in any model of theological education and training, residential or diocesan, is not adequate by itself. In order to address this void, the CPSA launched in 1994 an extensive Continuing Ministerial Education programme. The programme

169

is co-ordinated by the College of the Transfiguration, and draws participants, both clergy and laity, from all parts of the CPSA. Persons with
special skills are brought in to facilitate the programmes, and participants
are issued with certificates to acknowledge their participation in those
programmes.

The programme is three-pronged, consisting of a sabbatical programme
for those who are burnt out so that they can be re-energized; mid-career
programme for those who need fresh stimulation or are earmarked for
leadership in their dioceses; and vacation seminars designed for all clergy
and lay people who are prepared to take up new and more challenging
responsibilities and wish to acquire new spiritual and theological perspectives that would contribute to the formation of communities with a
capacity to respond creatively to their changing context.

The Federal Theological Seminary (FEDSEM)

A model of theological education to which no reference has as yet been
made is that of St Peter's theological college. St Peter's College was part of
an ecumenical venture consisting of Anglicans, Methodists, Presbyterians
and Congregationalists. This federal structure was founded in 1960 at
Alice, adjacent to the university at Fort Hare. FEDSEM came about as a
united attempt of the Churches in South Africa to fight against the policy
of Apartheid. In the 1970s FEDSEM had become so politicized that it
became a symbol of struggle and resistance against apartheid. It incurred
the wrath of the government, and consequently its property was expro-
priated in 1975. It moved temporarily to Umtata, and subsequently to
Imbali in Pietermaritzburg. How far FEDSEM was committed to resolving
the doctrinal differences that comprised its constituent colleges is difficult
to ascertain. What cannot be doubted though is that FEDSEM, more than
any other theological institution, was able to challenge and even defy the
racist laws of the country with unprecedented vehemence. As long as there
was one common enemy – apartheid – the staff and students of FEDSEM,
including the sponsoring Churches, were prepared to stand shoulder to
shoulder in opposing apartheid, and this they did with remarkable resil-
ience. FEDSEM became the matrix of the Black Consciousness Movement
and the Black Theology Project. As soon as apartheid ceased to be a rallying
point, issues of ecumenical concern that had hitherto been clouded by
national concerns became too glaring. Thus FEDSEM became an ecumenical war zone which culminated in its closure in 1995.

Contemporary challenges

Ministry to the informal settlements

In the past 50 years there has been an interesting phenomenon in South Africa – the sprawling of shanty towns or informal settlements, as they are sometimes referred to. Millions of black South Africans live in such settlements. The CPSA ministers to people in these settlements, but some dioceses lack skill and vision to handle this new phenomenon and pastoral challenge. The temptation is to build new church buildings from monies raised from these parishioners even though the majority of them are not only unemployed but also unemployable. Training institutions are also still trapped within the traditional models of theological education and ministry. This inability to equip persons to minister to such people is one of the serious flaws of the present model of theological education and training. This is a major challenge that currently faces the CPSA, an opportunity for creativity that would be regrettable if it were missed.

Indigenization

No model of theological education and training can succeed without taking into account the context of such education and training. In spite of many years of its presence in Africa, for many Africans, Christianity remains alien. Part of their very selves and lives remains outside the Gospel. This is the source of a certain double quality in living their beliefs, holding them divided between their faith in Jesus Christ and traditional practices. The new dispensation in South Africa has brought about additional challenges for the African Christian who is still burdened by the apparent perennial contradiction between the Christian faith and African culture. This calls for indigenization as a task that is not just urgent and necessary, but a priority. There is need to assure those people whose culture is trampled underfoot that there is nothing wrong with being African and Christian at the same time. And as such, models within the Southern African context should reflect the effervescence of its people.

Anglicanism in West Malaysia

Eddie Ong

On Christmas Day, 1995, Dr Mahathir Mohammad, the Prime Minister of Malaysia, made a house visit to Lim Cheng Ean, the newly appointed Anglican Bishop of the Diocese of West Malaysia. That visit by a Muslim head of government to a bishop, in my view, speaks of a fresh commitment to Christian–Muslim relationships. This is in a context where Anglicans comprise only 1 per cent of Malaysia's 21 million people in 1997; Islam is the official religion, while Chinese Religions (Buddhism, Taoism, Confucianism), Hinduism and Christianity are together a significant 45 per cent minority.

Economically one of the 'Asian tigers', Malaysia has been experiencing an economic boom, with average annual growth of 8 per cent for the past ten years. In 1996, it was the seventeenth largest trading nation in the world and hopes to achieve a fully-developed-nation status by the year 2020.

In the beginning

Christianity first came to the western part of Malaysia through the Nestorians. Merchants took advantage of Islamic advancement of navigation and freedom given to 'people of the book'. Nestorian ecclesiastical texts referred to Patriarch Ishoyab III's episcopal jurisdiction (AD 650–660) as stretching from 'India . . . to the country called Kalah' in West Malaysia. From the end of the fifteenth century, Malaysia had visits from three groups of Western Christians – Portuguese Reconquista Catholicism (1511–1641), Dutch Protestantism (1641–1824) and English Anglicanism (1786–1957). Unlike the peaceful merchants of Nestorian Christianity, Reconquista Catholicism (to differentiate from present-day Roman Catholicism) brought violence, greed and slavery. Although they built eighteen churches and one Cathedral, Francis Xavier (1506–52) lamented that in Malacca 'preaching was neglected, and the teaching of Christian doctrine had lapsed completely into oblivion'.

Reconquista Catholicism was violently replaced by Dutch Protestantism in 1641. It was certainly safer to be a non-Christian than a Catholic during the Dutch occupation of Malacca. Anglicanism came to West Malaysia following the Union Jack. While the coming of the British was generally peaceful, they lacked interest in mission. Merchants of the British East India Company were interested only in exploiting the virgin land of Malaya. It was policy of the EIC not to interfere in the customs and religions of the local people. This was made clear at the Treaty of Pangkor in 1874 whereby British Residents were appointed 'whose advice must be asked and acted upon on all questions other than those touching Malay Religion and Custom'.

Although this policy of non-interference may sound noble in inter-faith relations, it was certainly economically motivated. Any religious incident that would jeopardize the British hold on strategic Malaya was to be avoided.

When one J. Moore adopted Malay dress he was ordered to return to European dress and cease mission work amongst the Malays. Benjamin Purdy was prohibited from selling Scriptures to Malays. Clergy were appointed as chaplains, not missionaries. Their exclusive task was to minister to the spiritual needs of the English communities.

Although a few Anglican mission schools were established, this was generally against the EIC's policy of non-interference with local customs and religions. In contrast, Methodism and Roman Catholicism made inroads through school missions. In 1921, out of about 70,000 Malayan students, 28 per cent were in Methodist and Roman Catholic schools while the Anglicans had only 1 per cent.

Evangelizing the Muslim Malays is still prohibited today, and Anglican work is almost exclusively among the immigrant Chinese and Tamils. Following the Japanese occupation of the country (1941–45), the Anglican Church had some positive growth through the faithful evangelistic efforts of Indian and Chinese priests. In recognition of their work, eight of them were collated 'Canon' in 1945. Evangelism took on a more definite emphasis during the period of anti-insurgency called 'The Emergency' (1948–60), when Anglican missionaries arrived from China following the defeat of the Kuo-Min-Tang.

But village work established then was short-lived.

Efforts were made to indigenize in the appointment of the first local vicar (1952), archdeacon (1957), assistant bishop (1958), Bishop of Singapore and West Malaysia (1966), Bishop of West Malaysia (1970). But mission and evangelism remained a weak point in the life of the diocese. Thus, after almost 200 years of Anglican work, the Electoral Roll of the Diocese of West Malaysia stood at only 4,092 members in 1985 with one bishop and eleven clergy covering a region of 131,794 square kilometres (1970). Although Christianity was the fastest-growing faith in Malaysia, Anglican work was slow, according to Archdeacon Batumalai: 'Due to a lack of adequate staff, funds, certain restrictions, a limited freedom and a

Eddie Ong

lack of lay missionary leadership and for other reasons, we were not able to bring many people to Christ' (Batumalai, p. 143).

When the 518 bishops of Lambeth 1988 called for a decade of Evangelism, the Anglican Church in West Malaysia, while apprehensive of its poor track record, appreciated the reminder that evangelism is the primary task given to the Church. Bearing in mind its tiny presence in West Malaysia, evangelism became a top priority in the diocese.

Launching of the Decade of Evangelism

The Diocese of West Malaysia launched the Decade of Evangelism on the first Sunday of 1990, quietly and discreetly. A bookmark with a Collect for the Decade of Evangelism was distributed within the walls of Anglican churches. There was no newspaper publicity nor any banners proclaiming her evangelistic intentions. Five years later, statistics showed some significant increase:

	1990	1995	Growth
Church buildings	47	68	44%
Clergy	50	62	24%
Electoral Roll	4,292	6,171*	44%
Finance	RM 0.8 million	RM 1.6 million	100%

(* The figure 6,171 is based on the 1992 statistics as the 1995 figures were not available at time of writing.)

The Bishop reported confirming 590 people in 1995, which is about 10 per cent of the 1990 Electoral Roll. New Anglican work among rural Chinese villages was reported from one villlage in 1993 and from ten in 1995. Evangelistic work among the Hindus also has had some success. The Anglican church in Banting, Selangor reported the number of converts up from two in 1986 to 24 in 1992, 52 in 1993, 62 in 1994 and 70 in 1995. The Electoral Roll of the parish grew from 78 in 1985 to 170 in 1990 to 550 in 1995. In addition to 21 new churches begun, outreach work has been carried out in 108 centres since 1990. The number of parishes likewise increased from 20 (1984) to 29 (1995); and Missionary Districts from seven (1984) to 17 (1995). Home-cell groups operate in most of the parishes.

Reasons for growth

In my view, there are at least three major factors for recent growth in the Diocese of West Malaysia: external factors, charismatic renewal and family unity.

External factors

The process of implementation of an Islamization Policy beginning in 1983 caused non-Muslims in Malaysia to feel that their religious and legal rights were gradually eroding. This was followed by the Enactment on the Administration of Islamic Law 1989 in a number of states legalizing the conversion of a non-Muslim to Islam, so long as that person has attained the age of maturity. Much to the relief of non-Muslim parents, the Supreme Court deemed the legislation as contradictory to the Federal law of Malaysia. The proposal from an opposition group for 'hudud' ('restrictive'– a small section of the Shari'ah) laws in the State of Kelantan in 1993 further accentuated apprehensions of non-Muslims and justified their suspicion that their future is uncertain. Although 'hudud' laws were set aside by the predominantly Muslim Federal Government, such feelings of vulnerability only strengthened the faith of Christians.

Anglican charismatic renewal

When the charismatic renewal came to Malaysia in the 1960s, the diocesan leadership was hesitant about how to react, feeling that less diversity in churchmanship was needed, in the interests of unity. In some parishes, it was either rejected or discouraged. A number of Anglican charismatics left the denomination. Clergy who had this renewal experience had to confine their experience to the 'private'. However, the year 1990 saw a turning point when Anglican Renewal Ministries (ARM) was accepted at the Diocesan Synod. A survey in 1992 showed that 71 per cent of Anglican Churches in the Diocese had incorporated a 'praise and worship' section within the setting of either the main service or an evening service. Most of the Anglican parishes that are growing rapidly are led by charismatic-renewed priests and parishioners. Critical developments had also been the experience of healing and renewal of Bishop Savarimuttu, who consequently gave a strong charismatic lead in the early 1990s; and at the same time, the growing influence from Singapore and other parts of what became the new Province of South-east Asia, which were strongly charismatic, and where Anglicanism had been growing fast, particularly within the Chinese community which was also a significant part of the Diocese of West Malaysia.

A sense of a family

The identity that we are Anglicans of diverse yet acceptable liturgical traditions seeking the long-neglected growth of the diocese has helped forge a family spirit of togetherness. This was observed by Bishop Lim

175

Cheng Ean during his visits around the diocese. This harmony has its roots in the Seminari Theoloji Malaysia, Kuala Lumpur, where nearly all Anglican clergy receive their theological training. A sense of Anglican comradeship, family unity and encouragement prevails.

Into the third millennium

In my view, the leadership of the Anglican Church in Malaysia will need to focus on three areas of concern.

Relating to Muslims

While Christians are prohibited from preaching, propagating or persuading Muslims towards Christianity, Christians are not prohibited from reflecting afresh on their understanding of Islam. The Church (including the Anglican Church) needs to view Islam and Shari'ah not from the perspective of insecurity, fear, polemics, suspicion or prejudice, but as fellow committed citizens with a common concern to turn Malaysia into a peaceful, harmonious and God-fearing country. The Prime Minister is on record as asking non-Muslims 'not to misunderstand Islam' and encouraging Muslims to adjust to modern changes. Confrontation as it had happened in history is neither necessary nor desirable. Christians need to be able to see Islam and Muslims and say: 'We understand you are different but we also understand your differences.' As George Carey put it, when receiving at Lambeth Palace Dr Muhammad Sayed Tantawi, Grand Sheikh of Al Azhar, Cairo, 'The answer to fear and suspicion is always a closer contact ... through friendship, not hostility; understanding, not ignorance; reciprocity, not exclusivism; and co-operation, not confrontation' (*Church Times*, 23 May 1997).

This does not mean compromising our beliefs. It means a responsibility to respect differences. Could not Christians and Muslims work together on environmental issues, refugee problems, relief work, Jubilee 2000, poverty, family values, rehabilitation programmes, the welfare of those on the edge and building peaceful religious co-existence? Could not Christians and Muslims begin to reflect on the positives and what is common in each other's faiths? A study of early historical Muslim–Christian relations will help to foster better relationships than there are now. It will also help sincere parties to avoid the pitfalls of the past.

Ecumenical relationship

The Church in Malaysia is historically fragmented by denominations and it needs to give a united witness as well as to make a positive contribution to a multi-racial and multi-religious country. Ecumenical relationships in Malaysia made a great advance when the Roman Catholic Church, the Council of Churches and the National Evangelical Christian Fellowship combined as the Christian Fellowship of Malaysia in 1985. Almost all denominations and Churches in both East and West Malaysia belong to this body. Apart from looking after the interests of the Christian community, this body has brought Christians to more co-operation in Church life, witness and ecumenical projects.

Releasing God's frozen Anglicans

The third area where the Anglican Church will need to continue its focus is the laity. The diocesan theme of 'Mobilizing every Member for Mission in Malaysia' needs regular motivation, emphasizing wholehearted commitment from each. Men and women, clergy and bishops need to 'defreeze' themselves from a tedious, lethargic, stress-filled understanding of the Christian life to becoming mature disciples of Christ. Until and unless God's frozen Anglicans are set free, dioceses and Provinces will be filled with the mundane task of keeping the structures going, rather than being freed for mission.

Conclusion

The way ahead for the Anglican Church in Malaysia is to combine the Great Commandment and the Great Commission. At the heart of *missio Dei* is love. Effective evangelism must be preceded by and accompanied by good neighbourliness, what Archdeacon Batumalai has called 'neighbourology'. As the Church looks at its past, it must renounce the colonial version of the Great Commandment. It should reflect on the Nestorians – peaceful, quiet but zealous. Malaysia needs the Gospel of love, compassion, care, harmony and justice. This Gospel needs to be shared sensitively, responsibly and prudently. As it looks into the third millennium, the Anglican Church in Malaysia will need to focus clearly and positively on its relationship with Muslims. While its future looks humble, I believe the Anglican Church will remain significant. It will be a leading body in fostering Christian–Muslim relations because of Anglican via-media perspectives.

P. Victor Premasagar

Further reading

Ghazali Basri, *Christian Mission and Islamic Da'wah in Malaysia* (Kuala Lumpur: Nurin Enterprise, 1990).
Sadayandy Batumalai (1990) *A Malaysian Theology of Muhibbah* (Kuala Lumpur: S. Batumalai).
R. Alan Cole, *Emerging Patterns in the Dioceses of Singapore and Malaya* (China Inland Mission, 1961).
John C. England, *The Hidden History of Christianity in Asia: The Churches of the East Before the Year 1500* (Delhi: ISPCK and Hong Kong: CCA, 1996).
Robert Hunt, Lee Kam Hing and John Roxborough (eds), *Christianity in Malaysia: A Denominational History* (Petaling Jaya, Malaysia: Pelanduk Publishing, 1992).
Mahathir Mohammad, 'Islam: the misunderstood religion', *Journal IKIM*, vol. 4, no. 2 (Kuala Lumpur: Institute of Islamic Understanding Malaysia; July/December 1996), ch. 1.

Anglicanism and the Church of South India

P. Victor Premasagar

Historical reflections

Union negotiations for a united Church in South India took 28 years and, from the beginning, the Lambeth Quadrilateral, including the requirement to adhere to the 'historic episcopate', was made central to the discussion. Indeed, for the seven Anglican negotiators, this was mandatory, and the other partners accepted this.

When details of the scheme were public, there were varying reactions from the Anglican side outside India. William Temple welcomed it as an unprecedented enterprise, and commented 'it is at least possible that unprecedented expedients may be legitimate and appropriate' (Address to Canterbury Convocation, January 1944). The Derby Commission, set up by Archbishop Fisher, disapproved of certain aspects of the scheme, and could not suggest full communion with the CSI, but felt the scheme should go forward, and that there should be no censure on Anglicans who joined the united Church. CSI bishops were not invited to the Lambeth Conference, SPG, because of its statutes, could not officially aid the new Church, though it set up a special fund for this, and some churches in England put up notices that CSI members were not welcome to communion. The first moderator, Michael Hollis, told of a visit to Ridley Hall, Cambridge, where he was not allowed to celebrate the Holy Communion Service because he would not give an undertaking that he would not do so also in non-Anglican churches during his visit to England. These were some of the prices the CSI paid for the union, and the uncertainties introduced for some Anglicans by the union scheme itself, with its '30-year clause', by which non-episcopally ordained presbyters were recognized, for this period, without being 're-ordained'.

Gradually full acceptance has come, and the CSI is now a member of the ACC, its Moderator comes to the Primates' meeting, six of its bishops came to the Lambeth Conference of 1988, and all are invited in 1998. Both Robert Runcie and George Carey have visited the CSI and been welcomed by thousands, including people of other religions, who saw them as 'Jagadgurus' (world spiritual leaders). Archbishop David Hope preached at the Golden Jubilee Eucharist in 1997.

After the last Lambeth Conference in 1988, the next Primates' meeting in Cyprus was asked to consider changing the Lambeth Quadrilateral, which forms the basis for any union negotiations in which Anglicans are to take part, from 'historic episcopate' to 'apostolic succession'. I argued strongly against this, since it was because of the phrase 'historic episcopate locally adapted' that the non-episcopal partners were able to enter into the union. The term 'apostolic succession', I believed, would make any future unions almost impossible. The term 'historic episcopate' was retained.

Contemporary issues

Full membership of Anglican structures enables us again to learn to challenge and be challenged on certain common issues, through the experience of Anglican partners, from whom, to some extent, we had been cut off. These are some examples:

(a) The union negotiating committee discussed at length about 'parity of ministries' but did not sufficiently consider the key question of 'authority in the Church'. This is discussed in almost every Lambeth Conference, and there is a large bibliography on this from Anglican circles. These discussions could be a great help to us, since the CSI needs to address the issue in detail and in depth, to minimize confrontations and the misuse of power, which has become endemic.

(b)   I participated for nine months in the weekly seminars of the Centre for Anglican Communion Studies (CEFACS) at the United College of the Ascension, and Crowther Hall, in Selly Oak, Birmingham. Here, critical study is made of the issues confronting the Anglican Communion, not least those of authority. A similar centre could be set up in India, both for training experienced presbyters to consider the issues in a reflective rather than irascible manner, and to enable bishops both to hear from others and to reflect together.

(c)   New patterns of ministry are urgently needed within the complex multi-religious context of India, with its thousands of village pastorates. Much can be learnt from varied patterns being developed in numerous parts of the Anglican Communion, including the Church of England.

(d)   The 'locally-adapted' episcopate meant a new and simpler style of life and dress. These were indicated by the saffron robes and stole, which were a reminder of the renunciation pledge made by the ancient sages of India. But in recent years, purple has become fashionable again, and some of the style of life associated with the regal orientation and wealth of the Western Church, and indeed of secular officials in India.

(e)   Elections and democracy within the Church have become the occasion for the display of how far we have deteriorated in terms of all sense of spiritual values. It would be helpful to study how checks and balances work in this area within the Anglican Communion, in both its historical Churches and its newer members. For a solution to this question is vital, if the Church is to maintain credibility in its multi-faith context.

(f)   In 1982, the CSI set its priorities in mission, and invited its partner Churches to partnership, beckoning them to help with resources and ideas. They are invited to periodic evaluations of such priorities. This has not often been reciprocated. As Moderator I often asked our partners 'You are generous in the sharing of your resources, but you never share with us your mission priorities and invite us to assist you. I am sure that God has endowed the Indian Church with gifts which may be of help to you in your mission.' To receive such would be a sign of mature partnership.

(g)   The Anglican heritage of worship and liturgy are a great asset to the CSI. But the comment of the Derby Commission of 1946, that the CSI could have been more radical and more Indian, is still pertinent. The CSI liturgy of 1950 was a pioneer among the products of the modern liturgical movement, and was important in bringing our traditions and language areas together. But it had few Indian features. The same can be said of the first revised liturgy, which was a mere simplification of the 1950 Eucharist. The recent new liturgy, prepared by the Liturgical Committee, takes strongly into account our cultural and religious heritage and the context of poverty within and around our Church. But it has not been widely used in India (though appreciated in Britain, where it has been reproduced in USPG's book of liturgies from around the world), and has not yet been translated from English.

(h)　There is a concern within the CSI about its 'Anglicanization'. This is seen in the continuing use of the 1662 Prayer Book in many ex-Anglican Churches, and a tendency for some to call themselves still 'Anglicans', and to have a kind of 'superiority air' about them. It is seen in the unfortunate recent schism of some congregations in Tamil Nadu, who have called themselves a continuing Anglican Church, and some members have received ordination through an Indian bishop ordained through such a group in the United States. In the past such schisms have been short-lived, and on the positive side, the Diocese of Nandyal, in Andhra Pradesh, which stayed out of the union and maintained its Anglican links, eventually joined the CNI, and now has transferred to the CSI. Perhaps more seriously, the Anglicanization can be seen, both in the growing power of the episcopacy (as noted above) and in the tendency, in areas which were never Anglican, to build towers on churches, to install bells and organs, and to emphasize a separation between laity and clergy, thus devaluing other traditions that joined the CSI.

(i)　To end positively, the Union has remained and indeed inspired further unions in North India, Pakistan and Bangladesh, all countries where the imperative of both survival and mission is central in their minority multi-faith contexts. In the CSI we are also encouraged that other union negotiations are proceeding in various parts of the world to which we related. Perhaps we have something to offer to those negotiations, from our experience. We long to see the day when the Churches who brought the Gospel to India would also be united as one Church. We believe that the unity of the Church is a foretaste of the unity of all people and of harmony in the whole of creation.

Further reading

Guenther Gassmann, 'Quadrilateral at one hundred' in J. Robert Wright (ed.), *Anglican Theological Review*, Supplementary Series, no. 10 (March 1988).
Michael Hollis, *The Significance of South India* (London: Lutterworth, 1966).
Wendy Robins (ed.), *Let All the World Sing* (London: USPG, 1990).
Bengt Sundkler, *Church of South India: The Movement Towards Union, 1900–47* (London: Lutterworth, 1954).

New wine, old wineskins

A look at possibilities for a rural diocese in a changing society

Oswald Swartz

A snake must shed its skin in order to survive. However this change of skin is never violently done; it isn't that the old skin is impatiently and brusquely ripped off to allow the new one to appear. On the contrary, while the old is still in place, the new skin slowly and gradually begins to take shape until the point is reached where the old simply falls away. It becomes obsolete, to give place to the new.[1]

This parable used by José Marins in a very useful book on Basic Ecclesial Communities provides much food for thought when I pose myself the question *Quo vadis*, CPSA [Church of the Province of Southern Africa]?

South Africa, a changing society

We are experiencing what is for me the most thrilling period in the history of my beloved country, South Africa. Not so long ago it was a country that cried. We wept tears of frustration for a country, so rich in natural and human resources but impoverished by an evil system. We wept in a country that has a motto: *Ex unitate vires* – unity is strength – and yet tried to keep people apart. The strength which should have been because of the rich diverse cultures was never realized because our 'differentness' was emphasized. Our tears mingled with children's blood in Soweto and elsewhere as the young people vowed not to be bound by the yoke that robbed generations of their full humanity.

Tears of mourning have turned into songs of joy. The Rainbow Nation is on the move. It is a wonderful sight to see bumper-stickers on cars owned by both white and black people displaying the new and lovely flag accompanied by the words: Proudly South African.

Holding on to 'Anglicanism'

The Church of the Province of Southern Africa has a black membership of more than 80 per cent. Although we do not 'count heads by colour', it is a simple fact that the majority of the members are black. Despite this fact the Church has been tardy in seeking to provide the means and the space for the majority of its members to express themselves in ways that are relevant and meaningful.

It is not going to be easy to redress the situation. It will take lots of hard work, much energy to be expended in re-educating a people who have been subtly (though not always deliberately and in a sinister way) indoctrinated to believe that Anglicanism meant 'Englishness'. In my first parish as Rector I was taken to task by the elders when I suggested that the language of our worship should be the language of the community – Afrikaans. 'Father, this is the English Church.' That 'coloured' community was convinced that by using the language that they all understood and used daily and were taught in, they would be losing something of the character of their Church. Maybe I was comfortable with that situation; maybe it let me off the hook – for it was only very much later that I was liberated – ironically, during a visit to the UK I suddenly became immensely proud that I could be African and Anglican. The sky did not fall on my head! I should add that all this was happening during those heady days of our first democratic elections.

Did we cling to the Anglican ethos (as we understood it) because it gave us a definite identity in a country where the whole system was geared to depriving us of our identity? In our Church, we felt we belonged – we were Anglicans. Was not our 'Big Chief' the archbishop of a country which gave our oppressors, the Boers, so much grief? Were not our champions those liberal clerics who gave up the comfort of life in Britain to fight by our side?

One can understand why it would be difficult for dyed-in-the-wool Anglicans to make a shift and to get to grips with the concept of enculturation.

But we need to shed the old skin in order to survive. Painful as it may be for many of us we must wriggle out of the old skin. The story of the snake is encouraging because it reminds us that it need not be too traumatic an experience. It does not need to be violent. But it must happen. It should not be too slow. It calls us to be alert, to recognize the signs, to move when it is required to do so.

Our attempts at enculturation, if not properly interpreted and implemented, will be like pouring new wine into old skins. At some point the process will blow up in our faces and we will be left with a useless mess.

Restrictive structure

How can we in the Northern Cape shed the old skin so that we can get on with the job of enabling God to pour in his invigorating wine?

Democracy is the buzzword in South Africa and we as the Church are being urged to get on board. We delude ourselves if we believe the answer is as simple as that. Democracy as we understand it is a Western concept. The Westminster style of government on which our synodical system is based is not only foreign to Africans but also complex and confusing.

There is a little booklet published by the Ecumenical Literature Department Trust in 1977 on behalf of the publishing department of the CPSA called *How to Succeed at Synod – for Beginners*. Under the section 'Synod and its Standing Rules' it says: 'Though at first sight they may seem complicated, these rules are all in fact based on common sense.' Far removed from common sense, they remain complex for many people. During debate you have to make your point succinctly. You have one chance only to speak. If you have blown it, you've had it. A technicality can rob you of a satisfactory solution. This is quite different from the *kgotla*,[2] the tribal council, where you can make your point taking as much time as you wish; where you can 'put down your straw' (resting your case for a while and indicating you have a further point to make) to pick it up again. You are allowed to 'smoke your pipe' thus reserving your right to speak for a while (with the right to resume after your 'pipe session'). The debate can go on until the matter is thrashed out and when the council is dismissed there is a general consensus and it would not be unusual for the participants to spend much time afterwards over a pint.

The provision that allows a member who thinks that a motion has been debated sufficiently to move ' ... that the motion now be put', that is 'be put to the vote', is also not in the spirit of *kgotla*. It is also confusing to 'vote to vote' on an issue.

We sometimes hear disparaging remarks about 'African time' when people refer to the laid-back attitude (often a generalization) of black people, but there is great truth in the retort: 'You whites have watches, but we have time.' At one elective assembly I attended, people dispersed on a bad note because of, I believe, our reluctance to set aside enough time for the things of God.

Technical knockout

Technicalities inherent in our present structures make it difficult for the Church to minister effectively and for the people to understand the nature of the Church. The trustees of the diocese took longer than a year to settle a case concerning money held in trust for a resettled community. The eloquent and lucid argument of the Chancellor centred around the point that the Trustees have to be absolutely certain that the money is released to the proper claimants and that they would not be surprised by any further claims. This particular community had been removed from their abode and dumped in very inhospitable terrain. They did not like the site and appealed to a Homeland leader, who allowed them to move to another site. Compensation for the initial move was handed over to the diocese to administer. The community, being aware that money was held in trust, now wants to build a church on that third site.

At first sight the Chancellor's argument made sense because not all of the original families are at the present location, some having managed to slot into other communities. But it does not take into account that it was government policy to resettle *communities* not *individuals*. They simply moved in and removed a community *en bloc* as they went about eliminating 'black spots' and creating black reserves called 'Homelands'. (Black spots were those reserved for whites but still being occupied by black people. The homelands – Bantustans – were areas demarcated for blacks which were supposed to operate as 'independent States'.)

It took the Trustees a year to realize that the community has a legitimate right to the money and that individuals could have no claims on the money. Indeed a slow sloughing of the skin!

A happy ending to a sad saga? Not quite. The technicalities persist. Are the Trustees to hand over the money as a grant, or a loan which is refundable? Although the original church building for which compensation was received was erected by the community with their own resources, it did not belong to them technically.

All of the property of the CPSA is vested in the Trustees which are there ' . . . for the purpose of exercising powers on behalf of the Provincial Synod for the management, control, and disposal of property' (Canon 42.1).[3] Every diocesan Trusts' Board ' . . . shall . . . exercise, on behalf of the provincial Synod, the powers designated . . . in respect to property given or acquired for the benefit of the Church in that Diocese'. Canon 42.11(a) in the Diocesan Regulations states that 'The Board of Diocesan Trustees shall exercise all the aforementioned powers with reference to . . . all other property (which shall include money) given or acquired for the benefit of the Diocese, and which is entrusted to the Board of Diocesan Trustees by the donor or by Diocese synod' (Diocesan Regulation 19, 9).[4]

People cannot just understand why they need to get their own money back as a loan to be repaid. This affects their giving to the diocese and also discourages them from investing their money through the diocesan agents, something encouraged by the Trustees and infinitely better than having resources dotted all over the place.

Such technical points make it difficult for the Church to be an enabler, especially in helping people deal with the legacy of apartheid.

Another parish has a debt of some R70,000 which was incurred when they had to build a new church. They had an adequate building but because of forced removals they had to replace their church. Compensation offered does not take into account escalation in building costs. The parish has asked for the debt to be written off, but it does not make economic sense and messes up the bookkeeping. Again, Western technicalities.

How can the administration of this diocese enable new wine to be poured into new wineskins?

A demoralized people

It is going to require much effort to wriggle out of the old skin in this part of the world. In Northern Cape (the largest of the provinces in the new South Africa) we have a high rate of unemployment. Our school drop-out rate is also among the highest and it is therefore no surprise that illiteracy is also a major factor in the retardation of progress.

A majority of the young people have to go away to study and most of them take up jobs elsewhere. Many of those who return are 'the ones who have not made it'.

A great section of the diocesan population is made up of people who are demoralized. This is reflected in the many instances of substance abuse, gangsterism, rape and child abuse. One of the local townships, Vergenoeg, was considered to be the most violent township in South Africa in May 1997, as revealed in a study commissioned by the *Sunday Times*.[5] The alarmists think there was a sudden upsurge in violent crime, but it only shows an increase in the number of reported crimes, since police charge offices are now more readily accessible and the police force has become more 'people-friendly'. (Police stations were usually few and far between in the townships during former years – the reverse being true of the suburbs – and the police were not quick to react to reports from those areas, so that it seemed a futile exercise to report crime and also to risk the ire of the aggressors.) What we are seeing is the reflection of a trend which has been part of the lives of a demoralized people. The Church is there to be the bearer of good news; to be the channels of God's restoring and reconciling love.

Transformation Commission

The CPSA is attempting to take this task seriously. It has constituted a Transformation Commission to help us cope with change in a changing society. This commission is in the embryonic stage. Contact with it thus far suggests that it is moving in the right direction and that there is great potential for change. The breath of fresh air is on the horizon and we need to remind ourselves that we will not see staggering results overnight. The sloughing of 'old Anglicanism' and the emergence of a more authentic and African Church will be a gradual process, but a process requiring constant attention.

Grass roots approach

In order for this process to work properly it should fan the embers at the grass roots.

Looking at this particular diocese again – how can a largely demoralized people 'own' the church and allow a relevant theology to develop? Because synods and other important meetings are conducted in English, invariably the representatives from the local congregations are those proficient in that language. They are from the ranks of teachers and other professionals who often serve on many bodies in both church and community (some not doing justice to all their many portfolios).

A first step would be to empower the local congregation to send those they feel are truly representative and sensitive to the needs, hopes and dreams of the local situation. They should be selected for *who* they are and not *what* they are. The medium of communication should not be a limiting factor. In a diocese where four of the eleven official languages of South Africa are used it is going to be quite a difficult task to accommodate everybody. If we are going to be serious about empowering people then it should not be too onerous a task. By engendering a sense of belonging we will be well on our way to empowering our people.

Empowering the disempowered

Organizations which we have inherited from abroad need to be looked at afresh. The Mothers' Union is a good example. This organization with its high (Western) ideals of family and marriage has marginalized many

Oswald Swartz

women. In this diocese women are the 'backbone' of the Church. They keep things going while the menfolk work away – because of the local unemployment situation or the migratory labour system. Those men not otherwise usefully employed are caught up in the quagmire of low self-esteem and other related problems. Despite the vital role women play in the Church, they are often disempowered – as in the community, the workplace and the home in this patriarchal society.

By recognizing that society has changed; that the family has been redefined; that it is not only different but has a validity of its own; the Church can begin to become a potent force for empowerment. This will be true for other organizations/societies which will allow themselves to be new wineskins for new wine.

Conclusion

A process has begun. The exciting signs of new birth are around. Giving birth is not a hurried process and sometimes it is traumatic. But the process must run its course, otherwise there is the danger of a stillborn baby.

Those of us who can assist as midwives must seize the opportunity and tackle the task boldly. Just as the snake emerges a beautiful creature or the butterfly spreads its wings free of the constraints of the caterpillar, we must envisage a wonderful result. Our fellows in India and elsewhere have shown us that redefinition of Anglicanism does not necessarily lead to spiritual impoverishment. It is thrilling and yet humbling to be a co-worker with God in bringing something fresh, vibrant and beautiful into being in this part of the kingdom.

Notes

1 The BEC process, from José Marins, *The Church from the Roots: Basic Ecclesial Communities* (London: Cafod, 1989).
2 *Kgotla* is the Setswana word for Council or meeting. The chief and his advisers get together to thrash out some issue concerning the community. Everybody is allowed to speak and time is given to present an argument.
3 Canon 42, 'of Trusts', in *Constitution and Canons of the Church of the Province of Southern Africa* (CPSA Publishing Committee).
4 Regulation 19, 'of Diocesan Trusts', in *Diocese of Kimberley and Kuruman Diocesan Regulations* (1994).
5 A weekly newspaper published by Times Media, Johannesburg.

Reflections from ecumenical partners

A Roman Catholic view: the Anglican Church – Federation or Communion?

Harcourt V. Blackett

I have had much contact with the Anglican Communion in many parts of the world. I was brought up in an Anglican household in Barbados and my whole life was influenced by Anglicanism. As a student of theology I spent six months in the Anglican theological college in Barbados, an opportunity to share my faith with Anglicans. I was well received by the community and established lasting friendships. This was continued when I was a student in Canada.

My next most important encounter with Anglicans came in 1992 when I was invited to be a visiting fellow at the College of the Ascension at Selly Oak. The time spent in Birmingham brought me into contact with Anglicans of all shades of opinion and from several parts of the World Anglican Communion. It also exposed me to the Church of England and to participate in its life and worship. It was here that I met the Anglican Bishop of Central Zambia. It was he who suggested me as Chaplain and Co-ordinator for the Leadership and Development Programme at the Mindolo Ecumenical Foundation. Here I have met Anglican clergy and laypeople from Zambia and from all over Africa. I have also had the chance to visit Kenya and Uganda and to see the life of the Anglican Church there.

I was in England during the time the Church there took the decision to go ahead and ordain women to the priesthood. It was indeed a most traumatic experience for many, while others rejoiced at the arrival of the day they had longed to see. I have a great deal of sympathy for those Anglicans who are in pain as a result of the decision taken by the Church in England. And yet sections of the Anglican family have been ordaining women to the priesthood for years and were now involving women in the episcopal ministry, so the idea of women's ordination was not something new to Anglicans. I was left to wonder how they viewed those parts of the Church that had taken that decision years ago. It was this that led me to ask whether or not the Anglican Church was a Communion or a Federation.

Sometimes the Anglican Church presents itself as a Church with all the answers and at other times as though it has no answer at all! Despite its limitations I have found a great love for the Word of God in the Anglican Communion. There is a rich heritage of studying and proclaiming the Word of God which has helped so many on the road to salvation. My great love for the Scripture comes from my contact with Anglican Scripture scholars.

The Anglican Communion is a communion at prayer. The prayers of the Anglican Communion, and its regular celebration of the Eucharist, reflect a deep sense of doxology and truly reveal the beauty of the liturgy. Sung Evensong in the Anglican Churches in Britain continues to inspire many Christians. Anglican theologians do their task seriously.

The Anglican Communion is very concerned for the unity of all Christians. It should be commended for its important role in the modern Ecumenical Movement. Because of its Middle Way position it is able to facilitate dialogue between Roman Catholics and other Christians. The Anglican Church is also ready to collaborate with others for the advancement of people. In my recent visit to Uganda I visited a joint project for giving men and women skills which would help them to become employable or start their own business. In Zambia the St Francis hospital, formerly Anglican, is now both Anglican and Roman Catholic. Anglicans have a great sense of mission and are involved in furthering the Kingdom of God in the world.

The Anglican Church has shown a great respect for the sacred traditions of the Christian Church. The creeds and councils of the early Church are valued as the deposit of the faith and the early Church Fathers are studied and used by many today. I think of the contribution of Bishop Mark Santer of Birmingham to my own appreciation for the early Church Fathers.

The fastest-growing section of the Anglican Communion is on the continent of Africa, but what kind of contributions are these Churches making towards the Anglican understanding of itself? My experience of the Anglican Church in Africa is that the Church tends to carry on the traditions of whatever missionary group evangelized it (mainly CMS or USPG) without any question. The people have become very loyal to the two schools and are prepared to defend one position against the next.

For me the Anglican Communion is a very significant part of the people of God. As part of the people of God it is on pilgrimage with the rest of humanity towards the Kingdom of God. Since the Anglican Communion, like the rest of the Church, lives in the world and comprises men and women of the world it stands in need of constant reformation in order to fulfil the call to holiness. This pilgrim people of God at times runs ahead of the rest of the Church and at times becomes complacent and gets bogged down in its own complacency.

Anglicans often feel that the Roman Catholic Church is over-bureaucratic and that this limits freedom of expression. Of course too much authority can impede progress but no authority at all can lead to disaster. In the Anglican Church there is no clear position on many important moral issues and in some sections of the Anglican Church, clergy, including many bishops, seem not to be accountable to anyone. Decisions taken at Lambeth or even at Provincial meetings are not binding and therefore appear to be exercises in futility. How are these situations going to be rectified in the absence of authority?

The Anglican Church should now concentrate on those elements within its own Tradition which make Church Church: the Word of God, a life of prayer; theology; ecumenism and mission; and so offer the world what it is capable of presenting.

Although many Anglicans protest at the idea that the Anglican Church is a Federation and not a Communion, I would still make that claim. I suggest that Anglicans face this reality so that they can move forward. The desire for Communion is a real desire which has to be worked out in practical ways. In whatever way, the time has come for the Anglican Church to move from Federation to Communion.

A Methodist looks at worldwide Anglicanism
Diane Clutterbuck

From 1991 to 1997 I worked as the Overseas Service Secretary of the Methodist Church in Britain. In the course of my work I visited partner Churches around the world, some Methodist Churches, others United Churches in which British Methodism is a partner. There is no Methodist equivalent of the Anglican Communion: British Methodism relates church to church. Also we do not have an independent mission agency in the way that the Church of England does. Every member of the British Methodist Church is also a member of the Methodist Missionary Society – mission is the concern and responsibility of everyone. It is from this background that I share my insights in worldwide Anglicanism.

In 1972 I went as a student to The Queen's College in Birmingham. It had recently become the first ecumenical theological college in Britain, but still retained much of its Anglican ethos. Here I caught my first glimpse of the worldwide Anglican Communion. It seemed to me little more than a ghostly survivor of the British Empire, chaplain to those who had stayed on after the sunset. That image was confirmed when in 1979 I first worshipped in St Luke's, Laucala Bay, Fiji: it was a memorable, but incomplete image.

The Anglican Communion may not be the remnant of Empire, but there is something to be said for comparing it with the Commonwealth. The international unity of Anglicanism is valuable as testimony and symbol,

Diane Clutterbuck

expressed in the regular prayer for different parts of the communion. This can be expressed politically: during the apartheid years, the Church in South Africa was assured of moral and material support from overseas. This sense of belonging, spiritually and politically, to a body that has members throughout the world is a major strength.

But there are some aspects which need to be questioned. What justification is there for the Archbishop of Canterbury retaining the role as head of the Anglican Communion? Why does the Lambeth Conference always meet in England? Why is the structural focus in the Church of England? If partnership in mission is to be more than talk, the Church of England must let go its central position and move out to stand alongside other members, taking its turn in providing leadership.

Nowhere is the model of partnership in mission better expressed than in the international community of the United College of the Ascension in Selly Oak, Birmingham. A United College came into being in 1996 thanks to the courageous vision of the Methodist Church and the United Society for the Propagation of the Gospel. For me this has been such a different experience of encounter to the one I had in Queen's 25 years ago. Then overseas visitors were a small minority, and there was little expectation that we might receive something from them. When visiting the United College, I am part of a small white minority. The worship and community life rejoices in cultural and national diversity. Everyone is changed by this experience. There is an emphasis on the exchange of gifts, the sharing of insight and real dialogue.

In 1997 a couple, a Methodist minister married to an Anglican priest, went out from the United College of the Ascension to work in Zambia, the minister to teach in the theological college of the United Church of Zambia, the priest to work with the Anglican diocese. They go to work with separate Churches. No doubt there are good historical reasons why the Anglicans have not participated in the United Church in Zambia, as they have not in Canada, Papua New Guinea or Australia. There are parts of the world where different types of Methodist fail to unite, for example in Tonga. But are there questions to be asked about the effect belonging to the Anglican Communion may be having on the willingness of Anglicans to participate in the creation of united churches? Although Anglicans were fully involved in the creation of the Church of South India in 1947, it was not until 1972 that the Church of England entered into full communion with the CSI. To Methodist eyes this seems to be rather half-hearted ecumenism.

It is often said that the Anglican Communion is the worldwide Anglican family. To an outsider it looks as if the Church of England is the matriarch. If a mother is too protective of her son, he may find it hard to leave home, or even find a wife. It is hard to let children grow up, to make mistakes, and become adults in their own right. Is there something in the relationship between the Church of England and the other Churches of the Anglican Communion that makes it hard for them to break free? Does the reluctance of the Church of England to engage in close ecumenical relationships with other British Churches affect the willingness of other Churches to become part of united churches? The value of belonging to a worldwide Church is immeasurable. The Church of England will always be mother, but she has to decide what kind of mother she will be as her children reach maturity. The same is true for the Methodist Church. The great strength of the Anglican Communion is that there is enough which binds member Churches together to save them from being congregational in their ecclesiology. We need to read the Bible through eyes other than our own, to hear the prophetic voices speaking to us out of different cultures. In a world that is divided in so many ways it is good that the Anglican Communion exists to speak when individual voices are too weak or oppressed to be heard. What a powerful force for wider ecumenical unity the Churches of the Anglican community could be. Let us pray that one day the prayer of Christ will be answered: 'that they may all be one . . . so that the world may believe that thou hast sent me.'

A Lutheran looks at worldwide Anglicanism
Aasulv Lande

I

My first encounter with Anglicanism was as a WCC ecumenical scholar at St John's College in Durham 1962/63. The World Council of Churches had offered me an Ecumenical Scholarship for one academic year.

Trained in a conservative 'confessional' Lutheran seminary in Oslo, I did not find Anglicanism immediately attractive. There seemed to be a lack of theological seriousness! One day I participated in a class on baptism. I was curiously awaiting an exposition of the Anglican doctrine on this matter, to compare with the careful exposition of Lutheran doctrine, between 'papist' and 'spiritualist'. 'Now we arrive at the crucial question in infant baptism', announced the lecturer, with a pregnant pause. I listened carefully, somehow waiting for a significant statement. 'The crucial question is: how to hold the child'! Not theology but the performance of a practical rite was considered most crucial! This was a complete surprise to me. Later I came to appreciate more the Anglican appreciation of theology – not least the fact that they opened up for me an appreciation of wider aspects of my own tradition – for example, Schleiermacher or Bonhoeffer; not to mention my fellow Norwegians, Torleif Boman (a biblical scholar whose 'unorthodox' views had led to his exclusion from academic life), and Sigmund Mowinckel, the great OT scholar; Anglican openness to more philosophical perspectives on the Bible presumably offered less biased views on Scandinavian thinking than Scandinavians themselves could come up with. Anglicans appreciating attitudes to what I considered neglected elements of my own tradition thus provided an inspiring push to appreciation in return. Thus Anglicanism at first appeared friendly, rather vague and theologically confused; later I saw that it could mediate a wider, more inclusive faith.

II

My second period of exposure to and contact with Anglicanism lasted from 1965 to 1980. During these fifteen years I was based in Japan, where I worked as a Lutheran pastor in congregations but also served in the field of inter-religious dialogue. I recall three basic impressions of Anglicanism in the Japanese context. Initially I felt that the Anglican presence in Japan was weak. Not simply weak in numbers – that was true of all Christian groups. But rather, Anglicanism gave an impression of being weak in communicating with others. They appeared isolated, not engaging too strongly in social matters, not speaking too decisively in doctrinal issues.

It is difficult to be too critical of another Christian tradition, because my own tradition also had its weak points! For example, the hopeless disunity of the different Lutheran groups (American, Norwegian, German). The Anglicans on the other hand were united in one Church body. Unity is strength, but they nevertheless appeared invisible. I am inclined to think that the apparent 'invisibility' was partly due to Anglican emphasis on worship. Worship is not a strong and visible activity like social statements or doctrinal absoluteness. Another reason for the isolation might be historical. When Japanese religious laws in 1941 forced Protestants to unite in one organization, Anglicans refused to join. For this courageous and heroic attitude they suffered a precarious existence as a non-recognized Church body during the war years up to 1945. The heroism led to isolation from Japanese society. It also implied isolation from Japanese Protestantism, which as a whole took another course during the war years, and was based on a different theology of ministry, which could appear arrogant to other Christians.

On the other hand, the worship-based Anglican particularity could also appear surprisingly different from isolation. Anglicanism could draw on a much wider Church approval and support for inter-religious dialogue. As one case I recall the much-disputed joint worship event which occurred on 3 February 1977 at the Omoto sanctuary in Ayabe where Anglicans and believers from Omoto – a Japanese religion in the Shinto tradition – were the main partners. It was basically an Anglican service, led by a Japanese priest, Revd Sekimoto; the surprising thing was that it could take place in the Omoto shrine. 'We had great fun the other day', Sekimoto joked with me later.

The idea of worship as 'just for fun' matches the image of invisibility and worship-centred Anglican identity. It reminds me of the work of the Reformed theologian, Jürgen Moltmann, in developing a 'Theology of Play'. But worship for fun could hardly be done in Lutheran bodies. I am much impressed by the joy, courage and interfaith experimenting which Anglicanism has offered, despite its image of isolationism!

III

My third period of close relationships with Anglicans begins in 1990 when the Lutheran World Federation appointed me the Lutheran lecturer at Selly Oak Colleges in Birmingham. During this time the Porvoo agreement was signed, with its mutual recognition of ministries between Baltic and Scandinavian Lutherans and British Anglicans, an important statement for the self-understanding of both communions. It could well be that the idea of a common mission, expressed in the Porvoo agreement, should have a high priority in the process of actualization of the agreement. I will particularly comment on the implications for mission. The Anglican work with the partnership idea since the Toronto congress in 1963 and the organization of 'Partners in Mission' in 1973 are most significant in this connection. Anglicans have pioneered the concept of dialogue, from the creative ideas of 'Christian presence' put forward by CMS in the 1960s. But ecumenical openness towards sisters and brothers far away is one matter. Local ecumenical inclusivity is a quite different process. And what about Lutheran–Anglican relations in other areas where both are important Christian communities: places like USA, Tanzania and Namibia?

I will conclude my look at the Anglican community, with which I have been involved for more than 30 years, by pleading for continued and deepened fellowship between the two communities. The importance of this is one of my dearest concerns, as it has shaped my whole Christian self-understanding.

Further reading

Anglican–Lutheran Relations: Report of the Joint Working Group of Cold Ash (London: Anglican Consultative Council, and Geneva: Lutheran World Federation, 1983).

Aasulv Lande

In Good Faith: The Four Principles of Interfaith Dialogue. A Brief Guide for the Churches (London: Council of Churches for Britain and Ireland, 1991).

Aasulv Lande, 'Contemporary missiology in the Church of England' in Aasulv Lande and Werner Ustorf (eds), *Mission in a Pluralist World* (Studies in the Intercultural History of Christianity, no. 97; Frankfurt am Main: Peter Lang Publishers, 1996), pp. 25–64.

William A. Norgren and William G. Rusch, *Implications of the Gospel: Lutheran Episcopal Dialogue*, Series III (Minneapolis: Augsburg, and Cincinnati: Forward Movement Publications, 1988).

On the Way Towards Visible Unity: Meissen Statement 1988 (London: Church of England, 1988).

Lars Österlin, *Churches of Northern Europe in Profile: A Thousand Years of Anglo-Nordic Relations* (Norwich: The Canterbury Press, 1995).

The Porvoo Common Statement: Conversations Between the British and Irish Anglican Churches and the Nordic and Baltic Lutheran Churches (London: Council for Christian Unity, Church of England General Synod, 1994).

Section Three

The Church in society

An Anglican view of ecological issues in the Australian context

Christabel Chamarette

Environmental awareness among Australians generally is a phenomenon which arose in the late 1980s. Unfortunately despite or perhaps because of Australia's status as a 'developed' nation and its immense wealth of natural resources, the economic forces of globalization have frequently over-whelmed the attempt to translate environmental awareness into ecological responsibility. The major political parties, the Australian Labor Party (which governed federally from 1982 to 1996) and the Liberal/National Coalition (currently in government), have shown a remarkable coincidence of interest on globalization, free trade, Aboriginal rights and labour law. It is in this context that the Anglican Church, through its parishes, its agencies and its bishops, has assumed an increasing role of a dissenting voice towards government policy on the interconnected issues of social justice and the environment.

While the Anglican Church has always had critics of government policy within its ranks, they have tended to be idiosyncratic. The Church, in common with other major denominations, has more often been closely allied to 'establishment' interests through, for instance, its role in provid-ing education through private schools, many of which are elite. Consequently, there is a tension between speaking for those who are oppressed in the Gospel way, and the economic interests of the Church's congregations, who remain typically Anglo-centric and affluent. The fact that at least some bishops are prepared to speak out despite the tension is illustrated in the 1997 public debate on the Federal Government's Native

Title Amendment Bill, when one Federal Member called for a boycott of the Church by its members.

In relation to ecology, Australia presents the startling contrast of a frontier mentality of massive environmental destruction through forestry, mining and industrialization which continues apace alongside one of the strongest forms of ecological spirituality ever known. While Australia has much to learn from the mistakes of Europe and Western civilization, Aboriginal spirituality offers the world a unique opportunity to learn a deeply spiritual ecology.

The interconnection between social justice and care for the environment becomes marked when we see in the Australian context that Aboriginal spirituality derives from people's relation to the Earth as their mother. Simply put, Aboriginal people have values of care for the earth and care for each other which Europeans would do well to emulate and without which the future for humanity as a whole looks bleak. Australia has a particularly fragile, ancient and unique environment. Vast areas of Western Australian lands have been rendered useless to agriculture by an attitude of unbridled exploitation. Difficulty and denial in accepting Aboriginal humanity, prior occupation and sovereignty of the land of Australia seem to parallel the brutal treatment of the land as simply resource to be exploited and plundered. The same destructive values, quite contrary to the Gospel, are at work. Aboriginal spirituality challenges us to return to the radical core of the Gospel in a way that makes Christianity not only relevant to contemporary ecological issues but also prophetic.

Learning to be the prophetic Church, Anglicanism is being pushed to the periphery as far as the majority is concerned. The search for meaning of young people and the past failure of the Anglican Church to offer experience which appeals to the dissenting young have been triggers for a new progressiveness.

Community-based change is a sign of hope. Within congregations the willingness to work on integrating the theological with the controversial political is an increasing trend, particularly in parishes which retain a youthful congregation. The demonstration of the relevance of faith to the needs of society and political issues is not unrelated to young people feeling that the Church and faith are relevant to their world and seeking active involvement in political activism as an expression of their faith. As Margaret Mead said, a small number of people can bring about real change.

Over recent decades the Australian Anglican Church has been rediscovering a theology which respects creation. Members of the Western Australian Anglican Social Responsibilities Commission produced and launched the 1990 Social Justice Statement, entitled *Justice for the Earth*. The statement addressed the topic of a theology of the environment and was supported by a series of case studies on concerns such as air pollution, waste, salinity and de-forestation from around Australia. 'GOD IS GREEN – Says justice statement' was the headline in the *Anglican Messenger* of October 1990.

It was an auspicious and hopeful start to the last decade of this century and members of the Social Responsibilities Commission, of which I was Chairperson at the time, were elated and hopeful. However this expressed Anglican view on ecological issues was more progressive, political and prophetic than it is widespread, practical or reflective of any significant shift in Australian community and government attitudes. There is still a very long way to go. Since that time I had the unique experience of entering the political arena and observing at first hand how great was the distance to be covered for a prophetic document to be translated into prophetic action.

My role as a known Anglican Christian as well as a Member of Parliament has not been without criticism from within the Church itself. My stand as a Green is one which integrates my politics and my theology. However, we can expect the Church to mirror the wide diversity of political views within the community and not to have a monopoly on the truth. Sometimes I have been seen as a liberal political activist corrupting the Anglican Church's historic mission of spreading the Gospel rather than having a prophetic Christian voice. There were also some exciting moments when I saw the Church (often at an ecumenical level) exerting a leadership role from the community towards the political arena.

Two examples given by me in the Parliament on 26 October 1995 were an Earth Day mass on St Francis' Day which was an occasion of celebration, reverence for life and joy in which parishioners brought their animal family members for blessing and focused on our mutual needs to love and care for the earth and a similar service called the 'Celebration of the Gift of the Forest' held at the first logging site in Sydney by a group of people from different Churches called Christians for the Environment. The services like the two I have mentioned were joined by calls from churches and Church leaders across all denominations. An open letter was sent to the major political parties from religious leaders, calling for a stop to all logging of old-growth forest. I believe it is an indication that a very significant threshold has been reached.

Church leaders and groups involved in Christians for the Environment are concerned about the fate of our forests and see responsibility for the environment as fundamental to their faith. Christians everywhere are beginning to become aware of their responsibility for the restoration of God's creation and the need to actively support these issues.

There is a spiritual dimension to the forests, as well as a biological, social and economic one. The political agenda must take this spirituality on board: we must value God's creation appropriately. Forests are a vital part of this creation and of its ongoing sustainability.

The inter-relatedness of healthy forests and life – including human life – on this planet is testimony to the fact that forests are more than gifts from God for human beings to exploit. Our God-given human calling is to work responsibly with the rest of creation for human well being. But human well being in the long term is integrally related to the correct, sustainable use of God given forest resources.

Christian faith suggests that we are to work with God for the redemption of the whole world. Theologically and socially we argue that it is vital for us to nurture existing native forests and their biodiversity in order to work for a sustainable life style. The destruction of forests has an impact beyond the immediate areas where logging has taken place. The loss of old growth forests and wilderness areas means a loss to a whole diverse ecosystem of which human beings are a part. Loss of forests is a loss to this whole community of living things.

This statement was supported by New South Wales Ecumenical Council, the Uniting Church of Australia, the Sydney Anglican Social Issues Committee, and the Catholic Church.

It is a most beautiful and moving statement. I believe it marks the point where concern on this issue transcends not only Church boundaries, but also the boundaries of political parties.

I often make the statement that politicians are not leaders in the community; we follow the lead of the community. I believe the community is making a call to all politicians who may be involved in the decision-making processes that are leading to the inevitable destruction and loss of our precious old-growth forests and the rare and endangered species within them. I urge that we be obedient to the call and be led by the community, instead of leading it down a path of destruction.

Christians have always believed that the natural world is God's creation and that its beauty and complexity mirror God's splendour. To destroy irresponsibly the natural world, for whatever purpose, is to distort one of our most precious images of God.

In the past in Australia, through ignorance of the ecological complexity of our country, and through greed, we have already destroyed much of our natural inheritance. However, with better knowledge and a heightened ecological sense, we have no ethical justification whatsoever to continue destroying the natural world and distorting the creation of God.

It is clear to us that Australia's old growth forests are both ecologically precious and of great natural beauty. They also are home to rare and endangered species. As such, they mirror the creativity of God.

Therefore to continue to log them, for whatever purpose, must be considered ethically and even morally wrong. The text of the Book of Genesis, often referred to by those seeking to justify such destruction ['be fruitful and multiply, and fill the earth and subdue it; and have dominion' (Gen 1:28)], does not grant to humans the right to exploit, let alone to destroy, God's creation. To use the text to justify environmental destruction is a fundamentalist misreading of the text.

Part of the task of becoming the body of Christ is becoming relevant to our times. There is no way of avoiding environmental crises globally and locally. Tentative steps taken provide hope that ecological spirituality will be integral contributing both to healing the earth and healing the nations/world.

The authentic body of Christ is a prophetic church which plays an active role in community issues and concerns and has a particularly Christian, biblical or spiritual perspective to offer the wider community. The eco-logical crisis can only be resolved by spiritual renewal. Australian politics in itself has no credibility in this area. An example is the Liberal Govern-ment's insistence on continuing the increase in greenhouse gas emissions in the face of global crisis. The Anglican Church has taken steps by acting as a prophetic voice to address the unwillingness of governments to act on these crucial ecological issues sometimes only on an individual basis but also at a congregational, Church leadership and community participation level.

Minority ethnic Anglicans in Britain

Glynne Gordon-Carter

Trumpet call of the Black Anglican Celebration

When nearly 400 people met for the weekend of 22–24 July 1994 at the University of York, the Church of England took a step without precedent in its history. This was the first ever national Black Anglican Celebration, convened after three years' planning by the General Synod's Committee for Black Anglican Concerns, and attended by representatives of every diocese, with bishops from most dioceses, and guests from other Churches. Its main purpose was to celebrate and affirm the participation of black Anglican Christians in the task of the Decade of Evangelism, and to enable them to make common cause with each other for this purpose. Two-thirds of the participants were themselves black Anglicans, with an even balance between the sexes, a lay presence far greater than the clerical, and a distribution of ages weighted towards the younger end. The Celebration was addressed by both Archbishops, as well as by practised experts from minority ethnic men and women who gave a hard-hitting lead about the tasks facing black Christians today.

From the results of this work the black Anglicans with the support of all others at the Celebration issue this trumpet call:

To the Church of England and its leaders, we say:

Black people are people. Black Christians are Christians. Black Anglicans are Anglicans. Our ethnic origins may lie in Africa, the Americas, Asia, or the Caribbean Islands, and a few of us are visitors from these lands, but mostly we ourselves are English, a large proportion of us born in England, and glad to be Anglicans here in partnership with white Christians. We belong to this land and to every corner of it. Make us more visible within the life and leadership of our Church. Racism contradicts our Lord's command to love our neighbours as ourselves. It offends the fundamental Christian belief that every person is made in the image of God and is equally precious in his sight. Racism has no place in Christ: it creates nothing but hatred and fear.

Every Christian person in every generation has an individual responsibility to oppose and resist racism in all its forms, striving to reflect that divine Love which alone fills our lives with meaning and hope. So let all discrimination against us, knowing or ignorant, latent or overt, cease. Let us reach our own fullness in Christ as ourselves. Let our gifts and calling be recognized and affirmed, our partnership in the life of the Church of England be evident and welcome. We seek to walk confidently in Christ, one in him with all of every ethnic group, tribe and tongue who name his name. Let the whole Church of England by deliberate will live this doctrine in practical love. Without it there is no gospel message of God's love for us to live and proclaim.

To our English society, we say:

Black people are people. Black English are English. But there is as yet no real equality in jobs, housing, health, educational opportunity or the media and their message. True justice is too frequently missing from police methods and administration of the law. Institutional racism is deeply rooted, and we fear for our children if it is not rooted out. We are here; we are English; we are part of the community. Give us justice.

To ourselves, we say:

We have a responsibility to ourselves, our young people and the wider community to take up the challenges that we have met this weekend – the challenges like growing in confidence and leadership potential; and taking risks in order that we might grow; and offering this confidence as a gift to the whole Church. Risks that will allow us to create our own space and not leave others to create it for us. The risks to use our gifts in whatever way possible especially in the task of Evangelism and Mission. We are ready to play our part in reclaiming our rich biblical inheritance for both black people and white people. We are ready to encourage the Church to live the Christian faith authentically and therefore to confront our society in areas of racial injustices. For us evangelism and caring go hand in hand: we are committed to demonstrating and proclaiming the gospel. We are determined to encourage young black Anglicans to remain and become involved in our Church at all levels.

To our God, we say:

We have sounded our trumpet call to redress wrongs done to us, yet we are humbled before your love and are only seeking your glory. Let your trumpet call now guide our feet, your judgement and justice cry out to the skies. We meet in your love to do your will. We place our cause in your hands. Do your will in us that your world may be transformed. Amen.

The Trumpet Call has been presented in this chapter as it is still very relevant, provides an understanding of the past, present and future and the context within which this work is being done by the Committee for Minority Ethnic Anglican Concerns (CMEAC), formerly the Committee for Black Anglican Concerns.

During the post-Celebration period, there was a great deal of reflection on that event, as well as on the future of the Committee's work. This led to revised Terms of Reference, and the change of the Committee's name. Members decided on 'minority ethnic' as a more inclusive term which would encompass African, African-Caribbean, Asian, Black British, Chinese and many others who felt that they were still being marginalized by the Church on grounds of colour, culture and ethnic origin. In reference to the re-designation, Bishop John Sentamu, CMEAC's present Chairman, said 'The word "black" in twentieth-century multi-ethnic Britain is no longer inclusive or useful for all minority ethnic people in the country who face racism in all its varied forms. The parallel term here is the word *man*. Let the reader understand.'

The past

The Archbishop's report *Faith in the City: A Call for Action by Church and Nation* (FITC) identified racism as one of the ills in the society which still had to be overcome. Evidence given to the Commission called for the Church of England to stress the importance of compliance with the laws against direct and indirect racial discrimination.

Many Black Christians told the Commission that 'they had felt "frozen out" of the Church of England by patrician attitudes. Some had left the Church, yet others were still solid Anglicans. We have heard repeated calls from the Church of England to "make space" for and so better receive the gifts of black Christians.' Bishop Wilfred Wood (first Chairman of the Committee), in the foreword to *Seeds of Hope*, remarked that many Caribbean immigrants were used to worship in a Church where the clergy and leadership were English and white, and so 'anticipated nothing but acceptance and even welcome in churches in Britain with whose liturgy and worship they were thoroughly familiar. They were disappointed.'

FITC made it clear that the Church needed to give a clear lead from the centre in response 'not only to racial discrimination and disadvantage, but also to the alienation, hurt and rejection experienced by many black people in relation to the Church of England' (p. 96).

The report set out three objectives to be achieved:

- that the issues of racial discrimination and disadvantage are given a clearer and more sustained emphasis in all that the Church says and does
- the promotion of a greater awareness of these issues, and associated socio-cultural aspects, throughout the Church
- the removal of barriers to the effective participation and leadership of black people at all levels of Church life, particularly in relation to the ordained ministry.

Organizational changes and accountability within the Church structures and in relation to black Anglicans would be vital. Changes should work in tandem, otherwise 'race issues' might be compartmentalized or merely considered to be just one more pressure group. Significantly the report recommended that complementary initiatives to be taken should include 'the establishment of a wide-ranging Standing Commission on Black

Anglican Concerns'. This recommendation was narrowly defeated at the General Synod (GS) session in 1986; however, the GS voted overwhelmingly for the setting up of a Committee for Black Anglican Concerns (CBAC), with the status of a sub-Committee of the GS Standing Committee. CBAC (redesignated CMEAC) would help the Church to work at combating racism in its structures.

The GS also agreed that the Board for Social Responsibility (BSR) should set up a permanent Committee, to address racial justice issues in the wider society. BSR's Race and Community Relations Committee works mainly in areas such as employment, asylum and immigration issues and the promotion of the annual commemoration of Racial Justice Sunday by all denominations.

The present

CMEAC's work within the structures

CMEAC's principal tasks are to monitor issues arising, or which ought to arise, in the context of the work of the Standing Committee, the Central Board of Finance, the GS Boards and Councils, and of the GS itself, as far as they have policy implications for minority ethnic groups, within the Church and the wider community. The Committee assists bishops in developing diocesan strategies for combating racism.

From its inception, the Committee understood that priority should be given to tackling the under-representation of minority ethnic Anglicans within the synodical structures.

In his keynote address at the 1994 Black Anglican Celebration for the Decade of Evangelism, the Archbishop of Canterbury said 'I am very encouraged by the ways in which, increasingly, black people are holding positions of leadership within our Church, both as clergy and laity. But I am also aware that there is still much to be done . . . I long to see many more black Anglicans offering themselves for the Ordained Ministry or serving on Parochial Church Councils (PCCs), General Synod and Diocesan Boards and Committees.' He also noted that 'one gift which black Anglicans may offer to God's Church is to help us towards a better understanding of the true nature and right use of power. This will become clearer as more black people take up positions of responsibility in the structures of the Church.'

The survey report *How We Stand* identifies parishes in which minority ethnic Anglicans are worshipping, and their level of participation at all levels of Church life. The survey revealed that there are approximately 27,000 minority ethnic Anglicans. 'In two ways, the survey contrasts with statistics for the Church as a whole. In general, electoral roll membership exceeds usual Sunday attendance in a parish. Among black Anglicans, the comparison is reversed, with more attending than appear on the rolls. Black Anglicans also bring a higher proportion of children to church. Nationally, there are ten children for every 41 adults in church on a Sunday. Among black worshippers, the ratio is ten children to sixteen adults.'

In 1994, the survey recorded that there were 92 clergy, 39 readers, seventeen Church Army officers, 536 Eucharistic assistants, 673 group leaders, 213 churchwardens, 1,654 PCC members, 2,092 sidesmen and women, 237 members of deanery synods, and 38 members of diocesan synods. Currently there are fifteen members of General Synod. Non-registration on electoral rolls may be one reason why minority ethnic Anglicans are numerically under-represented on PCCs and synods.

Minority ethnic Anglicans are serving in the following senior positions: three bishops, three canons, a prebendary of St Paul's Cathedral; lay canons, vocations advisers, Advisory Board of Ministry selectors in some dioceses, an Assistant Secretary for Anglican Communion and Ecumenical Affairs to the Archbishop of Canterbury.

The future

While acknowledging the positive response and action taken by many dioceses, it is important to note that there are still some dioceses, deaneries and parishes which do not consider this work of any relevance to them. We think that there can be no room for complacency.

FITC had made no specific recommendations about changes in diocesan structures but does recommend that dioceses review their structures to ensure 'that black Anglicans have a voice in decision making or advisory processes, and that a concern for racial discrimination and disadvantage is reflected in policies and practices'. Also in his 'Message to Seeds of Hope', Bishop Sentamu remarked that the Report enabled the Church structures to ask themselves 'how truly they have lived up to God's vision of wholeness, freedom, order and peace. Do they visibly show what Heaven will be like? Have they managed to keep in balance the tension between the claims of earth and the eternal claims of Heaven? The Church can neither afford to treat race and justice questions as peripheral to the Good News of Creation and Redemption, nor adopt a defensive and knee-jerk response to them. Such attitudes have left the Church deprived and impoverished.'

Further reading

Peter Fryer, *Staying Power: The History of Black People in Britain* (London: Pluto Press, 1984).

Paul Grant and Raj Patel, *A Time to Speak: Perspectives of Black Christians in Britain* (London: Racial Justice (ECRJ)/Black Theology Working Group, 1990).

Maurice Hobbs, *Better Will Come: A Pastoral Response to Racism in British Churches* (Nottingham: Grove Books, 1991).

Kenneth Leech, *Struggle in Babylon* (London: Sheldon Press, 1988).

John L. Wilkinson, *Church in Black and White* (Edinburgh: St Andrew Press, 1993).

A South African reflection on the issue of homosexuality in the Anglican Communion

James GaOfenngwe Keetile

I do not presume here to be speaking on behalf of either homosexuals or the Church in South Africa. Rather, I have written this essay as a black heterosexual male who has become convinced that the Church must move into a constructive discussion with homosexuals. For this to take place some stereotypes need to be changed. Let me mention some of the heterosexual values that have shaped me and possibly many black South Africans.

I grew up in a small township of Mothibistad, not far from Kuruman. This community was for me a microcosm of South Africa. At a tender age I discovered that there were serious differences between 'mofies' (effeminate) and 'normal boys'. In this context the dominant value system was shaped by the ideas of the heterosexuals. As I moved to college I discovered that the pressure upon young men and young women to conform to sexual norms was very strong and that this exposed homosexuals or lesbians to a sense of oppression, and even abuse.

On reflection, from the mixture of traditional and cultural sources, the small community I grew up in developed a world order founded on political patriarchal principles of the complementarity of male and female.

Heterosexuality was part of this patriarchy, founded upon an ideology of difference. Many people in the Church know homosexuality only through the prevalent, predominantly pejorative stereotypes, including the common misunderstandings accepted by society as a whole. Chief among them is the mistaken belief that homosexual men are always attracted to boys under the age of puberty. The Church in South Africa and indeed throughout the Anglican Communion should help its members to draw a distinction between paedophilia and homosexuality.

Many of our people were socialized to accept homophobia as a way of life. The debate is often clinical rather than humane. Many think being heterosexual is more important than being human. I want to suggest that the second, fundamental challenge facing the Church is to change some of these stereotypes that have been institutionalized. Is there any possibility for an openness to the work and guidance of the Holy Spirit in a Church that has institutionalized its views and prejudices? In a democratic, non-sexist society which South Africa has become, homosexuals, rather than being somehow a menace to the values of society and family, should be regarded as part of God's creative plan. They have special qualities and gifts and a positive contribution in the building and healing of our nation. Perhaps this is also a challenge to our Church to assess how it should respond to the changing notions of sin among its members.

The problem of homosexuality is no longer the problem of those who have or seek same-sex relationships. It is the problem of those who cannot, or will not, understand that reality. The Church's discussion of this matter has been dominated by insistently ideological voices. When the subject is discussed we tend to ask not what people think, but how they feel, and feelings are non-debatable. In most cases when the issue is discussed there is always an underlying assumption that homosexuality represents a departure from man's proper nature, though in fact the Christian tradition is complex.

In the present Church there is, on the one side, the unqualified homophobic condemnation of homosexuals and all that appears homosexual, on the other the homosexual and lesbian rights activists demanding the Church's unconditional acceptance. And in the middle the 'liberal' who does not want to commit him or herself, keeps on asking questions like: Does Jesus pander to our desires? Most of the debate about the subject of homosexuality for the past few years has started on the premises of non-compromise and institutionalized prejudices.

In some communities these prejudices are justified by pointing out that homosexuality as a topic is ideologically suspect, and is determined by Western societal concerns. Many congregations do not acknowledge the existence of homosexuality in their ranks. It is rather a problem they feel is 'out there'. Thus when the subject of homosexuality is discussed it is not rare to hear phrases like *rona dilo tse re gola re sa di itse* (we have matured without coming across such things). A phrase like this reflects the conspiracy of silence that has for many years plagued issues of sexuality in the Church.

The history of sexuality in South Africa was thus also determined by the interests of those who were in power. As a way forward I believe the Anglican Church in Southern Africa can start taking the experiences of homosexuals as the starting point for a fruitful debate. In South Africa attitudes have been very diverse, ranging from reiteration of traditional blanket condemnation of homosexuals to expressions of variously qualified acceptance. Issues of justice towards oppressed groups is a particularly sensitive one in South Africa. The new constitution is particularly concerned to safeguard the rights of all sections of the population, not least homosexual minorities.

As the Anglican Church in the Southern African region discusses this issue, I believe it should be profoundly conscious of the guilt that the Church bears from its long-maintained judgemental and persecutory attitudes towards homosexuality through its theology and attitudes, in a social and ecclesiastical situation of institutional prejudice, such as sexism and racism. These theologies have also permitted the homosexuals to accept and internalize the values of heterosexuals. The mood in the Anglican Church when it comes to homosexuality has been one of liberalized conformity. Homosexuals have been encouraged to internalize their sexuality into a quasi-spirituality.

It is my belief that not only homosexuals demand for themselves the right to deal with the problem of homophobia, but also these problems need to be taken seriously and put on the agenda of the established heterosexual-dominated Church. The issue of homosexuality presents the Church with an opportunity to reclaim the beauty of sexuality as one of the powerful energies in the created order. It is my view that any understanding of Christian theology must therefore critically evaluate and reject all oppressive and marginalizing traditions even if they are deeply rooted in the Christian tradition and scripture.

The Anglican Communion will not survive long if it does not recognize and responsibly relate to the experiences of its members. It is my firm belief that a way forward is to affirm the experiences of homosexuals and assure the integrity of the Communion at the same time. While there is no good reason for excluding from the Church membership those who in good conscience have accepted their homosexual inclination, at the same time the Anglican Communion must be aware that like any other institution, it is a body which contains strong conservative strains, including people who without manifest prejudice hold sincere convictions that homosexuality is morally wrong. As the Anglican Communion prepares to move into the third millennium, the imperative confronting the Church is promoting a deconstruction of anti-homosexual theology and attitudes. The prerequisite to this is to recognize that we share a common commitment to the God revealed in Jesus the Christ.

'A sanctuary and a light'?

The Scottish Churches respond to violence against women

Lesley Macdonald

If it be your holy will, grant that a place of your abiding may be continued still to be a sanctuary and a light.

(from a prayer of the Iona Community, Scotland)

Anna is a Christian woman, a teacher, and a member of her local Episcopal church. She describes the architect she married as a charming man and a wonderful dancer. They had three children, and to all appearances enjoyed a pleasant and successful life. But for sixteen years, Anna's husband used verbal insults, threats, the withholding of money, and severe physical brutality to control and limit her life. She was hospitalized three times. Finally, she left the home she had worked hard to create and sustain. She and her children fled to the local women's refuge, where they found refuge and support to build their shattered lives. This is what Anna told me:

Fear is the most dominating emotion, because everything else is subject to it. I was paralysed by fear, and only a determination to protect my children released some energy to drag me out of that total erosion of personhood. For too long I accepted the humiliation and degradation. I kept thinking about the words of the marriage service: 'For better, for worse; in sickness and in health.' *I* was getting the worst, and *I* was part of the sickness, and somehow it all seemed to be my fault. Surely if vows had been blessed by God, I should have been helped through this? It hadn't occurred to me that a Christian marriage could be abusive. I felt like a failure, and that certainly added to the isolation. I was shamed into silence.

All over the world, women and girl children have been shamed into silence by gender violence. Perpetrators and victims of such abuse belong to no one class, religion, race or group. Abusers are not just the monsters or drunkards of myth and stereotype: they are ordinary men, living apparently ordinary lives. Worldwide, the dignity, integrity and very personhood of millions of women is violated: physically, sexually, psychologically, economically, structurally. Their space and opportunity to lead decent and fulfilling lives is attacked and denied. This is a fundamental issue of justice and human rights, as a UNICEF Report published in July 1997 makes clear.[1]

The United Nations Fourth Conference on Women, held in Beijing in 1995, acknowledged that efforts to prevent and eliminate violence against women, in all its forms, are both necessary and achievable. This is an important affirmation, because for too long, the evil of gender abuse has been accepted, trivialized, justified – and even sanctified by religion – as an inevitable aspect of relationships between women and men. It presents an urgent challenge to the Christian Church, which preaches the good news of shalom for all God's people; for there is a wealth of evidence that Christianity, in common with other patriarchal religious traditions, has been historically complicit in creating cultures and conditions which have colluded with abuse against women. Can the Church accept its pastoral and prophetic task, to name, condemn, and struggle against such abuse, in all its manifestations? Listen again to the voice of Anna:

> Once, I expected the Church to have answers to all my questions. But now, I think that I have answers to many of the questions the Church should be asking. And I know that may sound arrogant, but I've changed from being a victim to a survivor. I think my story – *our* story, all of us who have suffered violation and abuse – is a resource for the Church.

For the past two years, I have co-ordinated an action-research project at Edinburgh University's Centre for Theology and Public Issues. It is entitled 'Out of the shadows: Christianity and violence against women in Scotland'. The work of the project has been inspired, and to a large extent shaped, by the conviction that the stories of Christian women who have suffered violence are indeed a resource for the Church. Women who, with courage, clarity and insight, have found the strength to come out of the shadows and witness to their pain as well as to their capacity for survival, have so much to offer, as well as to receive, as members of the Christian and human community.

Central to the project has been a programme of extended interviews and ongoing contact with women who have had personal experience of gender abuse. There is now a large and consistent body of statistical and other evidence that male violence against women is not a matter of personal aberration, but is socially pervasive. It is probable that within every congregation, parish and denomination, there are victims, survivors and perpetrators.

The women who have spoken with me are of different generations, backgrounds, denominations and theological standpoints – as were their abusers. But what they share is a concern about how the Church responds to the reality of gender violence. Their voices recite a depressing litany: their value has been ascribed according to fulfilment of male need or desire, not on intrinsic worth. They have been counselled to be submissive and obedient; to preserve the marriage bond at all costs; to be willing to sacrifice their own interests and safety; unconditionally to forgive those who fail to acknowledge or repent of their own sin, and indeed who continue to wound them with impunity. Male abusers have rarely been confronted, challenged or sanctioned for their behaviour. And too many victims have simply been too afraid to share their problems within the Church, for fear of judgement or rejection.

Most of the women with whom I have spoken have been committed Christians. They have believed in a God of love. Their faith, and the community of the Church, have been formative influences in their lives. Most have suffered abuse in their intimate relationships. Several were married to ordained clergy, and suffered mistreatment at their hands. Others have been harassed, assaulted or abused in pastoral contexts – by Church representatives from whom they sought care and counselling, or with whom they worked as colleagues. For a small number, the Church was truly a source of empowerment and love at times of deep crisis and suffering. But for most, their experience of personal abuse was intensified by their sense that the institution and its representatives turned away from their pain, or protected the perpetrator, or failed to offer them refuge.

Above all, women who are refugees from abuse need *sanctuary* – a secure, holding but liberating space of safety, affirmation and encouragement; and they need *light* – to dispel the gloom and terror; to expose the perpetrators who lurk in the shadows of our indifference; to illuminate alternative possibilities and restored selfhood.

Surely it is a scandal to the Church's integrity and faithfulness that we so often fail to be a sanctuary and a light. One clergy wife, who was granted a divorce after suffering years of abuse, pointed out:

> Public opinion rests with the man. The wife is seen as guilty of abandoning him, while the assumption is that he is blameless as a man of God. Eventually one is so desperate that this is of no consequence, but it still hurts when church people ignore you or are cold to you. It feels so unjust. The system forces silence on us, even if we want to speak out.

Many of the women I know now find attendance at worship more painful than they can bear. When their need of sacramental community is most urgent, they have experienced the depth of abandonment, and they cry 'My God, my God, why have you forsaken me?'

When women are abused (especially by men who have position and status in the Church), they are too often locked into the silence of victim-shaming and blaming. Of course, there may be Christians willing to be their advocates and companions, but how are they to *know*? Has the Church addressed gender violence as a justice issue? Have we made strong public declarations that it is sinful and unacceptable? Have we held it before God as a concern in our liturgies? Have we confessed the Church's historical complicity and collusion? Have we campaigned for the political and legal changes required for female equality and safety? Where are the messages of hope for abused women:

- We believe you
- This is not God's will for you
- It is not your fault
- Your safety and well-being are our first priority
- You have the right to make choices about your own future
- You are not alone?

Because vulnerable and exploited people have rarely heard this kind of affirmation and reassurance in their church, they have remained burdened with stigma and silence. I believe that, as long as we perceive abuse of women to be a marginal, rather than a central theological and ecclesio-logical concern, the Church will have neither the motivation, nor the appropriate mechanisms, to impose effective sanctions on abusive men, and to transform its structures and attitudes. Until it commits itself to this radical process, it will rarely have the resources to be a place of true sanctuary and light.

There *are* signs of hope in Scotland. Through 'Out of the shadows', and other initiatives, Christians are much more aware that gender violence is an injustice which damages the corporate health of the Body of Christ. An ecumenical group, linked to NEWS, the women's committee of Action of Churches Together in Scotland (ACTS), has been formed to campaign for a co-ordinated and effective response. Vashti – Scottish Christian Women Against Abuse believes there are three priorities for urgent action:

1. training, education and self-awareness on abuse and gender issues (especially for those working as ministers, priests, and in positions of pastoral responsibility);
2. strategies to offer a safe point of contact, ongoing advocacy, and appropriate referral, for those whose experience of violence has been in a church context;

3. clear policies for prevention and intervention, codes of ethical conduct, and effective disciplinary procedures, to deal with harassment and abuse in professional/pastoral contexts.

Vashti hopes that the Scottish Episcopal Church, along with fellow members of the worldwide Anglican Communion, and other denominations, will take appropriate action. In our theologies, structures and pastoral ministry, let us bear witness as a sanctuary and a light – a safe place to share stories; to encounter and embody the love of God.

Note

1   Charlotte Bunch, *The Intolerable Status Quo: Violence Against Women and Girls* (UNICEF, 1997).

Resources for reading, reflection and action

Pamela Cooper-White, *The Cry of Tamar: Violence Against Women and the Church's Response* (Fortress Press, 1995).

Empowered to Love: Ballycastle Declaration from a Consultation on Violence Against Women in Europe, Held at Corrymeela Centre, Ballycastle, Northern Ireland, 1994 (WCC/Conference of European Churches – available from WCC/CEC, Geneva, or from CCBI, London. This was one of a series of regional consultations organized by the WCC during the Ecumenical Decade of Churches in Solidarity with Women 1988–98. Other declarations, and further information, from the WCC Women's Desk).

A. Gnanadason, *No Longer a Secret* (WCC Risk Publications, 1993; 2nd revised edn now in preparation).

Hands to End Violence: A Resource Book for Theological Reflection and Action (prepared by Women's Inter-Church Council; available from CCBI, or from NEWS, Scottish Churches House, Dunblane FK15 0AJ, Scotland, UK, tel +1786 823588).

Excellent training materials are available from the Center for the Prevention of Domestic and Sexual Violence, 1914 North 34th Street, Suite 105, Seattle, Washington 98103–9058, USA.

Church and State in Lesotho: reflections of a retired bishop

Philip Mokuku

The reflections shared in these pages are a product of priestly ministry in the mountain Kingdom of Lesotho, within the Church of the Province of Southern Africa. Geographically, Lesotho is totally engulfed by the Republic of South Africa. It is very mountainous with a rugged terrain, with some peaks as high as 3,500 metres, hence the intimation 'The mountain Kingdom'. There are two million people, 86 per cent of whom are Christians, and the remaining 14 per cent consists of Muslims and those who follow traditional religion. These statistics help to set the stage for Church and State relations.

Lesotho's encounter with missionaries was in 1833 through the Paris Evangelical Missionary Society. They were followed by the Roman Catholics and the Anglicans in 1846 and 1875 respectively. These missionary groups were invited by King Moshoeshoe the Great as agents of peace, in a Kingdom which was unstable and surrounded by warring tribes. The missionaries contributed to nation-building efforts by establishing schools to promote literacy and farming technology. Through their advice the King asked for Basotho protection from Queen Victoria of Britain in 1868, and Lesotho became a British Protectorate for the next 98 years. It was not long, though, before the Roman Catholic and Protestant missionaries engaged in unhealthy and divisive competition.

In 1966 the country gained its independence from Britain, adopting a Westminster style of government with the King as its head. Unfortunately, since that time the country has experienced serious instability characterized by coups and counter-coups. These bred intense hatred and prejudice among the people. The Churches which were already divided were also used to fuel this situation. Thank God, even in this confusion the Churches recognized that their differences were being exploited and that they were engaging in unhealthy politics. So they sought a better way of dealing with the situation. They mooted the idea of development projects with the aim of bringing people together, thus promoting unity and co-operation among the Christians. Thabakhupa, an ecumenical centre, was established as a result, offering a range of skills to all. This ecumenical movement was nursed by the Anglican Church, which also played a mediatory role between the Roman Catholic and the Lesotho Evangelical Churches. It also contributed, together with other denominations, to the promotion of justice, reconciliation and peace. In the late 1960s the Christian Council of Lesotho was established to intensify, extend and facilitate inter-denominational co-operation. The Council grew rapidly because of the selfless commitment of its leadership to unity, development and peace. It concerned itself with the limited job situation, the devastating poverty, the problems of migrant workers and their families, and social welfare.

The political situation was becoming more confused with political parties espousing divergent principles ranging from Marxism to Pan-Africanism which threatened the monarchy and amicable relations with the Republic of South Africa. The Pan-Africanist oriented party's government adopted a ruthless dictatorship with which the Church had to wrestle for well over two decades. In the confusion, a state of emergency was declared and a lot of people were either murdered, arrested or forced into exile by Chief Leabua Jonathan, then Prime Minister. In 1974 there was an attempted coup which saw the King placed under house arrest for sus-pected complicity. Some people's homes were burnt down in the process.

The Churches' response was to send a delegation to the Cabinet, comprising Anglican, Lesotho Evangelical Church, Roman Catholic and Methodist representatives with a message of caution and advice. This gesture was not welcomed by the powers that were. The Churches then issued a statement denouncing acts of harassment and appealed to the consciences of the Basotho people to 'carry each other's burdens . . . ' as a Christian community. It also called on Government to stop intimidations and wanton killings of its defenceless citizens. The Church was indeed taking up the role of being 'the voice of the voiceless', thus effectively using its public credible position. A pastoral letter was distributed to all churches in 1975 in which the Church leaders made a public confession on their own behalf for past failures to boldly represent Christ. This was done in the spirit of the Apostle James's injunction, 'Therefore confess your sins to each other so that you may be healed' (James 5.16). In the letter the leaders asked for forgiveness from the faithful as well as the nation and proclaimed their resolve to be true and faithful witnesses of Christ. It also called on all people to follow suit. Its first launch was in Maseru, the capital, at an ecumenical prayer meeting.

The pastoral letter's appeal was met by escalating violence, which became the primary concern of the Church. The Church had to translate its letter into action. It found ways of helping those who had lost their homes and property in the violence, with some leaders risking their own safety by offering asylum to the displaced. The government of the day considered this as a direct challenge, which it did not take kindly to.

Desmond Tutu's arrival as Bishop of Lesotho strengthened the Church. Though his tenure of office was short-lived, a legacy of passion for human rights which he inspired remains in the Church in Lesotho to this day. Inspired by a new vision, the Church made a fresh and passionate representation to Chief Jonathan persuading him to stop violence and enter into talks with other political representatives. When this seemed not to work, Church leaders introduced confidential bilateral talks with government ministers about the possibility of talks. Anglican and Roman Catholic bishops played a key role in this, resulting in the acceptance in principle of the much-called-for talks. The difficulty was that the exiled leader of the other party, Ntsu Mokhehle, was to be in attendance. Since the time was not right and the demand too heavy, the Church once again played a major role in easing the tension.

Once again hell broke loose: Government forces and exiled liberation armies were fighting each other, in the process killing and maiming innocent unarmed civilians. The Apartheid regime supported the exiled leader Ntsu Mokhehle and gave his army a base within South Africa. The situation was really out of hand. In a bid to promote peace among the Basotho, the Christian Council of Lesotho with the help of its Botswana counterpart established contacts with the exiled nationals. This meant that Church representatives had to travel the length and breadth of Botswana and South Africa in search of Basotho refugees. When located, prayers for peace were said and a message of goodwill from the Prime Minister of Lesotho was communicated. Initially this was viewed with suspicion by the exiles, but later it was accepted for what it was worth. Henceforth the Church delegation acted as an intermediary between Government and the exiles and helped to narrow the gap between them.

With the political scenario cloudy and foggy, Church leaders constantly appealed to the nation for sanity. Communication took the form of pastoral letters, press statements, ecumenical prayer meetings and sermons, all focusing on justice, peace and reconciliation. Such messages sought to exhort the faithful to prayer and fasting, asking them to stand firm against the forces of sin, evil, greed and selfishness, 'For we live and work in the confident knowledge that God, in his mercy and in the power of the Holy Spirit has brought us out of darkness into his marvellous light'. In 1985 Church leaders wrote a letter to the diplomatic missions in Maseru, expressing concern over what seemed to them apathy on the part of the missions who were turning a blind eye to the suffering of the Basotho. They also noted that some countries were constantly supplying arms to the warring factions, so that 'Mosotho killed another Mosotho; a person killed his brother. In fact the nation was destroying itself with outside help.' The letter ended with an appeal to all countries involved to desist from and avoid using Basotho as pawns. This made the heads of foreign missions recognize the mediating role of the Church in the civil conflict, and from then onwards they maintained frequent contacts with the Church leaders' secretariat.

Chief Jonathan's decision to align with the African National Congress, Nelson Mandela's political party, made him an enemy of South Africa. South African Forces raided ANC bases in Lesotho, adding to the confusion. These raids triggered a worldwide Church reaction: they were condemned outright. Church leaders registered their concern by writing a letter of protest to the South African Minister of Foreign Affairs stating that ' ... killing of innocent people was not a valid Christian response to any crisis whatsoever ... ' and that they believed that 'the way of Christ sought to preserve life rather than destroy it'.

The coup of 20 January 1986 brought to an end twenty years of Prime Minister Leabua Jonathan's dictatorial rule. Though it was a military regime, headed by King Moshoeshoe II and Major General Metsing Lekhanya, it brought great relief and expectations for true reconciliation and peace. It drew personnel for the Council of Ministers from a wide spectrum, and all exiled people, including leaders of opposition parties, returned to Lesotho. The Church welcomed the military takeover with caution. At an opportune gathering at Thaba-Bosiu the Church expressed the understanding that the military regime was transitional, and that members of its two councils should not entrench themselves. Later they also sent a memorandum to the King expressing their misgivings about his leadership of a military government. This made the Church the conscience of the nation in a true sense, and its efforts culminated in talks designed to return the country to a Constitutional government.

It was not long before the Church's misgivings were confirmed. The military government stalled progress towards a Constitutional government, a power struggle arose within the military junta, the King and the Chairman of the Military Council were at odds. This led to a second military coup, which exiled the King. Once more the Church had to pick up the threads, and champion the cause for reconciliation between the King and the military junta. The King was allowed back home in 1992. In March 1993 general elections were held, King Moshoeshoe II, who had been deposed in 1990, was reinstated in 1994 through the intervention of Church leaders and the heads of frontline states (Southern Africa).

The Church's responsibility has been to help the government nurture the fragile democracy. Power struggle within the one-party government ranks is threatening its survival. The new Prime Minister, Ntsu Mokhehle, has created a new political party, the Lesotho Congress for Democracy, and labelled it 'the ruling party'. This has created a lot of confusion among the electorate who voted him in as a Basotho Congress Party member. Church leaders have drawn the Prime Minister's attention to this. Archbishop Winston Ndungane has said 'I am hopeful that in a land in which the general salutation is one of peace (*khotso*), we will see the same progress and growth opportunities that are occurring in other Southern African States. This would be consistent with the resurgence of an African renaissance for which many political, business and religious leaders are vividly working on the continent.'

In democratic Lesotho, the Church has to search for a new role in society. The prophetic ministry should remain an essential part of its ministry. Co-operation between the Church and State in the educational and health areas has developed enormously in recent years. In times of need the government readily turns to the Church for help, a recognition of the Church's contribution to national unity. The Church is also working closely with the non-governmental organizations in matters of common concern and national interest. Clearly, the Church in Lesotho is no longer the only public voice, and so its role as 'voice of the voiceless' has become a shared responsibility in recent years. However, the Church and the State need to interpret each other's activities in a positively interactive manner since they both claim the loyalties of the people.

Khotso! *Pula*! *Nala*! Peace! Rain! Prosperity!

Resisting *vumilia*[1] theology
The Church and violence against women in Kenya

Esther Mombo

'Women are like matatus. If you miss one, you will always get another.'

Introduction

Violence against women in Kenya cuts across all groups regardless of their socio-economic background. Physical and/or psychological torture is rampant at home, school, office, market, matatu and even in church.[2] In most cases, the violence either goes unnoticed as 'normal' occurrence or is treated as a private 'women's' matter because it is deeply rooted in the traditional perception of women by men: a tradition reinforced by Judeo-Christian religion. The situation is also aggravated by past and present socio-economic situations characterized by greed and power inherent in the establishment that allows publicity of such violence in matatus. Yet women are expected to endure these insults without raising an eyebrow.

Violence in matatus

In Kenya, the matatu is one of the most popular means of public road transport. It is notorious for bribery, and for accidents, as vehicle drivers rarely obey traffic rules. They are known for overloading, over-speeding, poor maintenance and pollution. Passengers have no say on board, as the aim of the cut-throat business is to make quick profits. The system is increasingly becoming out of government control – hence the freedom to use any vulgar language (written or verbal) against passengers especially women.

Matatus are loud, musically and graphically. Most of the graphics include derogatory remarks about women, such as:

'A woman is like a cob of maize . . . any man can chew.'

'Women are like matatus, if you miss one, you will always get another.'

The abusive postings that are inscribed on the walls of matatus justify and encourage the various forms of violence against women in their everyday life. Nobody has ever taken action against this form of injustice.

The Church and *vumilia* theology

Although the Kenyan Anglican Church, like most other Churches, is known for championing acts of justice and as a voice for the voiceless, its own structure renders it incompetent as a good example in dealing with most issues that concern women.[3] Although women are a majority in church, they have remained on the periphery of the Church's decision-making bodies that deliberate on women issues. Women who work within the Church as Church Army sisters, deaconesses, deacons and priests raise issues of injustice and discrimination.[4]

Mothers' Union

Kenya boasts of a vast number of women's groups organized along economic and/or religious lines. Women organizing and working together owes its origin to traditional clan support systems. The multiplicity of these groups could be viewed as a good thing, but it also shows how women have been sidelined from the mainstream patriarchal systems characteristic of Kenyan ethnic groups and they have had to group together in order to voice their presence.[5]

The Mothers' Union (MU) is one such group and stands as the largest women's organization in the Anglican Church of Kenya (CPK).[6] Its members undertake many important initiatives with women. Never-theless, a brief analysis of MU shows some of the complexities involved in the issue of violence against women. It consists of members whose marriages have been blessed by the Church. Missionary wives founded the organization in 1918. In 1956, the first African women were admitted into Union. MU leadership remained in the hands of missionaries until 1970 when African women took over.[7]

The MU is structured in such a way that the wife of the Archbishop is its head. MU is used by the main Church as a fringe to disseminate its theology on family life as enshrined in these aims:

- to uphold Christ's teaching on the nature of marriage and to promote its wider understanding
- to encourage parents to bring up their children in faith and life of the Church
- to maintain a worldwide fellowship of Christians united in prayer and the protection of children to help those whose life has met with adversity.[8]

Since the aim of MU is to promote and support women to be 'good mothers and wives', it seeks to develop Christian values and foster positive attitudes among families. Because of its strong emphasis on the 'traditional family', MU sidelines certain categories of women such as single mothers. One would expect the issues of violence against women to be a priority to the MU and other Church groups. However, like the mainstream Church, MU gives an impression that its members are not violated and if they are, it is because the individual has a problem in managing her family.

It is in this relation that members of MU, to retain membership, conceal issues such as marital rape or wife-battering thus submitting themselves to the ideology of the organization. Preference to personal safety may mean leaving a family thus rendering a woman separated or divorced, contrary to the group's ideals. This means that few women develop the courage to speak up or leave a violent situation.

The conflict between encouraging women's participation in the MU and their enforcement of patriarchal values leads to a *'vumilia* theology'. This theology is implied in sermons and speeches given during occasions such as engagements, weddings and funerals. It is based on interpretations of certain biblical passages.[9] It encourages women's passive submission as good virtues of motherhood, and violence against women is women's fault as in the case of Tino cited at the end of this chapter. Invariably, women are encouraged to:

> Go back to him. ... Learn how to adjust to his moods ... don't do anything that would provoke his anger ... Christ suffered and died for you on the cross ... can't you bear some suffering too?[10]

Along the same line Rose Waruhiu has rightly observed that:

> In many Christian prayer meetings, which have taken root in religious revivals, women are perpetuating their own oppression by accepting that they must suffer and toil, as was 'destined' in the Bible. Women are for example unwilling to act against their husbands who batter them or mistreat the family.[11]

This kind of understanding has led most women to interpret violence against them as 'walking in the footsteps of Christ' or 'bearing the cross'. Much time is spent by the women praying for themselves and their molesters to 'change' or 'repent'. Most women do not reveal mistreatment, either because they are not trusted or because the Church is silent or because it will deny its occurrence.

The Anglican Church in Kenya has denied the existence of marital rape. A national task force looking at laws relating to women observed that the law shielded various forms of violence including marital rape. In reaction to this, the Archbishop challenged the Attorney General by arguing that he was interfering with the social lives of Kenyans by inciting women to rebel against their husbands. The Archbishop termed the views of the Attorney General 'westernised and impractical in the African social set-up'.[12]

The Tino–Nduko case

The following case illustrates *vumilia* theology, a basic Church problem-solving strategy, which continues to dehumanize women:

Tino (31) and Nduko (39) are members of a local Anglican church. Tino is a member of the Mothers' Union. When she received promotion at work, Nduko objected and instead asked her to stop working and stay at home with the family. They talked about this between them, but did not seem to come to an agreement. Tino argued that the family needed both incomes for an adequate living standard, but Nduko insisted that she stopped working, threatening her with 'discipline'.

He started to beat her each time she came home from work. Tino shared this with members of her MU, who then prayed with her. They promised to continue to pray. One night, Tino was badly beaten and sought refuge at a neighbour's house. Nduko followed her there to continue the beating. The neighbours protected Tino and brought her to a local priest. After hearing her story, he took her to her house and discussed the matter with the husband.

After listening to both, he read Ephesians 4.21 and gave a short homily stressing that Tino being a mother and a member of the MU should take care of the family. He than prayed for the couple and left. Nduko was glad that the local priest had brought Tino back to the house and had supported him by asking her to be submissive.

After a few days Nduko resumed the beating. Tino again sought refuge, and 'shared' testimony with the members of MU, who asked her to *vumilia* because 'that was life for most women'. Her life was becoming a misery, as she could bear no more. She decided to leave and escape this violence. But she was not accepted by the MU as she had broken her marriage vows. In a subsequent sermon the local priest urged the members of MU to teach 'young women' how to take care of their families and prevent break-ups even if they were economically 'independent'. Women had to obey the marriage vows, but he was silent on men's beatings.

Conclusion

This article shows that the patriarchal values inherent in both African and biblical cultures have produced a *vumilia* theology, which is disseminated through MU as one of the Church structures. It is being challenged by lone voices that are bringing to light issues of violence against women.[13] There is a need for women in Kenya to stand together to protest against the affront of human dignity. The potential of the strong religious groups exemplified by MU needs to be tapped to challenge society's understanding of what is acceptable. This movement must emerge from the cries of the women, and receive support from the Church so that the whole Church may move closer to the vision of Christ.

Notes

1 *Vumilia* is a Kiswahili word which means 'endure', and in this chapter it connotes passive submission.
2 The forms of violence include wife-beating, rape and sexual harassment, female genital mutilation, forms of marriage such as child brides.
3 Henry Okullu, *Church and State* (Nairobi: Uzima, 1984); David Gitari, *Let the Bishop Speak* (Nairobi: Uzima, 1993). Both books give emphasis to the prophetic role of the Church, especially in matters of the Church in society, but little is said about violence against women in particular.
4 Association of CPK Women in the Ministry (ASWOM) was formed in 1993 with an aim of being a forum through which the women working in CPK would share and raise issues that affect them and other women in that Church. The fact that this body was formed shows that there were no other ways in which the voices of these women could be heard.
5 Shanyisa A. Khasiani and E. I. Njiro (eds), *The Women's Movement in Kenya* (Nairobi: Association of African Women for Research and Development, 1993), p. 116.
6 United Society of Friends Women (Quakers), Women's Guild (Presbyterian Church of East Africa), Catholic Women Association (Catholic Church) and Women's Fellowship (Methodist Church).
7 *Rabai to Mumias: A Short History of the Church of the Province of Kenya 1844–1994* (Uzima: Provincial Unit of Research, Church of the Province of Kenya, 1994).
8 Ibid., p. 156.
9 For example, Genesis 2.18–25; the book of Ruth, which is quoted in most wedding invitation cards; Ephesians 4.21, etc.
10 Aruna Gnanadason, *No Longer a Secret: The Church and Violence Against Women* (Geneva: WCC, 1993), p. 1.
11 Rose Waruhiu, 'What do African women want' in Georgina Ashworth (ed.), *A Diplomacy of the Oppressed: New Directions in International Feminism* (London: Zed Books Ltd, 1995), p. 144.
12 *The Daily Nation* (17 June 1994).
13 The Circle of Third World Theologians, Kenya Chapter.

A Structural Adjustment Programme and its effects on the Zambian people and the Zambian Church

Robert Mumbi

Introduction

Zambia is a predominantly Christian country. The Anglican Church is just one, fairly small Church among the rich variety of Christian communities: Roman Catholic, United Church of Zambia, Adventist and Pentecostal. All Christians in Zambia, indeed all Zambians, are caught up in the problems which SAP has induced, and this account does not, therefore, single out Anglicans for any special treatment. Economic development or lack of it affects the lives of everyone, young and old, men and women, Muslim and Christian.

To understand how the Third World countries accumulated huge debts we need to go back through the years and find out the cause. In about 1973, there was a rise in oil prices and the commercial banks in the United States and Europe were flooded with oil money. The banks were desperate to find customers to borrow this money, as the banks wanted not to cause inflation but to make profits. They were interested in the countries that looked economically promising. Zambia, because of its copper, was one of them. The two multilateral financial institutions – International Monetary Fund and World Bank – were trying to help those countries considered very poor by encouraging long-term investment in economic reconstruction and development.

With so much money in the banks, the interest rates on the loans were very low. The beginning of the crisis began when the United States administration pushed up world interest rates in order to attract capital from all over the world to cover its mounting trade and budget deficits. As a result of this the 'price of many raw materials such as sugar, cotton, tin and copper collapsed dramatically because demand from the depressed Northern economies slackened while their suppliers attempted to produce more to compensate for their losses.

'Many [developing countries] began to run out of hard currency to pay the interest on their large foreign debts. Most tried to postpone default for

Robert Mumbi

as long as possible by borrowing even more heavily. But ... in August
1982, ... Mexico and ... other developing countries were forced,
reluctantly, to ask the commercial banks to allow them to repay their loans
over a longer period. The banks agreed, but insisted that the debtor nations
should first reach agreement with the International Monetary Fund (IMF)
and an "adjustment programme" ' (*Banking on the Poor: The Ethics of Third
World Debt*, pp. 8–9).

The IMF Structural Adjustment Programmes (SAPs) are intended to
help the countries involved repay their debt. The programme's main
characteristics are: liberalization of the market economy; removal of export
and import barriers creating a free market; devaluating of local currency to
encourage exports while discouraging imports and cutting public spending
to reduce budget deficit, remove subsidies on services and foodstuffs, and
then in the end increase interest rates to discourage borrowing.

Effects on the people

The implementation of SAPs in Zambia has caused great misery to the
people but successful adjustments from IMF's point of view. When the
Zambian government decided to follow strictly SAPs in 1991–92, the first
thing that was announced was for everybody to tighten their belts. Did
people know or understand what the government meant? I don't think so
because everybody was at first happy that they were to start paying back the
loan seriously. But a price had to be paid. Education and health were now
no longer to be free but to be paid for by everybody. The life-style of the
low- and middle-wage earners inevitably began to change in every aspect.
One problem led to another and the whole issue became complex.

Health

SAPs have increased the need among most people in Zambia for health care,
but it has become more difficult to obtain. Men and women are spending
more time in looking for food or the means of getting food. This has caused
the number of malnutrition cases in children to rise. Many people cannot
afford to go or take their relatives and children to the hospital. The number
of people dying at home has definitely risen. Don't ask for statistics on this
matter – just go and stand at the entrance of any government hospital and
count how many bodies of both young and old are brought in dead to the
hospital mortuaries every day. The price of essential drugs makes them
unaffordable for the average person. Curable diseases such as malaria have
become major killers because people's bodies are weak and they cannot

226

afford the drugs. Infant mortality rate has risen, partly because many women give birth at home, because they can't afford to go to hospital.

Education

Knowledge, whether formal or informal, means power to the people. When education is denied to the children, then you are not building the future of the country. With the government's withdrawal of subsidy on education and health, who will support those hundreds and thousands of children whose parents cannot pay for school fees? Where shall we take these children who leave school prematurely?

Who can give me answers to all these questions? Is it IMF or the Zambian government? Children who have dropped out of school have found their way into the street, and are exposed to drugs, abuse and child labour. Walk down any city street and you will find children carrying heavy loads on their heads, selling petty goods, or smoking.

There is a general campaign for the equality of women, but if we cannot prepare the young girls of today to take up the more challenging opportunities of tomorrow, then our fight is in vain. How can we help this campaign when girls lose school places because of inability to pay fees? There is a higher percentage of illiteracy among women compared with that in men. How do we fight this when the government has continually been cutting down the number of school places? When there is a shortage of money in the home, boys are given the first priority to go to school. Education is vital to everybody and denying some because they can't afford it is contributing to the under-development of the country.

Agriculture

Agriculture is the foundation to all development in the country: a nation that cannot feed itself cannot claim independence. Could it also be true to say that in leaving the agricultural sector entirely in private hands, the government is running away from the responsibility of feeding the nation? Zambia's staple food is maize and it is grown mainly by the peasant farmers. The removal of subsidy on all agricultural inputs has hit this group hard because they can no longer afford to buy fertilizers and other requirements. This has resulted in low yields, which ends up with the government importing maize from outside the country. Farmers produce on a small scale; they get very low prices and end up in debt to the bank. Because of the high interest rates in commercial banks very few farmers can manage to secure loans. Many co-operatives have collapsed. The liberalized market has seen the locally-grown crops not selling well on our market because they are expensive compared to cheap imported crops from South

Africa. For the government, cash crops have taken preference to staple foods because they raise foreign exchange to service the debt. When and how will our economy grow if we cannot produce food but rely on yellow handouts in the form of yellow maize from the United States, or cheap maize from South Africa?

Our agricultural market is not strong enough yet to compete with the foreign ones which still get subsidized. Zambia this year will import maize from Zimbabwe to meet the shortfall because many peasant farmers were either discouraged by the previous market price or could not afford the price of the inputs. In spite of these conditions the government will continue to encourage the commercial farmers to grow rose flowers for export to Europe to service the debt. If Structural Adjustment Programmes are designed to improve the economy for the benefit of the people, who will survive to enjoy the fruits?

Devaluation

Devaluation of the currency is meant to attract the foreign buyers of our copper and other raw materials, because this makes them cheap. It also discourages imports, which become more expensive. Yet how can our industry survive if we cannot afford to import spares to sustain the machinery? As a result our industries operate on half capacity. Agriculture is definitely affected when the currency is devalued, for the prices of both the inputs and machinery go up. This has discouraged farmers from growing maize. Farmers go for cash crops that will fetch high value but should they all grow one crop the price will fall.

Devaluation is supposed to encourage food production by making crops grown locally cheaper than the imported ones, but reality is the opposite. Devaluation has brought the rise in price for the essential commodities, leaving the wages and salaries of the people static. This has left the average person with no choice but to reduce the number of meals per day from two to one. SAPs have adjusted the lives of the people, making them without hope, rather than adjusting the economy of Zambia in any beneficial way.

Privatization

To many people in Zambia, privatization means closure of companies and declaring workers redundant. They also look at it as one way for the white man to come back to colonize Zambia, because he wants to run the national companies. To some it is a welcome idea in that it will boost liberalization and the competition of the market. When multinational companies come to Zambia to invest they have already the capacity, money, technology and the international standards. It is very unfair to allow such companies to compete with local firms that have neither the capital nor the technology, are insufficient in capacity and unaccustomed to international standards. Many local private and national companies have been closed down because they have been found not to be viable, e.g. Zambia Airways, the United Bus Company of Zambia, National Marketing Board, the Kabwe Mine, etc. When companies close, workers are thrown out of a job; as they lose a job they also lose a house, because jobs go with houses. In the case of United Bus Company of Zambia (UBZ) people in some remote parts of the country have been deprived of bus services. Many private bus owners do not want to work on the unprofitable routes. They choose where they can make money.

What has happened to all these people who have been working for the companies that have been closed? It seems to me that the government had not prepared enough, if it did at all, because many people now are on the streets looking for employment. The argument the government gives is that this will boost the informal sector, meaning that those being declared redundant will be re-employed running small-scale businesses. But how will our economy grow if everybody in the informal sector is dealing in buying and selling of consumer goods from neighbouring South Africa? Privatization and liberalization have definitely created a good market for South African goods. Whose economy will grow in such a country where most of the goods sold on the market and streets is foreign? How can our economy grow on children and women selling cigarettes, and rolls, milk, second-hand clothes? In short, privatization and liberalization have thrown many people into deeper poverty.

Change in life-style and direct effect on the Church

An average family in Zambia contains about seven members, with men as the bread winners. If a man loses a job then six other people more will have lost regular support and a house. When a man loses a job the pressure is transferred to a woman and children, because they in turn take up the responsibility of supporting the family. The life-style of this family changes, starting with the reduction of meals, selling the car and other items they can no longer maintain. Women are obliged to work longer hours in order to make at least a small profit to carry back home. The change of life-style often brings stress to families, particularly men who find themselves in a position of not supporting their families. There has been a lot of movement of people from one town to another. Traditional and cultural values of looking after one another are slowly disappearing because many people can no longer afford to keep relatives. The Church has become a refuge for those who cannot find help anywhere. It has found itself with more work, dealing with the people with stress, feeding the hungry and caring for the street children. And yet the Church has fewer resources, because the people who supported it financially have lost their jobs. It has become the work of the Church to try to prepare or give counselling to those who are about to be made redundant. Many men and women suffer from hypertension. Some have died from stress, leaving a widow and children. Mrs Maka lives in a shanty township near the city. She is a widow with three children; her husband worked in the mines before he was made redundant. After losing a job, he built himself a simple house in this shanty town because he could not afford a big one in a council township. Mr Maka died six months later, leaving his widow with children but no support.

Zambia accepted Structural Adjustment Programmes because it wanted to get out of the terrible difficulties that were caused by debt. Six years have passed but there is no sign of people living a decent life, yet the cost of living is getting higher and poverty increasing too.

Hopes for Jubilee 2000

For every $4 aid that comes to Zambia, $3 is used to service the debt and $1 for public use, such as health, education and social services. Of the population of 9.4 million, 6.5 million live in poverty. Zambia's external debt in 1996 was $6.57 billion compared to its GDP that was $3.5 billion. With such a figure of debt exceeding GDP how can Zambia pay back the debt, and when will it finish paying? In reality Zambia has already paid for its original loan and is now paying the interest accumulated over the years. How can Zambia develop its economy if 70 per cent of aid is used to pay the debt? Zambia needs aid for development, not to pay debt. Should the $6.57 billion be cancelled, Zambia would concentrate on building its economy. If Zambia were a person, looking at its GDP compared to its debt, it would have been declared bankrupt. But is there any law that would find a country bankrupt? No. Jubilee 2000 is campaigning for the cancellation of the unpayable debt for the countries like Zambia. When debt is cancelled the Zambian government should develop the agricultural industry for two purposes. First, to have enough food to feed the nation and to export to other countries to earn money. Secondly, this is the area that would create employment. It is only agriculture that can develop rural areas to de-urbanize the congested cities. Zambia is one of the most urbanized countries in Africa because of the copper mines and many people come to the copper belt to seek employment. With the privatization process in the country, many mines would be bought by the multinational companies who will take their shares out leaving the country with not much to develop with. If Zambia wants to develop, it must look at the people and compare their needs with the resources. Can the people sustain themselves without developing agriculture? No, I don't think it is possible. We badly need agriculture now and not mines. The government must protect the peasant farmers who produce maize to feed nations. It is only food sufficiency that will build our economy. The international institutions must see that there is a fair trade between North and South. In the absence of fair trade, the Southern countries will come back to the same position of heavy indebtedness.

Further reading

Adjustment in Africa: Reforms, Results, and the Road Ahead (A World Bank Policy Research Report; Oxford: Oxford University Press, 1994).
G. A. Cornia, Richard Jolly and Frances Stewart, *Adjustment with a Human Face* (Oxford: UNICEF and Oxford University Press, 1987).
The Debt Cutter's Handbook (Jubilee 2000, 1996).
Susan George, *The Debt Boomerang* (London: Pluto Press, 1992).
Susan George and Fabrizzio Sabelli, *Faith and Credit: The World Bank's Secular Empire* (London: Penguin, 1994).
Bob Goudzwaard and Harry de Lange, *Beyond Poverty and Affluence: Toward an Economy of Care* (WCC, 1995).
Peter Selby, *Grace and Mortgage: The Language of Faith and the Debt of the World* (London: Darton, Longman and Todd, 1997).

Male circumcision (*imbalu*) among the Bagisu of Uganda and the mission of the Church

Beatrice Musindi

The Bagisu are a people living in the eastern part of Uganda. They are also called the Bamasaaba, taking their name from the great mountain, Masaaba (Mount Elgon to the British), which dominates the whole area. The Bagisu are a diverse group of people, based on clans and, in pre-colonial times, without a single ruler. What has united them as a particular people, and distinguished them from neigbouring groups, has been the cultural rite of circumcision (*imbalu*), performed biennially throughout the tribe. This is the corporate initiation of adolescent males into manhood. In some parts of Africa, embracing Christ and his Church meant a radical rejection of African cultural values – in parts of Kenya, for example, circumcision became the focus of bitter conflict between culture and Christianity. But my experience as a Mugisu Christian has shown me that most, if not all, Bagisu Christians practise Christian rites alongside cultural practices. Bugisu is a strongly Christian and Christianized part of Uganda, with the Anglican Church of Uganda as a major presence. There is also an important Roman Catholic presence, and a stronger tradition of Independent Churches than has tended to characterize Uganda as a whole.

Amid all the changes of this century, *imbalu* is still of immense importance for all Bagisu. It distinguishes men from boys, and Bagisu from the neighbouring 'uncircumcised' peoples who surround them. It has profound social and political implications for individual and community and the Church cannot afford to ignore it.

Indeed, for many Bagisu Christians, what God has done in Christ is part of the wonderful thing God did in Abraham. The culture of circumcision practised by Bagisu brings the experience of Israel into their modern context. Both are seen as incorporating youth into the community. *Imbalu* gives the initiate a sense of belonging to a special tribal brotherhood commonly called *Bamakokyi*, which is responsible for teaching social morality and the secrets of the tribe. The moral code of the Bagisu is bound up with the custom of circumcision. The challenge for Christian Bagisu is to attach spiritual significance to *imbalu*, to adapt or integrate the rite into the Christian doctrinal tradition.

There are some aspects of the rituals that are incompatible with the Christian gospel. What seems clear about the Church's stand is that it regards various aspects of the ceremonies as obscene and degrading but does not object to the physical operation itself. During the ceremonies, a great deal of beer is consumed with subsequent loss of self-control. For initiates, normal rules of conduct can appear suspended, as their absorption in the dancing and the *imbalu* seems to make normal courtesies of everyday life irrelevant. Furthermore, the *kadodi* dance is seen by the Church as being too sexually explicit.

One response of the Church is to advocate circumcision in hospital as a child. This ensures care in operation, less pain, better treatment and the use of sterilized instruments. But many see this as emptying the rite of meaning. *Imbalu* is above all a test of courage and endurance, and this is more important than the actual physical operation. Moreover, each time a man faces problems, he is expected to recall the pain of circumcision and to face difficulties with determination. From this point of view, circumcision done in hospital is rather pointless. It is not, therefore, surprising that those who have it are not accepted as real men. They are referred to as *abafu*, literally 'dead men': cowards, those not respected.

The operation is embedded in a richly symbolic set of rituals associated with ancestral worship, invocation of spirits and sacrifices to the dead. This holds a profound significance to the candidates and their families. The visitation of ancestral graves and cultural sites entails veneration of ancestors and minor deities. In fact, many Bagisu believe that the ancestral spirits appear to circumcised men and to the candidates. This is viewed by the Church as an occasion of spiritual degradation, and coming under the condemnation of Deuteronomy 18.9–14, prohibiting all forms of soothsaying and divination. The traditional Gisu attempt to explain and control evil or misfortune by reference to witchcraft or sorcery is regarded by the Church as a baseless supersitition which should be banished. Likewise, the sacrifices which form an important part of ritual circumcision are condemned by the Church. The widespread belief about the role of the ancestors is questioned by the Church.

Nevertheless, the content and meaning of *imbalu* could be transformed into an indigenous experience of Christian faith. In fact consideration should be given to the feasibility of incorporating into the liturgy an order of service for circumcision ceremonies. In this regard it would also have to be decided whether the ceremonies should be held in the Church or should be done in the traditional or cultural sites. Cultural ceremonies such as the blowing, or spitting, of millet beer over a person (*khubiita*) and ceremony of smearing with mud (*litosi*) will have to be examined.

Wherever possible, the Church itself should arrange the ceremony and also the necessary care during the circumcision period. Traditionally, on the day following circumcision the candidates are given tribal teachings. In my view, the time for ritual ceremonies should serve as a time for offering Christian teaching and lessons from the Bible. Some of the families might have no contact with the Church, so it is an opportune moment for the Church to reach out to them.

The Bagisu ritual of circumcision should be capable of re-interpretation and reconceptualization. For example, the idea that *imbalu* is a personal test of bravery and self-control, publicly witnessed, should be given a spiritual interpretation as well. It would be the duty of the Church elders to visit the boys and give them Christian teaching. In regard to *imbalu* as a preparation for hardships in this world, it could be argued that in human strength we can do nothing except for Christ who strengthens us (Phil 4.12). If we consider the question of suffering, when Christians encounter it, they should always be reminded of the pain Jesus went through because of their sins. This helps the person to accept the privilege of sharing in the glorious walk with Jesus Christ, the Suffering Servant.

In its teaching, the Church should make reference to physical circumcision to illustrate the Christian transformation which can be referred to as the circumcision of the heart. Emphasis should therefore be put on repentance of the heart which leads a person to cut off the lust of the flesh. In these ways the Church should build upon and not destroy the earlier meaning of the ritual. The Bagisu should be encouraged to see Jesus as an ancestor who is the new source of human lineage. There is no doubt that *imbalu* has immemorial religious riches. The blood shed at circumcision binds the people together just as the blood of Jesus brings all nations together. As they sing and dance together, the Bagisu portray a sense of corporate solidarity and common ancestry. This endorses the concept that the self-understanding of the African is not simply as an individual but as part of a community. To ascertain this, life is both shared and celebrated, hence the emphasis on participation and initiation. The mission of the Church should be to strengthen this unity amongst the people. Love for one another and the unity of all God's people should be at the forefront of the Church's agenda.

The anticipation with which *imbalu* is looked forward to shows that this is one of the customs in Uganda that is not about to be discarded. The chorus 'Sheta umwana afane baba we' (Circumcise the son so he may look like his father) is as popular as ever. The ritual of male circumcision has positively affected the Christians in many aspects of their fellowship and love for one another. The strengthening of this fellowship through the outworking of love in the mission of the Church is vital. Clearly it is right for the Church to get involved in the circumstances that face society. It hurts when people find that the Church is not addressing the issues at stake. Mission in Christ's way calls for humility and obedience. Attitudes based on ideas of superiority ought to be abandoned. Indeed, as the saying goes, 'The Church ought to be scratching where it is itching'.

Spirituality and sexuality: Christians and sexual behaviour today

Michael Nazir-Ali

During the course of the debate on human sexuality in the General Synod of the Church of England, there were several statements of the Church's teaching, but none of them said *why* the Church teaches as it does. It is very important to explain the Church's teaching if it is not to seem like the mere repetition of old slogans.

Because of creativity and sociability, the range of human behaviour is very wide and, unlike with most other creatures, human sexuality pervades every area of our being. That is why we can talk of 'sexy' voices or movements and even of 'sexy' activities or professions. In our case, we simply cannot limit sexuality to its genital expression. It has to be understood in the context of the wholeness of our humanity.

Even in its physical expression, however, human sexuality has a 'unitive' aspect to it which promotes affection and love between persons. This experience of union, on which there is so much biblical reflection, has to be set alongside the procreative dimension of sex. Both St Augustine and Thomas Aquinas acknowledge the companionship and love which exists between sexual partners, and some of the Reformers, such as Calvin, see this unitive state as one of the building blocks of society.

It is true, of course, that friendship, companionship and even love are not limited to sexual partnership and may be experienced over a wide range of human experience and relationships. For example, at different times and in many cultures, there has been an intensity of love and friendship in same-sex relations which has enriched society and which has sometimes been missing in heterosexual marriage.

Family life takes many different forms in different cultures and ranges from the nuclear to the extended family and even to wider kinship groups. Whatever the form, the union of a man and a woman for fellowship and for the nurture of children remains at the heart of authentic manifestations of family life. Without this, there can be friendships and even 'family-like' structures for support but not the stable and committed relationship which is needed for the nurture of the young.

If human sexuality is ordered towards the 'goods' of marriage which include that experience of union which is open to the creation and nurture of life, then, it can also be said, other manifestations of the physical expression of human sexuality will not be seen as normative and may be seen as lacking in the fullness of God's purpose for human sexuality.

We must be careful, however, of jumping to moral conclusions. Even if a certain kind of sexuality cannot be seen as normative and lacks something of God's will for human sexual expression, this does not mean that people have freely *chosen* such a sexuality for themselves. We do not, for instance, know of all the causes of homosexual orientation and behaviour, but it seems fairly clear that homosexual orientation is often fixed in childhood and that, in many cases, reorientation is difficult, if not impossible. On the other hand, there are those in the radical lobby who see it precisely as a matter of choice and of the right to choose. There is some evidence that exposure to a homosexual environment can 'trigger' homosexual practice for a number, though prior 'disposition' may also be a factor in such cases. Such a disposition may account for the presence of homosexuality in cultures such as traditional Muslim societies, where the environment itself is hostile to homosexual orientation and practice. These are aspects of the issue which need to be taken into account when questions like the age of consent are discussed. The legal age for consent is determined by a complex of factors which include the age at which sexual orientation might become 'fixed', the possibilities of exploitation by people in a dominant position, and by society's attitude to sexual behaviour of a certain kind.

In terms of pastoral care, it is paramount that the Church should assure all of God's love and acceptance of who they *are* (even if this does not imply acceptance of all that they *do*). While the Church should continue to teach clearly that God's purpose for us is to express our sexuality within an ordered pattern of life which involves either marriage or singleness in a way that is both sacrificial and fulfilling, it should also continue to make sensitive pastoral provision for those who struggle with the Church's teaching and their sexuality.

In particular, all should be welcome in church to hear God's Word, to participate in Christian worship – and to be strengthened by the friendship and fellowship of Christians. Recognizing the importance of conscience, the Church will encourage people to reflect constantly on their life-style in the light of God's Word. It follows from this that the Church will have to respect the decisions of an informed conscience even where it cannot agree with them.

At the same time, it is clear also that those who hold public office in the Church should exemplify the Church's teaching, particularly in a matter as fundamental as the expression of human sexuality. This is not, as is commonly believed, a matter of 'double standards'. Scripture is clear that an exemplary life-style is required of those who lead the Church and who have a special responsibility in teaching and preaching. The response of the clergy to this may only be a feeling of inadequacy and a desire to cry out 'Lord have mercy!' The ideal and the standard are clear, though it is only through grace that we are able to live them out. We know also of God's forgiveness when we fall short of divine standards and the possibility of a fresh start. The fact that those who hold public office in the Church are called to be 'examples to the flock' implies, of course, that they are examples *to others* in the Church. The teaching is for all but some are called to be especially vigilant in embodying it in their lives and families.

Clarity about the Christian position in this area, as in other areas of moral concern, is crucial in the context of dialogue with people of other faiths. They are often puzzled by the diversity of Christian opinion and need an account from Christians which is clearly based in a sound theological anthropology. Indeed, it is this which saves the Christian position from being merely an arbitrary set of rules which can easily be set aside.

It is important that sexuality should be seen both as a gift from God and as affected by human fallenness and frailty in the same way as our other faculties and affections. This means, on the one hand, that sexuality cannot be seen as an unmixed blessing. Like everything else, it has potential for great good but also for much evil. On the other hand, we must be careful that we do not set sexual sin, of whatever kind, in a category of its own. It has, rather, to be understood in the *total* context of our calling as persons and our failure to live up to this calling.

Youth and the Anglican Church in Madagascar

J. Bruno Ndriamahafahana

Of Madagascar's population of nearly 13 million, some 55 per cent are less than 20 years old.[1] The majority live in rural areas and are relatively unskilled. Nevertheless the proportion in schools is high when compared with many sub-Saharan African countries, and the gap between the genders is low.

There are four major Christian groups: Roman Catholic, Lutheran, the United Protestant Church (basically Presbyterian) and the Malagasy Episcopal Church. There is a small Muslim community. A good percentage of the population still belong to traditional religion, with a belief in Zagnahary – God the Creator.

In Malagasy culture, the meaning of the word 'youth' is very relative. Almost anyone can be considered young – even at 50 – especially if their parents or older siblings are still alive. A younger brother is less likely to be considered a 'youth' even if he stays with an elder sister than the other way round – Malagasy society is still male-dominated.

Fewer than two Malagasy out of every three have been to school for any period of their life. The rate increases to 81 per cent for the province of Antananarivo (around the capital), down to only 38 per cent for Mahajanga, in the mid-west. Rural areas are disadvantaged, partly because teachers are less motivated to work in what they consider to be remote areas, inaccessible to motor car or even push bike. Where teachers are content to live in rural areas it is often because of personal commercial interests such as farming rather than interest in teaching rural children. Few children reach secondary level, and it is reckoned that only 15 per cent of the population has any fluency in French – mostly these are from urban areas and between 35 and 50 years old. This is an indication of the decline in educational standards in more recent years.

From a total of about 6 million people reckoned to be employed, nearly 5 million work in the agricultural domain. Less than half a million work in factories – and even in this sector there is increasing redundancy and unemployment as technology advances. Commercial activities provide about 300,000 jobs – but often these are jobs in the informal economy, scraping a subsistence in petty trading and the like. The number of civil servants is about 164,000 (one state employee to every 75 inhabitants). Urban civil servants tend to have a privileged situation. In the private sector, many are engaged in low-paid domestic activities.

Though the term 'unemployment' is common, it is worthwhile asking: who are the unemployed? In fact, unemployment is essentially an urban phenomenon. One can see it in the villages, true, especially as a result of excessive division of meagre plots of land. But no one in the village will fail to have food, because of the communal nature of life. As education in rural areas is so precarious, youngsters leave for towns hoping for a better life. But lack of qualification prevents them from getting jobs. In the end they have to return to their home villages to live with their parents and become a burden to them. The opportunities for children born in the towns is slightly better, in that they may have had better education over a longer period, and they can afford to hang on, living with their parents in the town while looking for jobs. In recent years inflation and the high cost of living has meant that even the formerly privileged civil servants find it hard to make ends meet – most of them go in for secondary jobs of various kinds. Social insurance benefits are elementary and are non-existent in terms of retirement pensions, paid holidays, sickness benefit, written contracts or compensation after injury at work.

This situation means that child labour is common. Girls in rural areas are often asked by parents to walk around their village to sell buns, fried fish or sweet potatoes each morning before school or in the evenings. They might be exempted on Sunday because of church services. Young boys from the age of nine usually take cattle to the fields. In urban areas they have the same problems, selling ground-nuts, especially near venues for video-shows (these are small commercial rooms with a video-TV, which in many places have almost replaced the older cinema halls).

As churchgoers reflect social life, Church life itself reflects and refers to what happens in society. The majority of people in society are youth – and that is true also of the Church. Many are economically deprived, fighting for the minimum of food and clothing. They are, of course, God's people longing for education and training. They are God's creatures, answering his call and turning to the Church. They are God's flock. In the tiny cathedral of the Episcopal Church at Antsiranana (at the northern point of the island) the majority of the 300 congregation will be children – packing into the church, standing outside for the major festivals. They are also the majority filling the parish church of Avanatranjoma Antananarivo every Sunday, or swallowed by the small Cathedral in Mahajanga, and so forth. As each parish has got eight congregations at least, and many do not have regular access to a priest, young people are often indispensable. They often care for congregations, pay pastoral visits, prepare candidates for confirmation and take services. In the Diocese of Mahajanga, young people are involved in evangelistic work, pioneering in areas where there are no Episcopalians. The *Tafika Masina* (Holy Army) is a group for young people. In the dry season they walk long distances to evangelize every weekend.

Humanly speaking, the future of the Church in Madagascar is precarious and uncertain. Everywhere in this cosmos, economic issues persist, even in developed countries. The question is: is the situation of the Church the same in the two worlds, the economically rich and the deprived one? If anyone is tempted to say 'yes', just consider the empty churches of the North. How can Christians in Madagascar, with their spiritual wealth, help England? After centuries of financial dependence, should we expect to get support from overseas forever? Is the Church in Madagascar condemned to dependence on the UK and the USA, on USPG and PIOSA (Province of the Indian Ocean Support Association) for ever? Is not this the right time for all dioceses to run viable and durable development programmes and projects? To pay adequate salaries to teachers and evangelists? Adequately to support church institutions and hostels? Indeed, nobody will say 'no' to these questions. But how will these programmes and projects be done and run? Certainly training, both at home and abroad, is essential. And prayer is essential.

Note

1   The statistics included in this chapter are derived from a 1993 report of the Institut National de la Statistique, and from *L'Emploi, le chômage et les conditions d'activités dans l'agglomération d'Antananarivo* (June 1995).

The Church as a source of identity: reflection from the Caribbean[1]

Las Newman

Understanding Church

However the Church may be understood, theologically or sociologically, central to its nature and function are the issues of community and communion. The Church was instituted by our Lord, the Christ, as a new community anticipating and manifesting the Kingdom of God, in and over against the old community of the ancient world. This community was to be built up on a chief cornerstone. The *raison d'être* of this community was the reconciliation of humanity to its Creator, to their fellows, and to their environment and the provision of a new basis for communion between the Creator and his creatures, who were made in his image and likeness. At the heart of the understanding of the Church-as-communion was the understanding that this is what gives true identity, through Christian Baptism and participation of the Eucharistic Feast, the Mass.

The Church and identity in history

As the early Church of Jewish origins began to spread throughout the Roman Empire through its missionary endeavours, it inevitably ran into the problem of identity. First of all, it had to face the problem of its own identity. Was the Church to be inclusive or exclusive? Was the Church to be Jewish, for the sons of Abraham, or was it for all people without distinction, those who would identify with the 'new Israel of God' (Gal 6.16)? Then it had to face the question of what to do with non-Jews who wished to join this 'new way' in the ancient Graeco-Roman culture. Galatians 2 and Acts 15 indicate the centrality of this question for the early Church. Paul devoted much of his Christocentric theology to this issue (Rom 9 – 11; Gal 3.1 – 5.15; 6.11–18; Eph 2.11–22; Col 1.15; 2.23), arguing most emphatically for a new identity in Christ for Gentile Christians and the legitimacy of this new identity in the plan of God.

Andrew Walls has argued that Church history has always been a battleground for two opposing tendencies, the indigenizing principle and the pilgrim principle. The reason, he says, is that 'each of the tendencies has its origin in the Gospel itself'. The indigenizing principle ensures that each community recognizes in Scripture that God is speaking to its own situation. This tendency helps the Christian community to associate with the particulars of its culture and group. The pilgrim principle, on the other hand, equally of the Gospel and in tension with the indigenizing principle, associates them with things and people outside of the particular culture and group. This tendency helps the Christian community to associate with the universals of the Christian faith.

The impact of the modern missionary movement since the discovery of the New World created a problem of identity for the Church quite unlike anything it had experienced before in its history. For the first time the European missionary movement was faced with the problem of a non-European identity as the Church spread deep into Asia, Africa, Latin America, the Caribbean and the Pacific Islands.

As the Mission Church began to develop and search for its own identity, soon the need for indigenous theology to deal with issues of Gospel-as-brought-by-European-missionaries versus local traditional culture, contextualization, indigenization, and inculturation began to give a new face to the Church. Walls points out that 'within the last century there has been a massive shift of the centre of gravity of the Christian world, so that the representative Christian lands now appear to be in Latin America, sub-Saharan Africa, and other parts of the southern continents'. This means that Third World Theology is now likely to be the representative Christian theology.

The Caribbean context

In the Caribbean context, the peculiar experience of the Caribbean Church has demonstrated the reality of the Church being a source of identity formation and transformation.

The peoples of the Caribbean have had to endure more than four centuries of European colonial domination, with its particular social features of the imposition of a regime of feudal plantation society, the introduction and practice of modern slavery, the development of mono-culture, elitist economies, and the suppression of local, indigenous culture. The effect of this on personal identity was devastating, particularly for the native Indian and transplanted African populations. As Harvard sociologist Orlando Patterson argues, in the case of the enslaved African population, the series of adjustments the transplanted Africans were required to make upon their enforced arrival across the Atlantic led to major distortions in personal identities. As part of survival strategy the African Caribbean person developed two selves; an Afro-centric self and a Euro-centric self.

Las Newman

Both were inauthentic but perhaps necessary for survival. Both became part of the African Caribbean personality.

In this milieu, the Church-as-planted-by-European-missionaries becomes a great source for the re-formation of identity for the African population. The conversion to Christianity was extensive. By the mid-nineteenth century many mission societies in the Caribbean reported great success in their endeavours. Brian Stanley points out that in the case of the Baptist Mission in the West Indies: 'the West Indies Mission occupies a unique place in the nineteenth-century history of the Society (BMS). Alone in the early fields, the West Indies were not wholly unevangelized territory. BMS missionaries came not primarily as evangelists of the "heathen", but as pastors and teachers of an existing Christian negro community. In no other Baptist field during the nineteenth century was Church growth so spectacular, and nowhere else was progress towards the autonomy of the indigenous Church so rapid, nor so firmly insisted upon by the Society.'

So significant was the impact that within four years of the abolition of slavery Baptist Christians in Jamaica bade farewell to the Baptist Missionary Society and Theological Training Institute, and began to recruit African-West Indian Christians for the newly-opened mission enterprise in sub-Saharan Africa. Other denominations such as the Anglicans followed suit.

What accounts for this remarkable transformation? There is every evidence to suggest that the Church as community in communion, through the proclamation and application of the Gospel, answered the ontological question for a people enslaved in a hostile environment. It helped to answer the existential question of identity in the form of kinship, familial networks. As Jesus himself said, 'my brother and sister and mother is whoever does the will of my Father in heaven' (Matt 12.50). But the Church-as-brought-by-European-missionaries, though important, was not the only factor in this process of identity transformation. As Caribbean historian Monica Schuler demonstrates, the presence of the Church provided an opportunity for the African population to recover and reassert its own African religious cosmology and ritual significance. Religion was central to everything in the slave community.

When Emancipation occurred, after more than one and three-quarter centuries of the existence of a slave society, the challenge facing the Church was how to help with the construction of a new society in freedom. The Church, as a major social institution undertook the task of social organization and development, involving itself immediately in land-reform, education, health, housing, and poverty alleviation programmes such as skills training for productive employment opportunities. All of this contributed to the process of personal identity formation and self-definition, this time in a new society of freedom.

This freedom was what the African slaves struggled and fought for during the nearly two centuries of slavery. Slave resistance and revolts on the one hand, and slave conversion to Christianity on the other, are part of a continuum of a struggle for existential identity. The Church was a new instrument in this struggle, which added an ontological dimension in the quest for identity. This explains in part why after a few years of freedom, the African population began to distance themselves somewhat from the European Church structures and asserted their own 'native' Churches, complete with Christian and traditional African symbols. Bisnauth refers to this as the process of the 'Africanization of Christianity' in the Caribbean context.

At the same time as this process was taking place, a Black Christian elite was being prepared through education for leadership in Church and society. This element had to work through its own identity issues and decide to which side of the decolonization process it would direct its intellectual energies. By the time of Independence in the 1960s, one external observer could speak of the alienation of Black intellectuals in the Caribbean from the Church and what steps the Church needs to take to restore credibility to this and other sectors of the society.

Three decades have now passed since Caribbean countries gained political independence. In this period the Church in the Caribbean has undertaken three major projects in an attempt to understand and define its role in a post-colonial society.

The three major projects were (a) the development of ecumenical Church organizations and theological training institutions (The Caribbean Conference of Churches, and the Caribbean Association of Evangelicals; the United Theological College of the West Indies and the Caribbean Graduate School of Theology); (b) the attempt to construct a Caribbean theology (a project which lasted a decade and produced half a dozen documents and then dissipated); and (c) the establishment of an agenda for its role in social and community development.

None of these directly addressed the public issue of identity, as one of the lasting legacies of the colonial and slave society. Indeed, if the Church in the Caribbean attempted to address the identity at all, however indirectly, it did so with a great deal of reluctance and scepticism. The Church's ambivalence on the issue was due in part to the heavy and sensitive political climate at the time as well as to its stress on the meta-ethnic nature of Church. The reality was more likely, as E. H. Jay said at the time, that 'the churches have lost their old militant radicalism and have settled down to a respectable conformity. Their western bias has been enhanced by the fact that many of their members, descendants of slaves, have moved up the social scale into the middle classes and have been taught to despise their African ancestry and to cultivate Anglo-American customs and cultural

243

patterns.' In post-Independence Jamaica, the Church found itself in a majority culture, a position for which it was ill-prepared. The very Black elite it had helped create now turned on it with savage criticism of its institutional life, its 'outworn traditions which are irrelevant to the social, cultural, and spiritual needs of the country'.

The public issue of identity during this formative period of Caribbean life was pursued not by the Church but by non-Church social forces such as the emergent Rastafarian movement (with its messianic identification with Ethiopia as Zion and reggae music as the cultural weapon to 'beat down Babylon'), a renascent Pan-Africanist movement, and militant Black Power advocates (inspired by the Civil Rights movement in the United States), which gave an international dimension to the struggle to bring about 'Black man's redemption'. These forces emerged out of self-conscious awareness of the persistence of structural poverty, increasing marginalization, and Third World dependency.

Today, the Church in the Caribbean finds itself at a crossroads. Like the State apparatus under which it operates, three decades of institutional experimentation and failures, and a long history of external domination before that, have left it squeaking like Ezekiel's valley of dry bones. There are voices, internal and external, crying for reform of Church and State. In the case of the Church, there are voices calling for reform and renewal of its theology, its liturgy, its pastoral care, and its mission.

Vital questions

There are four questions I would like to draw from this overview. First, how does the Church avoid the danger of intellectual captivity and remain open to the Spirit of the Church to bring about renewal and change? At times in the past the Church became culturally captive and was seen to be mono-ethnic in character and tied to certain civilizations. Whenever this has occurred, it has meant real danger to the true understanding and expression of the Church.

Second, how does the Church affirm identity in a post-modern world and find freedom from the historical legacy of patriarchy, racialism, and hierarchicalism? The Church was intended to be for all nations, for all people groups, for all ethnicities (Gal 3.26–29). That is to say, the Church is to be a multi-ethnic, multicultural redeemed community 'from every tribe and language and people and nation' (Rev 5.9). At the same time, the Church was intended to be a meta-ethnic, metacultural redeemed community with a transcendent identity in Christ.

Third, how does the Church in a dominant ethnic-specific cultural environment treat minorities in its midst? It seems to me that both the Old

Testament and the New Testament have a lot to say about the treatment of strangers and aliens in the community. In the modern urban centres of today's society the Church-as-community has a real opportunity to rediscover its true nature and role in the world. Community is not to be idealized. Every true community must live with differences which cause dissonance and tension. The goal of community must be health and wholeness from the discovery of what is truly held in common.

Finally, how does the Church achieve its true mission as an agent of reconciliation in the world? As the Body, Building, and Bride of Christ in the world (Ephesians), the Church has been mandated to bring about reconciliation (2 Cor 5.19). The beatitudinal exhortation to the disciples as they listened to the Sermon on the Mount, 'blessed are the peacemakers, for they will be called sons of God' (Matt 5.9), is very much part of this mandate.

In the Caribbean context, the social history of plantation slavery provided a fertile environment for demonstrating the Church as a source of identity formation and transformation. The evangelization done by European missionaries before Emancipation was a welcome opportunity for the enslaved African population to redefine themselves. Their ready acceptance and appropriation of the Gospel and participation in the life of the Church effected a process of transformation and reconciliation in their being.

This early role in the Church in the Caribbean region has not been sufficiently appreciated. Indeed, in the long process which followed Emancipation and decolonization, the Church in the Caribbean played an important role in racial reconciliation, identity formation and community development. If today, post-Independence, the Church in the Caribbean has apparently lost sight of its role as agent of transformation, a few voices are calling for reform and renewal. Perhaps, in due course, they will be heard and new life may yet burst forth.

Note

1 This chapter is an edited version of a paper published by EFAC (1995).

Further reading

Kwame Bediako, *Theology and Identity: The Impact of Culture upon Christian Thought in the Second Century and Modern Africa* (Oxford: Regnum Books, 1992).
Dale Bisnauth, *A History of Religions in the Caribbean* (Kingston Publishers, 1980).
Idris Hamid (ed.), *Troubling of the Waters* (Trinidad, 1973).

Jürgen Moltmann, *Human Identity in Christian Faith* (Stanford University Press, 1974).

Katrin Norris, *Jamaica: The Search for an Identity* (Oxford University Press, 1962).

Andrew Walls, *The Missionary Movement in Christian History* (Edinburgh: T. & T. Clark, 1996).

Polygamy in the African Church today: a Kenyan woman's perspective

Edith Njoki Njiiri

In the past, polygamy – the practice of having more than one wife at the same time – was a much more common and accepted tradition in almost all African societies, but Christianity has made the practice less common and less accepted. However, that does not mean that polygamy is not practised in such Christian communities. As Mbiti has observed, the polygamous institution of marriage is found in almost every African traditional society, where the rate of such marriages may be as high as 25 per cent.

Traditional factors such as childbearing, economic status, sexual continence and security, which made polygamous marriage so common and accepted, may seem outdated but there are many communities where these factors keep polygamous marriage alive today.

Contemporary factors

Traditional heritage

Very high on the list of priorities leading to the continuation of polygamy in Africa today is the fact that, though Christianity and Western education are prevalent, there are some traditional beliefs and practices which continue. Highest on the list is the African philosophy of marriage: to bear children, to be a husband and father or wife and mother, to be an elder in the community.

In a recent research of over 300 Kikuyu men and women, 296 of those interviewed expressed the desire to have children in marriage. Not all desired many children; three was the average number. Childlessness is still a big problem. It can lead to marriage breakdown or polygamy. Unfortunately, even Christians quote the Bible (especially the Old Testament) as approving polygamy in the case of childlessness. Mbiti observes that the Churches teach and emphasize procreation as an important aspect of marriage. In the Anglican marriage service of 1662 still widely used in Africa, the first reason for marriage is the procreation of children. Thus, barrenness becomes an excuse for retaining polygamy.

Urbanization in Africa

Given that men have been more privileged in most families, they have had more of an opportunity to have a formal education than women. More men than women go to look for employment in urban centres. Very commonly, we find that those men working and living in the urban areas have wives in the country. They go home once a month or so. Wives in rural areas take that state of affairs as normal so long as the husband is maintaining the family. But the men take other women to live with them in their work location. Thus the men have rural wives and urban 'wives' at the same time.

Education and social status

In the past, status had to do with wealth in terms of animals and agricultural farms. In modern Africa, the difference in formal education resulting in social status is another forceful factor leading to the continuity of polygamous marriages. A relatively well educated man, married as a jobless school-leaver, may leave his wife behind both in academic qualifications and in the search for work. Employment gives him opportunity and education to improve himself. The Managing Director finds himself with an uneducated village wife. Such men often take other wives of their new social status.

Theological interpretation

As a woman priest, wife and mother, I think that African theologians and Church leaders have contributed to the continuity of polygamy by the way in which they have interpreted and taught the biblical view of marriage. Being Africans themselves, some of whom have come out of polygamous families, African theologians tend to sympathize with polygamy in a manner that can encourage it. For example, both Mbiti and Archbishop Gitari agree with other scholars that the Bible does not explicitly condemn polygamy. Mbiti further remarks that 'polygamy enhances the traditional concepts concerning the purpose and meaning of marriage'. Bishop Okullu argues that in some cases taking a second wife may improve the behaviour of the first wife.

To add to the theological interpretations, the Anglican Church of the Province of Kenya readmits lapsed Christians who, for one reason or another, have become polygamists. Sometimes, this is done with very little pastoral counselling. I can understand the pastoral concern of admitting and even baptizing repentant converts who are polygamists, but for lapsed Christians who become polygamists, the Church must take a stand. People say that these days one needs to get out of the Church for a while and after being recognized as a polygamist, seek readmission. In fact, this is becoming almost a tradition.

Given that the Church can do very little if anything to change these factors, then the Church should give marriage-counselling and education extra attention. Both men and women need to be given more counselling through family life education programmes. It would be good to see a specially-trained marriage counsellor in every parish.

Where possible, the Church should show good examples of family unity by not posting husband-priests far away from their families. It is odd for a priest to be posted in a parish where he or she cannot afford to see his or her family more than once a month. In some dioceses, where both the husband and wife are priests their posting is considerate, but the same consideration is often not shown to couples where both are not priests. It is not a good example to have family problems caused by such separations. African bishops should observe African geographical home-concepts when posting clergy.

African theologians and Church leaders should reconsider their biblical and theological views of marriage. It is now ten years since Archbishop Gitari, then Bishop of Mount Kenya East, presented a paper on polygamy to the Provincial Board of Theological Education and the Lambeth Conference. What impact has it had? What changes in pastoral practice that recognize the problems of women will be introduced?

Further reading

Archbishop David Gitari, 'The Church and polygamy', *Transformation*, vol. 1, no. 1 (Jan.–March 1984).

T. N. Njuno, 'The challenges of childlessness to Christian marriage in Kenya' (unpublished study done through the Oxford Centre for Mission Studies).

Township women united in prayer

Martha Nkoane

I am a product of my own world, that of township life in South Africa. Women, especially black women, form about 80 per cent of attendance in our churches. As a member of the Anglican Women's Fellowship I have come to appreciate the benefits and values of women praying together and interacting with the word of God.

In the past, South Africans, including women, were torn apart by apartheid. Even those women who share a common belief of Christianity and the same confession that 'Christ is Lord and Saviour' were also segregated even during worship. Though there are Churches which did not subscribe to segregation, the way of worshipping differs in terms of singing and praying. As an example, in black Churches, the congregations are more extrovert in terms of their spirituality and singing is one of their greatest ways of praising God.

Effects of transformation on religious women

During colonialization, missionaries spread Christianity among the indigenous people of this country. This created adjustment problems. People could not cross over from one culture to the other easily. As a result there emerged a religion whereby Christianity is mixed with indigenous beliefs and practices. This is displayed at events such as weddings and funerals. For example, a traditional marriage is arranged whereby rituals such as paying lobola, slaughtering a beast and dressing up of the bride in traditional gear are performed. Thereafter, a Christian ceremony in church is celebrated.

Women's primary roles are still to a great extent looked at as those of housekeepers, caregivers, mothers, subordinates to their husbands, as in the past; the negative effect of this to women is that it instils the feelings of guilt, insecurity, and inability to develop in many aspects of their skills and personalities to their full potential.

There are visible changes though, as women priests are now being ordained, but as yet only a few rise to the heights of rector. There are however a large number of women ordained as deacons. While this is encouraging, there are anomalies which occur. At a recent all-women's service I attended, it was a male priest who conducted the service! It is surprising how women frequently oppose and oppress their sisters. When women seek to make a difference they are frequently criticized by other women.

The political factor

After 1994, a number of women have emerged as political, civic, trade union, educational and Church leaders. Over these extraordinary years, women have coupled standing for their rights with practising their faith. An interpretation of the scriptures which says 'all people are equal in the eyes of God' helps to empower and liberate women in terms of their rights. But the rate of women's assault and rape escalates daily. Abused women, however, are often stigmatized by other women. Our human rights are shrouded by 'culture'. As women in the Church we should work to bring dignity and justice to survivors of physical, sexual and emotional abuse that women frequently experience in their homes, street and workplaces.

Family life

Women, the bulk of the Church, attend services and prayer meetings with their young and nursing children. However when these children come to adolescence they are lost to the Church. It lacks appeal for them. Men are in the minority, and some go to the lengths of forbidding their wives from attending church or joining church groups. This is a form of spiritual abuse.

Women's groups are very important. They unite women in prayer, sharing and learning from the word of God. In these groups women share their problems, pray for each other and give each other advice. They provide strong support systems in times of grief or social and marital crisis. In these groups many women learn to realize the power of prayer.

Home visits are very comforting. In the township if a member has suffered a loss of a loved one through death, the other members visit daily until the day of the funeral. The aim of these visits is to pray, offer condolence and comfort the bereaved. Sick visits to hospital and home for prayer and cheer also occur. These groups are therefore genuinely therapeutic.

Health issues

In most Churches, AIDS and HIV are discussed openly. There are still many misconceptions around these illnesses, however. There is a lot to be done. Other abuses such as alcohol, drug and substance abuse are a real problem as well. Further, because of culture and taboos, sexuality tends not to be spoken about in black Churches. Hence gay men and lesbians do not get out of the closet easily. Many young people now attempt or commit suicide.

Finance

Many township women are unemployed. They are creative, however, in finding funds. Some sew blouses, hats and school uniforms and sell them to their friends and neighbours. Others bake cakes, or sell ice cream or soup in makeshift booths. If a member of the Women's Fellowship suffers a loss, a set sum is set aside to help the bereaved with the funeral expenses. Townships like Soweto have both rich, upper, middle-class and poor, but this is not clear in the Church.

Change and future challenges

There is a need for more programmes to address the development of women, and improve their economic, educational and social condition. Literacy classes, assertiveness workshops and life-skills classes are all called for. From AIDS and HIV-awareness to simple instruction on nutrition, the Churches have a wonderful opportunity to help in the health of the nation. Our youth need to be taught morality, be instructed in sex education and sexuality and helped to value themselves. The ability to say 'no' to many of the temptations of crime, drugs and promiscuity is vital. We could do so much to help in building marriages, resisting despair and suicide, and help in the peaceful resolution of domestic conflict. We need more home carers, to help with the care of the destitute, chronically ill and dying. Finally we need to encourage our children with nursery and pre-school care, coupled with Bible study, so that they are ready for school and church.

Women in the Church have stood up and made a change. But there is still so much to do, and the stereotypes of women and their role frequently block further progress in Church and society.

Refugees and worldwide Anglicanism[1]

M. Louise Pirouet

This chapter will begin in Egypt where a small group of Sudanese refugees is cared for by the Anglican Cathedral in Cairo. Nothing could be more fitting. More than three millennia ago Joseph's family found refuge in Egypt; their subsequent enslavement and God's rescue of them is still a defining experience for the Jewish people and a basic metaphor of salvation for Christians. More than a thousand years later it was in Egypt that the Holy Family found refuge from Herod's persecution. The themes of exile, refuge and suffering are embedded in biblical thinking. The obligation to treat the stranger well is grounded in this experience, and in the command to love the stranger as one would oneself (Lev 19.33–34), regardless of who the stranger is. It rests in our common humanity: all are created in the image of God, all are fellow members of the human family and equally subjects of God's love.

The Christian responsibility towards refugees is threefold. First there is the responsibility to help create conditions where people may live in peace and security. We pray 'Thy kingdom come', and accept a responsibility to work for peace and justice now as a demonstration of the coming of God's eternal kingdom.

Then there is the need for states to establish just procedures for determining whether or not people should be recognized as refugees. Most Western governments have enacted laws aimed at preventing people seeking asylum. People in need of protection are forced, if they seek refuge in the West, either to lie in order to get a visa, or to purchase false documents and bribe their way onto flights. This is contrary to the spirit of the UN Convention on Refugees and to the spirit of the Gospels. And thirdly is the need to care for refugees during their exile.

It must be emphasized that refugees themselves are not the problem. The problem is the conditions of extreme poverty and repression (often inseparable) which force people to flee, the failure of states and international organizations to deal with these, and too often a failure to treat humanely those forced into flight. Mrs Sadako Ogata, UN High Commissioner for Refugees, rightly argues that dealing with the 'root causes' of today's refugee crisis is a priority. There are some 15 million refugees in the world and at least as many more displaced within their own countries.

Anglican bishops have sometimes had to make a costly decision to speak out on behalf of their own repressed people as Archbishop Desmond Tutu did for years in South Africa, and as Archbishop Gitari of Kenya did in his enthronement address in January 1997 when he repeated his call for human rights to be respected in his country, and as he has repeatedly done since.[2] In Congo/Zaire in early 1997 some Anglican bishops suddenly found themselves caring for hundreds of destitute people driven from their homes by the fighting. Bishop Ochola in Kitgum, northern Uganda, is working to keep open lines of communication with rebels in order to help bring peace.

Bishops and clergy in such fraught situations may need support from other parts of the Church. The Archbishop of Canterbury has visited oppressed Southern Sudanese Christians, and in mid-1997 protested at the violation of All Saints Cathedral, Nairobi, Kenya.[3] Bishop Keith Sutton of Lichfield visited South Africa as the Archbishop of Canterbury's envoy in 1985 at a very critical moment.[4] But anything smacking of political action is shunned by many Christians even when the ethical imperative seems overwhelming.

The conditions of today's world are very different from those in biblical times when the command was given to show hospitality to the stranger. The world's population is vastly greater and resources are limited; refugees may be a serious political embarrassment; governments find it hard enough to see that their own citizens are provided for; it may not seem right that refugees should have handouts from international agencies when nationals are desperately poor; some refugees may even be 'bogus', making false claims in order to cash in on free hand-outs. The granting of asylum is the prerogative of national states, and the Church is frequently told it should not interfere in politics.

But those who seek asylum are not the problem. They would almost invariably have stayed at home had conditions not become intolerable. This applies to many so-called 'economic migrants' who are branded as 'bogus asylum-seekers' by rich Western nations who have forgotten that whole continents have been populated by economic migrants from the West, sometimes at the cost of great suffering to the indigenous populations. And some of those same rich nations are at the same time cutting back on overseas aid while selling arms to states which repress their own populations.

If states find difficulty in granting asylum it is usually because of shortcomings in their own social provisions: because failed housing policies mean they cannot house their own people let alone refugees, because of high levels of unemployment, because of racism; or perhaps because of the poverty they have been forced into by international debt and structural adjustment programmes, and the failure of the international community to support them as it should.

So the gospel imperative remains. *Love*, the norm in personal relations, translates into *justice* in public life. Christians have a responsibility to work for just laws justly administered. In Uganda in 1982 during Milton Obote's second Presidency, the Uganda government encouraged the pillaging and expulsion of thousands of Rwandan refugees in the south of the country. Bishop Festo Kivengere took a lead in trying to stop this action, and in alleviating the suffering, in spite of the danger he ran in doing so.[5] Anglican bishops in the British House of Lords spoke on behalf of all the Churches against harsh and unfair asylum legislation introduced in 1993 and 1996.

Christian giving is another response to the Christian imperative to help refugees. In the wealthy countries of the West, Christian giving helps refugees in many parts of the world. This may be channelled through an ecumenical agency such as the British Christian Aid, or through denominational agencies such as the Presiding Bishop's Fund for World Relief in the USA. The USA's chief responsibility has been to refugees from Latin America, and the sanctuary movement began in the States. In Canada the Primate's World Relief and Development Fund works in partnership with Churches in many parts of the world, giving both emergency and long-term aid to refugees. It undertakes advocacy work in collaboration with others, supporting a network of volunteers who educate parishioners about refugees and campaign for just refugee and immigration policies. In many poorer countries people have been equally generous. For years Malawi, with a population of under 10 million, hosted 1 million Mozambican refugees. This required toleration and generosity of a high order.

The Anglican Church has a presence in many countries where there are refugees. By far the largest proportion of the world's 15 million refugees are found in the poorer countries of the Two-Thirds World such as Malawi, Pakistan and the countries of Indo-China. In some delicate situations help must be given quietly or even anonymously. A tiny minority of refugees finds its way to the West and to Australia and New Zealand. As it is impossible to survey Anglican work with refugees comprehensively, we will look at some areas of activity in which individual Anglicans and the Church as a whole are discharging their duties of love and justice.

A survey of refugees from the conflicts in Sudan will take us on a global journey. Because of civil war in the South and massive repression throughout the country, Sudanese refugees are found in many countries. As well as 1 million internally displaced, a further half to 1 million are refugees in surrounding countries and perhaps 20,000 are in the West.[6] In Uganda, which has hosted tens of thousands of Sudanese for decades, the Anglican Church has a full-time Refugee Officer. Ever since the early 1960s, that Church has been involved in relief and pastoral work with refugees. The most recent influx of some 250,000+ Sudanese has been concentrated in the north-west of the country. The Bishop Allison Bible School was sited at Koboko, and it was a devastating blow when this was burnt down by Ugandan rebels, and the area became too dangerous for the aid agencies to function. In 1997 many Sudanese were led home by their bishop when the Southern forces made huge advances, freeing large areas of Equatoria Province.

We have mentioned the help given to Sudanese in Cairo, where local Christians have worked with Church Mission Society personnel. CMS workers in Moscow, together with St Andrew's Anglican church, have also found themselves called on to help stranded Sudanese refugees. Fifteen families, Russian and expatriate, have joined a monthly envelope scheme to pay the costs of a drop-in centre where volunteers teach computer skills, and where warm clothes for the Russian winter have been provided.[7] Giving a completely different kind of support, the English Diocese of Salisbury is twinned with the Episcopal Church of the Sudan, and has for years provided help of many kinds for Sudan and its diaspora, and has made visits which have brought great encouragement to people tempted to feel the world has forgotten them. The visit of the Archbishop of Canterbury which we mentioned earlier was also greatly appreciated, as was that of Archbishop Robin and Mrs Eames from Ireland in 1997.

Karin Ayok-Loewenberg, who works with Sudanese, has described the disruption to family life when refugees and displaced people have constantly to move, the effect on children of knowing nothing but conditions of violence, and the ways in which Christians help one another.[8] Refugees are not simply objects of charity: they have resources and must be worked *with*, not *upon*.[9]

In Kenya Sudanese refugees at Kakuma Camp in the far north of the country have suffered such severe food shortages that health has been undermined. In April 1997 the Church Mission Society asked their supporters to write to the UN authorities about this, and many did so; a simple but effective piece of political action. Kakuma receives occasional pastoral visits from the Bishop of Eldoret and Bishop Nathaniel Garang, as well as by Marc Nikkel of the CMS/ECUSA. For many in the camp a Christian identity serves to arm them psychologically over against their Muslim oppressors. This needs careful handling by those who provide pastoral care.

This brief consideration of Sudanese refugees in just some of the countries where they are found illustrates the different ways in which the Anglican Church is involved with refugees: congregations (in Cairo and Moscow) are involved at a personal level; a diocese sets up a link and provides support of various kinds (and receives back as much as it gives, though in different kind); Church leaders provide encouragement by high-profile visits; a mission society asks its supporters to take political action; Uganda has a full-time Refugee Officer and years of experience; Kenya has no comparable organization, but a bishop includes refugees in his pastoral care programme. But help is patchy: should the Anglican Consultative Council or some other body be mandated to co-ordinate Anglican work and thinking about refugees?

The International Affairs Commission of the Anglican Church in Australia is undertaking a major survey of what is being done at parish level to assist refugees, and a report to General Synod has identified a need for education at parish level and recommended greater involvement in advocacy work. An excellent leaflet has been prepared, both challenging and informative.[10] STARTS (the Society for Trauma Victims) was begun by the Revd Martin Chittleborough, an Anglican priest (there is Christian support in many countries for those who have survived torture). The Anglican Church in New Zealand has a representative on that country's Refugee and Migrant Commission, and helps with resettlement.

The UK hosts nothing like the number of refugees which many African and Asian countries host. In 1996 the whole of the European Union (population 350+ million) received just 214,000 applications for asylum most of which would be refused, of which the UK (population 56 million) received 27,875. Since the collapse of Eastern Bloc Communism, Western Europe has been increasingly hostile to people seeking asylum. Even admissions from neighbouring Bosnia were strictly limited. In the West refugees are not put in camps and housed and fed by the UNHCR: the state is able to afford to give them access to social security benefits. But in 1996 the UK enacted legislation which deprived most asylum seekers of this, leaving them without food or shelter, claiming that most were 'bogus', and 'economic migrants'.[11] The Roman Catholic Bishops' Conference came out with a clear statement condemning the refusal of social security as inhumane,[12] as did both High Court and Appeal Court Judges when judicial action was taken to test the law.[13] In September 1996 the courts ordered Local Authorities to provide emergency assistance under the 1948 National Assistance Act. While many bishops and other prominent Anglicans gave a clear lead, and the bishops in the House of Lords attacked aspects of this legislation, the Church of England made no comparable statement on behalf of the whole Church. A significant gap was revealed in the corporate thinking of the Church. It was left to individuals and to parishes in areas where there were concentrations of destitute asylum seekers to make what provision they could to deal with the emergency. In London they mostly did so through an ecumenical network set up through the Social and Pastoral Action programme of the Roman Catholic Diocese of Westminster, which also led the way in raising funding. Individual churches, the ecumenical Churches Commission for Racial Justice, the

Refugee Council, the Red Cross, the Jewish Council for Racial Equality and the refugee agencies struggled to cope with the emergency. Westminster Abbey, through its One People Fund, paid for a report into the destitution caused by the withdrawal of social security, and gave a total of £6,000 towards the emergency Day Centre run by the Refugee Council and the Diocese of Westminster. It continues to help fund the Central London Interfaith Refugee Network.

Eventually some refugees are able to return home. In recent years exiles have returned to Zimbabwe, Mozambique, South Africa, Namibia, Chile, Argentina, and elsewhere. Those who returned to Yei in Sudan at Eastertide 1997, led by their bishop, would have understood perfectly the psalmist who wrote 'When the Lord turned again the captivity of Zion, then were we like unto them that dream; then was our mouth filled with laughter and our tongue with joy'. They then had to begin the hard work of rebuilding, and of praying that war would not return to that place, nor land-mines claim too many lives. But return is not always possible. Numbers who fled from the horrifying conflict in Bosnia now have no homes to go to, and are being granted permanent status in the West. Refugees are perhaps most in need of loving hospitality when hope of return home finally fades.

Notes

1 I wish to thank the following for information and help: Cristopher Carey, John Evenson, Cherry Gertzel, Jean Holm, Storrs McCall, Michael Mayne, Elsa Tesfay Musa, Philip Ridsdale, Nicholas Sagovsky, Sally Thompson, Patrick Tugume and Philip Turner.

2 Sermon summarized in *Yes* (Church Mission Society; April/May 1997).

3 *Guardian* (14 July 1997); *Church Times* (18 July 1997); *Tablet* (19 July 1997).

4 Shirley du Boulay, *Tutu: Voice of the Voiceless* (London, 1988).

5 Jason W. Clay, *The Eviction of Banyarwanda: The Story Behind the Refugee Crisis in Southwest Uganda* (Cambridge, MA: Cultural Survival Inc., 1987); Anne Coomes, *Festo Kivengere* (Eastbourne: Monarch, 1990), pp. 419–22.

6 UNHCR, *Refugees* (1994), II, 6; (1996), I, 9; *International Anglican Family Network* (Lent 1997).

7 Robin and Penny Minney, CMS *Link Letters* (June and October 1995).

8 *International Anglican Family Network* (Lent 1977).

9 Barbara Harrell-Bond, *Imposing Aid: Emergency Assistance to Refugees* (Oxford, 1986).

10 'Report to the General Synod International Affairs Commission on Anglican Involvement in Refugee Resettlement', prepared by Susan Campbell (4 March 1997); *Refugees and the Australian Church: What Do You Know About Refugees?*, prepared by the International Affairs Commission of the General Synod of the Anglican Church in Australia.

11 *Guardian* (12 October 1995); *Independent on Sunday* (29 October 1995); *Guardian* (8 January 1997), etc.
12 Statements made by the Catholic Bishops' Conference about asylum legislation from 1991 onwards are quoted in the paper issued by the Conference's Office for Refugee Policy, 'Catholic social teaching, the General Election and refugee policies' (1996).
13 *Guardian* (27 March 1996); *Times, Guardian*, etc. (22 June 1996); *Times, Guardian*, etc. (9 September 1996). Mr Justice Collins described this as 'the most draconian piece of legislation this century ... I find it impossible to believe that Parliament intended that an asylum seeker, who was lawfully here and who could not lawfully be removed from the country, should be left destitute, starving and at risk of grave illness and even death because he could find no one to provide him with the bare necessities of life.' (The then government made it quite clear that this was precisely what they intended: *Times, Guardian*, etc. (18 February 1997).) The measures removing social security were 'so uncompromisingly draconian' that 'no civilised nation can tolerate it' according to the Appeal Court judgement quoted in the *Times* leader (18 February 1997).

Women within Church and society in India

Krupaveni Prakasha Rao and Julie Lipp-Nathaniel

It is common knowledge that patriarchy has profoundly shaped the theology about the place and role of women in society in the major world religions. 'Na Stree Swatantra Marhati' ('Woman is not eligible for freedom') is the Sanskrit saying based on the religious laws of Hinduism which summarizes the position assigned to women over centuries. Seen to be placed lower than the man in the natural order of living beings, from birth to death she was put under the custody and protection of a male member of the household: first her father, then her husband, and finally in her old age her son. Her identity was defined in terms of being an obedient wife, a good mother and a thrifty housekeeper. Only if she bore sons did she fulfil her most sacred duty and would she earn the respect of her family. If she had only girls she would be considered a curse.

Happily this low regard of women in India is increasingly a thing of the past. Independent India has recognized that the development of the country 'depends on the participation and development of both men and women in its social, cultural, political and economic fields'. Legislation which gives women the vote and equal rights with men, and abolishes such malpractices as that of dowry, is in place. Government, non-government organizations and the Churches have launched many programmes to see that the woman who was oppressed over the ages now can be released to play her full part. Still it remains a huge task. The impact of the age-old, male-dominated religious and social practices and values goes very deep. What in government schemes and project plans, and in feminist social theory and womanist theology, is fully convincing often falters in being translated into action. The men feel they have a lot to lose, and women themselves have so internalized their subservient role that they are often the ones to most staunchly guard and perpetuate the unequal gender order.

The disadvantages and discriminations which to a great extent still mark the lives of women in India begin from the day a baby girl is born. Where the beating of drums and feasting hail the arrival of a son, a female child is received in silence and the mother will shed hidden tears. The key to bringing about changes for the improvement of a woman's lot has been education, both formal and informal. A second major thrust has been to create opportunities for women to be economically more self-reliant. And thirdly the focus has been to build up women's self-awareness in terms of knowing their rights and equipping them to take responsibility and leadership in the family, the Church and the society as a whole.

The 1991 census showed a bare 40 per cent of the women being able to read and write. In 136 of India's 386 rural districts the female literacy rate falls below 10 per cent, as a recent World Bank study revealed. On the other hand in the south-western state of Kerala just under 90 per cent of women are educated. Not only early women missionaries on the west coast but also the rulers of Travancore and Cochin were keen to promote education amongst their subjects. Furthermore, for this most populous part of India it is the people who are perhaps its chief export: men and women who because of their good qualifications easily find jobs throughout India and beyond. A good qualification is of high value also when it comes to calculating the dowry a bride is expected to bring with her at the time of marriage. In urban areas generally, especially among the middle classes where the drive to participate in the economic and technological leap into the twenty-first century is acute, the realization is growing that it is worthwhile to invest in the education of daughters as well as of sons.

The vast majority of girls throughout the length and breadth of rural India and the slums of the cities, however, still cannot dream of such educational opportunities. Girls are considered a misfortune, at best a burden on the family. So at an early age they are kept back from school, made to do the household chores of fetching water, washing clothes by the river, cooking and minding the younger siblings while both parents work for daily wages. Others have to earn their livelihood as domestic servants in the homes of the more well-to-do, or in the factory sector as child labour.

The early missionaries of the eighteenth and nineteenth centuries had put the task of bringing education to the ordinary people high on their agenda. Schools for girls and work among women, for instance through the Zenana Mission, made a considerable and lasting impact. In some parts it was said that parents had difficulty in finding an equal match for their well-educated daughters! The role of these pioneers continues to be well recognized. Today the Church in India carries forward this tradition of providing education of a high standard through its schools, colleges and technical training institutes, and boarding homes, all of which assist girls as well as boys.

Job-oriented training for women has in the past tended to be confined to the traditional areas of dress-making, embroidery and secretarial courses. With India taking the lead in the software industry and fast catching up in many other sectors, and with women increasingly taking their place alongside men in every sphere of work, the Church is challenged to explore the possibilities of diversifying the opportunities it offers to women of the poorest communities. These include, of course, Dalit and tribal women as well as men.

The All India Council for Christian Women (AICCW), which is the women's desk of the National Christian Council of India, is energetically promoting programmes which enable women to realize the dignity into which they have been created. It has played a vital role in taking the message of the Ecumenical Decade of Churches in Solidarity with Women to the individual Churches. The degree to which these have made its concerns their own varies, but it is true to say that the women's organizations within these Churches have responded with enthusiasm and energy.

The Church of South India has in its dioceses numerous self-employment schemes for women, especially within the programme known as VELCOM (Vision for Equipping Local Congregations in Mission) which enables the grass-root congregation members to share in the decision-making and carrying through of the mission of the Church. In solidarity with the Women's Fellowship the CSI has made a mandatory provision that women should be given a 25 per cent membership in all the administrative and decision-making bodies from the local congregation up through the diocesan council to the synod. Despite the fact that some dioceses still have not ordained women, the constitutional hurdle was removed as far back as 1979. There are today around 100 women presbyters, few compared with their male counterparts. The Association of Theologically Trained Women of India boasts a membership of around 800. This association does excellent work in promoting the development of women through theological education.

Two projects, the Jagruti Tribal Development Project and the Adegaon Development Projects in the Church of North India Diocese of Nagpur, can stand as an example for others. It is worth quoting from the letter written by Elaine and Peter Streatfield, the USPG missionaries working in the area:

> Women's groups were formed which fought for their rights and recognition with the result that a number of them entered the male domain of the village committee as representatives. Three of them even became leaders of their respective village area councils. There are now over fifty women's groups which meet every month to discuss the local situation, share their problems, hopes and aspirations. They make loans to help one another and to improve the overall situation in home and village. Every month members deposit 10 to 20 rupees (between 33p and 66p) in the group account. From these central pools loans are given as needed, thus cutting out the loan sharks who used to bleed them dry . . . Over the past two years the women have deposited more than 250,000 rupees (£4,207) in the local banks. The International Fund for Agricultural Development recently began providing credit to the rural economy through such women's groups, so the local bank managers, who have to implement the scheme, are very keen to provide these same women with credit. This type of activity has boosted the morale of the women no end. Becoming economically independent of the men has emboldened them to step into areas hitherto dominated by them. In some villages women have destroyed the illegal breweries, prevented the transportation of liquor and closed down the liquor shops with the result that atrocities against them have decreased significantly.

The Women's Fellowship of the CSI has an intricate network of branches which spread into the remotest villages of southern India. Encouraged by the goals set out by the Ecumenical Decade of Churches in Solidarity with Women, it launched conscientization programmes through its regular meetings as well as through special conferences, seminars, leadership training camps and the like.

Before some illustrations of the concrete programmes are given, it is worth recalling just two of the specific aims of the Decade spelled out by the WCC:

- empowering women to challenge oppressive structures in the global community, their country, their Church;
- affirming – in shared leadership, decision-making, theology and spirituality – the decisive contributions women are already making in Churches and communities.

In the Diocese of South Kerala the Women's Fellowship conducted a survey which showed 40 per cent of Christian families living under conditions of severe stress. Unemployment and poverty coupled in many instances with alcohol problems of the husband were some of the major contributing factors. As a result wives and children were all too often the victims of battering and abuse. Many men had walked out on their families. In order just to provide for one square meal mothers would have to work long hours in the fields or on building sites. The Women's Fellowship is tackling these problems at several levels. Firstly it recognized the need for a more professional counselling service. For this purpose it sent a married couple for training at the Christian Counselling Centre (CCC) in Vellore. They were employed in a new counselling centre of the diocese. At regular intervals short courses in counselling skills are organized for selected couples from the congregations. The aim is to give these basic skills to trusted and respected people in the locality who could assist the presbyter in his or her role of pastoral counselling. Seminars and workshops are offered on such subjects as 'How to handle an alcoholic husband'. Women are helped to become economically self-sufficient without having to sell their labour under value. They are trained in skills that they can employ in their own homes, among other things in cooking and catering, artificial flower-making, tailoring, making leather handbags. A scheme of giving loans enables others to start a petty business such as selling vegetables and other basic commodities or to start rearing cattle or poultry. To relieve them from the care of their babies and toddlers while they are working, day-care centres are provided. Here the children are well looked after and encouraged in their development by trained crèche nurses. Through the day-care centres and in health camps mothers are given instruction on health and hygiene.

Untold numbers of women in India spend their whole life never questioning their traditional roles and never knowing what their legal rights are. To redress this the South Kerala Women's Fellowship offers regular conferences and seminars on such subjects as the malpractice of giving dowry, discrimination against women and the girl child, property rights of women, laws pertaining to rape.

Susheela is a woman whose life has been a long road from oppression and humiliation to being a person who can hold her head high. Susheela is the mother of three young children. Her husband earns a daily wage of about 60 rupees (less than £2) a day. Of this he would give her at the most 15 rupees. The rest would be spent on alcohol. Yet he would come home and demand that she cook him his favourite fish curry. If, as was so often the case, she could not produce it because of the price of fish, he would beat her and the children. Through the petty loan system Susheela was helped to start a small business. She buys and sells rice, raises vegetables and fruit in her own back yard. This has made her not only economically more independent, but has strengthened her sense of her own worth. Today she can say with Mary 'My soul magnifies the Lord for he has done marvellous things for me'.

Finally, women need to be equipped for leadership in Church and society. Verbal recognition of this is fulsome; putting it into concrete action means surmounting many obstacles. Nevertheless, women's organizations and groups in the Church are themselves giving it priority attention. Again the examples are drawn from the activities of the South Kerala Women's Fellowship, but they stand for similar initiatives in other dioceses in India.

Women workers of the diocese are trained in how to lead devotions and use innovative Bible-study methods. They reflect together on women leaders of the Bible and discuss issues such as 'The woman's role in Church and society'. One conference was held under the title 'This is not a time to keep silent'. Every year Family Week is observed in the diocese with a set theme. It is the women's groups who plan and organize it. Women are also being encouraged to tell their stories. To this end conferences are organized to develop women's creative writing. They learn to speak before a public audience, to chair meetings and take the minutes. To be part of this process is an exciting but also humbling experience.

Gender continues to be a pressing challenge to the Church entering the twenty-first century, enabling women to come to grips with their own problems. It is no wonder that the highest-ranked Christian in the political field in India, the Speaker of the Parliament, in giving his address at the Jubilee Celebrations of the CSI in Madras (September 1997) said that the empowering of women was the most important task facing the CSI in the next 50 years.

Further reading

Lily and Sam Amirtham, *A Praxis for Human Development* (National Christian Council of India Publication), and various articles.
Anjali Bagwe, *Of Woman Caste: The Experience of Gender in Rural India* (London: Zed Books, 1995).
P. Caplan, *Class and Gender in India: Women and Their Organisations in a South India City* (London: Tavistock, 1985).
Madhu Kishwar and Ruth Vanita (eds), *In Search of Answers: Indian Women's Voices from Manushi* (London: Zed Books, 1984).
John C. B. Webster, Deborah Premraj et al., *From Role to Identity: Dalit Christian Women in Transition* (Delhi: ISPCK CTE 13, 1997).

Living as a minority in Pakistan[1]

Mano Ramalshah

Pakistan was created in 1947 to be a homeland for the Muslims of the Indian sub-continent, perhaps the first example where a religious state was created, followed by Israel in 1948. I hope this will not be repeated as it denies a person the basic human freedom of his or her own faith. Mohammed Ali Jinnah, the founder of the nation, advocated freedom for each individual to practise his or her own religion. Sadly that freedom has been eroded as a programme of Islamization has been implemented by successive governments. Former President Zia ul Haq amended the existing law resulting in the notorious Section 295-C of the Pakistan Penal Code. This introduced the death penalty for anyone found guilty of making offensive remarks against the Holy Prophet of Islam. In practice people have used this law to take revenge on their enemies or settle their personal disputes. It has become an encouragement for people who want to stir up bigotry and hatred. The effect of this seems to be cumulative; each outrage is worse than the last. For example in 1997 a Christian village, Shantinagar, was attacked, houses and shops were looted and burned and livestock were killed by a mob of 30,000.

The statistics for the quality of life in Pakistan do not make happy reading. Officially the literacy rate is 36 per cent but it is much lower in rural areas and among women. Infant mortality is high at 91 infant deaths per 1,000 live births. Per capita GNP is only US$430. Two-thirds of the population have access to safe drinking water but less than 50 per cent have access to sanitation. There are ten times as many soldiers as there are doctors in Pakistan. The government spends more than a quarter of its total budget on the military. Compare this to the allocation for education, 2.7 per cent, or health, 1.8 per cent of the Gross National Product. Life expectancy at birth is less than 62 years and the national average for years at school is less than two years.

The population of Pakistan is about 140 million and is growing by 3 per cent annually, one of the highest growth-rates in the world. According to official figures non-Muslims account for 3–4 per cent of the population. This includes Christians, Hindus, Buddhists, Sikhs, Ahmadis and Parsis. One Christian scholar estimates that 1.9 per cent of the population of Pakistan is Christian; that is, 2.8 million people.

The Church of Pakistan was formed in 1970 as a result of a union between Anglicans, Lutherans, Scottish Presbyterians and Methodists. We are unique on the world stage in that believers of such different backgrounds are together in a united Church.

In St Matthew's gospel, chapter 25 we read the Christian manifesto to the 'less fortunate' that has become the norm for mission in the last 200 years: feeding the hungry, giving a drink to the thirsty, providing hospitality to the stranger and clothes for the naked, ministering to the sick and imprisoned. This is seen as the way of sharing Christ with the little ones of the world. The story of the Good Samaritan has encouraged us in this so that we almost romanticize poverty. Too often we have an emasculated picture of the Good Samaritan as simply someone who helps the unfortunates of the world. That is charity, not mission. Mission for many people today means helping those less fortunate than ourselves, 'the least of the brethren': in mission we seek out the poor so that we may serve them. This is a caricature that limits the Gospel: the Gospel of Christ is for the salvation and liberation of all humankind, of rich and poor, and yet we persist with an idea of mission that needs the poor. We seek to serve the poor but they remain poor, powerless and indebted; we heal the sick but they return to unsanitary living conditions; we clothe the naked, but still they can barely afford life's basic necessities. We serve the poor, but we rarely empower them so they can escape from poverty. We do not challenge unjust systems that keep the poor from benefiting from opportunities. We seek to follow Christ's command in our service of the poor, but we do not have the prophetic insight to see what the problems really are. And if we cannot even ask the right questions, how can we dare to give the correct answers? How can the Church respond to the needs of the people it seeks to serve? How can the Church express other values of the Kingdom such as liberating the captives? Before we can answer these questions, we need to explore the history and context of the Church in Pakistan.

Missionaries arrived in South Asia along with the European colonial powers. During the second half of the nineteenth century large numbers of low-caste Hindus, mainly Chuhras, were converted to Christianity. Today's Pakistani Church is made up of the descendants of those Punjabis who were converted to Christianity. They were poor, and they were forsaken within their own social and religious system. In his classic novel *Untouchable*, perhaps the finest observations written in English by an Asian, Mulk Raj Anand writes of the humiliation suffered by the sweeper Bakha when he accidentally bumps into a high-caste Hindu in the bazaar. Physical contact with an Untouchable meant his impurity and uncleanness was transferred to the other person. Even today in Pakistani Muslim society that caste-consciousness means that Christians are still associated with the uncleanness and untouchability of their forefathers. Their conversion has not allowed modern-day Christians to escape from the stigma of untouchability. Even the term Chuhra, which used to be a name for a group of people, has become a term of abuse. When missions needed avenues of *diakonia*, of Christian service, they looked for the lowest of the low so they could share God's love with them. The Chuhras were certainly among the lowest of low, the least of the brethren. Missionaries' contact with these people was a manifestation of the incarnated love of Jesus.

The majority of Pakistani Christians work as street sweepers or toilet cleaners. Throughout Pakistan over 86 million people have no access to sanitation, so people still expect them to perform that most menial of tasks. They live mostly in squalid sweepers' colonies that are often little more than fetid slums. To live like this for generation after generation is to be dehumanized. After 200 years of preaching and teaching the Christian Gospel, why is this so? Why have these people's lives not changed in all aspects? Even after two centuries there has been little development and certainly no liberating transformation of the Christian community. Is this not an insult to the Gospel? Why can't these people have decent shelter and be able to live reasonable lives? Is being untouchable an integral part of being Christian? If not, why after 200 years have so few escaped from their situation of poverty and powerlessness?

Aiming for community uplift and development is not a new idea. Pioneer missionaries founded educational and medical institutions as instruments of diakonia. The whole community needed health care and education and this movement led to the creation of a whole network of schools, colleges, clinics and hospitals across South Asia. It is worth remembering that these schools and colleges also provided the British Raj with the clerical workers it needed to administer their greatest imperial possession at low cost. Great work has been done and continues to be done in these institutions. The hope was that through education Christians would be empowered and enabled to escape from the quagmire. Today we are proud that at least some Christians who, but for education, would have remained untouchables, are represented in the professions as lawyers, doctors, clergymen or engineers.

But when we look at the overall picture the number of Christians able to get decent jobs through education has been relatively small. Only a few have escaped from the vicious circle of dehumanizing jobs and squalid housing. The truth is that despite 200 years of missionary activity and more than two decades of education specifically targeted at poor Christians most of them are still locked into lives spent in a foul environment and going out to carry human excrement for their livelihoods. As Christians we are followers of Jesus Christ, the son of God who became human. Yet in Pakistan we see many of his followers have to live lives that are less than human. This is a grotesque perversion of the Incarnation. All we have done is simply educate some people who in turn become totally dependent upon the public sector and government agencies for employment. In Pakistan this sector is already over-stretched. It is also a sector which governs life and makes rules according to religious identity. If you belong to the majority, you can claim a share, however small. But those of a different religious persuasion are complete outsiders. In Pakistan people say 'Majority has authority'.

In a world where the global trend is to cut down on government and to privatize more and more functions that were once run by the state, who will suffer when the jobs, even the bad jobs, are cut? What do you need to do when you are at the mercy of the majority, however that is defined, whether by race or religion? Common sense tells us that the minority must become less dependent on the majority. Because of their prejudices the majority may not be benevolent and the minority must find their own niche, otherwise they will become a target for the hatred of the majority.

Education is necessary, but education by itself will not lead to social and economic development. There must also be access to opportunities along with preparation and training to exploit these opportunities. It is safe to conclude that for the foreseeable future Christians will not get equitable treatment in Pakistan. Tokenism from the government or even changes in legislation will not ensure equitable treatment. Does that mean that Pakistani Christians will never experience a total and holistic liberation of body, mind and spirit?

The only way forward for our community is to acquire a new paradigm, a new model for the way we live our lives as Christians in Pakistan at the dawn of the new millennium. In the new paradigm people will change from being fodder for the state-run service sector to becoming their own masters. A successful example of this already exists in Pakistan.

Ismailis, a small Shia Muslim sect, are found either in Karachi or in the Northern Areas. Karachi boasts the Aga Khan Hospital, the most modern medical institution in the country, and the prestigious Aga Khan University. In the Northern Areas the Aga Khan Rural Support Programme has brought revolutionary changes to the area due to a whole slate of social and community development projects. Ismailis are involved in banking and finance and own some of the top hotels in Pakistan. They have a reputation as hard but honest bargainers and as people who help their own kind.

Do we see these values among Christians in Pakistan? Is the Christian community motivated to facilitate this change to a new paradigm? The answer is no, at least not on the surface. This begs the question 'Why not?' The answer is that they have been dehumanized to such an extent that they have given up hope. The flame of hope that flared when their forefathers became Christians, of the same faith as their British rulers, has largely died. That is not to say they do not have hope for salvation, for eternal life gained through following Jesus, for many of these people are faithful and expect God to deliver his promises. But those same people have lost hope for a life with dignity, a life with opportunity or a life with justice. They know better than to expect these things. They believe in salvation, but cannot imagine liberation.

If the Church is to respond to the needs of the people it seeks to serve, the first task is to rekindle hope and to motivate them for change, for transformation. The gospels tell us that Jesus made a difference to people's earthly lives. He touched people who had been marginalized by sickness or disease and made them well and clean so they could fully participate in the life of the community. He went to people who were disregarded by the establishment and gave them dignity in allowing them to offer hospitality. We, too, must use this Gospel model to encourage people to walk on this road to achieve the new paradigm for our community. Christians in Pakistan have found false security in their menial jobs and squalid houses. Now we have to embark on a journey full of risks but we must break out of the dungeons to see the open spaces of opportunity that await us. The Christians of Pakistan need to embark on their own exodus from humiliation to liberation. Doubtless many will be reluctant to leave the false security they know. There will surely be many complaints along the way from those who look back to the old days and the old ways. Yet God's people must struggle to shake off the fetters imposed on them if they are truly to live life to the full.

There are two models for us to explore. The first is setting up small businesses or micro-enterprises. Already in my diocese one project is involved in this activity in a very small way as an extension to its main purpose of technical training. This programme is designed to involve young men with small businesses while they are still under training. So even with relatively small amounts of money, typically around US$60, young Christians are setting up their own small-scale, labour-intensive workshops and businesses. They are increasing their earnings and even now creating employment in the informal, skilled micro-industry sector that supplies much of Pakistan's needs, whether as tailors, plumbers, mechanics or electricians.

The second model is altogether more adventurous. It could involve the Church, or a Church agency, setting up medium-sized industrial units to fulfil the hope that accompanies the new paradigm. Such a venture could provide Christians with an entry point into the life of their own country instead of remaining part of the underclass. This is an achievable goal, something that has been seriously investigated. Investment in such a venture would involve local and foreign sponsors, loans from various agencies and public subscription. This is in keeping with the principles of nation- and community-building exhibited in the Church's continuing diakonia in health and education programmes.

Is what I have been saying sound? Are these dreams reasonable and in tune with reality? A statement by the United Nations Development Programme lists 'Four Essential Components For the Human Development Paradigm', which reads as follows:

- *Productivity*. People must be enabled to increase their productivity and to participate fully in the process of income generation and remunerative employment.
- *Equity*. People must have access to equal opportunities.
- *Sustainability*. Access to opportunities must be ensured not only for the present generations but for future generations as well.
- *Empowerment*. Development must be *by* people, not only *for* them.

These components fully reflect and complement the ideals I have outlined for the Christian community in Pakistan. And to achieve these ideals the Church must become pro-active and intervening. It is a huge task, but one that I believe the Church is called to undertake if it is to incarnate Kingdom values in its people. But our resources are very limited and we need to enlist the help of public and private agencies for training, planning and funding. We need advocacy to influence government policy. Facilitators and project workers need training so that they can act as motivating agents in the community. They must increase people's awareness of their situation and challenge them to work out solutions. Existing and potential entrepreneurs need business-skills training to improve the effectiveness of their operations. The few Christian businessmen must be encouraged to help other Christians by offering employment or contracts for work. Our Church institutions have to promote the idea of entrepreneurship and inculcate this culture in our people. We need to discuss this whole issue with people in the Church, for it is they who must realize the urgency of the situation. They must realize for themselves that the current situation is one of false security that ultimately degrades and humiliates them. And crucially, we must ensure that there are opportunities for our people so that their hopes and dreams can be realized and not dashed and destroyed.

How does the Church in Pakistan interface with Muslims as a faith community? How do our people witness to their own faith? Since Christians exist on the margins of Pakistani society, opportunities for witness, dialogue and evangelism are limited to exchanges in our schools, hospitals or some community development programmes. In their day-to-day lives Christians are often unable to witness simply because they are socially invisible. Our people have to become visible, to become legitimate, accepted citizens contributing to the life and economy of their country. This is the new dream. This new paradigm will create a new instrument for diakonia and mission. The transformed Christian community would be able to interface as equals with their fellow countrymen and women. They would come out of the dungeons, leave the margins of society where they

Mano Ramalshah

have existed for so long. They would be able to sit at the same table, to have dignity and be able to reclaim their humanity and become effective instruments of mission.

Note

1   Much of the material in this chapter is taken from a paper, 'A new paradigm', by the author. It is available from Diocesan Centre, 1 Sir Syed Road, Peshawar, NWFP, Pakistan, 25000.

Further reading

M. R. Anand, *Untouchable* (London: Wishart 1935; Penguin Books, 1940, 1986).
D. Frost, *Skills for Life* (London: Intermediate Technology, 1991).
J. P. Grierson, *Vocational Training and Self-Employment* (Cranfield: Cranfield Institute of Technology, School of Management, 1988).
L. D. Hayes, *The Crisis of Education in Pakistan* (Lahore: Vanguard, 1987).
A. Hope and S. Timmel, *Training for Transformation*, Book 1 (Gweru: Mambo Press, 1984).
Dr A. Hussain, *Poverty Alleviation in Pakistan* (Lahore: Vanguard, 1994).
P. S. Lall, 'Pakistani Christians: population, employment and occupations' (paper presented at Human Rights Conference, Lahore, 1993).
P. A. Neck and R. E. Nelson (eds), *Small Enterprise Development: Policies and Programmes* (Geneva: International Labour Office, 1987).
State of Employment in Pakistan (Islamabad: Policy Studies Institute, 1987).
P. H. Streefland, *The Christian Punjabi Sweepers: Their History and Position in Present Day Pakistan* (Voorpublikatie nr 6, Afdeling Zuid- en Zuidost Azie, Anthropologisch-Sociologisch Centrum, Universiteit van Amsterdam, 1973).
Mahbub ul Haq, *Human Development in South Asia 1997* (United Nations Development Programme; Karachi: Oxford University Press, 1997).
L. Vemmelund, *The Christian Minority in the North West Frontier of Pakistan* (Rawalpindi: Christian Study Centre, 1972).

The healing ministry of the Anglican Church: medical work through institutions

Fannie H. Storr

The healing ministry of Jesus was inseparable from his preaching and teaching ministry. He came to make men and women whole. 'Heal the sick, raise the dead, cleanse lepers, cast out demons' (Matt 10.8). Miraculous healing has been a part of the Christian tradition ever since but it is a gift given to very few.

The Anglican Church's ministry and mission of healing has followed a parallel path of evangelism and service. Its purpose has been to bring to people in need all that can be done to relieve suffering, to heal and prevent disease in an atmosphere of Christian love and compassion. In all parts of the world there are Christian centres seeking to make men and women whole, including many that are ecumenically based, but in which the Anglican Church plays its full part. Some of these provide outstanding leadership and training in the countries in which they are based.

In the early days of the Anglican missionary societies' work there was considerable discussion and indeed disagreement on how much of the Churches' resources should be committed to medical work and the establishment of hospitals and clinics. These decisions became particularly acute when Western medicine began to develop and the cure of many diseases became a distinct possibility, as did prevention through vaccination. Some societies, like UMCA (Universities' Mission to Central Africa, now part of USPG), saw the establishment of hospitals as integral to their mission from the first. Others, like CMS (Church Mission Society), at first saw medical mission as a relatively small part of their work, only establishing hospitals and health work in specific regions and not giving it the same priority as their programmes of evangelization and education.

The problem of cost is even greater now than it was then, even in the wealthier nations where the drugs are manufactured, where expensive research produces new treatments and where the state or private insurance has taken over the financial responsibility for the treatment of disease. In poorer nations, where drugs must be imported and poverty increases the risk of disease, there is no way that the people can meet the cost of Church hospitals and health projects.

In some countries, governments had also taken over the Churches' medical work, but in the majority they undertook to share the work of the mission hospitals and many were integrated into national health programmes.

National independence has been paralleled by the independence of the Anglican Churches in the South, with the responsibility for the health care projects and hospitals being undertaken by the local church. The Churches are proud of the clinics and hospitals established by missionaries over the years and see their continuation as a high priority. New dioceses wish to establish health care projects as part of their ministry. Many bishops have already led centenary celebrations rejoicing in the Christian service the former mission hospitals have given to the community, often at very little cost to the recipient or even to the local Church. Yet, with many others, the Ghanaian theologian Kofi Appiah Kubi can ask: 'If Jesus came that we might have life and have it more abundantly, where is this abundant life in the midst of increasing poverty, misery, sickness and suffering?'

The costs of medicines and equipment used in Church hospitals have soared. Governments, faced with the Structural Adjustment Programmes, are cutting public spending. Some governments are even asking the Churches to take back hospitals they took over as thriving, well-equipped and structurally sound buildings, and which are now almost derelict. They are no longer keeping up with the payment of grants agreed with Church hospitals and staff salaries are not being paid. Local doctors in Asia and in Africa cannot afford to live and bring up their families on either irregular government or low Church salaries. They go into private medicine. There is a desperate lack of qualified doctors in Church hospitals especially in Africa. Missionary societies are being asked to recruit doctors who are prepared to work overseas, but there are fewer available. A question now being asked is: should Anglican missionary societies be recruiting non-Christian doctors to work in Church hospitals? We know that compassion and love are not the prerogative of the Christian, but these hospitals were founded as a Christian ministry.

Under Structural Adjustment Programmes poverty increases and with the resultant malnutrition overwhelms the effectiveness of those very expensive drugs from the North. Most foreign exchange goes on debt repayment and government drug stores are empty. Malaria and tuberculosis grow more virulent and no longer respond to the cheaper drugs. On top of all this has come the HIV/AIDS pandemic, sweeping through Africa and Asia.

So where does all this leave the Anglican Church's healing ministry?

A team of Malawian midwives continues to encourage young mothers to come in to the maternity hospital. They know that all the local midwives

are still not practising safe hygienic deliveries in spite of training programmes. They also know that they do not have sufficient supplies of
gloves, nor even enough test kits to check if the mothers are HIV positive.
They continue to care for the labouring mother because she needs them,
even though it means unprotected contact with her blood. Their delight in
the safe delivery of a healthy baby is no less than that of their colleagues in
the West in spite of the risk they run; in fact it is probably greater.

The Church of Uganda has responded to AIDS through medical care in
its hospitals and clinics, and through pastoral care of those affected and
their families. Teams work out in the community supporting families
caring for their relatives at home, bringing eggs, fresh linen, dressings,
with comfort and encouragement. While making a firm moral stand by re-
emphasizing the Christian teaching on marital fidelity, Anglicans join with
other denominations to provide loving care for those who are dying of
AIDS, struggling to create dignity in this most undignified of deaths.

In Tanzania staff continue to work, even when the hospital has not
received the government grant for their salaries for three months. They do
not just do the bare minimum, but admit patients on to mattresses on the
floor when all the beds are full, and they try to stretch their meagre
resources still further. If the only doctor is away with their only vehicle, the
administrator will go on his motorbike for several hours on rough roads
through a rainstorm to get the doctor from a neighbouring hospital in an
emergency, because that is the caring tradition of their hospital. They
struggle to keep a basic standard of care with a frightening lack of
resources. Miracles do happen and reports are filled with stories of how fresh
supplies such as infusion sets arrive just as the last one has been used; but
sometimes it does not happen and patients die because they cannot be
treated.

Former Anglicans are members of the Churches of South and North
India and are part of the whole healing ministry of those Churches. The
Christian Medical Centres of Vellore and of Ludhiana provide skilled care,
leadership, training and innovation in health care. In Vellore there is a
programme of Community Health and Development. CHAD has encouraged village communities to take responsibility for the improvement of
their own lives, linking socio-economic, agricultural and health concerns.
Hundreds of visitors come each year from all over the world to learn more
of this successful primary health care project backed by the Medical
Centre.

In 1994 The Board of Mission of the General Synod of the Church of
England published a paper on mission called *A Growing Partnership*. It
recognized that the experience of the Churches of the South has emphasized
the importance of the close relationship between mission, justice and all

aspects of development in a society. Anglican Communion thinking sees work for justice and development as integral parts of the Church mission inseparable from evangelism and Christian nurture. The experience of Churches in poor and oppressed societies has contributed to drawing together what the Churches of the North had separated, but they are frustrated by the divisions, especially when the provision of funds is involved.

Recognition without specific action is not enough. The holding together of the spiritual, cultural and physical aspects of being is crucial for the healing ministry of the worldwide Anglican Communion, if it is to continue Christ's ministry of making men and women whole into the twenty-first century.

Can the Anglican Church meet the cost of these health issues?

Further reading

Margaret Dewey, *The Messengers* (1975).
Jocelyn Murray, *Proclaiming the Good News* (1985).
Gillian Paterson, *There Rest Thy Feet: The Chad Experience* (New Delhi: CMAI, 1989).
Report of the Church of England Board of Mission, *A Growing Partnership* (1994).
John Wilkinson, *Making Man Whole: The Theology of Medical Missions* (London: Christian Medical Fellowship, 1990).

Childhood challenges

Key issues affecting children and young people throughout the Anglican Communion

Sally Thompson

Most of all, O Lord, we do not care for your children as we should. We let too many of your young people struggle with hunger, danger ignorance, violence and hopelessness.

But you are the God who saves Isaac from sacrifice, and cures Jairus' daughter, and says, 'Let the little children come to me'.

Challenge us, O God, that all our children shall be taught by you, and great shall be their prosperity.
(Extract from the prayers at the opening celebration of the 42nd Triennial Meeting of the Episcopal Church Women, Philadelphia, USA, July 1997)

Since 1992, the International Anglican Family Network (IAFN) has been publishing newsletters on key issues affecting families in the Anglican Communion. These are now incorporated in the Communion's magazine, *Anglican World*. Articles are submitted by people from all over the world working in projects linked with churches. Their insights and their work provide the basis for this chapter.

The United Nations Convention on the Rights of the Child was drawn up after the last Lambeth Conference in 1989. In summary, it states that all children have the right to:

1. love and security
2. food
3. survival and development
4. parental care
5. a decent place to live
6. health and health services
7. protection from abuse
8. education
9. rest and leisure

Although the Convention does not refer directly to the spiritual well-being of the child, it nevertheless sets out practical goals which all people of faith – as well as those of no faith – can aspire to. The reality of the experience of many children in the Anglican Communion is very different: homelessness; poverty; the breakdown of family relationships; the devastating effects of the HIV/AIDS pandemic; abuse. One recent report has described children as 'the most vulnerable members of our society'. The scale of the problems may vary considerably: millions of street children, homeless, without means of support and succour, in South America, Asia and Africa: thousands in the more affluent societies of the UK, USA, Australia and New Zealand. Worldwide, throughout the Anglican Communion, the catalogue of vulnerability and disaster for many children is horrific and depressing. But at the same time the IAFN newsletters tell of the work and struggles of many Anglican Churches and Christians to help and support children – and their parents – in distress. There is hope as well as despair as the followers of Jesus, who was himself a helpless child, seek to obey his command to 'Let the little children come unto me'.

Street children – those for whom the street is (for a shorter or longer

period of time) their home and their upbringing – are not a new phenomenon. But their numbers are growing. There are now more than 100
million street children around the world who live in fear every day of their
lives. In Brazil, about 25 million children live and work on the streets,
about 40 per cent of Brazil's total child population. In the USA on any
given night the population of homeless children is larger than the total
number of children in Pittsburgh. In Port-au-Prince, Haiti, 5,000 children
live in the streets, 85 per cent not knowing who their father is.

In Africa, street children are a more recent occurrence in cities. Numbers
are now increasing rapidly due to massive population displacements,
through war and famine, the AIDS pandemic, and rapid urbanization. In
Asia many of the numerous street children are being sexually exploited –
often by Western tourists.

A former Anglican bishop once said that to despair of being able to do
anything, or to refuse to do anything, is to be guilty of infidelity. Many
projects to help street children have been started by Anglican churches.
One is St Alban's church in Dar es Salaam, Tanzania, which started up a
soup kitchen and clinic in the church grounds. Three evenings a week
children came for their evening meal and medical attention. When the
numbers grew too many, with the help of a non-governmental organization
a home was purchased to accommodate the children. There is now a drop-in
centre as well. The organizers write that some children live in the shelter
for a while, and then leave because they cannot conform to rules, or because
they do not want to attend school, but the change in those children who
have been there since the start of the project is 'amazing'. At Harare in
Zimbabwe, the diocese has established a project called Outreach based at
the cathedral. This feeds some 300 street children as well as providing some
basic education and skills such as carpentry or sewing in the hope of
creating employment opportunities for them. In South Africa, the author of
an article for IAFN's *Street Children* newsletter, writing of a project linked
with St George's Cathedral in Cape Town, states that poverty, unemployment, alcohol abuse, lack of privacy in homes, physical abuse, and
everything that results from these are the reasons for young people taking
to the streets. The public views the children, victims of the apartheid
system, as a burden and nuisance, and treats them as such. They have no
effective rights and are thus a vulnerable and marginalized community.
They are not as tough and streetwise as they pretend to be. But there is
hope. For the article on the work of the Homestead and the Salesian
Institute in Cape Town goes on to state that once the confidence of the
street children is built up, they respond with willingness to resolve the
difficulties in their lives. Each is a rough diamond that needs the right
handling to reveal its inner worth, to let life grow where it has been
smothered.

This hope is echoed in the work of projects in Bangalore, India, where the Bosco project, linked with the Roman Catholic Church, believes it is education that can help street children live with dignity. Meeting the children in small groups on different street corners led to the idea of street classes. Another innovation is the waste paper management project, which is run by the boys themselves, who then benefit from the income. It is in South America that the despair seems most acute. A Brazilian bishop writes of the street children – sons and daughters of 'street adults' – who find protection in small groups or gangs and turn to a life of petty theft and prostitution. They find shelter in the sewers. They are children born of injustice and poverty, who become little thieves who fight for survival while they are still young enough to suck on a soother. A project worker in Rio de Janeiro, who has established a day centre for street children, describes the four categories of street children: those abandoned by parents or relatives; those who are homeless, living on the streets with their parents; those who are rented; and those who have run away and chosen to live on the streets as life at home is intolerable. Even in such conditions, where children compete with vultures for food from the rubbish dumps, Christian commitment can bring change. An article from Peru tells of Mayaco (the name means 'rotting fish'), who, after some time and much distrust, came to the Centre run for abandoned street boys by Scripture Union, Peru. The Gospel changed his name and his life. With the help of the Centre he managed to obtain a birth certificate and become a legal citizen of Peru. He is now in the army, with work, hope and a future.

There is no doubt that a major underlying cause of children living (and dying) on the streets is poverty. Every minute of the day 47 babies are born into poverty, and it is estimated 800 million people in the world go hungry. For children, even short periods of undernutrition can affect their behaviour, cognitive development and future productivity. (Information from the Presiding Bishop's Fund for World Relief, USA.) A recent report by the World Health Organization points to poverty as the world's biggest killer – especially of children. It is not surprising that the IAFN newsletter *Tackling Poverty in Families* received more articles than any previous issue. Again the stories sent in were of efforts being made by Churches and individual Christians to alleviate the suffering. In Bukedi Diocese, Uganda, the Mothers' Union started a tailoring project to train girls who will then go and help other children to have the skills to earn money both for themselves and their families. Also from Uganda there is the story of Kungu, who left home to fend for himself on the street. His mother, desperately poor, had no way of keeping him home. Single, she struggles to bring up the family of five on her own in the Nairobi slum of Pumwani. Kungu started to come to the St John's community centre, run by the Anglican Church. He joined a special education programme run by the centre for children who have missed out on many years of school. After some time he became a Christian. Through the mediation of the St John's worker, Kungu returned to his mother and began to live at home again. His mother was helped by the loan scheme run by St John's to help families and she now makes a living selling sukuma wiki (a leafy vegetable) wholesale. The manager of the centre says that many people are so used to poverty that they find it hard to believe that they really can change their lives. But for some the miracle is happening.

Even in the richer countries there are many who are poor and the numbers are growing. This was recognized by the United Nations Social Summit held in 1995, at which world leaders pledged themselves to work for both the eradication of absolute poverty and the reduction of relative poverty. Again, children are often the worst affected. More than 21 per cent of US children under age 18, and 25 per cent of children under age 6, are poor. According to a recent report, a third of all children in the UK now live in poverty, with over two million aged under 10 living in families which depend on income support. There are many projects, linked with churches, seeking to give practical help such as running projects on depressed estates to build up skills and confidence, encouraging self help. Women's advice sessions, food co-operatives, credit unions all help families and their children. Others work to bring political pressure to try to ensure that public policies are more supportive of family life and so of children. In New Zealand, a Family Centre in Lower Hutt, run by Anglican Social Services, undertakes research to show the effects of government policy on poor families. The workers feel that the Church needs to play a part in working for a just social policy, and it is to help this that they are researching the experience of people and trying to put numbers on the problems that those setting policy would rather ignore.

Marriage breakdown is another key issue affecting most of the countries of the Anglican Communion. The articles in IAFN's newsletter on *Strengthening Marriage* show that dismay about the rate of such breakdown and the resulting suffering caused to both adults and children is widespread. But the message is that something can be done. Marriage Encounter in Chile, Mothers' Union work in Africa and rigorous marriage preparation in the USA are all helping to strengthen marriages and provide a stable base for the bringing-up of children. In some countries efforts are being made to train and enlist 'ordinary' people from the churches to help support married couples and work to prevent the escalation of problems. Deep and difficult issues are involved in modern marriages: the changing roles of men and women; how to parent; how to grow in relationships; how to resist pressures of materialism and individualism; how to cope with poverty and unemployment. A previous newsletter on the theme of *Women and Violence* made clear the possibility of misery and inequality within the marriage bond. Such disastrous relationships inevitably impact on children. An article from New Zealand told the story of Billy. At 8 years old he was an angry little boy: stealing, verbally abusive and unable to concentrate at school. He was placed on a residential programme run by the Anglican Trust for Women and Children. It was soon clear that Billy's bad behaviour reflected the family's distress. The parents spent a lot of time arguing about how to handle the children and the boy saw his father as the one in charge because he was the one who wielded the strap. The mother's authority was often undermined by her husband, and because he escaped the ensuing stress by going fishing or working overtime, she was left to parent virtually alone. Deeper issues were addressed by the programme, such as the father's belief that his wife was inferior to him and that verbal abuse was an acceptable way of maintaining his power. There was also the wife's feeling of frustration and anger, aimed at her husband but more often directed at the children. With this help, Billy's stealing and aggression stopped and he began to do well at school.

Taking up this issue, *The Challenge of Parenthood* is the theme of another Family Network newsletter. All over the Anglican Communion pressures on parents are felt to be increasing. Some of these reflect social changes: as in Papua New Guinea and parts of Africa with the move to cities in search of work resulting in the fragmentation of more stable rural communities. Pressures of poverty and unemployment add to the difficulties of parents, with single parents often at the bottom of the poverty league even in the more affluent societies. Peer group pressures on children – the keeping of 'bad company', the resorting to alcohol and drugs – are described in articles from Africa and from the West. Projects to support parents range from education – a parenting pack to be used in schools produced by The Children's Society, a major non-governmental organization linked with the Church of England and the Church in Wales – to ambitious attempts for whole parish communities to offer support to parents in a Shared Action scheme in Australia. The vision of this is that all will benefit – single people in the Church community can feel part of a family, older members can become adopted grandparents, older children can learn to care for the younger. The resources of the Church as an inter-generational family can assist isolated parents, struggling to cope in a fragmented community.

Disease is another common enemy of children. The HIV/AIDS pandemic, affecting all countries of the Anglican Communion, devastates the lives of children as well as adults in the prime of life. By now it is expected that over two million children will have developed AIDS. Millions more will have been orphaned, the more fortunate looked after by other family members, many more left to fend for themselves or in the care of siblings – themselves little more than children. Increasing knowledge is a powerful weapon in preventing the accelerating spread of the infection. The newsletter *HIV and AIDS and Young People* tells of efforts in many countries at peer-group education where international Christian organizations like ACET (AIDS Care Education and Training), the Mothers' Union, and many individual churches work with children and young people through drama groups, education classes, and anti-AIDS clubs to spread the message of the dangers of sexual promiscuity and the virtues of fidelity.

Jesus stressed the importance of children: 'If anyone causes one of these little ones who believe in me to sin, it would be better for him to have a large millstone hung around his neck, and to be drowned in the depths of the sea' (Matt 18.6). Concern for children is an imperative for the Anglican Church throughout the world. Through its newsletters, the International Anglican Family Network tries to increase our global understanding of both the problems affecting children and families and ways in which the Churches are trying to help. The work being done by many Anglicans and other denominations, and other world faiths, should not be unsung: it is a right encouragement to us all. But the need to do more is clear – whether through specific projects, Christian education, or pressures to lessen unjust structures in society.

> We are guilty of many errors and many faults but our worst crime is abandoning the children, neglecting the fountain of life. Many things can wait, the children cannot.
>
> (Gabriela Mistral)

Further reading

International Anglican Family Network (IAFN) newsletters:

Refugees and Their Families (Spring 1993)
HIV and AIDS and the Family (October 1993)
Elderly People and the Family (March 1994)
Cohabitation – A Challenge for the Church? (October 1994)
Street Children (February 1995)
Tackling Poverty in Families (October 1995)

Since 1996 the IAFN newsletters have also been published in *Anglican World*:

Women and Violence (Lent 1996)
Strengthening Marriage (Michaelmas 1996)
HIV and AIDS and Young People (Advent 1996)
Moving Families: Migration, Immigration and Asylum (Easter 1997)
The Challenge of Parenthood (Michaelmas 1997)

Issues planned:

Young People: Risk, Exploitation and Abuse (Advent 1997)
Families and Disability (Lent 1998)

Other helpful publications

Amnesty International, *Childhood Stolen: Grave Human Rights Violations Against Children* (London: Amnesty International, 1995).

D. Barrett (ed.), *Child Prostitution in Britain: Dilemmas and Practical Responses* (London: The Children's Society, 1997).

Jo Boydon, *Children of the Cities* (London: Zed Books, 1991).

Thomas Chu, C. Kajawa and A. Rowthorne, *God Works: Youth/Young Adult Ministry Models: Evangelism at Work with Young People* (available from Morehouse Publications, Harrisburg, PA).

Fact Sheets produced by Office of Global Education, Church World Service (Baltimore, USA), e.g. *Children on the Streets, Children for Sale.*

J. Gabarino, K. Kostelny and N. Dubrow, *No Place to Be a Child: Growing up in a War Zone* (Lexington, MA: Lexington Books, 1991).

Jane Lowicki, *'We Can Help Each Other': Setting up a Global Child-to-Child Network* (Geneva: World Council of Churches, 1996).

Naomi Richman, *Communicating with Children: Helping Children in Distress* (London: Save the Children, 1993).

State of the World's Children 1997/Focus on Child Labor (New York: UNICEF Report, 1997). See also 'Child labour', *New Internationalist* (July 1997).

United Nations High Commissioner for Refugees (UNHCR), *Refugee Children; Guidelines on Protection and Care* (Geneva: UNHCR, 1994), available free.

UNICEF, *UN Convention on the Rights of the Child 1989*, available free.

Youth Violence Prevention, resource packet produced by the Ministries with Young People, Episcopal Church Center, New York.

Working with women in the Congo

Emma Wild

Monthly ecumenical women's meetings held in Bunia in north-east Congo display the vibrancy of Christian faith of Congolese women. Resplendent in their colourful vikwembi cloth, the women sing and dance with joyful enthusiasm. The preacher speaks with assurance and clarity. After the sermon, individuals testify to God's work in their lives. Open prayer follows, each woman speaking aloud her praise and intercession and, on occasion, praying for women who have never given birth. A meal is sometimes shared at the end. Notices given show the wide range of

Emma Wild

activities in which Christian women are involved, from communal cultivation of fields to the running of literacy classes and visiting the sick. Most surprising for me is to observe the Anglican women, whom I know well, taking part in all the activities with verve and confidence. They enter fully into the dynamism of these meetings; a stark contrast to the timidity displayed at the other women's meetings I have attended.

Siku ya wamama (Women's Day), held on the feast of the Annunciation, is an important day for the Mothers' Union. The local MU President leads a service and gives a short sermon under the watchful eye of the local clergy*men*. It is the only day during the year when a woman is expected to preach. Then the clergymen give talks on subjects like the obedience of Mary, good conduct in the home, and good relationships with husbands. The clergy also organize the elections in the MU committee to ensure, they say, that there are no arguments among the women. They conclude by holding a communion service. There are no female clergy in north-east Congo; so the clergymen often preside at the women's meetings. A meal is prepared at the end at which the clergy are invited to sit at the top table and are served with the only dish of meat. In a gesture of magnanimity they may invite the president of the MU to eat with them. Through all this the same women who are lively and confident at the ecumenical meeting are shy, demure, apt to giggle and to hang their heads with embarrassment when asked to participate.

The difference between these two meetings is not that one is ecumenical and the other is Anglican; the second scene is familiar in other denominations. The difference is between women-only gatherings and mixed gatherings. When women meet together without men present they are relaxed, open and vivacious. When women are in the company of men, even if they are the majority, they are quiet and self-effacing. Generations of teaching that a woman's place is in the domestic sphere has imbued women with a sense of unworthiness to contribute to public debate or lead a mixed group of people. They are socialized to believe that it is improper for them to speak in front of men. The Anglican Church in Congo has done little to alter these ideas.

Women make up the majority of committed members of a church. They are faithful in attendance and loyal in service. The role they play in the church is an extension of their role in the home: cleaning the churches, preparing parish feasts, looking after visitors. They are members of choirs, Sunday School teachers, and are on occasion asked to take the collection. Senior, respected women may be asked to read the lesson and there are rare examples of them receiving the title 'Deaconess'. Respect is usually given according to the position of their husbands or fathers. The Diocesan Mothers' Union Presidents are all bishops' wives and the capable Director of the Anglican Health Service is believed by other women to be doing the job, not primarily because she is good at it, but because her father was an important pastor. There are other talented women who are able to contribute to the development of women's role in the Church but, almost without exception, these women have this possibility because their husbands are pastors.

The MU has made an important contribution to the role of women in the Church. With its emphasis on marriage and the home it provides women with a model of behaviour which ensures harmony with the status quo. Irene Bahemuka, an urban woman who, on getting married, moved to a village, was grateful to the MU for providing teaching on customs (like that of women kneeling to greet men) because this enabled her to adapt quickly to her new situation. Within the MU, the older women organize seminars for teenage girls in which they learn how to be good wives and mothers. The MU offers a forum for women to meet, discuss those things which concern them, and study the Bible together. It runs self-financing projects which both provide money for the group and give women skills and a personal income. Many women appreciate the support the MU gives in the routine of their lives but a growing number of women would like to see it taking a more prominent and challenging role in the Church.

The provincial MU Trainer, Damali Sabiti, is one such woman. She finds that she cannot fulfil her remit of equipping women for leadership and she believes the stumbling blocks are the male leaders. 'The problem', she says, 'is that the head people are men, so they don't give us opportunities.' In the big cities like Kisangani she has seen women taking part in services, but generally there is little opportunity for women to contribute either in Sunday services or in church meetings. Mugisa Birungi, a teacher of the women's programme at the Provincial Theological College, agrees with Damali, saying that in a church 'if a man isn't present a woman can do nothing'. She knows that women have a vital role to play in all spheres of Church life and yet they are constantly denied participation. Church leaders willingly speak on the behalf of women without consulting them beforehand. They are surprised when women vocalize their problems and they are astonished when they realize how much women are involved in the active running of the Church in other countries. This realization has led to minor changes in the Congo Anglican Church. The Diocesan MU Presidents, the Provincial Trainer and the Anglican Health Service Director are now invited to the Provincial Synod. No other women are present.

Other women who would like more involvement are not considered. Those who believe they have gifts are never approached by the men who have the authority to allow them to participate, and those who attempt to involve themselves are regarded as forward and unwomanly. Because of this, Mugisa feels that they eventually confine themselves simply to household concerns. In their work, Damali and Mugisa are able to study these issues with women who have not had the same level of education. Mugisa's Bible teaching, for example, comes from her Congolese woman's perspective. When one class of women were finding their studies too demanding on top of all their other work they asked that some courses be cut. The one course above all others that they did not want to lose was Mugisa's 'Women in the Bible'. For the first time they realized that, far from being the cause of all evil, as they had often been taught, they were made in the image of God, equal with men. They saw that, like the women of the Bible, they could participate in God's work in many different ways. This fresh understanding of themselves gave them new self-confidence and an awareness of the injustices of their present position.

This marginalized position of women in the leadership of the Anglican Church in Congo has to be understood in its wider context. In Congo, education and health care are minimal, the infrastructure is crumbling and its inhabitants live at subsistence level. The Anglican Church is a relatively small and under-resourced denomination in this vast, chaotic country. Like most other Churches, it lived through the Mobutu regime by keeping its head down and avoiding conflict. Its attitudes reflect the basic aim of its members: survival. It offers a sense of security. Leaders are traditionally given great respect. In the Church this means that the clergy wield much authority; so lay men as well as women are limited in the contribution they can make to the Church. There has been neither the energy to encourage new roles within the Church nor the freedom to take up new challenges. In such an environment, women's issues have not been a priority for men in leadership.

This is borne out in discussions with clergymen on the position of women in the Church. Several reactions are given: the dismissive, the defensive, and the bewildered. Women's participation in leadership and decision-making is dismissed on the grounds that these are the natural roles of men. I was told with great seriousness on *Siku ya wamama* that men needed to be present to help run the event for women because Joseph had helped Mary. My informants completely missed the irony that we were celebrating the conception of Jesus which, according to the gospel accounts, did not involve a man at all. Others exclude women from participation in Church activities because they are not sufficiently educated. School education, or literacy at least, is considered a prerequisite for Church work, no doubt as a result of the traditionally close relationship in mission between education and evangelism. Economic constraints coupled with traditional values means that boys are chosen to attend school while their sisters remain at home.

The majority of women in Congo have been unable to attend even the first years of primary school. Women themselves perceive this to be a handicap in taking a public role. Clergy frequently encourage this sense of inferiority. Academic education has often merely widened the gap between men and women. Other clergy are defensive about a challenge to the traditional role of women in their Churches. They defend the status quo by saying innovations are contrary to African culture. They insist that women have refused to be involved in meetings or the leading of worship when asked, or that women have never expressed an interest in being involved. 'We've tried but it didn't work', they say. This timidity of women is a problem of society, they believe; so it is unfair simply to blame men. The bewildered clergy are those who would like to see more women taking active roles in the Church but cannot understand why women do not always respond to their requests for more involvement. These men believe sincerely in teaching men to love and respect their wives as well as vice versa. They organize events for women, not realizing that women need examples from their own sex.

All these reactions suggest that most clergy have not tried to put themselves into the shoes of the women with whom they are working. They have not asked themselves why one woman might refuse to take a public role, or what she might feel about having been socialized to accept that her father, brothers and her husband are superior to her and have a right to demand obedience and submission from her. Nor have clergymen understood why another woman might not be satisfied with all their efforts on her behalf. The clergy would do well to listen to the women in their congregations if they want all the members of the body of Christ to work together with their full potential.

A gradual change is taking place vis-à-vis women's roles. Joyce Muhindo, the first female graduate of the Provincial Theological College, is proof of this. She sees changes elsewhere as well. In the Aru area close to the border of Uganda, she met women whose husbands were supportive of their studying at Bible school, recognizing their call by the Holy Spirit. In her own Diocese of North Kivu there is a small group of women lay readers who have followed a course of biblical training. Unfortunately, they are not yet involved with leadership. Joyce has met other women who started a course only to leave without completing. In all of these cases Joyce points to the conflicting interests which are at play: the needs of the family and the desire to serve God in a leadership capacity. Joyce would like to see greater encouragement from Church leaders for the training of women. She believes an emphasis on Theological Education by Extension would enable women to study and remain at home where they can continue to look after their families. These women do not want to desert their roles as wives and mothers as their detractors suggest but they do believe they have other talents to offer the Church.

In Goma, one parish has been consciously targeting women. Realizing that women are reticent about taking a public role in the Church the pastor has been organizing seminars on 'How to lead services'. Claudine Muka-nirwa, a seamstress, was delighted to find that she was expected to take a larger part in church life. 'Before this', she said, 'I knew I didn't have a role to play in the church. I just wanted to deepen my personal knowledge of the Bible. But now I see the necessity of getting involved.' She also mentioned that the members of the MU were encouraged that the same pastor showed an interest in their group by popping in every so often and listening, 'as if he were a woman' (!), rather than appearing simply to lead the group. This example shows the prevalent desire of Congolese women to be encouraged by the male leadership. Their sense of worth is increased if their pastor takes an interest in their affairs. The Anglican Church would do well to appreciate this when considering women's participation. On the other hand women might observe from the experiences of others that men are generally reluctant to support women in projects which may lead to the diminishing of their control.

Anglican women in Congo already contribute greatly to the life of the Church. They comprise the majority of committed members, they work tirelessly behind the scenes for festivals, they provide hospitality for visitors and at synods. All this they do with good will. They are aware, however, that they are not consulted in the running of events, but are merely expected to carry out orders. In services where there are no male inter-mediaries women enter into worship of God wholeheartedly and show themselves just as able as men to lead, organize and take decisions. An increasing number of women believe that the Church would more closely represent the body of Christ if leadership were shared more equally between men and women and if the concerns of women were more clearly under-stood. They believe that they have God-given talents which have yet to be used to their full potential in the Church.

Corrymeela: healing the division

Trevor Williams

(The total population of Ireland, North and South, is just over 5.1 million. There are 3.8 million Roman Catholics, 382,000 Church of Ireland, 350,000 Presbyterians and 64,000 Methodists. However, 75 per cent of Church of Ireland members live in Northern Ireland, where Protestants form the majority. During almost three decades of violence in Northern Ireland, the Christian Churches have made it a priority to care for the injured and bereaved and to restrain the vengeful. The ministry of reconciliation has been pioneered by a growing number of intentional ecumenical communities. The Corrymeela Community founded in 1965 was one of the first. Corrymeela's membership represents all the main Christian denominations. In 1996 the Church of Ireland set up a Commission to investigate sectarianism within the Church. Trevor Williams is the first Anglican priest to be elected leader of the Corrymeela Community.)

The turning of a millennium presents an opportunity for reflection. The communications revolution and ease of travel have transformed the world into a global village. However although the means of communication are accessible, and the opportunity to meet across the geographical, cultural and religious divides has never been easier, we still live with division, misunderstanding, injustice, and violence. The cold war may now be slightly warmer, but the fear of a world war between superpowers has been replaced by the reality of ethnic conflict bringing unimaginable suffering. The roots of ethnic conflict are difficult to understand to the outsider. They lie deep within the life of local communities and personal memories. The observer is deeply disturbed at how neighbours, who have lived side by side for so long, can suddenly commit such atrocities on one another. The 'sound bite' of modern communication is inadequate for the task. Belfast is 'bomb city' and that's all that most people in the rest of the world know about Northern Ireland; it's a crazy place where Christians kill each other in the madness of a religious war. Our modern mass communications have become expert in showing the 'what' but poor in revealing the 'why'.

However, in Northern Ireland our communication is also flawed. We find it difficult to cross our cultural and religious groupings to understand the others. Rather, we blame them for the troubles we experience. And in finding someone to blame, we blind ourselves from our responsibility to find ways of living together with those who are different.

The roots of Northern Ireland's violence stretch far back into our history. What is important is that Northern Ireland, or the North of Ireland as others insist on calling it, is a 'contested' place. Like many other 'contested' places it is the legacy of settlement and colonization, where the historically-defined native and settler groups exist in relatively balanced proportions to one another. In Northern Ireland the contest remains unresolved through the inability of either group to finally dominate the other. What remains is an uneasy tranquillity. But beneath the apparent calm is uncertainty, caution and fear. Such insecurity leads to a perspective where life is viewed as a contest between 'them' and 'us'. There is little 'common sense' between the two sides. Each side claims to know the 'true facts' of any situation. At the same time nobody can agree on what are the 'true facts'. Two histories exist, two sets of attitudes and prejudices, two loyalties, two cultures, two sets of tradition. The common factor is a deep rooted fear of 'the other'. Education and employment become battle grounds for 'our rights'. Religious and cultural symbols can become badges of identity showing who belongs to us and who belongs to the enemy. The distinguishing political aspirations, for union with Britain or independence from Britain, is pursued by each side as a fundamental right and is non-negotiable. The differences between the two traditions are symbols of threat. Each new situation is interpreted to support the age-old truths, the battle between 'them' and 'us'.

Since 1969, this psychological distance has been increased by deep suffering, the result of 27 years' violence. Almost every family in Northern Ireland has suffered its own personal tragedy. These hurts and wounds have further hardened the hearts and minds. In the early 1970s housing estates where Catholics and Protestants lived side by side as neighbours were targeted by the paramilitary forces claiming to represent the majority tradition on the estate, making sure that the estate was 'cleansed' of the others. The trend 'to live with your own sort' has continued since then so that today the majority of people in Northern Ireland live in areas which are predominantly Catholic or Protestant. Because of segregated housing and schooling many people never meet those 'from the other side' during their formative years. The other side continue to be feared and blamed for the troubles. Those from one tradition cannot understand why 'the others' feel as they do. So the stereotypes generally held remain unchallenged, and attitudes and postures remain fixed. Political compromise is suspect and progress towards peace well nigh impossible. It's easy to fan a spark of fear into the flame of violence.

What I have been describing is not a story unique to Northern Ireland. Echoes of our experience can be found in many 'ethnic frontiers' in central Europe and elsewhere, and indeed between alienated communities in more settled societies.

The paramilitary campaigns of violence in Northern Ireland are based within the most socially deprived communities. Unemployment rates are typically over 80 per cent, where life offers little hope to young people, and where there are few facilities to enhance life. Lack of hope can even make violence attractive, as was expressed in this poem by a Belfast teenager.

> God no, please
> give me violence

again, to drown this silence
which is killing me.
... Big streets empty, full of little
papers, cigarette ends, decaying spittle
and walking here only causes dust to move.
... The big wind blows
all the dust to other footpaths,
nice and empty ...
The snobby sun thinks he knows
it all, looking down, and he can only see
someone spitting here.
It's only me!

The alienation of hopelessness where the excitement of violence, the commitment to a cause, the camaraderie which demands you risk your life for your friend, the esteem of the hero is so much better than nothing. Violence thrives in a vacuum.

Corrymeela is a Christian community of Catholics and Protestants who commit themselves to work together to find a way of peace and reconciliation in a landscape where politics is paralysed by fear and where religion is impotent because it is used as a symbol of tribal identity. The pastoral task of caring for a traumatized community has made it very difficult for many Church communities to undertake the costly task of reconciliation.

Corrymeela is seeking to find how faith can be part of the solution. In affirming the unique value of each individual and all life; in seeking to practise the gift of forgiveness which can open a new future liberated from the past; in providing a safe place where opposing sides can meet and recognize our common humanity, we have found that fear can be replaced by trust, ignorance by understanding, and that hostility can give way to peace.

Following Jesus Christ, his life of non-violence, his solidarity with the victim and the oppressed, his creation of an inclusive community of love, his call to walk the path of justice and peace, this is the way Corrymeela has committed itself to.

For the 180 members of the dispersed community, Corrymeela is about creating a 'safe space' where those who enter are not judged, but accepted as they are; where each one can learn of his or her unique value; where it becomes possible to meet others from a different background; where differences can be acknowledged, shared, examined, and sometimes appreciated; where it's possible to learn to live with difference, without fear. In meeting in this way, in sharing the stories of our lives, our joys and sorrows, our difficulties and accomplishments in small groups, from both traditions, Catholic and Protestant, a new way of living in Northern Ireland is being discovered. Instead of excluding 'the other', instead of fearing 'the other', blaming 'the other', demonizing 'the other', we attempt to bring the enemy close. We believe that if we come close enough to recognize our common humanity we can discover the first step of a new way forward together.

This process takes place in regular small group meetings of ten or so members of Corrymeela, as well as in large community gatherings. We find that it's in the journeying together with trusted friends of both traditions that we are open to learn of our own prejudices and stereotypes and are faced with the option and opportunity for change.

What we experience as members of Corrymeela, we wish to share with others. We wish our centre at Ballycastle to be a place of welcome and encounter for Protestant and Catholic groups, of young people, schools, family groups, community and Church organizations. The groups come and live as a community for two or three days, or longer, at our residential centre. Ground rules are explored and accepted by the groups with each person agreeing to treat others in the way they would wish to be treated. Common themes frequently emerge. No one is put under pressure to speak; no one is interrupted; if questions are asked, the person asked doesn't have to reply, and has a right to know what the interest of the other is in the question; people are encouraged to speak for themselves about their own experience. Generalizations about others are discouraged, and confidentiality is respected. As well as formal sessions, time is taken to find other ways of exploring new territory – from helping one another to walk safely up a river midstream, to finding new ways to express yourself in arts, crafts and drama. And sharing the household chores together.

The sharing of stories is a favourite pastime in Irish culture, and is central to all our work. Rather than discussing opinions, which in Northern Ireland so often leads to a sterile verbal battle, the shared story of human experience can create a sense of empathy and understanding. In the shared story you learn not only the 'what' but the 'why'. As personal stories are shared and heard, the seeds of a new community are sown.

Not long ago during a residential programme with two schools, one Catholic, the other Protestant, fifty 16-year-olds split into groups of eight, four Catholics and four Protestants. One of our volunteers was facilitating the discussion on 'How the years of violence have affected my life'. As is often the case, the discussion wandered a little at first. And then one girl had the courage to say 'My father was a member of the police and he was shot by the IRA'. She went on to talk about her father, and her feelings at his murder and how her family had been affected. In many contexts such a story could not be told in mixed company of Catholics and Protestants. The two communities have very different views on the police and this girl couldn't guarantee a sympathetic hearing for her story. But the others listened, Catholics and Protestants listened until she had finished. Then another young person told his story, and another, and another. In the end six out of eight of those young people told stories about how they had lost a close family member or friend as a direct result of the troubles. There were a lot of tears. And the pupils comforted each other. After that group session the six young people, three Protestants and three Catholics, couldn't be separated. They ate their meals together, they went on walks together. They had so much suffering in common, even though at another time and place they could be expected to regard one another as the enemy. However I believe it was more than shared grief which bound them together. It was being able to tell your story to a member of that community from which the murderers came; to experience the other listening and hearing, and being moved with compassion. Then in turn to realize their suffering, with so many opposites in it, was just the same. This was the real relief, that a new relationship was possible with those who had been the cause of so much terror. In sharing their grief together, they had glimpsed a new way of living in Northern Ireland, a way of sharing and hope, rather than division and fear.

We are a Christian community, and twice a day worship is held in our worship centre called the Croi, which is the Irish word for 'heart'. Everyone is invited to come, though no expectation is attached to the invitation. Worship is simple and short; it involves a reading from Scripture, relating to what has been happening in the groups, some singing and prayer. At the end of another residential the person was concluding worship and asked if someone was concerned about some other person, they might like to ask the group to pray in silence for that person. One girl responded and said 'I would like you all to pray for a man in prison tonight. He is very worried and his family is also very worried. He is about to receive his sentence. I would like you to pray for him.' Later she was asked 'Who was it you asked us to pray for?' She said, quite simply, 'He's the man who murdered my father'.

In Belfast there are huge barriers, 16–18-foot-tall walls, erected to keep neighbours apart. They run down the interfaces where Catholic areas meet Protestant areas. These huge structures mean that some people have to keep the light on in their kitchen all year round because they live in the shadow of these 'Peace Walls', as they are called. At the one time they are symbols of security and symbols of fear. We have been bringing families who live on both sides of the Peace Wall together. They had decided to try to do something with the fear, and find a new way forward.

The dialogue started with a feelings box. Each person wrote a single word on a piece of paper representing what it felt like to live in the shadow of the Peace Wall and put the paper into a slot in the box. Then the pieces of paper were taken from the box and read out anonymously. People were free to add something if they wished. It was impossible to tell from which side of the wall they came. Whether they were Protestant feelings or Catholic feelings. Sadness was the most common. Sadness at the loss of loved ones, the lost childhood for their young people growing up with constant violence on the streets where they lived. Several people put in the word hatred. As 'hatred' came out of the box one woman said 'I don't mean to say that I hate anyone. What I meant was that I don't wish to carry on knowing that I am hated, and that my children are hated.' That's what we hear, as the young people yell abuse as they see if they can throw bricks over the massively high wall.

The group went on to discuss what they understood as 'community'. Both sides had no problem agreeing what was important for them. They talked about what they hoped for in the year 2000. Both sides wanted peace, and better amenities for their children, and jobs. At the end of their residential the Catholic group and the Protestant group decided they needed to work together for the development of their area. One of their dreams was to have a common community centre where both communities could continue to meet and support each other.

Meanwhile the children were meeting. They watched a clown as he came into the room, dressed in an outlandish costume. The more the children laughed at him, the sadder he got. Until he was crumpled up on the ground sobbing. They recognized that feeling, being laughed at because you were different, and both sides talked about their experiences of bullying in school.

They then began talking about their favourite pastime, throwing bricks over the Peace Wall. Since they met a day ago on arriving at Corrymeela, Paddy and William, a Catholic and Protestant, had become the best of mates. Paddy was the best shot in the district.

'Paddy, what if you hit William?'

'Oh, I wouldn't.'

'How is that?'

'I'm a good shot. I wouldn't aim at William.'

'But sometimes you can't see who you will hit, the wall is too high.'

Paddy thought, long and hard. 'Yea, you're right. I'm going to have to climb up to the top of the derelict house where I can get a really good aim.'

'But Paddy, last weekend you could have injured William with a stone, because then you didn't know him. How would you feel about that now?'

'Bad!' said Paddy.

Eventually Paddy and the rest of the group decided that they would stop throwing stones.

The person who led that programme was passing through the area where they lived a couple of weeks later and saw some of the children hanging around opposite the one place where you could see through the wall. She was curious as to what was going on. So she stopped. The children said they wait there everyday on the way back from school, to wave to their new friends on the Protestant side. It's the way they keep in touch with their new friends.

When we hear one another, a new reality is created between us.

Corrymeela is about creating space for that new reality. Creating space where the new, the unexpected can be encountered as people meet, tell their stories and face new choices about their future together.

Further reading

R. Davey, *A Channel of Peace* (Belfast: Marshall Pickering, 1993).

D. Morrow and D. Wilson, *Ways out of Conflict* (Belfast: Understanding Conflict Trust, 1996).

J. Morrow, *Journey of Hope: Sources of the Corrymeela Vision* (Belfast: Corrymeela Press, 1995).

Section Four

Mission of the Church

Dalits and salvation

J. Aruldoss

Who are the Dalits?

D, a five-year-old girl from a small village in Tamil Nadu in south-east India, was badly beaten up by her schoolteacher and lost her eyesight. This child cannot now see the difference between a branch and a snake and was beaten up for no other reason than that she had drunk water at school from a glass reserved only for higher-caste communities. The normal practice in that school is that children belonging to the Dalit (so-called 'untouchable' or 'Harijan' communities) should be asked to cup their hands if they wish to drink, while someone else pours water into them. The sin committed by this poor child was to drink from a vessel.

M. is a fertile village just ten miles from the great temple city of Madurai. The cobbler community, a Dalit caste, live separately from the high-caste Hindus, have no land, and are in a state of bonded labour. They earn no money, only a share of the rice harvest. If they need money, they have to borrow it against that share of the harvest, or from an outside moneylender, at interest of 10 per cent a month. Their women are exploited in all senses of that word. For a period a number of families became Christian, attracted by the person of Jesus, by the concern of evangelists, and by the liberating possibilities in this new faith. Worship took place on Sunday morning and they were bonded to work seven days a week. When one of their number decided to go to church rather than to the fields, he was brutally beaten and forced back to work. The village were divided as to whether he should complain to the police, some saying that it was a matter of social justice, others saying that he had broken age-old rules of bondage (more or less slavery, and now illegal) and that they should keep quiet.

Under these pressures, it is not surprising that most have reverted to Hinduism, though in some other villages, converts can point to the wounds they have received, or those who died, in order to establish the right to worship on a Sunday.

These incidents, repeated a thousand times over each year, symbolize the plight of the so-called 'untouchables' of India, perhaps 18 per cent of the total population of over 900 million people.

There is much speculation and historical research into the origin of these people. Dr James Massey, a leading academic and Dalit activist from the Church of North India, in his book *The Historical Roots of Dalits*, establishes the view that Dalits are the early settlers of India or they share their historical roots with the indigenous people of India. There are many other scholars who substantiate this view. Dalits also descend from the people of the renowned early Indus Valley civilization. But later these indigenous people were subjugated by the fair-skinned Aryans who came into India around 2000 BC. They were degraded as outcastes and untouchables through the caste system introduced by the Aryans. In the British period, they were known as 'the depressed castes', and in independent India as 'Scheduled Castes'. Gandhi named them 'Harijans', people blessed by God. But in recent years they have themselves adopted the name 'Dalit'.

It is said in the ancient Hindu text, the Rig Veda, that the primal man was divided into four parts from which four sections of people were created. From the head of the primal man came the Brahmin, the priestly caste whose profession is education; from the shoulder the Kshatriya, who is a warrior; from the stomach the Vaisya, whose profession is trading; and from the leg and feet came the Shudra, whose occupation is serving the above three sections of people, as labourer. The first three are 'twice born' (through physical birth and through spiritual birth). In this stratification of society, the indigenous Dalits are not even mentioned. They had a different culture and religion, not part of this 'dharma' or caste system. They were later brought in, therefore, as outcastes, not part of this system of 'varna', a word meaning 'colour', which gave a racial basis to society, with a religious sanction. The indigenous people were brought under this system as 'Panchamas' which means 'fifth category' and were branded as untouchable. So evolved the caste system in India.

Concepts of religious purity, pollution and exclusion have further degraded their situation. They were seen as people polluted by the material world because their occupation included dealing with dead animal carcasses, cobbling and leather work, removing human excrement, providing services after deaths, including carrying the news and providing music, and general labouring work. This close contact with the material world affected upward mobility. They were excluded from most temple worship, public places and social gatherings, and were forced to live in segregated sections

295

J. Aruldoss

outside the main village. They could not use the same wells or drinking vessels. They were expected to give way in the village street to their 'superiors' and were not expected to use sandals, umbrellas or bicycles in the presence of the higher castes. They were addressed in a form of language suggestive of a higher to a lower person. A high-caste child should use such language of superior to inferior, even when addressing adults or the elderly from the Dalit community. Most are landless and many are 'bonded labourers', de facto slaves to the high-caste, with their women often expected to give their sexual services (strangely, here pollution is not taken so seriously!).

Pollution is not related primarily to physical cleanliness but to ritual and spiritual purity. They cannot change their position as it is related to their birth. Their birth in this world is determined by deeds in their previous births, through the belief in 'reincarnation' and in 'karma' (the fruits of one's deeds) carried with one in this life and from life to life. So it takes many births to change status by observing caste duties assigned. No change in this life is possible if one is born in a lower community. The present (1997) President of India is a Dalit, and remains such, in spite of his having one of the two highest offices in the country. Though outlawed by the Indian constitution of 1950, untouchability, open or covert, continues to differing degrees throughout India to this day. When atrocities are committed, a case can be brought, but proof is difficult and legal power and money power are with the higher castes.

Dalits originally had their own religion(s) and cultures, but gradually these were subjugated into Hinduism. Many scholars established this view, that Dalits are not in origin Hindus but were absorbed into Hinduism. Such scholars include J. A. Sharrock, T. E. Slater, James Massey, Theophilus Appavoo, Pupul Jeyakan, and above all Abraham Ayrookuzhiel. Abraham died in 1996, was from Kerala and had been ordained in England into the Anglican Church. He spent the last twenty or so years of his life researching the local traditions of the Dalit peoples and discovered a rich and diverse religious culture, mostly unwritten and found in song and poem and story, and often deeply dignified and liberative in its spiritual depth.

This was not the view of Gandhi, nor of other leading Hindus, who see Dalits as essentially part of the Hindu fold. But, disagreeing with Gandhi's view, their leaders have chosen the name Dalit in recent years. The word 'Dalit' means 'broken', 'oppressed', 'crushed'. The word indicates their sufferings, anguish and aspiration for liberation.

After their absorption into Hinduism they lost their religious identity. Their religion and culture were vulgarized and damaged, and oppressive culture and religious ideas were imposed on them. Their temples were gradually 'Sanskritized' (brought into the dominant Hindu system). Salva-

296

tion is impossible for them in this life as they are born as untouchables. In the not so distant past, Dalit ears and throats were said to be plugged with molten lead if they tried to learn the Vedas.

So the Dalits looked for opportunities to empower themselves. They embraced other religions as a social protest against the inhuman and unjust practices of Hindu society. They also embraced other religions for a means of gaining the real spiritual and salvation experience which has been denied to them. It was also a search for new identity within other religions. They converted to Islam, Buddhism, Sikhism and Christianity and now constitute a considerable number within each religion.

Dalits constitute a majority within all Christian Churches, over 90 per cent within the Church of North India, and well over 50 per cent in the Church of South India. They have come largely through group movements over the last two centuries. Liberation in Christ has not always led to liberation in the Body of Christ, where the Church remains often still divided on caste grounds. Efforts are now being made, by Dalits themselves, in all Churches, to rectify this, and the process is painful, but it seems it is a necessary part of the process by which a Church can eventually be achieved in which there need be 'no Jew nor Greek, no slave nor free, no rich nor poor', but all can be one in Christ.

Dalits, who were often known as 'Dasas', servants or slaves of the upper caste, after conversion started using names such as Christadoss, Jesudoss and Devadoss (slave of Christ, Jesus, God). There is the well-known hymn of D. T. Niles, 'Slaves of Christ, His mercy we remember'. My own name, Aruldoss, means 'slave or servant of grace'. Our names themselves are protests against Hindu caste imperialism.

The most important name for Dalits in recent times is Dr Ambedkar, a great lawyer from their community, who wrote the constitution of the new India, and who, along with several million other Dalits, converted to Buddhism in Maharashtra in 1956. More than a decade before this, he had announced that he would not die a Hindu, since there was no place for a Dalit there. After much reflection he rejected both Christianity and Islam as foreign religions. Sikhism was too localized, and his conversion to Buddhism, he felt, was conversion to an Indian as well as a universal religion. This movement, known by some as neo-Buddhism, has helped Buddhism become re-established in the land of the historical Buddha's birth.

Others have converted to Islam, including a fair number in recent years. New Muslims appear here to have found a degree of equality and acceptance from old Muslims that has greatly encouraged the converts. But the political backlash from Hinduism, where conversion to Islam is seen as a political move of national significance, has ensured that the movement remains small and largely symbolic. In response, certain cosmetic changes

J. Aruldoss

have been made within local Hinduism, to encourage Dalits to remain loyal
to what is claimed is the only true 'Indian' religion.

Many remain in Hinduism and some seek for liberation through reform
movements within the religion, such as egalitarian 'bhakti' groups (spiritual, charismatic-style movements). The majority of Dalits classified as
Hindus are practising a village religion different from the orthodox
Hinduism, which is classified as the 'little tradition' by scholars, as opposed
to the 'great' or Sanskrit/Brahminic tradition, much venerated by traditional Western orientalists and scholars of comparative religion.

Dalits and salvation

Dalits, as seen above, are not a homogeneous religious group. They
themselves are also divided into sub-castes, and in the insidious way of the
caste system, and indeed of human nature, these sub-castes have become
hierarchical, with de facto 'higher' and 'lower' Dalits. Religiously Dalits are
ecumenical and pluralistic. They have a different world depending on to
which religion they belong. There cannot therefore be one particular view
on salvation for Dalits.

But they share a common reality, that which they need to be 'saved
from'. The common reality is that they suffer from dehumanization,
oppression and injustice. Based on this common reality, which a Christian
could call 'corporate sin', or the oppression of 'principalities and powers' in
a very tangible sense, understanding of salvation has common aspects for
them, within each religion to which they belong.

Important common aspects of Dalits' understanding of salvation

For Dalits, irrespective of their religious background, justice, freedom and
liberation became the pre-condition for spiritual enlightenment or salvation. All should be trusted equally and there should be no discrimination
based on birth. Only with these preconditions can the Dalit experience
spiritual salvation. To achieve such is indeed a kind of spiritual liberation.
It is only if basic social needs are fulfilled that men and women can have the
possibility and space for contemplation and self-realization. As their
physical and social needs are fulfilled human beings can search for a level of
understanding of the divine. Such is a continuous process.

There are some theologians who see that social and spiritual dimensions
of salvation are two sides of the same coin. They cannot be separated.
Salvation and humanization are interlinked. This view is much expressed
by M. M. Thomas in his book *Salvation and Humanisation* (Bangalore,
1970).

298

The next aspect of Dalit understanding of salvation is that the divine experience of salvation has to be transformed into action. The God experience may differ between religions, but that divine experience has to become a tangible reality. It has to be experienced through action in this material world. Salvation according to the Dalit is a corporate experience. The whole universe, not only fellow human beings, has to be included, and only then can the individual's salvation experience become complete. He or she has to work for the salvation of the whole universe. The enlightenment experience cannot be a solitary one. Here, the ideas of Mahayana Buddhism are clearly to the fore, with the Boddhisattva concept, that the individual and potentially enlightened person, who is capable of realizing his or her Buddha nature, voluntarily renounces that possibility, and returns to teach others the way, since the salvation of one depends on the salvation of all. We can think too of Romans 8, with its ideas of the whole creation groaning for redemption.

Another aspect of the Dalit understanding of salvation is that 'nothing is final', every vision is partial and incomplete. Every vision about the divine or the ultimate is partial. Everyone has to respect the visions of others and try to be enriched by the vision of others, and also help others to be enriched by their own vision.

Dalits are among the most suffering communities in the world. Their suffering lies within each religion, where conversion so often has not brought the liberation for which they had longed. Christian Dalit converts, for example, find themselves known as 'Christian Paraiyars' or 'Christian Chamars', and often continue to face discrimination within the Church as well as within society. The most hopeful change in recent years is a growing self-consciousness of their situation, and a determination not to rely only on the law or on well-wishers from outside to help them, but that they are increasingly working together for their own salvation. In this the pluralism of the Dalit community, in their various communities, needs to be balanced by a solidarity across religious communities. If this is achieved, the Dalit understanding of salvation can become a model for others to be more inclusive and pluralistic, which is essential in an India where a healthy pluralism is increasingly under threat from political and religious fundamentalist forces.

Further reading

A. Ayrookuzhiel, *The Sacred in Popular Hinduism* (Bangalore: CISRS, 1985), and many other books and articles.
Dalit International Newsletter, published quarterly: PO Box 932, Waterford, CT 06385, USA.

V. Devasayagam (ed.), *Frontiers of Dalit Theology* (Delhi: ISPCK/Madras: Gurukul, 1997).
James Massey, *Dalits in India* (Delhi: ISPCK, 1995).
James Massey, *Roots* (Delhi: ISPCK, 1996).
J. Webster, *The Dalit Christians* (Delhi: ISPCK, 1992).
A. Wingate, *The Church and Conversion* (Delhi: ISPCK, 1997).

Anglican educational institutions and the mission of the Church

A case study of St John's College, Agra (Church of North India, founded by the Anglican Church)

Pervez Deen and Rina Deen

Anglican higher educational institutions were often a redeeming factor in regions with an otherwise doubtful or unpleasant history of British colonialism. A clear example is India, with its many colleges throughout the subcontinent. As India celebrates the fiftieth year of its independence in 1997, these continue to be of continuing importance, in spite of their ambiguous 'Western' origin, and their continuing Christian ethos. A report in the journal *India Today* (June 1997) placed five Christian colleges among the top ten in India, and St Stephen's, Delhi, the Anglican foundation, as in first rank in the country. Criteria were academic, popularity and facilities, and of course they are, through being in the list at all, clearly elitist in their ethos.

A recurring question arises, historically and in the present: is the vision of involvement to a high degree in secular education consistent with the Gospel mission of the Church? In 1929, John McKenzie, Principal of Wilson College, Bombay, observed 'There is no branch of missionary work which has been subjected to so much criticism as educational work', since to many it was 'difficult to understand why missionaries should give so much time and energy to secular education'. Questions here are not about lower-level school education, but about the development of university-level colleges and prestigious high schools. A further contemporary question is what is now distinctive, if anything, about such institutions, apart from their historical Christian foundation? To clarify such questions, we will look at the case study of St John's Agra, founded in 1850, in the city of the Taj Mahal, now in Uttar Pradesh.

The College was founded by the Agra Mission as a place of witness through works rather than just words. It was one of a number of institutions which included an orphanage, a printing press, Christian housing settlements and other educational institutions parented by the college. It was in Agra too that the first north Indian Christian to receive Anglican ordination, the famous convert from Islam Abdul Masih, became pastor of St John's church, which was opened at the same time as the founding of the college. Over the next 150 years, both secular and Church contexts have changed dramatically. A mission became a Church, the Anglican Church entered the Church of North India. Agra was in the epicentre of much of the struggle, beginning in 1857, with the Indian mutiny/insurrection, which ended with Indian independence 90 years later. A colonial and 'Christian' government gave way to secular India, with its Hindu dominance by population. As Zechariah Mathai asked in an important study in 1979, 'How do we react (in higher education) to a changed historical situation?' What continue to be its essential rationale and attributes?

The founding missionaries had believed that 'intellectual and spiritual illumination belong closely together'. This, we believe, still holds today. Even in mission terms, people are challenged more authentically by the Gospel where there is education rather than ignorance. A distinctive Christian character is given to an institution by both what it professes and the quality it delivers.

Christian principles are affirmed explicitly in general assemblies, staff meetings, chapel services, and voluntary moral and religious education classes. Emphasis is on interfaith understanding towards 'the peace of God that passes all understanding'. When communalism occasionally percolates college life, it is confronted, as daily prayer emphasizes human concerns and values and common vision.

The Christian ethos of the college is symbolized by the prominent cross at the centre of the main dome of this new building. Its architect, Swinton Jacob, worked largely without pay, as his contribution to a 'redemptive purpose'. When Michael Ramsey visited, as Archbishop of Canterbury, he commented 'This morning I saw the Taj Mahal, the ancient glory of India, and now I see [in St John's] the modern glory of India'. Prime Minister Nehru, visiting in 1959, said he was coming as 'a tribute to the good work the College had done for over 100 years'. He would have recognized the courageous stand of the first Principal, in insisting on providing refuge for Indians as well as British, defying British orders, in the 1857 period. In the same tradition, in the recent and equally terrible conflicts between Muslims and Hindus associated with the destruction of the mosque at nearby

Ayodhya, when hundreds died in Agra, the college provided a refuge for numerous people of all religions.

The founding Principal, Revd French, represented 'the high ideal of Christ ever present in their midst'. This description was of its time, and something more different is needed today, within the secular framework of the nation. Moreover, Principals ceased to be clergy long ago. Clergy are now usually underqualified for what is a distinguished professional role. However Christian a Principal may be, he or she must be professionally extremely competent, if the institution is to remain respected.

Structurally, it is the college–Church connection that provides the vital extra-academic dimension if Christian identity is to be maintained. The Bishop of Agra is the Chairman of the college, Principals are active lay Church leaders, Christian staff and students are committed to chapel and church worship outside, thus linking college and Church. Such a commitment has become even more important, as numbers in the college have risen sharply, while the proportion of Christians has fallen. Daily assembly with Christian prayer, Bible classes, moral and religious education programmes, Student Christian Movement activities and Christian festival celebrations, Christian Teachers' Retreats are all vital components of maintaining identity. All are voluntary, and, of course, other religions have their own programmes, conducted through the College Teachers' Association. In addition, social outreach programmes take place, linking spiritual concern with social action.

From as early as 1862, the College is recorded, in its history, as having 'taken a great moral stand against the tyranny of the Hindu caste system', by admitting people from outcaste groups (now known as Dalits). A heavy price was paid at St John's for this stance, as 180 students withdrew in protest, seven teachers resigned, and a parallel Hindu college was established in retaliation. Students from such 'backward' communities were helped over the years with easier access, concessions, books, guidance and vocational support.

A special concern was shown for the even larger and more deprived sector, women and girls, through the opening of St John's Girls' School early in the twentieth century. This was for the home-confined sisters of St John's boys, who were bound by 'the excuses of early marriage, purdah restrictions, family customs and the like'. Today, women in the college continue to receive equal educational opportunities, proctorial protection, and a separate common room.

The way Anglicans and afterwards the CNI have founded and encouraged institutions for women has been a pioneering story in a country where, around 1900, it was calculated in a special survey conducted by Pandita Ramabai that fewer than 1 per cent of women in British India could read. Ramabai was a Christian convert as important in her own way as the rightly renowned and venerated Sadhu Sunder Singh. It is perhaps because she was a woman that she was little remembered until recent times.

A convert from a high caste, influenced above all by the story of the Samaritan woman in John 4, and by her experience of social work seen in London with so-called 'fallen women', when teaching at Cheltenham Ladies' College, she returned to India and, besides becoming the first woman member of the Indian National Congress, she conducted this survey and, motivated by this, founded a women's university and several other institutions. It was in such a tradition that St John's Agra can be seen.

The character of this kind of special service to the disadvantaged sectors is all the more important when a national survey in 1986 showed that the so-called higher educational boom, instead of equalizing opportunities, had in fact legitimized or even aggravated inequality over the years.

Another radical step, taken as early as 1911 at St John's, was to end the segregation of students by religious affiliation. Until then, Hindu, Muslim and Christian students were housed in different hostels, in itself limiting Christian influence. Now, all were placed together, and Muslims and Christians at least ate together, with the Principal of the time declaring 'It is not the function of a Christian College to perpetuate caste restrictions, but rather to promote the Brotherhood of Man – and the time for a bolder advance in this direction seems to have arrived'.

In general, this non-sectarian attitude has been maintained, certainly compared with what is seen in many Indian institutions. Occasionally there is some reaction to what is seen as 'Christian bias' in appointments, accommodation or admissions. But this has normally been assuaged through a process of dialogue within what is valued by all as an open institution.

St John's is an active member of the association of Colleges and Universities of the Anglican Communion, which held its second international conference in Delhi in January 1997. Its present Principal, Dr Ipe, is on its steering committee. He sees this association as a way that St John's can interact in a global way, enabling mutual support, and sharing of resources, such as accommodation, hospitality, observation and research facilities.

The founder of the college had expressed its aim as 'character-building', very much in line with the Victorian ideals behind British public schools of that time. It was to give 'a liberal education through ... a distinctive Christian atmosphere, which would produce a new and higher moral type of character'. This was 'the supreme aim and object for which a missionary college should exist'. From the staff there can be expected even today both academic and faith commitment. These original aims can perhaps be reaffirmed in face of the recent letter from the Delhi Police Commissioner to 2,200 principals, stating 'The collapse of values in all walks of life has become a topic of common discussion ... and one's attention turns to the educational system' (quoted in *Times of India* (13 August 1997)).

In an India where Christian evangelism is increasingly difficult as communalism grows stronger, and where particularly in north India the influence of Hindu fundamentalism grows stronger, the role of the Christian college becomes even more important. Some will argue that, with strictly limited resources, the Church in India should concentrate on grass-roots programmes for the very poor, rather than colleges which, even if they include a minority of Dalits, remain largely the preserve of the rich, upper-middle-class and English-speaking elites.

From the beginning, missions varied in their response to this question. It was the Church of Scotland that most argued for the need to be in touch with these elites through its colleges such as the renowned Madras Christian College. It is through such colleges as St John's that generations of Hindu leaders in all fields in the new India have been proud to say that they had had a Christian education. And the English language is now seen as vital, not as a colonial imposition, but as the way for India to play its role within the international community at all levels. Certainly it would be culpable if resources went only to such institutions, and not to work with and for the oppressed. But the reality is that for a comparatively small Church, the CNI has a wide range of work with those sectors too. The important challenge is, we believe, not whether to continue with such colleges – they exist and, by any standard of measurement, are effective in their work. The challenge is to find ways, through their existence, to challenge those who come, both staff and students, with the wholeness of the Christian Gospel, in particular with the special concern in God's heart for the poor and excluded, such that this becomes part of their thinking, and may motivate them as they move on in their life, to see ways to challenge the wider society.

Further reading

Colin Alves, *The Christian in Education* (London: SCM, 1972).

Jeff Astley, *The Philosophy of Christian Religious Education* (Birmingham: Religious Education Press, 1994).

Compass Points (New York; publication of the Colleges and Universities of the Anglican Communion).

Margaret Cormack, *She Who Rides the Peacock: Indian Students and Social Change* (London: Asia Publishing House, 1994).

J. P. Haythornthwaite and T. D. Sully, *St John's College, Agra, 1850–1930* (London: Highway Press, 1932), and various other such publications.

Zechariah Mathai (ed.), *Seeking Christ in India Today* (Mysore: National Christian Council of India, 1979).

D. A. Thangasway and T. K. Thomas, *The Christian Teacher* (Madras: CLS, 1969).

Towards a wider world: partnership and the Church of Bangladesh

Martin Heath

> By nature all people are dwija – or twice-born – first they are born to their home, and then, for their fulfilment, they have to be born to the larger world.
>
> (Rabindranath Tagore)

Accidents

There were twelve of us in the small chapel of the Zendingshuis of the Netherlands Reformed Church in Oegstgeest as we broke from our consultation on Sunday morning to receive Our Lord in Word and Sacrament. We were there as the guests of the Reformed Churches in the Netherlands, constituting, if not a gathering of Parthians, Medes and Elamites exactly, then an ecclesia that would have earned the approval surely of the author of the Acts of the Apostles, representing as it did the traditions of Calvin, Cranmer, Luther, Newman and Wesley. We were meeting as representatives of the partner Churches of the Church of North India, the Church of South India and the Church of Bangladesh. Another ecumenical forum meets in relation to the Church of Pakistan.

At one level it could be said that the ecumenical regional groups that meet under the umbrella of the Church's Commission on Mission (of the Council of Churches in Britain and Ireland) are but a pragmatic response by the historical external partners of the United Churches to the fact of Union in the Indian sub-continent, who were obliged in their own continuing dis-unity to find ways of co-operating with one another, and of relating in new ways to the United Churches. Admittedly, in terms of response to our Lord's prayer on the night before he died (John 17), collaboration by autonomous members of his body might seem but a modest expression of unity. In terms of St Paul's theology of the body (Corinthians 12), however, collaboration enjoys a higher status, demonstrating the interdependence of the constituent parts in order that they may realize their potential and thus empower the whole body. So, while the origin of these ecumenical and international groups may derive from expediency and pragmatism, as a sacramentalist I prefer to see them rather as accidents, the external signs of

305

something infinitely deeper, and profoundly significant in the history of the Church. Besides, for those of us who have experienced these new expressions of Church there can be no going back, no remaining in the confines of denominationalism. Neither is such a low view of co-operation – of sharing in a common life and mission – consistent with the richness of our experience of the United Churches themselves, an experience that has frequently re-defined for us the nature of the mission enterprise. I choose now to offer some glimpses into the life of the Church of Bangladesh.

Phoenix

As East Bengal present-day Bangladesh was, until 1947, a part of British India. At Partition it became East Pakistan to be, with West Pakistan, a homeland for the Muslims of the Indian sub-continent. But government by West Pakistan, including an attempt to impose Urdu speech and script, was deeply resented by the Bengali (Bangla) population, who have a very strong sense of their distinct cultural identity. These resentments exploded in a terrible war in 1970, culminating in the ignominious defeat of the (West) Pakistan army and the establishment of Bangladesh as a sovereign state. Although only the size of England and Wales, Bangladesh is the second largest Islamic nation, with a population of 120 million.

With Bangladesh still classified as one of the world's poorest nations, there are signs of change in the wake of economic liberalization, with stock exchanges in Dhaka and Chittagong and a growing number of Asian companies establishing factories. While the quality of life in Old Dhaka deteriorates through overcrowding and pollution, New Dhaka is booming with building developments. Yet, if a pre-requisite for economic growth is a stable society, the prospects for politically turbulent Bangladesh are not promising. In the short period since independence, two of the country's four Presidents have been assassinated and a third ousted and imprisoned on corruption charges. Much of the political turbulence arises from a deep-seated animosity between the two leading politicians, both of whom are women and both of whom have inherited their positions. In a reversal of fortunes following elections last year, Sheikh Hasina's Awami League Party came to power, while Begum Khaleda Zia's Bangladesh National Party became the opposition. A deep animosity exists between these leaders, who seem to embody an irreconcilable tension deep within the Bangladeshi psyche, making present through an awful kind of anamnesis the young nation's birth and violent history, a legacy that refuses to be ignored and which continues to haunt and to confront.

The birth of the Church of Bangladesh (CoB) is synonymous with the birth of the nation. The CoB, as an autonomous Church, came into being in

1971 and for twenty years comprised the single Diocese of Dhaka, until the creation in 1990 of the Diocese of Kushtia. The Union comprises former Anglicans and Presbyterians with an estimated community membership of between 12,000 and 15,000. The largest Churches are the Roman Catholic and Baptist Churches, with estimated community memberships of 217,000 and 117,000 respectively. Thus the CoB is a minority Church within a tiny minority Christian population.

Kenosis

Those who have long experience in this part of the world will understand that the atmosphere has not been conducive to the upliftment of minorities. We have not been called on to play our part in the life of the nation. We have often been left alone, the remnant of foreign rule. However, all the odds have not overtaken us and the Church has not become some inward-looking ghetto. The Church is there to share the kenosis of Jesus Christ, in full solidarity with the people, living close to them.

Those words of Barnabas Dwijen Mondal, Bishop of Dhaka, are in effect the CoB's mission statement, expressing its self-understanding and the nature of its divine call. The reflections that follow have to be understood in the light of that awareness.

Oikumene

The form for liaison with the CoB is the Bangladesh Group (of the Church's Commission on Mission) which intentionally also permits fellowship with the Baptist Missionary Society and, through it, with the Bangladesh Baptist Sangha. Membership currently comprises the Baptist Missionary Society, the Church Mission Society, the Church of Scotland, the Council for World Mission, the Methodist Church, the Oxford Mission, the Reformed Churches in the Netherlands and the United Society for the Propagation of the Gospel. With the exceptions of the Reformed Churches in the Netherlands (for reasons of distance from Britain) the CoB's partners in Britain recently committed themselves to making all missionary appointments in Bangladesh jointly and ecumenically. All other mission issues, including funding, have long been addressed corporately. In the case of funding, each year partners receive a copy of the CoB's consolidated budget which sets out concisely and in categories descriptions of the work and amounts available locally, or from other sources. All the member bodies contribute undesignated block grants and, with some negotiating, it is usually possible for the member bodies between them to meet the full external funding requirement. In the case of personnel appointments to the CoB, and of appointments under the programmes of partner organizations whereby the CoB sends Church members to Britain for training, or for involvement in the mission of local Churches in these Islands, one of the Bangladesh Group member bodies acts as 'lead agency' on behalf of the others, for purposes of administration, preparation and pastoral care. In the case of appointments from Britain other member bodies are represented in the vocational exploration and selection processes. Thus, for example, Gillian Rose, an Anglican working as a nursing and midwifery supervisor at Bollovepur, is relating simultaneously through the Bangladesh Group to United Reformed Church congregations, Methodist Church circuits, Church of Scotland presbyteries and a diverse range of Church of England parishes.

As I reflect on more than twelve years' experience of working in this way, I cannot recall any instance of a theological or missiological dispute arising by virtue of ecclesial tradition. It seems that, when it comes to mission, we all speak to a common understanding about the nature of mission, and that our respective agendas constitute a common agenda. Only in worship do 'our differences' become apparent, but never in a negative way. My experience has been only of interest and mutual appreciation.

Less easy to assess is the readiness of the Churches in Europe to assimilate into their own local mission the fruits of what is on offer by virtue of their partnership with the Church of Bangladesh. Because of a tendency to objectify poor Christians as people in need and, let us be frank, because also of latent racism, it is not easy for many in the Churches in Europe to recognize that the materially impoverished Bangla disciple, with his hands outstretched, is not necessarily waiting to be given something, but is rather offering something instead, a pearl of great price.

For me that pearl has been in the form of an awareness that, just conceivably, nearly 2,000 years of doing theology from the top downwards might not be the best way to take hold of life abundantly. Here in Britain as a Christian I feel increasingly out of place, like the Church of Bangladesh, in danger of inhabiting a ghetto, cut off from the wider community whose values and lack-of-expectations I do not share, wondering whether it is possible to be prophetic without also seeming to be holier-than-thou. Such anxieties flow from the sense of separateness that exists by and large between the Church and the wider community. For me these anxieties have become focused on what it means to belong to the body of Christ.

Diakonia

In Bangladesh the Church is a tiny minority in an overwhelmingly dominant Islamic context. It could therefore have opted to keep its head down and devote its energies to survival and to caring for its own members. Had it done so, few would have judged it. Instead the CoB has evolved a theology of Church and a theology of mission that are drawn directly from the context. Instead of looking for that which separates it from the people around, it has identified that which it has in common with them, namely material poverty and faith in God. And between these twin poles it has seen the face of Jesus Christ who, though he was rich, yet for their sakes became poor. Thus the CoB has opted explicitly to model itself on the person of Jesus Christ and to be a Church of and with the people. Integral to this commitment to share the kenosis of Christ is the Social Development Programme (SDP) employing a staff of over 700, of whom more than half are women. The staff is made up of approximately 65 per cent Christian, 20 per cent Muslim and 15 per cent Hindu, and the SDP's activities include community health, agriculture, credit schemes, primary education, vocational training, women's co-operatives, adult education, social forestry and irrigation. The emphasis is on small-scale, community-based programmes, using participatory methods through group formation. Sometimes the CoB is criticized for a perceived emphasis on works, rather than on evangelism, but that is to interpret evangelism restrictively. If we understand, as the CoB does, that the evangelium is concerned with speaking to people as social creatures within communities as much as if not more than individuals, then we can see that the CoB's way of evangelizing is through service. Thus, in a ministry of disinterested diakonia to the whole community the CoB is committing itself to realizing in its own time and place the agenda for mission of Jesus himself, announced at Nazareth at the start of his own ministry (Luke 4.18–19). It is at the same time a demonstrating of the knowledge that, in Christ, all belong to and depend on one another.

Corpus Christi

It is not easy, within the space of 24 hours, to transfer from Watford to a room in the slums of Old Dhaka, about ten feet square and made of panels of woven cane. Moving the body isn't a problem; moving the mind is. But there I sat, cross-legged with Ms Khaleda Afroz and Mr Torun Mondal from the SDP, with more than a dozen women who, for nearly an hour, told me how Jesus Christ had changed their lives. Of course neither they nor my companions said that, or anything like it, but that was the reality. Because, and only because, the CoB understands itself to be, like its Lord, a servant bearing good news for the poor, committed to living with the people and, with them, to discovering new life, the fortunes of these Muslim women had undergone a profound change. In terms of their raised self-estimation, their ability to read and write, their enhanced awareness of what is happening in the world, and of their rights under the law, they were a new Creation, being moulded as Christ would have them be. But what they valued most of all, they said, was their solidarity with each other. And if we substitute communion for solidarity, we are surely not far from the heart of the Gospel.

St Paul's theology of the Body of Christ (Romans 12.4–5) demonstrates the inter-connectedness of all things, of how we need each other for wholeness. The theology of the body simply restates a principle of creation, that in Christ, all things hold together (Col 1.17). We are accustomed to interpreting Romans 12.4–5 as meaning that, by virtue of their confession and baptism, it is individual Christians who collectively comprise Christ's body. Equally though, can we not say that, whenever and wherever two or three people come together to do the things that Jesus did, then surely he is present among them? That being so, is it too fanciful to posit that each time two or three Muslims come together to do something that in some way fulfils Christ's teaching on Kingdom values, he is in their midst and that his body is thus reconstituted?

This theology of the absolute inter-dependence of all human beings on one another is present also in Jesus' story of the Final Judgement (Matt 25.31–46). There is nothing in this teaching about fine points of doctrine, nor about religion, nor even about a need to confess Christ as Lord (others said that, later), only that salvation is corporate, requiring that we serve Christ in one another and love, as he loves us. On the evidence of this story alone, the only condition for eternal life is whether men and women cared for each other in their basic human needs.

Dwija

If there is integrity in these reflections it means that we who are called to mission are by no means as isolated or unresourced as we may think. The logic and the lesson is that the body of Christ, the one who lives with and leads to God, is as present and as active outside the Church as within it. It means furthermore that, since salvation is corporate, and since the evangelium is multi-directional, we would do well ourselves to cultivate the practice of receiving from beyond the Church. To me this is simultaneously the realization and the anticipation of that wider oikumene to which we are called, union with God. Or, to use the language of Tagore, of being born to a larger world.

Further reading

K. Dutta and A. Robinson, *Rabindranath Tagore: The Myriad-Minded Man* (London: Bloomsbury, 1995).

D. O'Connor, *Gospel, Raj and Swaraj: The Missionary Years of C. F. Andrews 1904–14* (Frankfurt: Verlag Peter Lang, 1990).

Social Development by the Year 2000: A Review of Aspects of the Church of Bangladesh (Dhaka: Church of Bangladesh Social Development Programme, 1994).

H. Stafflier, *The Significance of Jesus Christ in Asia* (Anand: Gujarat Sahitya Prakash, 1985).

R. Tagore, *Letters to a Friend*, ed. C. F. Andrews (London: George Allen & Unwin Ltd, 1928).

'Called to one hope: the Gospel in diverse cultures'

Reflections on the themes of the CWEM conference in Salvador, Brazil, from the perspective of the Church in Wales

Enid R. Morgan

It was in 1994 that a poster announcing a conference sponsored by the Council for World Evangelism and Mission (CWEM) reached my desk. I'd have wanted to attend had the venue been in Birmingham. That it was to take place in Salvador, Bahia, Brazil made it irresistible. Many of the issues with which I had struggled in the previous 25 years related to the theme 'Called to one hope – the Gospel in diverse cultures'. At different times I had been called to live astride uncomfortable boundaries, having to affirm apparently contradictory values – Baptist–Anglican, Welsh–English, charismatic–sacramental. I had for seven years edited a weekly Welsh-medium paper for the Church in Wales, thus representing and articulating the viewpoint of a minority within a minority in Wales. In 20 years of parish experience, both lay and clerical, I had shared in the tensions of a

Enid R. Morgan

Welsh-speaking community coping with a tide of monoglot English immigrants. My political and cultural commitment was to that resisting minority.

It was odd to have taken the apparently contradictory step of becoming an Anglican. I shared the myths of identity of non-conformist Welsh Wales. But in Anglicanism I was finding the potential for a breadth and depth of spirituality and worship, an aesthetic and a theology that meant rejecting part of my upbringing. To do so did not mean forgetting the very real strengths of that background. But even as I was discovering Catholicity I found that there are many Anglican 'cultures' and some sub-cultures just as limited as the world in which I grew up.

Preparation for Salvador included reflection on Wales as the first of the English colonies – a Wales already Christianized, a land in which the names of Celtic saints were part of the social geography. We were the people reproached by Bede for refusing to evangelize our conquerors. At the time of the Reformation, the Bible was translated into Welsh for a community steeped in the world-view of mediaeval Christendom. The translations of the Bible and of the Book of Common Prayer in the sixteenth century were to ensure a political unity. Even as the Act of Union banned the language from the law courts and government, in the sphere of religion it was given an infrastructure of support. When the Church of England sank into state subservience, the evangelical revivals reinforced the connection of the language with religion. Welsh, no longer the language of government or law, came to be called the language of heaven.

In the nineteenth century the identification of the Anglican Church with English government led to a huge political movement whereby the affectionate title of 'Hen Fam' (Our Old Mother) changed to 'Yr Hen Estrones' (The Old Foreigner). Methods of language suppression in use in the far-flung empire were practised in Church and state schools of Wales. The struggle led to the disestablishment and disendowment of the Church in Wales in 1920. But no swift demise followed and although the Church has suffered the same deep decline as all the mainline Churches in Europe, the Anglican Church in the 1990s represents 30 per cent of Christians in Wales. But all the Churches of Wales attract less than 9 per cent of the population. A conference on the theme 'Called to one hope – the Gospel in diverse cultures' might address these two themes of a crisis of mission in a background of cultural division.

Although the council for Evangelism and World Mission is part of the World Council of Churches, it has a wider constituency because of the involvement of the Mission Agencies. People from Churches who mistrust the political and Faith and Order agenda of the WCC still want to be identified with mission. Yet another input was provided by delegates who stayed on from an earlier conference for indigenous peoples. Although the

Roman Catholic Church is not a member, there were a significant number of Roman Catholic observers too. In terms of cultural richness and variety, this was an unprecedented gathering. The difficulty was to hold together the Western-style processes with genuine human encounters.

Even so, there was not an adequate representation of the Afro-Brazilians, which was the reason for choosing Salvador as a venue, nor of Pentecostal groups which are such a remarkable feature of life in South America. The worship, which was beautifully organized and imaginatively thought out, would have been more spontaneous and perhaps less synthetic if they had been there.

The presence of so many indigenous people was one reason why the conference was more at ease affirming the values of diverse cultures than in defining the One Hope to which we are all called. We heard the cry of anguish of peoples torn between the pain of oppression and genocide, and a Gospel seemingly forced upon them by conquest. It was not for them to voice a warning about the ambivalence of culture. That warning came most humbly and appropriately from a German Lutheran, Cornelia Fullkrug Weitzel, who reminded us of the dreadful results of making an idol of culture.

This point had already been made by a Kenyan woman theologian, Dr Musimbi Kyonoro, who insisted that

> ... neither gospel nor culture is good news until it liberates. That is to say, there is no gospel or culture that is automatically liberating ... African women whose voices are only now beginning to surface, are calling the churches to go beyond a theology of inculturation and to put culture itself under scrutiny, in order to determine whether it promotes justice, life, peace and liberation or whether it diminishes and dehumanizes people.

While some cultures were affirmed, it was also time for the old cultures of the West to submit to the challenge and critique of the Gospel. How do we discover a confidence to proclaim the Gospel to our own people in the postmodern market of ideologies? For people can pick and choose to believe whatever they like. They can go for neo-paganism and astrology, their religiosity can go for the exotic and colourful, they can reject any authority and even the possibility of an absolute truth. As Kristin Ofstad – a minister in the Reformed tradition in Wales, who was one of the keynote speakers – demonstrated, people gather handfuls of jigsaw pieces and force them together to make a picture of their choosing, trimming the bits to fit as they choose.

The response of the young people towards all this was particularly anguished. They pleaded with passion to be included as agents and not as objects of mission; particularly, they asked the Churches to give priority to resource and support work with young people who are especially vulnerable to all the pressures of globalization, racism, marginalization, and domination systems of the world.

Apart from the main and sectional debates, the conference did a great deal of its most effective work in sessions called *encontros*. These were opportunities for people from different parts of the world to make presentations explaining, illustrating, analysing, their own cultures in a way which would make sense to others. How can we uproot our old false confidence?

Listening, however, did not guarantee understanding. For instance, following a brilliant analysis of sectarianism and violence in Northern Ireland which had made it clear that Christian doctrines have been deeply implicated in that conflict, an Orthodox delegate from Eastern Europe expressed her sadness that this should be the case because she was convinced that in the Balkans, the Churches had nothing to do with violence. . . . Despite that, the *encontro* method was a way of enabling people to reflect and listen, and the time spent in them was, for many, more valuable than the document-producing processes.

The most life-changing point in the conference came on the Saturday morning, when we met for worship at the quayside where, in 1550, slaves from Africa were first unloaded to be 'sorted', marched up to the front of a nearby church where water was thrown over them and words spoken in a horrendous parody of baptism in order to increase their market value. There we were given time to see ourselves in relation to the story. And it was a deeply painful experience to identify ourselves as inheritors of the oppressors or their victims. It was a time of grief and repentance and it was startling to hear an 'African Confession':

> We have words of repentance. But those who brought us here were not alone in the making of this tragedy. We Africans share in the responsibility. We have degraded ourselves by selling our brothers and sisters as goods. It is because we have never had the courage to recognise it and repent that we continue to do the same today, hence the disgraceful situation of Africa. We want to repent and ask for forgivenesss and God's mercy.

So we were all included in the blood, cruelty, greed, racism, oppression. We sang:

> Come healing river, pour down your waters,
> Pour down your waters, upon this land.
> This land is thirsting, this land is burning,
> Wash clean the blood from out the sand.

Some of the other points made earlier by Dr Musimbi Kyonoro kept coming to mind. It was she who spoke of the danger of 'flirting with hopelessness' and the need to move on from 'the lament of history'.

> if we want to build strong and reliable relationships in the whole of the world, we need to deepen our trust in each other ... For healthy diversity is based upon trust and a common understanding of the well-being of the whole community.

Home to the Church in Wales. What are the things I remember, and what are we actually acting upon? As I noted earlier, less than 9 per cent of our population worship on a Sunday. That number is declining. In the Church of Wales, it has declined at the rate of about 1 per cent for the last thirteen years. What does mission and evangelism mean for a Church tempted to hang on the rags and tatters of establishment? What does it mean for Churches very closely identified with the cultural and political struggle of the minority culture? We could learn from the experience of repentance and healing. For only through the healing of the Holy Spirit can we begin to leave behind us the lament of our history.

The commission of the Covenanted Churches in Wales, which includes the Church of Wales, is putting forward a plan for an 'ecumenical bishop' in a growing, urban part of South East Wales. The needs of the mission are acute and the divisions and mutual suspicions of the Churches hamper mission. 1998 will be a year in which the churches decide whether they can take this small but risky step forward. The Church in Wales and the Presbyterian Church in Wales are also embarking on a small project together in training for mission and evangelism. In different ways, both Churches have developed a highly clerical culture and this will be an effort to train laity and clergy for collaborative ministry at a time of drastic falling-away of vocations. We may learn to trust each other enough to seek the liberation of the Gospel. Our ecumenical thinking and theology need to be, as Donald Elliot has said, driven by missiology. How do we evangelize our people in the new century?

Welsh culture, though apparently secular and post-Christian and post-modern, is really unchurched rather than secular. It is faintly folk-believing, superstitious and still hymn-singing. We need to accept that for many people, Church is the problem, not the answer, and that we need to find a new way of being Church. The old Churches are seen as controlling and judgemental, unable to relate to the young, wanting to change them into being middle-aged before their time. Church is seen as being part of the heritage mind-set, not the hope of the new millennium. There is a longing to step into the future with a Church that is not hanging on to power, is not proud, but is a humble, serving Church, able to proclaim community by being community itself.

In tired Europe, the Lord who makes all things new is the source of hope for the future: Jesus the hope of the hopeless in a Europe which is willing to let go the old power models of church. Hope has a face and name and is alive. Christ is our hope – or in the words of the conference message:

> We have sought to understand better the way in which the gospel challenges all human cultures and how culture can give us a clearer understanding of the gospel ... this last great mission conference of the 20th century has clearly illuminated that the gospel, to be most fruitful, needs to be both true to itself, and incarnated or rooted in the culture of a people.

Further reading

Challenge to Change (Yr Her i Newid) (results of the 1995 Welsh Churches Survey; British and Foreign Bible Society, 1995).
Davie Grace, *Religion in Britain Since 1945* (Oxford: Blackwell, 1994).
International Review of Mission, vol. LXXXVI, nos 340/341 (January/April 1997). This volume is all related to the Conference.

The Anglican debate in West Africa on Christian–Muslim relations

Ken Okeke

When one thinks of debate of any sort on any issue, what immediately comes to mind are 'papers' and conferences and consultations. Within the Anglican Church in West Africa, they have never debated Christian–Muslim relations in this way. Attributing the lack of debate to the fact that both religions are foreign is probably correct, with one thing in common: to convert the people of West Africa. A fair understanding of how these faiths came into West Africa will help us understand why instead of debates there are unstructured informal discussions. Instead of debate, there is subtle confrontation.

Pre-Islam/Christian West Africa

Before both Islam and Christianity came into West Africa, society followed traditional religion, the beliefs of which permeated all life. Belief in a supreme being who created the entire cosmos, undergirded all other beliefs. This Creator generated the spirit force which animated the various forms of rituals incorporating the veneration of the ancestral spirits and the spirit forces of nature. They wove the dead and nature into one entity in which the living were a vital component. Because society was bound up in religion, each group of people functioned as both a social and a religious community with its rituals and rites designed to maintain unity and continuity. There were periodic initiations to mark the different rites of passage and these fostered communion with the spirit world. Religion also played a role in the political ordering of society. In some parts of the region they believed that monarchies ruled over the nation with the approval of the spirits. They had village chiefs and regional heads helping them, thus creating a religious political hierarchy within society. It was to this society that both Islam and Christianity came and in their different ways and methods found adherents.

Islam in West Africa

In many parts of the Middle East, the coming of Islam was often associated with fighting and conquests. The history of the origin of Islam shows that the founder and his followers had no choice, sometimes, but to fight. Coming out of a period of conflict and being militarily opposed, force became necessary. This helps one to understand why Muslims down the ages resort to armed conflict as a means of 'spreading' the Islamic faith. Force is not always necessary but is always an option.

Some suggest that Islam was brought into West Africa as a ruling force associated with trade. It was not religion that aroused interest in West Africa but gold stumbled upon during a military expedition. According to oral traditions, an Islamic ruler called Uqba extended his raids as far as the frontiers of the Sudan to safeguard the mineral. The considerably wealthy Kunta – family groupings of great religious repute who were dispersed throughout the region reaching Niger and Senegal – trace their origins back to Uqba. They claim that he conquered Biru (Walata) and Takrur. According to Levtzion: 'In the tradition of the Torodbe, Uqba appears as

Ken Okeke

the leader of the migration from the North East. Ibn Abi Zar' says that Banu Warith, a Sanhaja group in the neighbourhood of Adrar, were converted to Islam by Uqba b. Nafi.[1] Historians question the accuracy of these accounts. West Africa's initial contact with Islam was in the eighth century. If this is so, then Uqba b. Nafi, who died in AD 688, did not penetrate as deep as oral accounts claim.[2]

The popular opinion is that Islam spread in West Africa through merchants who invariably acted as missionaries. They established trade posts which attracted settlements around them. Muslim scholars who were judges, doctors and diviners later followed and played the role of religious, political and moral guides. As one travels in West Africa, it is still possible to see evidence of these early settlements in Islamic towns and cities. It is significant that most of these settlements are found in the northern parts of many West African countries. A characteristic trend of Islam in West Africa from the early periods to the nineteenth century is that most Muslim converts were from the ruling elite or the merchant class or town-dwellers as opposed to village folks. It seemed that there was little impact on the way of life of the ordinary people who dwelt in the rural areas. According to Trimingham 'although sources relating to the introduction of Islam into Western and Central Sudan are so meagre and unreliable, what is clear is the slow peaceful nature of its spread and the weakness of its impact upon Sudanese religious and social life. This is due to the peculiarities of its adoption as a class religion with a place within the ruling pagan structure defined in such a way that its effect as a religious law and spiritual transformer was completely neutralized.'[3] In most parts of West Africa reached by Islam, the conditions were very similar. We can describe only states with an Islamic ruler as 'Islamic states'. That state therefore belongs to Islam. This fact is very important in understanding Christian–Muslim relationships and interactions.

While we can state that Islam in West Africa did not initially come with violence, there were areas of conflicts in later years. Localized *jihads* took place in some parts of Senegal and northern Nigeria in the eighteenth and nineteenth centuries, after which Islam took deep roots in these areas. In recent years we do not hear of *jihads* in the countries of West Africa but of factional interreligious 'flashpoints' resulting in some destruction of property and loss of lives.

Christianity in West Africa

We must recognize that Christianity reached West Africa long after Islam had been established. This was formally in the eighteenth century through the activities of the then Society for the Propagation of the Gospel in Ghana

318

– then known as Gold Coast. By the nineteenth century, the then Church Missionary Society started some work among the freed slaves of Freetown in Sierra Leone. Largely vast areas still practised the African traditional religion, referred to by the early missionaries as *heathenism* or *paganism*. For whatever reason they concentrated the Christian contacts with West Africa on the southern parts of the different countries, beginning with the coastal towns. The Church Missionary Society began work in Sierra Leone in 1804, where the Methodist and Baptist Churches had congregations already. It is supposed that freed slaves formed these congregations in Freetown. The Baptist Missionary Society and the Wesleyan Methodist Missionary Society were in Badagry, Nigeria around 1842 while the United Society for the Propagation of the Gospel was in Ghana and the Gambia. Later missionary societies like the Sudan Interior Mission and Qua Iboe Mission also joined the race within Nigeria. From these various activities, Christianity began to take roots in West Africa, and the Anglican Church emerged as the largest Protestant Church group. We must note that the Roman Catholic Church already had a large following. For these Christian groups, those practising African traditional religion and the Muslims were two different sides of the same coin, unbelievers to be converted.

The Anglican Church in West Africa is a big Church with a membership of several millions. The numbers however, are not evenly distributed in all the countries. Nigeria contains the largest number, followed by Ghana. Liberia and Sierra Leone are sizeable but the Anglican Churches in The Gambia, Senegal, Guinea and the Cameroons are small compared to the populations of their respective countries. These several countries have many Muslims living side by side with both Christians and African traditional religion adherents, presenting a very interesting mix.

Christian–Muslim relations; the Anglican perspective

The Anglican Church in West Africa varies in churchmanship and tradition from country to country. However, though there has been no collective debate on Christian–Muslim relations, attempts have been made in different areas of the region to engage either in talks or in activities to promote peaceful interaction. Africans are gregarious beings and they love and cherish the idea of belonging and community. People live together in large family units or communities. They talk and relate on that social interactive plane. Africans are deeply religious people and, as we saw earlier, they seriously intertwine religion with everyday life. When the African embraces Islam or Christianity that also is serious business. One can therefore understand the strain that religious matters sometimes cause in families and communities when the same community contains people of

319

different religious affiliations. They tear people between loyalties. It may not be obvious but when violence or other types of disruption emerge those religious loyalties become evident. It is consequently that some within the Church stress that they should not allow religious differences to disrupt the harmonious relations of the community.

According to Momo B. Kpartor, Vicar-General of the Anglican Church of Cameroon:

> The Christian belief in Jesus is the parting point with Muslims. I am convinced that whatever path and direction these people follow to reach God, He will determine their salvation either through Jesus or Mohammed. The point before divergence is very important! If people embrace the idea of universal salvation and practise the virtue of tolerance, conflicts and tensions which lead to deaths, destruction of places of worship, etc., will be reduced. Muslims and Christians tolerate each other well in Cameroon and Liberia.

It is significant that this is the stance often taken where the Church is in the minority and does not always represent the thinking or the attitude of the dominant Muslim community. In areas such as parts of northern Nigeria, where the Church exists quietly, worshipping peacefully, all is well. Once it seeks to make disciples from the Muslim community, the invisible divide becomes visible and it may suffer some physical negative repercussions for such efforts.

The above is illustrated by Kpartor when he says:

> St John's Anglican Church in Yaoundé where I am the Priest in Charge is in the heart of a Muslim community. There is a very cordial relationship between us and the people who live in this community. . . . They are quite aware that we believe in God through Jesus Christ. To live well within such a community is to have mutual respect for other people's beliefs and faith, above all, never to be religiously arrogant.

It is possible that what informs the line of argument expressed by Kpartor stems from what the basic understanding of the Christian faith is and the readiness to accept the Muslim's understanding of Christianity. On this Kpartor has this to say:

> A good Muslim believes that Jesus is exceptional though he denies the fundamental belief by Christians that he is the Son of God. If the 'Sonship of God' has caused religious conflicts and misunderstandings between Muslims and Christians, can we consider a bend around the corner for a theological compromise? This, of course, will challenge the very core and fabric of Christianity! What goes on in church or mosque should not destroy humanity. The Muslims and the Christians have God

for their Father, the Christians have the Church for their Mother but the Muslims have the mosque instead for their Mother.

I am not quite sure that Muslims will put it that way.

A strong Church

In different parts of Nigeria and Ghana where the Church is strong, the situation is not as described in Cameroon and Liberia. In Nigeria, the picture is that of a Church on the move. The Anglican Church often sees itself as part of the Church that should have the freedom to engage in meaningful debate and yet with a freedom to engage in evangelism among all non-Christians, Muslims and all. In the southern part of the country where Islam is thin on the ground, evangelism causes little problem. In the northern parts the story is different as flashpoints occur as Muslims react negatively to certain evangelistic practices and challenge the right of the Christians to engage in some activities which they assume are right and proper. In some ancient Islamic cities of Kano, Sokoto and Bauchi, they allow no church building within the 'walled city' where the Emir or any ruling Islamic head has his palace or dwelling. Sometimes, they allow no Christian preaching of any sort. The Church respects this ruling. One wonders therefore how the Anglican Church managed to appear within the environment of these ancient Islamic cities. Those involved in early infrastructural development played a major part in bringing Christianity to these cities. Most of the workers sent there were from Christian southern Nigeria, so they took their Anglicanism with them. Whenever they arrived in these ancient Islamic cities, they were assigned to areas designated for non-Muslim 'immigrants', in the Hausa language *sabon-geri* (strangers' quarters). Thus all the Anglican churches and any other denominations that came after stayed in these areas. Some of these 'sabon-geris' are now more developed than the ancient-city part of the town where they are found and the churches are flourishing too. They are now beginning to get members from the indigenes of these Muslim kingdoms. We must remember that they declare an area a Muslim kingdom because the ruler of that territory is a Muslim. There are vast numbers of people from those territories who are not Muslims at all and some who are nominal Muslims. These listen to the preaching of the Christian message and few problems have been encountered.

Tension

Most Anglican Churches in West Africa will either describe themselves as evangelical or see evangelism and mission as vital aspects of their Church life. Those in Muslim areas feel the strain of obeying this calling. Many

Muslims will see any evangelistic move as aggression and will react physically. This has been cause for much of the violence in the past. Each area now tries to engage in talk with the Muslim community to ease tensions. The talk styles vary from place to place. Each Anglican Church leadership has to formulate a form of talk that will best suit its context.

Debate has to start at social level if it is to be effective. This relates to social coexistence: what to do to improve the collective lives of the community, provision of schools and medical care and issues of security. This goes on all the time in places like Sierra Leone where communities are suffering the effects of a senseless civil war. People are always happy to engage in this sort of exchange and are willing to work together. There is also religious dialogue, which is more delicate and intricate, requiring spiritual sensitivity. We must realize that Muslims regard non-Muslims as unbelievers who are to be converted to Islam. Some Muslim sections pursue this vigorously, though there has not been any full-scale *jihad*. The Anglicans also see all non-Christians, including Muslims, as people to be witnessed to and led to Christ. The result is an interesting tension characterized by respect.

Current situation

The Anglican Church in West Africa has varying churchmanship, as noted above. The Church Mission Society, the United Society for the Propagation of the Gospel, and the West Indian Association for the Furtherance of the Gospel in West Africa are primarily responsible for this variation. All these different Churches with their different traditions talk about expansion. In many areas this creates no problem. There are many encouraging signs of coexistence and co-operation between Anglican Christians and Muslims. Differences are there, depending on situation and context. Because Anglicans are sensitive in their evangelism, they attract some to their faith and vice versa. When some problems arise, PROCMURA (Project for Christian–Muslim Relations in Africa) exists as a body that can be approached to resolve conflicts. There are other sections of the Anglican Church that are happy with a type of maintenance ministry. These are the ones who mostly engage in social exchange, and would rather leave things as they are. At times those who act otherwise irritate them, concerned that peaceful coexistence will be threatened. Perhaps there is a place for such a stance as the Church moves from one level of being and engagement to another. They will endorse this since they see the situation as 'the halfway house' and the Church is simply waiting for a conducive situation and time to engage in carrying the gospel message forward. Disagreements within the Church arise when those who favour the coexistence model try to recommend it as the permanent way forward.

Outreach is complicated when some clans or communities decide to embrace one type of faith as a whole. Every other alternative offered them is rejected since no one person wants to go against the community. So when a community claims to be Muslim, whether they are practising or not, the Churches in that area, Anglican included, find it difficult to penetrate. This notwithstanding, most of the Anglican Churches in West Africa will try offering the gospel of salvation to any community within their territories. They also try to present the Anglican Church as a body concerned for peace and the well-being of the community. Many Muslims respect this.

Notes

1 N. Levtzion, 'Abd Allah b. Yasin and the Almoravids' in J. R. Willis (ed.), *Studies in West African Islamic History*, vol. I (1979), p. 82.
2 Ibid., p. 82.
3 J. S. Trimingham, *A History of Islam in West Africa* (London: Oxford University Press, 1962), p. 33.

Evangelism in the Anglican Communion: an overview

A prophetic signal and a call for action

Cyril Okorocha

Introduction

In September 1995, 120 representatives of the Provinces of the Communion met at the Kanuga Conference Centre, North Carolina, USA to report to each other on the progress of the Decade of Evangelism. Since that review conference, I have sent questionnaires to all the bishops, archbishops and provincial evangelism co-ordinators around the Communion to learn what visions and plans they have for mission and evangelism as we launch into the third millennium. This brief presentation is a report of the findings of those two surveys.

Evangelism – the central task of the Church

Reports at Kanuga and from my current survey reveal that evangelism in its various forms is moving to a more central place on the agenda of the Provinces and dioceses of the Communion, as a result of the call for a Decade of Evangelism at Lambeth 1988. They also reveal a diversity of understandings of evangelism and a wide variety of approaches as Anglicans seek to relate the Gospel to their local situations. On the whole, a holistic understanding of evangelism which takes mission and evangelism together as a seamless robe is emerging alongside rapid growth and increasing confidence in the Gospel.

For example, the Church of Nigeria responded to the Decade in 1990 by consecrating and sending nine missionary bishops, in one day, into largely Islamic northern Nigeria, to make disciples and share the love of Christ. In this way bishops, they argued, are first and foremost missionaries and 'vision bearers'. Some of these 'dioceses' had very little or no Anglican presence at the time of sending these 'missionary bishops' to them. But current reports reveal astonishing conversions and growth. The survey shows that whereas by the end of 1988 there were only three dioceses in northern Nigeria, today there are eighteen in that area and more growth is anticipated.

Pakistan is combining its usual outreach programmes with intensified ecumenical anti-drug programmes and church-building projects to provide a Christian presence for witness and rehabilitation. Korea started a programme of shelter for all through a house-sharing scheme as their expression of mission in context. In the USA, urban ministry and various forms of church-growth techniques were developed. In the UK, virtually all dioceses appointed Decade of Evangelism officers/missioners to encourage 'grass-roots' evangelism.

The Decade vision, while not saying that evangelism was beginning *de nouveau* in the Church, nevertheless gave a new impetus to an old theme. Anglicans suddenly realized once again that the Church exists for mission. Or, in the words of David Bosch, that 'evangelism (or mission) is not so much the work of the Church as simply the Church at work' (1991, p. 372).

We are also learning from the survey that even though responses to the Decade vision have been varied, there are nevertheless some underlying common themes. Whereas evangelism is generally understood as sharing the Gospel in order to awaken or re-awaken personal faith in Jesus Christ, this could not be done without relating to personal and social context. Evangelism is the cutting edge of the broader task of mission. Any Church not seriously engaging in mission is a 'disobedient Church' (Carey, 1995) and faces the risk of extinction and of becoming a mission field for other religions (Okorocha, 1992).

Evangelism impacts on wider aspects of mission. For example, it challenges the quality of life and welcome of the Church communities into which new believers come. It raises questions of Christian nurture. It raises issues about the role of Christians in society and their service to the world at large. It provides challenges to the economic and social injustices of our world, and to age-old issues like racism and neo-colonialism. This draws attention to Rwanda (and Burundi) which was the cradle of the East African Revival and yet where, in recent years, there have been most horrifying cases of genocide and inter-ethnic intolerance. That tragedy remains a pain in the neck of the Church in that region and in some way an anguish for the whole of the Communion. But we are receiving reports from Rwanda of efforts at reconciliation resulting from in-depth repentance and forgiveness and the courage all this takes.

Emerging issues and future directions

Reports from around the Communion identify the following issues as priorities to be addressed honestly if we are serious about our desire to become a mission-orientated Church.

Issues of training and nurture: from chaplaincy to prophetism

To shift the Church from maintenance to mission, we need to shift emphasis in ministerial formation from 'chaplaincy' to 'prophetism'. We seem to train our clergy to become 'community chaplains' committed to 'gentle nurture' and maintenance. They wait for people to 'come to church'. But a missionary congregation takes 'the Church', the ministry of the Church, to the people in the larger community. Both clergy and laity need opportunities to gain confidence in telling their faith stories.

Issues of spirituality and worship

There is a strong call for freer worship and contextualized liturgy. Our common pattern of Anglican liturgy has helped to bind us to a common tradition and heritage which is fundamentally European, but needs to be revised to reflect local cultures. Personal devotion and communal worship lie at the heart of renewal in evangelism – which often includes 'spiritual warfare'. Clergy and lay leaders need training in this direction. Creative prayer and imaginative worship are fundamental to effective evangelism and renewal. New converts in particular are very sensitive to worship styles and prayer, as a baby is to milk and love. Where these are missing the natural tendency is to drift in other directions in search of nurture. The result is that many Anglican evangelistic efforts end up in making converts for other 'Churches'.

Repentance and humility

There is an acknowledgement that because the Gospel is a message of forgiveness, humble repentance is a necessary precondition to bold evangelism. In each part of the Communion there is a need for the Church to repent of its past and present sins, to find ways of healing bad memories and hurts and prejudices of the past such as those coming from genocide, ethnic cleansing, racism and colonialism and economic exploitation and arrogance. Reports from the Two-Thirds World insist that evangelism in the Church into the next millennium must address the scandal and enslavement of international debt. Examples from Japan and New Zealand are positive challenges to other Churches, individuals and organizations.

The role of lay people

There is a need not merely to give tasks to lay people, but to empower them by truly delegating authority and encouraging and enabling them to get on with the job in their homes, places of work and daily lives. This cannot be overemphasized. The survey shows that the Church in the Two-Thirds World in particular is growing so rapidly that ordained clergy are unable to cope. Here the issue that is raised and that goes far beyond mere rhetoric is about lay 'presidency'. Elsewhere, economic pressures mean that fewer young people are offering themselves for full-time ministry and the burden of its success is with the laity. Clergy have often been advisors and catalysts. The important role of women in witness was particularly highlighted. In many parts of Africa, especially West Africa, women – largely through the ministry of the Mothers' Union – lead the Church's mission and form the wellspring of its social and spiritual life and witness.

A Church open to all people

So as not to lose gained ground, local congregations/Christian communities are challenged to become more welcoming, nurturing and open to enquirers. They are being asked to provide neighbourhood, home-oriented 'cell' groups which newcomers can join. The hierarchical structures of our Anglican Church need to be modified to allow a more equitable sharing of responsibilities so that mission and ministry can be seen to be the call of all baptized believers.

Leadership and visioning

Evangelism, our survey shows, demands courage and willingness to take risks and to make oneself vulnerable. It is not for cowards, argues Raymond Fung (Okorocha, 1995, pp. 145–52). Reports from and my visits to Sudan, Nigeria, Polynesia, Latin America and elsewhere in the Two-Thirds World corroborate this. The reports keep calling for strong and prophetic leadership from bishops. There is a need for them to demonstrate practically and financially their commitment to evangelism, and to articulate a clear evangelistic vision. Some of them pay a heavy price, especially in the Two-Thirds World nations, for their courage and witness. There is everywhere, therefore, a call to free both bishops and clergy, as vision bearers, from administrative burdens, so as to exercise their prophetic ministry for the people, as they lead the people in mission which includes social transformation.

Youth

'Youth', argue the reports from the youth workers, 'do not believe in theories, they follow sketches, the life of the leadership.' What a challenge. They are at once the Church and missionaries of today and tomorrow. India, Pakistan, Korea and Nigeria are responding positively to this challenge and their youth are active in mission at home and overseas.

Co-operation with other Christians

I have found mission to be a strong bond that draws Churches together. In the second half of the Decade, provinces need to reassess their ecumenical co-operation in evangelism as urged by Lambeth 1988. My observation shows that mission can be a pragmatic instrument to Church unity.

Other faiths, ideologies, unreached people

The reports show that the term 'mission' is no longer exclusive to Christianity, and religious pluralism is no longer confined to Africa and Asia. There is special concern to understand as well as encourage our witness among people of other faiths. Approaches differ according to context but there is a call to move from the negative attitudes of xenophobia on the one hand and naive universalism, often precipitated by a 'guilt trip syndrome', on the other, to creative dialogue rooted in an evangelistic consciousness. Mention is also made of the challenge of materialism and secularism as new forms of religion in the modern world. In England, for example, a national football team poster advert inviting fans to a game reads 'Football is our religion'.

Cyril Okorocha

Issues of social and environmental justice

If evangelism is the central task given to the Church, this means a call to live like Christ in concern for the poor, the weak, the oppressed and to uphold the integrity of Creation. Churches are urged to pray and work to overcome structures and systems that perpetuate poverty, oppression and environmental degradation. The challenge comes especially from the Two-Thirds World where numerical growth in the Churches does not seem to be matched by equal positive social impact.

Some practical suggestions for mobilizing the Church:
1. A worldwide review of theological education curricula.
2. Exchanges of personnel, in all directions.
3. Team and group visits, to learn from each other's experiences, for example those between the Dioceses of Malaysia and Lichfield, England.
4. More resources in languages other than English.
5. Sharing stories, of faith, pain, martyrdom, and successful and unsuccessful efforts in evangelism.
6. Regional gatherings, for support and celebrating our oneness and rich diversity.
7. Electronic networking, including helping those acquire this tool who do not have the know-how. In some places, this is the only 'safe' method of evangelism.
8. Measurable goals and means of evaluation. Examples are Sabah Diocese's Mission 1-1-3: each member to work and pray to bring another worshipper in three years. Texas Diocese Mission 1-1-10: similar to Sabah's but a different context and the time scale is ten years.
9. Budgets, which indicate our commitment to evangelism.
10. Prayer as central both to evangelism and to sustaining work against injustice.

Five key observations

'Doing' and 'talking'

Those Churches that have been most creative and productive in their evangelistic efforts debate and write the least about it. They simply get on with the job. Since the beginning of the 'Decade' very few, if any, major books have come out of the growing Churches of the Two-Thirds World. Perhaps they are too busy doing evangelism to debate or write about it!

A *demographic shift*

The survey reveals a phenomenal growth and vibrancy among the younger Churches, suggesting a dramatic shift in the 'centre of gravity' of the Church, in terms of numerical growth and liveliness, away from the traditional places in Europe and North America to Asia and Latin America and especially Africa. It further reveals that in spite of material poverty, political and social marginalization and persecutions as well as pressures from other religions, Christianity in Africa seems to be growing faster than the population.

A *reversal in missionary movement*

Missionary statistics argue that on a global level, there are more missionaries and evangelists going out in India in recent years than any other nation of the world. Next in line is Korea. Recently, the Church of Nigeria responded to the evangelistic and missionary vision of its laity and launched a Church of Nigeria Missionary Society (CNMS) with a view to sending missionaries overseas.

It looks as though there is a new missionary movement following the demographic shift in the world Church. It is as yet unstructured and mostly spontaneous. Christians from the 'South' coming to the 'Global North' as students, migrant workers and economic refugees suddenly find themselves impelled by the power inherent in the faith they embody and from their experience in their home Church into becoming 'unofficial missionaries in their host countries'.

In the UK for example there are over 130 individual Nigerian missionaries working mostly among their own countryfolk – students and immigrant workers. As we consider the place and nature of evangelism through our Communion into the next millennium, we need to take this reality into consideration. But we should also ask, should this new movement be allowed to remain haphazard, from 'everywhere to everywhere', or should the older mission agencies lend their experience to make it more creative? Or will structuring and bureaucracy stifle the move of the Spirit? What is the Spirit saying?

Leadership for the younger Churches

We saw the need to train relevant and qualitative leadership for the Churches of the South. This is to help secure the future of the whole Church, to make partnership meaningful as it will then be more on the basis of equality, mutual acceptance and respect, and to mobilize and share God-given resources in the Church for mission.

Confidence in the Gospel and in the power of God

It looks as though the Church's honest engagement with evangelism at any age is directly proportional to its degree of confidence in the validity of the Gospel and of the message of the Bible for that age.

The goal of our evangelistic efforts into the next millennium should be more than a number-counting exercise. It needs to emphasize transformation as the prophetic import of evangelism. Thus our vision for evangelism is more than reaching the unreached or gathering and nurturing more and more compliant believers on our pews Sunday by Sunday. Success will be measured in terms of how much we have become absorbed in God's prophetic vision and how much we have been able to mobilize every believer into joyfully and courageously becoming vehicles of God's Good News. In this task, the Church of the Two-Thirds World is likely largely to make the pace and champion the vision.

Further reading

David Bosch, *Transforming Mission* (Maryknoll, NY: Orbis, 1991).
Richard Kew and Cyril Okorocha, *Vision Bearers: Dynamic Evangelism in the 21st Century* (London: Mowbray, 1997).
Cyril Okorocha, *The Cutting Edge of Mission* (London: Anglican Communion Publications, 1996).

The mission of the Anglican Church among the indigenous peoples of northern Argentina

Helena Oliver de Wallis

A difference between Argentina and other Latin American countries is that until comparatively recently the existence of the few Indian tribes who survived the military campaigns of the last century was *completely unknown*. In school we were taught about the Indians who had inhabited what is now Argentine territory, but the fact that there might have been survivors was hardly ever mentioned. It was therefore to an unknown world that I went 25 years ago, when I journeyed by tractor to Mission Santa María. I felt as though I was living through a fairy tale. As I got off the tractor everyone greeted me, but I didn't understand a single word. Was I still in Argentina?

A large number of children, young people, women and men came running to welcome us; it was obvious they felt great affection. Not a word of Spanish was spoken. The English missionary and the Argentine Indians exchanged fluent conversation, while I, an Argentine born and bred, did not understand a single word. The missionary spoke to me in Spanish so that I could understand.

Yes, she said, they will let you stay on two conditions, one is that 'you live with us' and the other that 'you believe what we say'. I asked her to tell them that yes, I accepted these conditions and that I would return soon. The government of the province of Salta needed a social worker to take charge of the final stage of a Project of Integral Development (a social policy in fashion during the 1960s and 1970s) which had received a huge amount of money destined for the community of Santa María. Funds had run out and the project needed to be 'brought to a good conclusion', by showing that the Indians had learned to sow seeds, to operate machinery, to organize themselves for work and that they were ready to 'provide for their own needs'. This project, devised and directed from Buenos Aires, the capital of Argentina, over 2,000 km from Santa María, had been a great burden for the Indians and was now being handed over to the province for its final stage.

In Santa María there are two villages, one Indian group living in the Mission and the other a *criollo* one living in what is called 'the town' (*criollos* are 'white' settlers who first came to this area at the beginning of this century; many are traders, others raise cattle). They had raised my tent in the middle of the Mission: a bed made of leather strips, a chair; outside it a simple safeguard, a fire.

All around were simple, cool houses, made out of what was provided in that place. Without secrets or furniture, they were merely places of refuge against the night and the cold. In the centre was a big house with mud-brick walls and a roof made of branches and earth. It had many openings along the sides (windows) and an entrance door.

In the morning the sound of an iron bar being struck called us. Some men went into the big house. I heard beautiful songs. Someone read something. More singing. I didn't understand a single word. The men came out and came up to greet me. Later the fire was lit, the first fish arrived, people brought water and wood and from that day onwards it has always been so. Like ministering angels they left their provisions and carefully withdrew.

They didn't expect any payment or thanks. I tried to learn this word in their Wichi language; with all my heart I wanted to say Thank you! Thank you! After more than 25 years, I still haven't found the right word. So it's clear that *thanks* are due only to God. What is given is a pure gift, and when it is given in this way there is no room for evil influences within the soul (pride, avarice, etc.).

Day-to-day living

'José, have you been to work today?' No. He was returning from the river with his string bag (made of cactus fibre) full of fish; it had been a good day. After standing hours and hours barefoot in the water in that winter cold. . . .

Weeks later. . . . 'Benjamín, have you been to work today?'

'No, today I didn't work.'

It was a hot day in October, sometimes up to 50 degrees and more. Benjamín was coming back from the scrub forest, having gone out very early with his string bag and his dogs. Thirsty and tired, he was bringing back one or two iguana lizards, delicious food for his family. But he had not been working! The women came home with heavy loads of wood on their backs, or fruit from the forest, but they never went to work.

I don't know, I don't understand! The word 'work' is oppressive in itself, perhaps because when we work we have to show some result and account for what we have done. But our daily bread which we gather is a gift from God. He put it there and it can't be accounted for. We can't pay for it. It always brings joy, even when it has to be collected with suffering.

P. came back from the river with no fish in his string bag. I was worried.

'P., wasn't there any fish?' 'Yes, I sold it to Oscar.'

'Did he pay you?' 'Yes, this much sugar (almost half a kilo) and flour (a kilo). . . . ' (He had given away about six fish for a very small amount of sugar and flour.)

'P., that's not fair!!! It would be better for your children to eat the fish and for you not to be deceived by Oscar.' (Oscar is a man who buys and sells fish while travelling about.)

'Calm down, calm down, Oscar didn't deceive me! I know he sells fish for a lot of money and gives me very little goods in exchange. But he doesn't deceive me. I'm fine but Oscar isn't, every time he needs fish he has to come to us because he always wants more and more money and he doesn't know how to get fish from the river himself. But I do; every time I need fish I go to the river and God gives them to me; if there aren't any now there will be another day. You see, when Oscar dies he can't take the fish or the money with him, poor Oscar doesn't know where he's going, but I do know ... '

... and around the fire, every day and every night, we used to gather and talk. ...

'When we were wandering nomads and didn't know God, we were always fighting, there were always wars and we used to kill each other.'

'When we used to drink too much we didn't always recognize each other and sometimes we killed our own brothers.'

'The criollos used to chase us. We would defend ourselves but they had more powerful weapons and we didn't want to go on fighting.'

'Once the border police put us all in a line.'

'They were going to kill all the men over 18. A criollo had accused us of stealing one of his cows, but it wasn't us, it was another criollo, they knew that. When we were all standing in front of the police so they could shoot us, we heard the sound of a vehicle and it was the missionary. The police were dismayed. When the missionary arrived, he said that if we were all going to be killed because we didn't own up to the robbery, then he would stand in the line with all of us. So they didn't dare kill us.'

'If it weren't for the missionaries you would not be able to live with us. We have forgiven the white people.'

What was it about these people? They responded to contempt with love, ... to poverty with gratitude, ... to pain with faith, ... to need with joy.

I had been living with the Indians about a year. One day Z., the pastor of Santa María and my adopted father, said something like this: 'It's a long time since you came to live with us. You love us, don't you? We love you, but this love will come to an end, when we die, if you aren't marked with Jesus' blood.' A few days went by. ... I had so much traditional religion and family ties in my past. ... But God had more than that, His eternal love, his infinite mercy and grace. One day I asked Zebedeo 'What do I have to do?' 'Be baptized. Repent and be baptized.'

The following Sunday there were nineteen baptisms, all Indians with me among them. The church, that large building in the middle of the Mission, was full. Through the openings along its sides God sent us his light.

No non-Indian person had ever been baptized in that church. Many children of God had been born there, all Indians. (Zebedeo said later that they had caught 'a white fish for the Lord'!) When the ceremony is over everyone greets the new believers. All along the entrance path to the church there were two lines of people through which the nineteen newborn Christians passed. What rejoicing! When I reached Ochiati (which means grandfather in Wichi – we had adopted each other), certainly the oldest man in the community, I looked up ... there were tears on his cheeks ... he looked at me and said 'you're not my grand-daughter any more ... now you're my sister'. .... We embraced.

The Wichi people are numerous, scattered over that vast region of forest and rivers. In 1914 the first missionaries arrived at Mission Chaquena (Algarrobal). They stayed, their children grew up with the Indian children. From the central Mission (Algarrobal) the seed grew and spread. The ground, so carefully prepared, accepted the seed. Indians from all parts came nearer in search of these white people 'who told us we had a Father in heaven who loves us', as they still remember every day, adding 'they didn't bring money or clothes or food or projects, only the Word; they didn't deceive us'.

'Before, we lived surrounded by evil spirits, they threatened us constantly.'
　'The spirits attack us in dreams, they roam at night.'
　'Didn't you see it? they were flying through the mission last night.'
　'No, I didn't see anything.'
　'Didn't you see it? they were walking round at dusk.'
　'No, I didn't see that either.'
　'It was standing there like a huge black dog, it wouldn't let me get near to help Chris (my husband, injured mysteriously by a machete).'
　'You white people see things differently, you can't see Satan with your eyes, but we can ... He walks around like a roaring lion. ... '

Evangelization

The Anglican missionaries who had come across the sea walked great distances, and even the Indians who had been converted to Christ could not stop. From one side of the Chaco region to the other, without any thought of payment, they would make, and are still making, truly missionary journeys. The Indian pastors of the diocese do not receive a salary. In my view this is by the grace of God. Those who decided this matter were guided by the Holy Spirit and bravely obeyed him. They always say that it will be different when the pastors are paid a salary.

　Faith among our Indian brethren is not inherited. It's also clear that, as Zebedeo once said in a sermon, 'Religion can't save us, nor the Church, nor the pastor, nor the missionary, nor even the Bible, but only Jesus Christ can save us, and that's why we should repent and follow him'.

Service of Praise and Teaching of the Word has no fixed hour; it begins at a certain time and may continue for hours. Everyone who is in need, or far from God, or who is following him, comes to the Church. We are all in need. The pastor listens, to the girl who fell into the hands of the white men, to the alcoholics, to the mothers with dying children, to men and women with terrifying fears. On one of those nights, when the service finished at about 2 in the morning, I said to Zebedeo 'That was long . . .'. 'Yes', he said, 'it was a very deep surgery; when we began we didn't know it was so bad. It's like the doctor who opens someone to do a simple operation and discovers a cancer, you can't leave it open but you have to carry on to the end. That's what happened tonight.'

Anglican mission and the Indians

The Anglican Mission in Argentina came first to the Indians, but not only to them, for today there are Spanish-speaking churches in many towns and cities. The Indian Church has 70 congregations with about 80 pastors. The Urban Church has sixteen congregations with eight pastors. There is a diocesan bishop, an Indian auxiliary bishop and an Argentine auxiliary bishop. There is also a missionary team working on translation and in medico-social and pastoral areas, as well as pursuing land rights.

An anthropologist began his thesis for a doctorate, studying the Wichi and the loss of their culture. One of his theories was that the influence of the Anglican Church had destroyed the Indian culture of the region. He has been very surprised to discover that if it had not been for the Anglican Church the Wichi would have disappeared and their language would not be spoken. The Indians of north-east Argentina have become well known. They are known in the churches for their faith in Christ. They are known in international meetings when they demand the rights of their land.

The evangelistic work of the Anglican Mission expanded but the conditions in which the Indians lived worsened. God had equipped his creation with everything necessary for native peoples to eat and live healthily and with abundance. But as the Argentine (*criollo*) population moved in with their different customs (and animals) the riches of the earth were gradually used up and the relationship between the two groups of people became complicated.

The Mission anticipated the need to find new ways of subsisting through carpentry, agriculture, handicrafts and other occupations. Medical help was developed and a health service organized; educational work grew from writing the Indian languages down, to making translations of the Bible, to helping the Indians to read and write their own languages. Now they have the New Testament in Wichi (Mataco) and Chorote.

Plans were implemented to encourage socio-economic development. A new missionary team was organized to follow up these plans. In certain cases land was bought for those groups who had nowhere to live in peace. These development projects were very concentrated and provided an opportunity for the Indians to share in a new experience alongside their Christian brethren. Government development projects, on the other hand, usually give very little opportunity to participate and to understand from the inside the processes and the consequences of the changes that come about through such efforts.

One of the long-term benefits is the awareness of the need to obtain land rights, and the unity which has grown regionally between the different groups in order to persevere in their claims for land over many years and in spite of many painful rejections. The majority of the land is fiscal, or government-owned. Any decision therefore has to be made by the government. Apart from a few exceptional cases where the people have already received the deeds, the vast majority live in complete insecurity and daily persecution.

Although in practically all the Indian communities there are government primary schools and in some a health centre attended by nurses, in both these services the Indians are still treated with discrimination. The presence and help of the few Anglican missionaries and Argentine brothers and sisters is a great encouragement in times of emergency and pain.

Traditional Bible studies, organized in every mission and guided by local leaders and the visiting missionary, have had to be replaced by the teaching of the Word in the church in daily services. All those who can read always want their own Bible.

In Church organization one can perceive a certain style handed down by the missionaries, but the dynamic is Indian and the style changes.

Years ago all women missionaries returned to their own country, but groups of women carry on meeting to read the Bible and pray together.

Since people continually talk about the Lord and his Word, I feel that the birds and trees, the river and the earth have all had the chance to hear the Gospel. How much more so the children.

This evangelization transcends the boundaries of the Indian peoples when they travel to take part in meetings with other groups, or when sick people come to the city hospitals and read the Bible and pray, or when they pursue their land claims with gentleness and with prayer, or when they visit Spanish-speaking churches and give their testimony or preach the word.

It's true that not all the Indians in northern Argentina have been converted to Christ; nevertheless there is that feeling that all of them come from the generation that opened themselves to God and that knows him. Two things that still cause the Indian peoples suffering are spiritual attack and rejection by the white man, but hope has opened the doors, as Bishop Mario Marino said: 'The suffering is the same, but the difference is that now we have hope!'

Further reading

Catherine Makower, *Don't Cry For Me Argentina* (Hodder & Stoughton, 1989).
Wendy Mann, *An Unquenched Flame* (SAMS, 1968).
Maurice Sinclair, *Green Finger of God* (Paternoster Press, 1980).
Maurice Sinclair, *Ripening Harvest, Gathering Storm* (MARC STL Books, 1988).
Phyllis Thompson, *An Unquenchable Flame* (Hodder & Stoughton, 1983).

The Church in Sri Lanka and relations with other faiths

Jayasiri Peiris

The Church of Ceylon originated because of the missionary efforts of the Church Missionary Society (CMS) and the Society for the Propagation of the Gospel (SPG). It consists of two autonomous dioceses in Sri Lanka: namely Colombo, founded in 1845, and Kurunegala, founded in 1950.

For four centuries, until 1948, Ceylon was ruled by a succession of Western powers, Portuguese, Dutch and British. Missionaries from these countries entered the land and propagated the faith. The majority of these missionaries considered that the people of the land were uncivilized and failed to recognize the richness of the cultures and religions of the people. This attitude led to clashes between Christians and non-Christians. Buddhist and Hindu revivals took place in the latter part of the nineteenth century as a response to this reality. In the controversies, the Christians were accused of being Western and unpatriotic. The situation changed in the twentieth century. In this chapter we will examine the different approaches taken by the Church of Ceylon within this context, in relation to other faiths. We will present a few models that we consider are important in Sri Lanka today.

Different approaches to other faiths

In the area of inter-faith relationships, there are four approaches to other faiths.

- The exclusive approach – in this approach, one considers that one's faith and religious texts are unique and the other faiths and other religious texts are in error.
- The inclusive approach – in this approach, one considers that God is the God of Creation and therefore God reveals and works in other faiths and histories outside.
- The pluralist approach – a study of other faiths with openness and an awareness that God is revealed in many ways, and all are valid, and no one has the right to condemn other faiths.
- The pluralistic-inclusivist approach – this approach recognizes the need for each faith to welcome the contribution other faiths can make to its own self-understanding, and helping it towards the fulfilment of the spiritual and theological content of one's own faith, in and through the contribution of other faiths, as all are living faiths.

Most of the foreign missionaries who served in Sri Lanka introduced Western expressions, culture and ethos. The people in the land accepted them fully without questioning them. Therefore, the architecture, music, forms of worship, the dress and the vestments were imported. The Church and the people imitated the West. There were a few exceptions, who did not reject the Sri Lankan cultures and religious thought-patterns. They were looked down on by the majority as rebels and heretics. However, in the midst of opposition and rejection, they felt that God called them to a different kind of ministry: to identify with the people of the land and relate their faith in a different way.

In the nineteenth century, Bishop R. S. Copleston studied Buddhism, as he realized that he should know what Buddhism is, in a land where the vast majority of people are Buddhists. Later he published a volume on Buddhism. His work could be considered extraordinary, taking into consideration the Christian attitude and theology that prevailed at that time with regard to other faiths.

In this century, Bishop Lakdasa de Mel, with the assistance of Deva Surya Sena and his wife Nelum Devi, did important work in indigenizing the liturgy. J. W. Samarasinghe contributed by composing a devotional chant using Sinhala Buddhist folk melodies. Indigenization in Tamil took place under the leadership of the Anandanayagams (husband and wife). This is referred to as the 'Anandanayagam setting'.

In the area of architecture, the Church had the Gothic style, which was alien to the people of the land. A. P. S. R. Gibson pioneered the use of traditional Sri Lankan architecture in one of the Church schools in the 1920s. Similarly, the Cathedral of Christ the King in Kurunegala, built in 1950, and the Cathedral of Christ the Living Saviour in Colombo, constructed in the 1970s (to replace the old Cathedral in Mutwal), were built on Sri Lankan architectural patterns.

In all these endeavours, the kernel of the Gospel did not change; only the outer husk. With the blow of a 'new' cultural wind in 1956, connected with a revival of Buddhism, the Church 'lost' its privileged position. The Churches in general, and the Church of Ceylon in particular, had to undergo a process of unlearning and relearning how to live with people of other faiths.

As a response to this reality, John Cooray took the name Yohan Devananda. He dropped his clerical title and took instead the term 'Sevaka' (servant), used in the Christian ashram tradition. He founded the Devasaranaramaya, on the Christian monastic tradition of St Anthony and St Benedict. Devananda incorporated the ashram and arama traditions: the Hindu search for the ultimate reality through intense spiritual activity and experience of divine powers, and the Buddhist path to an awakened and liberated mind, combined with a rigorous dedication to self-control and discipline. He felt that God had called him to get away from the Western-dominated, English-speaking elite of the towns to the Sinhala- and Tamil-speaking people in the rural villages. After a period of time, the peasants who were influenced by the aramaya felt that this Buddhist–Christian dialogue did not meet their needs. In the context of unemployment in 1969, Devananda initiated a half-day seminar on unemployment. Buddhist and Christian texts were read, a dialogue sermon between a Buddhist monk and a Christian clergyman was preached, and the Eucharist was celebrated. Later group discussions followed. At the end of the day, the peasants came to the realization that they had to move from contemplation into action; in particular that land reform was necessary.

From this time, the aramaya moved towards a collective farm. Devananda actively participated in peasant work and has also worked with people of other faiths in areas of human rights and peace work. The New World Liturgy which is used at Devasaranaramaya (and occasionally by others) has incorporated Buddhist, Hindu and Islamic texts as well as texts from Karl Marx, Che Guevara and Mao Tse-tung. This liturgy commences by honouring Hindu sages, Buddha, Jesus Christ, the Prophet Muhammad and Karl Marx.

Donald Kanagaratnam (Archdeacon of Jaffna, died 1995) appreciated the Buddhist and Hindu religious thought patterns. He emphasized the use of other faith symbols, and used them to expound the Gospel. By this way, he showed that other faiths are not alien to Christians and Christians should be bold enough to draw from these resources. He advocated a simple life-style and often said that Christian clergy should follow the model of Buddhist Sangha (monks), living on the alms of the people. A monk lives in the village, does not rush from one place to another, uses public transport, walks through the village. Therefore, the Buddhist monk is in constant touch with the people. In one of his articles, he spoke of the need to have a Theology of Lotus; theology of presence.

Kanagaratnam lived in a border village during his last fourteen years of ministry, engaged in a ministry of reconciliation; reconciliation of Sinhalese, Tamils and Muslims, Buddhists, Hindus, people of Islamic faith and Christians. He felt the need to work to take away suspicion (both ethnic and religious) and reconcile the people on trust, in order to build a new Sri Lanka. His work in the area of other faiths became important, because the people were able to see in him a person with whom they could dialogue about their faith. Kanagaratnam's respect for other faiths and races motivated him to work very closely with people of other faiths. When he was a lecturer at the Theological College, he also looked after a parish nearby. There he was able to work very closely with the Buddhist monks.

The third person who has given insights is Bishop Lakshman Wickremasinghe, a man from an affluent family, who had done his theological training in England. In the initial stages of his ministry, he realized the need of inculturation, with the intention of finding a new identity for the Church in Sri Lanka, and very specially for his diocese. Soon Bishop Wickremasinghe realized that evangelism and dialogue are not exclusive. In his lecture on 'Togetherness and Uniqueness', he says that each religion should be allowed to claim the uniqueness of that religion. He believed that these claims need not bring aggression and conflict among adherents of different faiths.

Divergent basic convictions will lead to mutual criticism and this must be absorbed with seriousness and receptivity, so as to lead to a reconception or reformulation of these basic convictions in the light of such criticism. On the other hand, each should seek to commend and communicate to the other his or her own uniquely central vision, so that the other accepts it by a process of conversion. Wickremasinghe understood conversion as a vision of Transcendent Reality who gives the possibility to learn from the togetherness of shared life. He was able to understand conversion in that way, as he himself had to unlearn and relearn, according to his own words. Wickremasinghe was not only a philosopher, he was also an activist. He put his visions into practice. He had very close relationships with Buddhist monks.

Once he was asked to speak at the ordination of a Samanera monk. He also gave the leadership to invite a Buddhist monk to speak in the Cathedral at Kurunegala at the interment of the ashes of Bishop Lakdasa.

Bishop Kenneth Fernando (the present Bishop of Colombo) was the Director of Ecumenical Institute for Study and Dialogue, before becoming the Bishop of Colombo. He is firmly convinced of the need to continue this spirit of dialogue and understanding between religions, as well as developing common approaches to the political and social issues affecting all our people.

Further reading

Devananda, *Living Dialogue: Documents of a Development Movement Among Peasants and Youth in Sri Lanka* (Hong Kong: World Christian Student Federation, 1977).
E. R. Sugirtharajah, *Asian Faces of Jesus* (London: SCM, 1995).
C. E. G. Weersuriya (ed.), *Indigenisation of Church Worship in the Church of Ceylon: A History 1945–95*.

Anglicans and inter-faith relations – a historical retrospect

Israel Selvanayagam

Introduction

I have been involved for 20 years in inter-faith dialogue, and been strengthened by advanced study of religions, particularly Hinduism. I remain deeply committed to the Christian gospel, and absolutely open to the visions and experiences of people of other faiths. I claim to be both 'evangelical and dialogical'. In reaching this position, I have been helped by historical examples from the Anglican tradition. For reasons of space, and in the light of the earlier chapter 'Salvation and other faiths' (pp. 4–12), here I merely introduce some of those who have provided such inspiration.

G. U. Pope

Buried in a tomb in Oxford that bears the inscription 'A Tamil Student' is
G. U. Pope (1820–1907), a missionary of the Society for the Propagation of
the Gospel (SPG), who worked in Tirunelveli, an Anglican mission field in
south Tamil Nadu. In the course of his language study he came across a
Hindu devotional text of the Tamil Saiva tradition, the *Tiruvasagam*. Its
devotional appeal moved him so greatly that he translated it into English.
He advocated that his fellow missionaries 'should take pains to know
accurately the feelings and convictions of those for whom, and in the midst
of whom, they work'. With reference to his own case, he says, he had never
ceased to say 'there in India, and here in Oxford' – to successive classes of
students 'You must learn not only to *think* in Tamil, but also to *feel* in
Tamil, if you are to be intelligible and useful among the Tamil people'.

Pope was not simply proposing a missionary strategy but a new
theological outlook in the context of religious pluralism. In the preface to
his translation he states:

> In matters of religion the greatest hindrance . . . is the spirit of ignorant,
> unreasoning, unsympathetic antagonism. Every system has its truths
> and profounder thoughts; and these lie deeper than 'full fathoms five' in
> man's nature; and must be fundamentally and essentially in large
> measure the same for all men, and for all time. It is only by recognising
> these *common truths*, and making them the basis of enquiry, as to further
> alleged Divine communications, that it is possible to gain a true
> religious development.[1]

While the Saiva scholars continue to praise Pope for his invaluable
translation of the most famous part of their scripture they do not fail to
point out certain shortcomings of his translation. Such shortcomings seem
to reveal the inner struggle of a Christian missionary to accept Siva, the
God of the Tamil Saivas, as supreme and universal. For instance, he
translates Hymn 4, lines 163, 164 as

> Civan, Lord of the southern land, – praise
> King of our country folk, – praise.

But the Tamil term for 'King of our country folk' actually means 'O God
to people of every country', as one of the later translators has put it.
Nevertheless, such shortcomings do not invalidate his respect for other
religious traditions and the empathy he had in understanding their
feelings.

Charlie Andrews

Kenneth Cracknell, in his recent excellent study of 'Theologians and missionaries encountering world religions',[2] highlights several Anglican missionaries, including Charlie Andrews. Charles F. Andrews (1871–1940) began his life in India, in 1904, as a SPG missionary and after ten years he left its service. He became more Indian than many Indians and built up profound association with great figures like Tagore and Gandhi. His 'missionary years' earned him the title *Dheenobandhu*, 'Friend of the Poor', which continues to be popular in India. His study of Hinduism and other religious traditions prompted him to take a position in line with Pope and Lloyd:

> We must believe that God has not left Himself without a witness for the thousands of years among the most religious people in the world. We must believe that holy men of old spoke as they were moved by the Holy Ghost, and we must no longer despise the Holy Ghost by speaking slightly of their message.[3]

Andrews found in the Hindu scriptures a true *preparatio evangelica*. He advocated, for Christianity, a stripping of 'foreign accretions and excrescences' and of the position of an exotic plant 'unacclimatized and sickly, needing the continual support and prop of the West'. His own indigenized personality was a silent call for the Indian Church to become indigenous, to be built on the ancient spiritual foundations of India. He saw the power of the eternal Word enlightening the great teachers and traditions of that land without denying the unspeakable degrading practices found in lower forms of religious life. He found Christ fulfilling the pathetic yearning of Hindus but without destroying all their good values.

F. D. Maurice and Brook F. Westcott

Cracknell writes of two Anglican nineteenth-century theologians. Frederick D. Maurice (1805–72) was influenced by many missionaries encountering world faiths. For him Christ before and after his manifestation in Jesus is the hidden principle which enlightens every human being and brings forth every good value. He appreciated Islam for its timely emphasis on the primacy, self-existence and unity of God who wants to purify his universe of all human-made gods and evils. Despite the apparent perplexing complexity of Hinduism, Maurice saw in it God's witness 'as evident in reflection, wonder and awe, high facets of culture and profound questions about the ultimate reality'. He found in Buddhism a certain divine intelligence which is manifested in the contemplation of divinity and heroic saintly sages. Above all his 'ten principles for Christian relationships with other religions' clearly reveal the mind of a great theologian, for whom people of other faiths are not simply the objects and targets of Christian mission but contributors to the enrichment of Christian theology.

Brook F. Westcott (1825–1901), Regius Professor of Divinity at Cambridge, New Testament scholar, one of the founder-leaders of the Cambridge Brotherhood at Delhi and famous Bishop of Durham, sought to build up his theology on the foundation of some of the early Church Fathers. He interpreted the Johannine statements like 'I am the Way, the Truth and the Life' and 'no man comes to the Father but by me' with the incorporation of insights coming from other religious traditions. For him Christ is the only door or agent to the Father. But he goes further, saying 'It does not follow that everyone that is guided by Christ is directly conscious of his guidance'. Westcott's 'Gospel of Life' starts from the 'gospel of creation' which includes the whole of humanity and human history which is dynamic and developmental as yet finding its consummation and fulfilment in Christ. He points out, in line with Justin Martyr, that all religions reflect, in some way, the seminal word implanted or inborn in every human heart. However, he observes, in the case of the Chinese, 'children crying in the dark' waiting for satisfaction in the gospel. He did not fail to take note of the 'sterile theism' of Islam and the 'shadowy vagueness of Hindu philosophy'. But the missionary response for him lies not in condemning them but in Christian communities demonstrating 'the free and generous relations of Christian brotherhood' with 'the spirit of self-repression and self-sacrifice, which gladly accepts a preparatory and transitory function', and 'which rejoices to leave a free course for the unforeseen operation of the Holy Spirit'.[4]

Bishop Appasamy and Sadhu Sunder Singh

A. J. Appasamy (1891–1975) emerged from the area where G. U. Pope worked. He and his father (a convert from Vaishnava Hinduism) were fascinated by Tamil Christian poets' works which reflected incorporation of literary and theological elements coming from the Vaishnava devotional texts. Appasamy took seriously the suggestion made by Westcott that 'Indian thinkers would be able to interpret fully the Gospel of John'. Hence his advanced studies in the Gospel in Oxford. He interpreted Christianity as *bhakti marga* (way of devotion) and the goal of human life *moksha* (release or salvation) as exemplified in Jesus' relational oneness with God and the Christian's faith-union with Christ.[5] He found raw materials for his interpretation of the Christian faith not only in the Gospel of John but also in the writings of poets, both Christian and Hindu, and the philosophical exposition of Ramanuja, a great Vaishnava teacher. Like some other Indian Christian theologians he found the Hindu concept of *avatara* (descending of God) to be helpful to interpret incarnation but suggested certain safeguards in order to maintain the uniqueness of divine incarnation in Christ. Appasamy was made a bishop in the Church of South India in Coimbatore Diocese (1950–58) and is acknowledged as 'one who has in many ways endeavoured to bring about mutual respect, understanding and sharing between Christians and people of other faith' and 'Christian forerunner and prophet of the emerging Inter-faith dialogue in India'.[6]

Appasamy's interest in interpreting the gospel with the help of Hindu categories and in developing an authentic Indian Christian spirituality was further evidenced by his close association with Sadhu Sunder Singh, a Sikh convert and wandering preacher. He collaborated with B. H. Streeter in writing a book on Sunder Singh's life and writings.[7]

Sunder Singh (1889–1929) was baptized in an Anglican church in Simla but he always claimed to be a member of the universal Church. Although his conversion was entangled with so much of struggle and ordeal he had a great respect for his Sikh mother who, he said, had made him a monk even before conversion by bringing him up in the Hindu–Sikh devotional life and without whom he could not conceive of a heaven after death. Known as 'the Apostle of the Bleeding Feet', Sunder Singh moved freely among the company of Hindu and Buddhist monks and sought to present 'the water of life in an Indian cup'. His writings[8] reveal his openness to people of other faiths and commitment to communicate the gospel using the Indian experience and resources. For him every living soul breathes in the Holy Spirit although Christ is the open light to which all must move for fuller life and fulfilment.

Conclusion

Ending where I began, I refer again to G. U. Pope. When I visit the state capital of Madras, and walk along the world-famous Marina Beach, I can see a whole series of statues erected in recent times to those who have made outstanding contributions to the development of the understanding of Tamil culture and religion. For me, as an Indian Christian, it is of immense pride to see there a bust of G. U. Pope, and to know that the Chief Minister of Tamil Nadu had given the privilege of unveiling the statue to Bishop Lesslie Newbigin, a close colleague in developing the modern city of Madras. As a contemporary Indian theologian, I am proud to stand as an inheritor of this tradition.

Israel Selvanayagam

Notes

1 G. U. Pope (trans.), *The Tiruvāçagam* (Oxford, 1900), p. x.
2 K. Cracknell, *Justice, Courtesy and Love: Theologians and Missionaries Encountering World Religions, 1846–1914* (London: Epworth Press, 1995).
3 Ibid., p. 176.
4 Ibid., p. 70.
5 The two books 'which are perhaps his best and most original': A. J. Appasamy, *Christianity As Bhakti Marga: A Study of the Johannine Doctrine of Love* (Madras: CLS, 1928) and *What Is Moksha? A Study in the Johannine Doctrine of Life* (Madras: CLS, 1931).
6 T. D. Francis, *A. J. Appasamy: A Christian Forerunner of Inter-Religious Dialogue in India* (Madras: CLS, 1991), p. 13.
7 A. J. Appasamy, *Sadhu Sunder Singh: A Biography* (Madras: CLS, 1958) and *The Cross Is Heaven* (London: Lutterworth Press, 1956).
8 T. D. Francis (ed.), *The Christian Witness of Sadhu Sunder Singh: A Collection of His Writings* (Madras: CLS, 1989).

Section Five

The Church and the future

All about Eve: woman of Africa

Brigalia Bam

I am told that the majority view among scientists is that human beings originated in Africa. Genetic evidence is of human life starting on the continent while the oldest fossil suggests that first human existence was indeed in South Africa.

The most convincing genetic evidence is relevant to the female lineage and points to the existence of 'Mitochondrial Eve' living in Africa between one and two hundred thousand years ago, at least thirty, perhaps forty, thousand years before some of her descendants moved into Europe and began to change their pigmentation.

Eve of Africa. This is where human beings originate – with a native woman, very probably of South Africa. This is the womb, the nurturing centre, the place of birth for humankind. On my continent we often speak of 'Mother Africa'. We now know that Mother Africa is the mother of all.

I too am woman of South Africa. I know the same rocks and shores, hills and valleys, rivers and streams, fertile soil and desert wastes of her background. It is mine as well. She truly is my mother. But, of course, she is also yours and belongs to everyone in the same way as everyone belongs to her.

Strange to consider our common mother as a black woman of Africa. For when we consider her we have to consider the way in which those whose pigmentation is black and all those who are women have been treated by that which we call the civilized world. To be black is to be second-class and to be black woman is to be doubly cursed.

Mitochondrial Eve calls to us from our past to remind us who we really are.

347

Common humanity of unique individuals

She is a reminder of our common humanity, our family relationship, where none is greater than another and none has right to lord it over others. She is also a reminder of our uniqueness for from our same mother we have the growth of our different natures and cultures, customs and practices. We have different gifts and skills to offer one another. We are human.

In some parts of Africa the Mopane tree grows profusely in the wild. Its leaves are fascinating for each leaf is in two parts joined together on one stem – a fragile joining of what seem to be two separate parts but where each is in fact dependent on the other for its life and sustenance. As one half lives the other lives, as one dies the other also dies. Is this a picture of our humanity? We are unique and independent people tied together by a fragile common humanity by which we all live or die.

Over many thousands of years Eve's children scattered through the world. A diffused family of people, unaware of the existence of others apart from close neighbours and competing tribes. It is in the last five hundred years or so, only minutes in the clock of human existence and seconds in the space of creation, that we human beings have learnt of one another, growing eventually into a global village of fast travel and electronic communication. A world we now know we share and where the death of one is the death of all and new birth is new life for all.

South African experience

We can certainly testify to the reality of this kinship in the South African experience. When black people were denied their freedom, their oppressors, the whites, were not free either. One could not be free without the other. And when we in the Church of South Africa sang our hymns of praise calling on God for strength or cried through our laments of grief, our voices were joined by those of the world Church, feeling our pain, joining our prayers, and standing with us in a time of great need. We were one. We are one.

We do not forget that and we are grateful for the experience of our unity as one people under God that makes our claim to be a 'rainbow nation' a worldwide symbol that goes well beyond the borders of our own new democracy.

We are grateful for the missionaries of the Church who brought us the gospel of the Lord Jesus Christ. The Society for the Propagation of the Gospel, the Society for Promoting Christian Knowledge and the Church Missionary Society made their contributions to the early years of our

Church here in South Africa. It is this experience of Jesus that brings us, you and me, together so closely in this one family. The Church sent us many of its best people in recognition of our common humanity and our common Lord. The values they taught have helped us – as our President Mr Nelson Mandela has so often acknowledged – to develop a respect for individual freedom on the one hand and common accountability on the other.

We are grateful to the people of the Church who did much for the development of this land in bringing us education and health care, sharing skills and resources to the glory of God and for the good of us all. I am a member of the Anglican Communion. I am glad to be able to say that. My great-grandfather was baptized and confirmed in this Church and with experiences of joy and pain in that membership over the years my family has been pleased to call itself Anglican since that time.

I am Anglican. But I am not English and I am not male.

Contradiction

Can you hear me as I face the contradiction of wanting to truly belong to, and be obedient to, the Church I love with all my heart and soul and yet, at the same time, cry for freedom to be me – black woman – in this Church. And also, I may say, in this new nation of South Africa.

Scripture tells us to honour our father and mother. How best can we honour our mother Eve – black woman of South Africa? Surely it is time to let her and all her children be free. It is time to loosen the custom that has made the world a place that belongs to white men, and from the tradition that has trapped the Church into reflecting a similar position.

As we in South Africa search for ways in which to live out the democracy we struggled so hard to attain, we discover we are having not only to examine and transform national legislation and social structures but also to look very closely at attitudes and behaviours between one another as individuals and as members of the different groups that make up this rainbow nation.

There are two major issues facing us here in South Africa. We have the urgent need of reconciliation and we have the need for the open recognition of the present and potential contributions to be made by each and everyone. Within these two major issues lie the huge problems of poverty and unequal sharing of the riches of our land, crime and violence, and the dreadful – almost satanical – abuse of women and children.

What role has the Church to play in facing these challenges? A large role obviously, for these are both issues that lie at the heart of Christian values and practices. Reconciliation can almost be claimed as a 'Christian' word.

Recognition of the dignity of others is a gospel imperative. The Church must be at the forefront of the movement toward a new democratic order of peace and cordial relationship.

Truth and reconciliation

The Churches in South Africa have been making their submissions to the Truth and Reconciliation Commission, under the chairmanship of Archbishop emeritus Desmond Tutu, to recall the way we acted in the days of apartheid and give some indication of our role for the future. The submissions differ in emphases and content but there are some basic agreements – that we did not do enough to eradicate apartheid and also that, by and large, the Churches reflected the society in which we live.

This meant that the Churches had members who were pro-government, some who actively opposed, and a majority who simply enjoyed or endured the status quo. We can make many claims about statements and sermons, special services and Church leadership challenge to the government of the day. We can *not* claim that the Church at heart portrayed a different society where colour did not matter and where declared status was not equated with privilege. We can *not* claim that the Church was a model of an alternative society.

We speak with pride in the Anglican Communion about those of our number who made a stand against oppression and racism. People such as Archbishops Huddleston, Selby Taylor, Tutu, and de Blank for their courageous prophetic roles, Dr Mampela Rhampela for her willingness to stand against oppression and suffer with the poor, and the Revds Calata and Gawa who were pioneers in the African National Congress. And there are many others whose witness to justice and righteousness is quite remarkable. At the same time we have to admit that the Church echoed society in the accepted disparities between white and black, and between men and women, in a form of institutionalized racism and sexism.

The South African Council of Churches (SACC) made a great contribution in the struggle against apartheid through its prophetic role, its work for the victims of apartheid and its determination that the world should know the truth of what was really happening to our people. It was, however, some individuals within the Churches and not the Churches as a whole who supported the ideals and participated in its activities. To claim otherwise and speak generally of the Churches' stand against apartheid is to deny the real truth.

And let it be said that it was the women of the Church who so often bore the brunt of the stand against apartheid. It was the Black Sash and the YWCA that gave advice and encouragement, education and moral support to so many. It was the Mothers' Union that played an active role in the support and care of those of its members, and other women too, who were torn from the lands of their birth, faced poverty and loneliness as loved ones were incarcerated, and cried at the death and maiming of their children.

When many people were killed in a dreadful clash in Bisho of the Eastern Cape in 1993 the nation was filled with accusations and counter-accusations, speeches and disputes. In the meantime it was the Church women's groups of the township who held the people together, consoled the grieving, supported the needy and showed compassion in a practical way.

Church women united

There is no doubt that those same women and their groupings must now face the challenges of the creation of a new democracy. We have an important role to play. A role in the transformation of the legislation and structures of the land, and a role in the transformation of attitudes and behaviour toward one another.

It was in recognition of this role that the SACC organized a Church Women United Conference in Johannesburg in June 1996. We came together because we knew that no single denomination can face the enormous responsibilities that stand before the Churches. We need one another and we need to recognize the different skills and resources we can bring together in one movement to serve the nation.

A network has been established working within what we have called a Women's Ecumenical Conference. The challenge to the women's move-ments in all our Churches, including the Mothers' Union, is to accept the need we have for one another and break down the denominational barriers between us. Ecumenism may not be a favourite exercise at the present time, but without it we are poor withered Mopane leaves that will die.

Women in the Church

It was obvious that we should be concerned about the place of women in the Church. This within the context of the role of women in our new society where legislation assures them of their equal place, but attitudes still remind them of the secondary nature of that position. This was expressed not only by those in the informal or commercial sectors but even by members of parliament. We have a high percentage of women in parlia-ment but the numbers do not reflect the influence and positions of power.

The same was also expressed about the Church.

Figures in our own Church show that there are a majority of female members and that it is the women's organizations that provide much of the financial support. But it is not the women who make the major decisions and choose the priorities for our Church.

Are we again to see a Church that reflects the society in which we live, where legislation allows for one style of life and attitudes create another? If the Church is to be a change agent in our new democracy, bringing about the healing of our nation through reconciliation, it has to be a model of that sought-after society where we are sisters and brothers under God.

The Church must be transformed if it is to play its role in the transformation of society. If we are to be leaders and provide a role model of the rainbow nation it must be reflected in leadership and opportunities for leadership. In a society where more than 80 per cent are black the Church still has a majority of white bishops, and not one a woman. There is need for inculturation in the modes and practices of the Church. This is not a criticism of the practices and traditions of the past, but a cry for the Church in Africa to be African and display its particular character and thus give input to the benefit of the worldwide communion. This can be an experience of our sharing and of our different pertinent gifts and offerings to one another.

I want my Church to be a model, a taste, an example of what it means to live together as equal brothers and sisters under God. I have to admit that as a black woman of some standing I feel better recognized for my abilities and input in our secular society than in the Church.

Women are now allowed to be ordained throughout most of the Anglican Communion. Are they allowed, however, to be women priests with their special gifts and nurturing attitudes or placed in a position where they are women acting out roles positioned by men? Is Eve the priest fulfilling the task that the Adams of the world have set for her? Why is it that there are some places where Anglicans are allowed without censure to refuse to receive communion from a woman priest? Perhaps it will only change if the women break the silence and refuse to accept communion from men!

We have many fine women theologians in our Church. Their place is acknowledged within the structures and debating courts of the Church. Their allegiance seems, however, to be with women ministers and priests of other denominations more than within their own communion. This is good for inter-Church relations but a sad reflection on the true acceptance of the new ordinances of the Church.

We seem trapped in traditions and attitudes that have no place in a truly free democratic structure where all are equal not only before God but among ourselves as well. We are trapped in a traditional attitude toward

women which fills the Church with contradictions that deny our witness to
the new society for which we struggled against apartheid.

Mother Eve calls to us through the years of human existence. In laying
claim to Eve we lay claim to our own being, to our own dignity and worth
and to the dignity and worth of all other people of whatever colour, creed
or gender. We lay claim to *ubuntu*, an African expression of the extended
family relationship in which we live not only *with* one another but also *for*
one another in recognition of rights and responsibilities of each and every
one.

Ubuntu, Mother Eve, the voice of Africa will not remain silent.

Note

I wish to thank Trefor Jenkins, Professor of Human Genetics at the University of
the Witwatersrand, and Revd Bernard Spong, former Head of Communications at
the SACC, for their assistance in information and editing for this chapter.

A vision for theological education in North America

Martha Horne

Theological education has been the subject of many conversations, articles
and books in the United States and Canada in recent years. Faculties of
seminaries and divinity schools, once charged primarily with the preparation of young men for the ordained ministry, now find their classrooms
filled with women, middle-aged students and retirees. Past generations of
seminarians were steeped in the religious traditions of the Christian faith.
However, students seeking admission to Episcopal seminaries in the
United States are frequently unfamiliar with the Bible, the history of
Christianity, and the theological and liturgical traditions of Anglicanism.

As these demographic changes pose new challenges for seminaries and
divinity schools, other concerns have appeared as well: How do we teach the
Christian faith in an increasingly pluralistic or secular culture? How are

men and women formed – spiritually, intellectually, morally – for leadership in the Church? Is theological education a form of *paideia*, geared
primarily to the spiritual and moral formation of Christian character, or is
it *Wissenschaft*, aimed primarily towards the creation of church professionals
through rigorous and critical academic study and research?[1] Other questions are more pragmatic: How do we develop a curriculum that provides
students with a working knowledge of the classical theological disciplines,
a supervised 'hands-on' experience of ministerial education 'in the field',
and those skills necessary for the leadership of worship and the practice of
ministry? How do we shape the seminary curriculum to meet the needs of
those who are new to the Christian faith or the Anglican Communion? Do
older students require different methods of teaching and learning?

The purpose of this chapter is to offer a personal vision for the future of
theological education in the United States. There are three main questions
to which I respond. What qualities do we want in the people who are sent
into the world as messengers of the Gospel of Jesus Christ? What resources
do they need in order to be responsible and effective leaders in the Church
and in the world in the twenty-first century? How can theological education develop and implement practices which form strong leaders for the
Christian community?

This author's vision for theological education is built on two assumptions: it assumes first that students and faculty are engaged in the enterprise
because they want to know God more deeply and because they are
committed to the mission and ministry of the Church. It assumes also that
theological education is not intended to be an end in itself, but is
instrumental in nature, having as its goal the formation of leaders for the
Church, and the proclamation of the Gospel.

Seminaries and divinity schools must be, first and foremost, places of
formation. Theological education requires far more than the acquisition of
academic degrees. In order to be faithful to the Gospel, theological
education must engage students in an intense process of inculturation into
Christian thought and practice. The process is both intellectual and
existential; questions like 'What am I to believe/think/teach as a Christian?' are considered alongside others: 'How ought I to live/act/serve as a
leader within the Christian community?'

Formation is an arduous process which seeks to integrate the intellectual, spiritual, moral and emotional dimensions of human life in such a way
that a person is conformed more closely to the image of Christ. Formation
encourages the development of certain habits – the nurture of the spiritual
life through the reading of scripture and a discipline of personal prayer and
piety, for example – yet more is needed. The development of certain
necessary skills of speaking and listening is important, as is the ability to

354

think critically about one's faith, one's culture, and one's own assumptions and biases. Passive assimilation of the values of the prevailing culture, without a careful critique of that culture, runs the risk of being idolatrous; thoughtful and careful examination of one's self and social location, over and against the claims of Scripture, is mandatory.

The preparation of strong leaders for the Church demands that students and faculties be actively engaged in the world around them. Like other academic institutions, seminaries are often criticized as being 'ivory towers', distanced from the concerns and cares faced by 'real people' whose work is in the world. Like parish churches, seminaries sometimes attract those who are seeking refuge from the world, a place to come 'for solace only and not for strength, for pardon only and not for renewal'.[2] The challenge is to provide an environment in which students can be free enough from the distractions of the world so that they can immerse themselves fully into the formation process while not losing sight of the needs of the world they are called to serve. Seminaries must keep before their students and faculties the missionary challenge and charge of the Gospel, lest they become too complacent, too distant, too comfortable with the status quo.

This vision insists that theological education should always include a significant ecumenical dimension. The power of the Christian witness to the world is seriously diminished by internal conflicts and disagreements, often public, sometimes hostile, which pit Christians against one another. In some places, Catholics and Protestants keep alive ancient hostilities and commit acts of violence against one another. Many of us engaged in theological education lament this separation and acknowledge both the importance and the difficulty of achieving the goal of 'ecumenical formation' identified by the World Council of Churches and other bodies.[3] Understanding Christian traditions that are not our own helps us to appreciate and claim the strengths of our own denominational loyalties, while also drawing us closer to other members of the Christian family who share the central tenets of our faith.

Effective Christian leadership requires an understanding of the increasingly pluralistic nature of North American culture. Theological education that fails to take into account the growing racial, ethnic, and religious diversity of the surrounding culture is inadequate and ill-equipped to prepare men and women for their ministries. Familiarity with other major religions of the world becomes an urgent priority as our families, schools, and neighbourhoods expand to include those of other religious traditions, and as temples, mosques, and shrines spring up among the Christian churches and synagogues of North America.

The challenges of Christian ministry in the midst of a diverse and pluralistic North American culture are matched by the challenges of living in a world where the globe is rapidly shrinking. Globalization requires us to think about the interconnectedness and interdependence of human life. Theological education should offer an opportunity for students to begin to experience and to understand people of other cultures and other faiths. Evangelism and conversion may comprise a part of the conversation we have with one another, but co-operation and collaboration around values we hold in common should also flow from those conversations.

The formation of Christian character, the ability to think theologically and critically about one's traditions, one's surroundings and one's self, an active engagement with the world around us, a commitment to ecumenical dialogue and partnership, and an appreciation of the pluralistic and global character of modern life: all are important components to theological education in the coming years. They are no guarantee of strong leadership for the Christian community, however. The Church must raise up, call, and support the preparation of candidates who have the potential to be strong leaders: women and men of deep faith and unswerving commitment to Christ who will be faithful in their prayers and passionate in their preaching, individuals who are willing to work hard for the sake of the Gospel, servants who want to follow the example set by their master.

These are turbulent, terrifying, and exhilarating times for those of us who have the work of theological education as our primary vocation. Many of us sense that the Church of our parents and, indeed, of our own childhood is no more. We strive to prepare men and women to serve a Church whose future shape we perceive only dimly – as through a glass darkly. We send students forth to proclaim the Gospel to a world that may greet them with bored indifference or with unmasked hostility. We see Christians dying for their faith throughout the world, even as others die for lack of faith.

It would be an impossible task, this work of theological education, were it not for a reality known in our hearts, but sometimes forgotten amidst the round of daily duties. Like the disciples whom Jesus first called to follow him, we do so knowing that the mission is not our own, but belongs to the one who sends us; that the Church exists through the mercy and providence of God, and that in God's time, all things will be accomplished and brought to their fulfilment.

Notes

1 David H. Kelsey uses these designations to discuss two contrasting models of education operative in North American theological schools. See David H. Kelsey, *To Understand God Truly: What's Theological About a Theological School* (Louisville: Westminster/John Knox Press, 1992), chs 3 and 4, pp. 63–98; and *Between Athens and Berlin: The Theological Education Debate* (Grand Rapids: William B. Eerdmans, 1993).

2   The phrase is taken from the Book of Common Prayer of the Episcopal Church (New York: The Seabury Press, 1979), p. 372.
3   In 1993 a study document was issued by the Joint Working Group between the Roman Catholic Church and the World Council of Churches, entitled 'Ecumenical formation: ecumenical reflections and suggestions'. See *Theological Education*, vol. 34, Supplement (1997), pp. 55–62.

Further reading

Mark D. Chapman, 'Scripture, tradition and criticism: a brief proposal for theological education', *Anglican Theological Review*, vol. LXXVIII, no. 2 (Evanston, IL; Spring 1996), p. 27.
Alice Frazer Evans, Robert Evans and David Roozen (eds), *The Globalization of Theological Education* (Maryknoll, NY: Orbis Books, 1993).
Edward Farley, *Theologia: The Fragmentation and Unity of Theological Education* (Philadelphia: Fortress Books, 1983).
Edward Farley, *The Fragility of Knowledge: Theological Education in the Church and the University* (Philadelphia: Fortress Books, 1988).
David H. Kelsey, *To Understand God Truly: What's Theological About a Theological School* (Louisville, KY: Westminster/John Knox Press, 1992).
David H. Kelsey, *Between Athens and Berlin: The Theological Education Debate* (Grand Rapids, MI: William B. Eerdmans, 1993).
John B. Lindner *et al.*, 'Ecumenical formation: a methodology for a pluralistic age: the care of the Ecumenical Institute at Bossey', *Theological Education*, vol. 34, Supplement (Pittsburgh, PA: The Association of Theological Schools, Autumn 1997).
Barbara G. Wheeler and Edward Farley (eds), *Shifting Boundaries: Contextual Approaches to the Structure of Theological Education* (Louisville, KY: Westminster/John Knox Press, 1991).

Women, Church and ministry in the coming decade

Penny Jamieson

The last ten years have seen significant developments in the position of women within the Anglican Communion. Since the debates at Lambeth 1988 a number of countries have begun ordaining women to the priesthood, including Australia, South Africa, England, Scotland, Ireland and Wales. In 1989, Barbara Harris was consecrated Suffragan Bishop in the Diocese of Massachusetts, and a year later I became Bishop of the Diocese

Penny Jamieson

of Dunedin in the Anglican Province of Aotearoa, New Zealand and Polynesia.

Dunedin is the southernmost diocese of our Church, and is consequently at one of the far edges of the Anglican Communion. It has been helpful to be away from the centre of the debates about the ordination of women, away too from curious eyes and critical minds beyond these shores. This is a sturdy and hospitable diocese, and I have been grateful for the opportunity to work prayerfully into the call that God put on my life.

This country received the Christian faith through the energy and commitment of the early CMS missionaries. Like other Churches within our Communion, our ancestors, both Maori and Pakeha,[1] faced the tension between holding to the fundamental principles of the faith and the challenge of communicating the vibrancy of the call of Christ effectively in this new context and a new country.[2] It is the challenge of mission, the challenge of particularity, the challenge of the Incarnation, of God with us in all times and all places.

Like other countries in our Communion, we have seen many changes in the last 30 or so years.[3] As the monolithic structures of the British Empire and of the Church that accompanied it began to evolve into local expressions of life and worship, so the Church in this and other countries has moved from its single commitment to white male clerical, professionally trained leadership, to a Church in which the leadership of both Maori and women, lay and ordained, is honoured and truly part.

And equally, in cultures where the leadership of women has not moved beyond the domestic sphere, it is a similar sense of honouring the local that has made some Churches decline with confidence to consider ordaining women to positions of leadership. We in Aotearoa/New Zealand are particularly alert to the subtle interplay and sometimes incompatibility of Western with indigenous values. We have learnt that there is no absolute value or integrity in any given position on the ordination of women. There is, rather, the constant challenge to use well the human resources that God has given to the Church for the spread of the Gospel of Christ.

This year [1997] this Church is celebrating the twentieth anniversary of the ordination of women to the priesthood. For us, this was a comparatively easy step: we have been living with its richness, possibilities and pitfalls ever since, and now 25–30 per cent of our priests are women. However, I am currently the only bishop who is a woman. I am ever hopeful that the next round of episcopal elections will see more women elected.

Our vision for women as for men has expanded, reaching beyond consideration of the numbers admitted to the privilege of ordination. Our experience of women in ordained ministry has shifted our understanding of priesthood; it has challenged the social construct of priesthood and made us ask what it really is.

Vision forms where the light falls, and so in this chapter I shall explore three shafts of that vision that has emerged out of the experience of women, myself included, in the Church in Aotearoa, New Zealand and Polynesia. With women in our Church, I offer these shards to our Communion in the hope that they might assist in the perception of the vision that God has for us all over the next decade.

Our vision of priesthood

The move to ordain women has become such a struggle in so many parts of our Communion that I think there are many cases where the achievement of this goal has obscured the reasons it was sought. It has been the experience of some lay women that when their friends became priests they lost not only their friends but their companions in the Christian venture: participation in the rites and collegiality of priests has excluded the unpriested. This is indeed a serious loss of vision. But a more distanced, dare I say, more mature experience of the ordained priesthood of women sharpens our understanding of the place within the Christian community of the priesthood of Christ.

Both the priesthood and the episcopate are strong symbols, and as we in our province have lived with and reflected on the interaction of ordination and gender, we have come to fresh realizations of the way the Church appropriates symbols and is in turn formed by them. This mutually formative interaction is seen most clearly in the symbol of the cross, given to us by the Son of God, which has been powerful in the shaping of our identity for nigh on 2,000 years.

The priesthood of Christ is a powerful gift to the people of God. Ironically, as access to the ordained priesthood has widened, we have seen more clearly that the privilege of the priesthood of Christ is present and is shaping the whole Church. As women have struggled to have their call to the ordained priesthood heard, they have made the point very clearly that they are called not to privilege and power, but to make real, through the symbol of their priesthood and the experience of their lives and their being, the reconciling, redemptive, renewing actions of Christ continuing to live through his body the Church. For some men and women this includes the ministry of priestly leadership. Just as bishops claim that priesthood continues to inform the character of episcopal ministry, so the Church as a whole embodies the priesthood of Christ and some amongst us are called to be signs and icons of this presence.

When priesthood is placed within the community, the hierarchical place of priesthood shifts from somewhere above halfway on the scale of leadership and thus the whole paradigm is questioned. In its place is growing a

359

slow culture of mutuality, generosity and trust in which all find the environment to share their gifts and to live under the headship of Christ. I have seen excellent lay leadership develop and I have seen communities grow and thrive.

It is no accident but rather, I believe, God-given timing that those parts of our Church which developed Mutual Ministry (or Total or Local Ministry)[4] are those parts that have been ordaining women for some years. Mutual Ministry does not thrive in a hierarchical model of ordained ministry, but grows surely and steadily where a context of the mutuality and complementarity of both lay and ordained emerges, and with it a reciprocity of difference.

This has powerful flow-on implications for our vision and practice of episcopacy. I believe that the vision of women within this Communion is to point to a style of leadership that has less in common with the 'rulers of this world' and more affinity with the servant Lord, who warned us that, although among the gentiles the great shall make their authority felt, 'it shall not be so among you'.

But, it has been so among us, which is why episcopacy, with its un-Christlike tendency to pomp and self-importance, is held in sceptical contempt by many who are altogether outside of the Christian faith. Women who are confident in their call and have no need for the false confidence that emulation pretends to, have no time for these monarchical models. For us it is a ministry of pastoral oversight, with a ready eye to chart the direction of the people of God. It is exercised in personal, collegial and communal ways, and it belongs to and is the responsibility of the whole people of God. Bishops are called to be signs and icons of this communal responsibility.

This vision of priesthood is shared widely in our Church, among men and among women. However, I believe that it is easier for women and through no merit of our own. In general, women are not accorded the support of social prestige and so it can be easier for us to grasp that it is intrinsic, not extrinsic authority that commends our leadership. Whether as bishops, as priests or as laity, we know that for us there is no easy resting on gender-derived esteem; it is the quality of leadership that counts, not the office held; it is our ability to articulate the purpose of the Christian community that matters, not our place in the pecking order.

Our vision of Church

It has been the experience of many of the Churches in our Communion that their engagement in decision-making on the ordination of women has tied up the Church with its own internal organizational business, and has reduced the focus on mission.

In practice the only justifiable motive for the ordination, or indeed the baptism, of *anyone* is to expand the Christian community and make the Gospel of Christ relevant to the here and the now. No priesthood should either be privileged or serve as a chaplaincy to the privileged, but must enable, through structure, calling and passion, the spread of the Gospel. There is here a profound honouring of evangelical effectiveness.

Perhaps the strongest critique of the privilege of ordination is that it can become more engaged in keeping the context of that privilege alive than in joining with others in common cause for the spread of the Gospel. My experience in this country suggests that it is bishops who find inter-denominational activities most difficult. These are embraced with ease by many lay people, who sit more lightly on our institutional structures. Undoubtedly the extra-parochial missions in which our Church is engaged in schools, hospitals, universities, prisons and industry, benefit from being organized and administered through a single Christian structure. Nothing demeans the Gospel more to secular eyes than the spectacle of Christians fighting for a place in the secular sun.

I have noticed that many women come to ordination with a passion for the Gospel that is despite, rather than because of, the welcome they receive from the Church. They have a seemingly natural ability to form partner-ships with Christians from other denominations, and this tendency can survive ordination. As a generalization, I would say that women lean less heavily on denominational structures. We do not need them to protect our position or even our view of the faith. However I must admit that I have noticed in myself, that my protectiveness of the Anglican Church has increased on becoming a bishop!

The touch of the Church expands as the range of those in visible leadership increases. Undoubtedly the ordination of women to the priest-hood has made both the Church and God more accessible to women who, often painfully, critiqued the monolithic male leadership of the Church. Perhaps, like Mary, we have enabled the Church to speak more humanly of the immanence of God as a balance to the transcendence of God. But over the years since women were first ordained in this country, this critique has sharpened. It would be true to say that many of us working and praying within the Church experience an increasing gap between our position and that of our more feminist sisters. This has been a humiliating experience; we have had to realize that, despite our commitment, the Church is still extraordinarily patriarchal, and that we are not able to save it: only God can do that. We have wept to find ourselves caught up in an institution that appears to be so irredeemably patriarchal, and we have wept at the loss of our friends who have found our continuing association with it quite incomprehensible. The communication that maintains relationships has at times been an intolerably stretching experience.

But, somewhere in the midst of all this pain, we have re-found and been re-found by the God who hung with us in all the pain of humankind, the God who was stretched, and in that stretching found birth.

Our vision of holiness

While we live with an inherited system of patriarchal and monarchical leadership, the widespread reality and effectiveness of women in ordained ministry means that we are less inclined to regard *male* (and white) as the normative way of being human, with the consequent definition of women (and other races) as *other*. From this we have acquired a wider, less restricted understanding of what it means to be made in the image of God. Our sense of the inclusiveness, embraciveness that is the heart of God is widened beyond recognition.

So it is no accident that the introduction of women into positions of leadership has led to the discovery, the rediscovery, of many holy women from our past and present, and thus has widened our horizons of holiness immensely.

As the debate over the use of inclusive (non-gender-specific) language has proceeded in the Church, we have discovered anew the inadequacy of *any* human language to talk to God. Images and metaphors for God have multiplied in liturgy and theology as we seek to define the indefinable. We stand in awe of the incomprehensibility of God, the transcendence of God shines through and as we worship thus we are less inclined to own than were our patriarchal predecessors, less able to be gate-keepers of God; the uncontrollable magnificence of God defies our puny efforts at control. It is less easy to claim unique access, ownership or privileged affection with a God who is *beyond gender*.

Holiness is thus freed from control and becomes much more fun. There is an almost playful delight in the exploration of the wildness of God, far more fun than surfing in cyberspace and much more companionable, for others journey with us. Holiness is not grim seriousness, but rather the totally unreserved enjoyment of the love of God that embraces all creation.

And it is mutual, it is generous and it is trusting.

Notes

1 *Maori* are the indigenous people of New Zealand; *Pakeha* are the people of mainly European origin who live in New Zealand.
2 Alan Davidson, *Christianity in Aotearoa: A History of Church and Society in New Zealand* (Wellington: NZEFM Board, 1989).

3   Brian Davis, *The Way Ahead: Anglican Change and Prospect in New Zealand* (Christchurch: Caxton Press, 1995).
4   This ministry, which includes the ordination of priests and deacons from local communities to form, with others, ministering communities, draws much of its inspiration from the writings of Roland Allen, and has developed widely in many provinces of our Communion, albeit in differing ways.

Further reading

Alan Davidson, *Christianity in Aotearoa: A History of Church and Society in New Zealand* (Wellington: NZEFM Board, 1989).

Brian Davis, *The Way Ahead: Anglican Change and Prospect in New Zealand* (Christchurch: Caxton Press, 1995).

Carter Hayward, *Touching Our Strength: The Erotic as Power and the Love of God* (San Francisco: Harper, 1989).

Penny Jamieson, *Living at the Edge: Sacrament and Solidarity in Leadership* (London: Mowbray, 1997).

Rosemary Neave (ed.), *The Journey and the Vision: A Report on Ordained Anglican Women in the Church of the Province of New Zealand* (Auckland: The Women's Resource Centre, 1990).

Hannah Ward and Jennifer Wild, *Guard the Chaos: Finding Meaning in Change* (London: SPCK, 1995).

Beyond revival: a proposal for mission in the Church of Uganda into the third millennium

Amos Kasibante

A traditional, conservative ethos informs the conception of salvation in the (Anglican) Church of Uganda (COU). This evangelical emphasis has its roots in the Church Missionary Society who brought the Gospel to the Kingdom of Buganda. It was enhanced later in the 1920s by the Balokole, the East African Revival Movement. The Balokole was a movement of the Spirit with several dimensions. While many of its facets can be traced back to the traditions of the Keswick Convention and the Cambridge Inter-Collegiate Christian Union (CICCU) to which missionaries such as Dr Joe

Church and Dr Stanley Smith belonged, its great success lay in both the manner of its transformation of individual lives and the translation of its message in terms that Africans could understand. A few examples will suffice here. There was a stress on repentance, public confession, and belief in the efficacy of the Blood of the Lamb, in washing a person clean of sin. Then again, the Balokole formed a strong bond among themselves, calling themselves people of the same clan. The term 'brethren' was an English translation of a single African word (e.g. 'Aboluganda' in Luganda) which meant both brother and sister. The way the Balokole understand the Gospel rotates around the ideas of being reconciled with God, with fellow human beings, living with Christ in daily life, and living in hope of the supernatural reality over and beyond this life. With their stress on living an exemplary life and being 'separate', the Balokole aimed to create an alternative society. They worshipped alongside Christians who had not made the type of confession and commitment that they themselves had made. But they were not prepared to regard these other Christians as right in their own way. They would not tolerate a 'two-integrities' Christianity, but rather challenged all to get saved.

The non-Balokole, on the other hand, either decided to be just 'good Christians' and admitted their daily failings – sometimes even justified them – or called the Balokole hypocrites who spoke as if human beings could be free of sin. Nevertheless even these people tend to operate with the conception of salvation established by the Balokole. For them salvation may be an ideal to aim for rather than a present reality. But for both groups, it is the individual Christian who is the object of salvation, with the Church as the locus of salvation.

True to evangelical doctrine, the COU emphasizes divine grace as essential for salvation. Good deeds are necessary, but not sufficient for salvation. This can be heard in the sermons and the hymns sung in church. But while the Balokole would insist on personal testimony of both your lips and actions (Romans 10.10), the 'non-saved' Christians tend to emphasize personal morality and a sense of religious duty.

All Christians encounter the Church at critical moments in life. The Church, whether Catholic or Protestant, succeeded in being present at and sometimes taking over the traditional rites of passage such as birth and naming, marriage, funeral and post-funeral and inheritance rites, as well as thanksgiving occasions such as recovery from a serious illness, acquiring an educational qualification, surviving an accident or the homecoming of a distant child or relative. So, the 'non-saved' Christians are not redundant where Church is concerned. Nor are they passed over by divine grace. In addition to having a religious faith – Christian religious instruction mixed with African traditional insights and, sometimes, Islamic views – they also have the opportunity, indeed the responsibility, of giving financial support to the Church and to Church projects. This is especially true of the 'heavyweight' members. A rich or prominent person who does not give substantially to the church or mosque will be regarded as mean. It is partly for this reason that political and other civic leaders usually get involved with, indeed meddle into, the affairs of the Church.

The Church also seeks in this way to exercise an influence on people in government and other important places. For access to sources of power and funds and ability simply to get things done, a local bank manager or headmistress may be more powerful or more effective than a government minister or university professor. The Church is seen and sees itself as the servant of the people, either initiating projects that help the community, or providing an infrastructure for the channelling of development, education and health, working in collaboration with the State. Indeed the State will be miffed if the Church threatens to withdraw from this unwritten contract.

The picture presented above shows a soteriology in which the individu-alistic, personal experience of the Balokole provides the soteriological norm by which even those who do not belong to the fellowship measure themselves, but the ordinary Christians also give the concept a wider locus as participation in the Church and in the community. This participation is given symbolic expression by the representation of religious leaders at major national or local occasions. Similarly, political leaders are represented at important religious functions: ordinations, the consecration of a bishop, the official opening of a church.

And yet, the question of how the Gospel impacts upon the lives of individuals and of society is one that is not clearly articulated in the COU. These days, the Church wants to boast that it teaches that the human being is a unity of body and soul, that you need to heal and provide for both. The new emphasis was in part a reaction against the accusation of liberation movements that the Church emphasized the abstract soul at the expense of the body, thus wittingly or unwittingly turning the believers into passive subjects who acquiesced in their oppression both under colonialism and in the face of post-independence tyrants. These may be sweeping general-izations, but often the propaganda is so insistent and one-dimensional that it presents itself as the whole truth. The truth, however, stands that the COU has expended so much energy in trying to create the imagery of peace-lover, unifier and reconciler, that it has tended to subdue the prophetic vision of justice that is so clearly vivid in Jesus' Gospel, especially as presented in the manifesto of Luke 4.18–19 or the Magnificat, Mary's Praise Song. For all its new-found emphasis on soul–body unity, its participation in education and medical work, its re-think on the position of women in Church and society, the teaching and preaching of the COU lacks a theology of individual and social transformation, one that reflects on

365

how social, political and economic reality impinges on the individual. The COU knows a lot about original sin and of the solidarity of humans in a state of sin, but it has not sufficiently appreciated the fact of structural sin and that this form of sin needs to be addressed. When it attempts to do so, it uses concepts that can only be judged as presumptuous.

The COU is the second largest Church in Uganda, after the Catholics. During the colonial era the Church of Uganda, the Native Anglican Church as it was then called, enjoyed semi-established status. Most prominent rulers and all the kings of the central kingdoms were Protestants – the term was and is used specifically to talk of Anglicans in Uganda, in contradistinction to the only major rival, the Catholics. As independence drew near, both Churches became identified with rival political parties. Since independence, the COU has been closely identified with whatever has been the regime in power – apart, that is, from Buganda, where the overthrow of the Kabaka by the central government in 1966 led to constant friction between the government and all elements of Kiganda society, including the Church. Museveni's National Resistance Movement has strongly attacked the Churches' sectarian role in the past and claims that government should be neutral as far as religion is concerned. But even here there have been complaints about the perceived bias of government towards the Protestants. For its part the COU, in a Joint Pastoral Letter of all the Bishops in February 1996, declared that the Church should act as 'the conscience of the state' because it had 'the responsibility of guiding the society and the government in doing God's will'. This position is repeated in the Provincial Canons of the COU of 1997: 'The Church of Uganda acknowledges the sovereignty of the State and conceives itself as the conscience of society' (Canon 1, para. 16).

Three questions arise here. First, does the COU conceive itself as the conscience of society to the exclusion of the other religious traditions in the country, including the Roman Catholic Church? What is its basis for making such a claim? Second, the words 'conscience of the state' were commonly used by Archbishop William Temple in the 1930s when he defended the Church of England's right and duty to provide the Christian principles for the organization and realization of a just society. Would his claim, made in respect of the established Church of England, apply in the same way in a country, like Uganda, whose Constitution does not give a privileged status to any particular religion? Would Temple have used similar words were he writing in England today? Thirdly, did the COU intend to proclaim that defence of fundamental human rights is part and parcel of its Christian witness? In which case the arrogation to itself alone of the role of society's conscience is in need of revision. How would the COU feel if they were to read from a statement of the Roman Catholic Church that they, the Catholics, are the conscience of society, given the history of bitter rivalry between them, as well as efforts at co-operation and ecumenism, especially after Vatican II? Perhaps it is to be conceded that in trying to follow closely the theology and practice of the Church of England, the Church of Uganda has sometimes been hampered in its mission.

The COU as nation's conscience presents a certain irony in that while it has been victim and made to bear the burden of refugees and other displaced peoples, yet it is the Church itself which has lagged behind in matters of equality (e.g. between women and men), accountability and transparency in administration, as well as failing to confront ethnocentrism within its ranks, especially in the choice of bishops. There are large numbers of educated youth leaving the COU to join the new Pentecostal and Charismatic Churches. This may be a challenge to the liturgical style of the Church, but it does also reflect a hunger for moral and social transformation which is not very much in evidence in the COU. Will these youths be convinced that the COU is the conscience of society? Providing that the Church has a duty to challenge society's conscience and cultural mores or even seek to protect these, should it engage in more serious study of society than it has done hitherto? For instance, what is Ugandan society today? What social, political, and economic forces have impinged on it in the recent past and how have these impacted upon people's choices, their views about right and wrong, and their understanding of the Christian faith?

There is no doubt that the Church of Uganda recognizes that it has to play a social role. Yet this is not to be a mere continuation of the role it played in the past when it ran a string of schools and hospitals and when loyalty to the Church earned one some privilege and influence. In these things the Church is now a junior partner and, where it is allowed to participate at all, it is usually on terms set by a secular agency. Often, because of scarcity of resources, it is the Church which has to struggle to keep to the legal and financial standards (such as a minimum wage) set by the government. The COU may regard itself as having accomplished a great feat if it should bring itself to criticize government policy, apart from preaching generally against corruption and divisions in society. Perhaps if it did, as happened during the regime of Idi Amin, its posture would be criticized as being political, or too political. This charge was indeed made against Archbishop Janani Luwum and led to his death. But the circumstances surrounding those events were very untypical of the COU's normal relationship to the State. The COU in fact too often strives to be on good terms with the government, and successive governments have assumed it to be subservient to the state. Deflection from this assumed role, or failure to show deference to a government representative, is sure to incur the ire of the State or of certain individuals in government.

In trying to work for individual and social transformation according to the ethical vision of the Gospel, the COU would do well to reflect on particular issues. It must rediscover the holistic teaching of salvation/liberation as taught in the Bible. It must learn and teach that justice and righteousness are coterminous, and that justice is not of secondary importance to the Gospel. It must rediscover the relation between salvation and creation so as to avoid a dualism. It needs to revise its language, especially since religious language often fails to communicate. For example, one could find acceptable the 'biblical' statement that Jesus came to save the world, but the same person may be puzzled, even disagree, if it is said that the Gospel aims to humanize people. People so used to attending church and reading the Bible daily may fail to see any connection between salvation and liberation, between healing and social transformation. And the Gospel may be so wedded to conventional morality and dominant trends in society that it becomes difficult to discover Jesus, the saviour of the marginalized and ostracized. For all its concern for orphans, refugees and the sick, the COU (and it is not the only culprit) has tended to see this concern in terms of charity rather than justice. What is being said here is that as the Church begins to conscientize the people about these issues instead of or in addition to calling upon people to get saved, people and the government will then not think that the Church is overstepping its legitimate limits if it speaks about conditions in the prisons, the gap between rich and poor, the subordination of women, the unfair distribution of resources between urban and rural areas and heavy military expenditure at the expense of health, education and development.

The COU must realize that Uganda is a secular and not a theocratic state, although religion plays a big influence on people's lives. It has to realize that it exists and operates in a multi-ethnic and multi-religious culture and that it cannot impose its will on society. Thus, in teaching its distinctive message and living its social reality it will be operating alongside other organizations that comprise civil society: women's groups, youth, student movements, political affiliations, the press, etc. – some of whose language and methods it has to learn or even employ in addressing the people. Above all, it will need to rediscover the theology of 'presence', of getting involved where the people are while at the same time pointing to the transcendent God who is the creator and to whom all creation, including ourselves, do ultimately aspire.

The Nippon Sei Ko Kai today and its future task

Samuel Isamu Koshiishi

Around fifty years after the end of the Pacific War, a movement to review its past history and actions and also to look forward towards the next century began to develop among the people of the Nippon Sei Ko Kai (NSKK: The Anglican Church in Japan). One of the motives for this movement was the desire of Church members to respond to the current mood in Japan of a developing respect for human rights to realize peace and justice throughout our society. A distinctive issue of human rights in Japan is the discrimination which has developed from the time of modernization and imperialism and has been practised against people who are seen to be not a true part of society – Koreans living in Japan, Okinawans, Ainu, and the 'buraku' people. One cause underlying this discrimination is the systematized and idealized rule of the emperor as a divine king, and the Tenno (God of Heaven) ideology which accompanies this. The NSKK had not dealt with these problems of discrimination as our own mission task; therefore we have found ourselves faced with the task of reviewing our own historical mission and especially our attitude towards the Tenno ideology.

As a result of this awareness, the General Synod of NSKK resolved to hold a Mission Consultation to review our historical position and actions, including our attitude towards Tenno ideology. Based on this resolution, all eleven dioceses of NSKK held a joint Mission Consultation in August 1995, in co-operation with overseas partners including those countries in Asia which had been occupied by Japanese forces during the Pacific War. A Joint Declaration was adopted by the Consultation and this document formed the basis of the 1996 General Synod Resolution which called for the NSKK to make a confession and apology for its involvement and acceptance of the actions of the Tenno ideology and militarism. Although this kind of resolution was epoch-making, still it was not sufficient in giving a basic Christian theological analysis of why these things were allowed to take place in the lives of our parents and grandparents, and what practical concrete tasks should be accomplished in the future to implement our new feelings and complete our responsibilities. These two points will be further examined.

The Consultation participants should have been made aware of the historical statement made by the Primate Bishop Paul Shinji Sasaki on the occasion of the first special General Synod of NSKK held in December 1945, at the end of World War II:

> The life of our Church was at a very low level. We didn't have a clear theological understanding of the relationship between church and state. We couldn't clearly understand the importance of 'episcopacy' in holding together the tradition of church life and the basis of the Sacraments. We allowed some indecent personal actions by a few people during discussions of government-forced church unification at the beginning of the war.

This statement by Bishop Sasaki should not be understood simply as a negative criticism of our lack of theology, but as a statement that our own cultural bonds are always in play and are enacted on us, regardless of our Christian beliefs. We are always surrounded by the structures of cultural control (deemed orthodoxy), which exclude minorities who stand out against such control (heresy). We should consider modernism as a force which was prevalent in those days on a worldwide scale, to understand the cultural bind that led Japan into World War II. Political leaders in Japan tried effectively to modernize the nation in a very short time and tried to avoid struggle and division among the people by making use of traditional exclusivism, and a systematized mutual-surveillance programme. These two points gave people a strong xenophobia which made them close their eyes and ears to anything from outside, and at the same time forced the people into a hierarchy in which Tenno was at the apex. Thus, at least up to the close of the Pacific War, the Japanese-dominated cultural regime didn't allow Christian belief to relativize its own culture. And further, if this statement is correct: 'The conversion of Christianity in Japan was basically motivated by the fact that the old ruling class, who had lost their political leadership, were forced to look into the possibility of leadership in the moral area corresponding to the new age.' If that is so, any way of receiving Christianity was itself already compromised by the local cultural regime of that time.

In this regard Bishop Sasaki's analysis seems to be related to this understanding of the processes of conversion to Christianity in modern Japan. And this in turn is related to the issue of authority. Should Christians see political leadership as authority? Or the truth that has been revealed by the cross and resurrection of Jesus Christ as the real authority? This is indeed a political and a theological question. And even more basically it is a subject that has a deep relationship with ecclesiology. Human beings by their fallen nature cannot be instruments of God's work in this world. Yet, because the Church was itself formed by Jesus Christ and the Holy Spirit was sent to guide the Church, so through the power of

God's redemption and guidance, human beings are given the power to become God's instruments, despite their weakness and inability. If we overlook this theological perception and understanding, we may very easily fall into a deadly dualism.

The 1996 Synod Resolution dealing with the war apology reflects the endeavours of those people who are trying to portray the history of modern Japan from the viewpoint of democracy. This position is very negative and severe on those who believe the Tenno ideology and support the government. The average people in Japan are caught in the dilemma of dualism between the two poles of secular democratic values and nationalist ideology; and are often guilty of 'selective inattention'. Recently there is appearing now in Japan from the nationalistic sector a new and different view of recent Japanese history. Both sides (secular democracy and nationalism) are bound up by the beliefs and presuppositions of logical positivism which fuels the struggle and continues the same basic structures of secular values. Both sides are neglecting the present situation of the human condition and existence.

The Nippon Sei Ko Kai has developed a new relationship over recent years with Churches in Asia and has heard first-hand experiences from people who lived through the ordeal of war. According to these stories there has been no redress or compensation from the Japanese Government for indignities and losses suffered; Japanese industry has resumed its push in Asia for profit; tourism has abused local people. All of which has caused devastation of local communities, without the visible gain that was promised. This is a new kind of nationalism and imperialism, which has replaced the old Tenno ideology, making use of the same structures. Modernism, using money as the basic value system, has taken the place of Tenno as the unifying force for the people of Japan to conceal the dichotomies of the reality of life. This has caused new criteria to appear as the basic measure of judging humanity – making money.

If we continue to pursue our task based on the proposals of the 1996 Synod Resolution, then we should look at those people who have been cast aside and discriminated against by society. We need especially to focus on the youth in schools, where the demands of education are still structured in the old way and have caused much distress in families who have children suffering from mental stress disorders and bullying. The old system of family life has been altered so that youth have difficulty finding role-models and adults with whom to consult and seek advice. This is true of many people who are now church members. We need to reach people where they are and stress the new community of believers who find their ultimate value and authority in the truth of the cross and resurrection of Jesus Christ.

A vision for the religious orders in the Anglican Communion in the next century

Una Kroll

There are many ways of serving God. The religious life, one that is lived under vows to God, is only one way. It is no better than any other. Yet, for someone called by God to such a life, it is a fulfilling and rewarding way of living. The vows bring with them certain freedoms that are precious. What are these freedoms?

The freedom that comes from the vow of poverty

This vow enables an individual and a community to travel light. Those who have few possessions are able to be mobile. Those without ambition can uproot themselves from one task to serve God in another. This is as true of the solitary and enclosed contemplative as it is of the missionary who travels all over the world. Such freedom is given to individuals, and to whole communities, so that nothing, nothing at all, should get between them and their ability to follow Christ wherever he leads.

The freedoms that come with the vow of poverty enabled most of the founders of existing Anglican religious orders to be remarkably adventurous when they started their work for the love of God. Looking back at the histories of such orders, it is obvious that most of them started out as innovative communities. Their members were willing to go to places where others did not want to go. They lived with people who were poor, ill-educated, outcast, unimportant. Many left the countries of their birth. They went to live and die far from home. They undertook work that needed doing because it was not being done by anybody else. Some of them pioneered the contemplative life of prayer, and paid a considerable price for their convictions.

The founders' successes, however, have had variable consequences. Some religious orders became too successful. They grew too large. They became well established and acquired charitable status and responsibilities. Their community acquired many possessions. It became settled in its ways. Such orders find practical difficulty if they want to change direction, even if it is obvious that God wants such a change. Unfortunately, many religious orders that expanded their work during their successful years have now found themselves with too few members to carry out all that they want to do. Recently, many religious orders have tried to solve some of these logistical problems. They have, for instance, welcomed people who have no intention of taking vows to live alongside the vowed members of the community, to share in its work and contribute to its life. This development has dangers as well as advantages. Those who are not in vows cannot be asked to go to places, or do things, that are only done by permanent members of the community. Moreover, persons living alongside a community can become dependent on it. On occasion this fact may prevent its vowed members from making changes, or from taking risks that should be taken. Without wishing to do so, 'alongsiders' may weaken the structure and stability of community life. Moreover, the core community may come to rely upon their help and find itself devastated when such people move on to other pastures.

Many Roman Catholic religious orders and some Anglican ones have already discovered this. They have resisted the temptation to try to carry on 'at all costs'. They have undertaken the painful process of renewal. They have recovered the visions of their original founders and have found new ways of putting those visions to work, even though their numbers have reduced, and some of them have begun to grow again.

All this has caused changes. Many members of religious communities are already living in small family-sized communities. They are living among the people they serve. They go out to work, earn money, become unemployed, worry about money, get sick, go to hospital, just like the people who are their neighbours. Many are living alone. Some are doing specialist work with those who have AIDS. Others are working with drug addicts, homeless people and the unemployed. It is likely that this trend will continue. New areas of need will be uncovered. Appropriate responses can be made, providing that the freedom that the vow of poverty affords is claimed, and that there is enough flexibility and consensus within the community to take the appropriate action.

That kind of renewal will continue, yet it seems that something still more radical may have to happen. Some orders may find out that the vision and work of their founder are no longer needed in the twenty-first century. They will need considerable faith and courage to make good provision for their elderly members, close their novitiates and be content to end. Those who have to make such decisions, before it is obvious to all that the order is going to die, will need much courage. They will also have to find the generosity to encourage potential members to develop new visions in ways that are apt for their time.

Una Kroll

The freedom that comes from the vow of chastity

Chastity is more important than celibacy. It sets one free in a way that celibacy cannot. Chastity means total commitment to fidelity, either to God or to one partner. This kind of commitment is sorely needed in a world where people are being torn apart by complex emotions, be they those that come from living in polygamous societies or those that are currently prevalent in a society where serial monogamy is the norm. Chastity is encouraged in Christian religious communes and associations where married people live with those who are committed to remaining single. These networks and communities have a very important role to play in the life of the Church in the twenty-first century. Nevertheless, there is still a great need for religious orders whose chaste and celibate members are free to offer to die for the sake of God.

It is true that those who are chaste and in a stable partnership may decide between themselves that they are free to die for God. If, however, they have children, such freedom may be compromised. Here, I am speaking primarily of physical death, but I am also thinking about the 'living death' that is an essential component of the prayer and witness of contemplative monks and nuns. The religious orders, and the Church as a whole, need to cherish that right to offer to die.

In the twenty-first century there will be many places in the world where Christians will be persecuted, simply because they are Christians. Christians who are members of a religious order and thus free to offer their lives for Christ will be needed. That does not mean that Christian parents and children will be spared from death. It does mean that some people will be more free than others to go into dangerous places and situations voluntarily and eagerly. They will not court martyrdom. Instead, they will seek to share in the lives of the Christians who are there. This kind of solidarity with others applies as much to those who also work outside their monasteries and convents. This is an important contribution that voluntary and chaste celibates can make in today's world. It is a sign that anticipates resurrection life by living in it. It witnesses to the goodness of giving one's life energy to God. This great leap of faith abides in time as well as in the memory.

The freedom that comes from the vow of obedience

This vow is made to God, not to a superior, nor even to a rule, although there is virtue in giving loyal obedience to a superior or to the rule in simple matters. The vow of obedience is the one that causes most difficulty to a number of individuals living the religious life. It is all too easy to sink into unquestioning obedience. It is also easy to rebel for the sake of rebelling. It sometimes seems that individualism can be as strong and as destructive within a religious community as it currently is in secular society. If someone claims the freedom to follow Christ, to obey God and no other, there needs to be careful evaluation. When people listen carefully and prayerfully for the voice they may be able to discern the will of God for both individual and community. Religious orders of all kinds will have to find new ways of being community. It seems likely that the best way forward lies through the development of small groups of individuals who live under vows. This style of living will allow future structures to be less hierarchical and more cellular in nature. There will be a search for ways of making decisions that rely less on authority from on high and more on consensus. There will be a deeper understanding of mutual interdependence on God that enables calculated risks to be taken with a good heart.

The essence of the religious life, its emphasis on simplicity of life-style, attachment to God above all else, and obedience to the will of God wherever it might lead, will remain the same. There is no evidence that God does not want the religious life to continue, but the expressions of that life can and will change. Already many people are wanting to live vowed lives outside formal communities. Many within existing communities are discovering the goodness of living in small groups within an identifiable larger organization. This trend will continue. New forms of religious life will, I believe, emerge in response to the needs of Church and society in the twenty-first century. The last section of this chapter will point to some of these needs.

Current and future needs of Church and society

Planetary ecology

Our planet will die unless we find better ways of living in harmony with creation. The wholesale destruction of rain forests, global warming and other climatic changes, pollution of the environment and agricultural genetic engineering all constitute serious threats to this planet. Moreover, our race will die unless we find better ways of sharing the earth's resources justly so that people may live human lives. We need religious orders who will preach the Gospel without compromise. Their members will be at the forefront of efforts to secure the future of our planet. They will live in ways that can be a sign to others of what may one day become possible for all. They will also be concerned with peace and justice issues as they relate to human affairs.

Human and moral needs

Our humanity will die unless we find out what it means to be a human being in relation with others. We need Anglican religious orders who will focus their attention on all the great moral issues that currently beset us. We need people who are willing to study human genetic engineering. They will consider the problems of over-population. They will look at the ethical implications of longevity. Some of them may be able to do some serious theological reflection about the nature of human bodies and their limitations. There is a real need for scholarly orders who will tackle such a task on behalf of the Church. Its members might come up with questions and some answers that will be taken seriously by ordinary members of society.

There is also a need for the development of Anglican religious orders who, for the love of God, will engage with the addictions that threaten the health and lives of so many young people in Western society. Members of these orders will live and work in areas where unemployment is high. They will know at first hand the problems of overcrowding. They will see drugged men and women on the streets. They will know what alcoholism and addiction to gambling can do to families. They will try to help those who are promiscuous. They will also care for the victims of those various evils.

Anglican Christians' needs

Our Christian Church will die unless we can find ways of helping people outside it to see that Christianity is relevant to them. So there is a need for monks and nuns who will live at the heart of the world and be part of it. These men and women will strive to understand the language and concerns of the people among whom they live. They will be able to live and work alongside those whose insights lead them to take political and social action in solidarity with their neighbours. They will spend time finding better ways of communicating the Gospel to people in an indifferent society.

It also seems likely that in Western countries there will be a growth of individuals living as solitaries. In times of social and moral breakdown God seems to call many individuals to live alone either in rural solitude or in an urban neighbourhood. These people live by alternative values. Some take vows, some do not. All try to be faithful to their lives of prayer. Such solitaries already exist in the Anglican Communion. They are growing in numbers. There are, as yet, no supportive structures that can help them to avoid isolation, attrition and all the other hazards of the solitary life that weaken vocations. The Anglican Church, and especially its bishops, need to take these vocations seriously. Bishops and established religious orders need to encourage good practice in formation and ongoing support for those who do not train through prior membership of an order.

The religious life is an exciting adventure, willingly undertaken for the love of God and one's neighbour. However, if Christians who have dedicated their lives to God by religious vows are to fulfil their role within the life of the Church during the next century, there will have to be considerable changes to present-day structures and ways of working. There will have to be a refocusing of energy. Existing work, however well established it is, may have to be turned over to other people so that pioneering work can be undertaken. Large buildings, corporate wealth, and a certain amount of respectable work will have to go. Instead, those who undertake such a life for the love of God will need to seize the freedoms that are inherent in the religious life and use them to the full. The signs are good. Please God, it will happen.

Further reading

Gerald A. Arbuckle, *Out of Chaos: Refounding Religious Congregations* (Mahwah, NJ: Paulist Press/London: Geoffrey Chapman, 1988), p. 226.

Joan Chittister OSB, *The Fire in These Ashes: A Spirituality of Contemporary Religious Life* (Kansas City: Sheed and Ward/Leominster: Gracewing, 1996), p. 178.

Augustine Roberts OSCO, *Centred on Christ: An Introduction to Monastic Profession* (Petersham, MA: St Bede's Publications, 1979), p. 170.

The Mothers' Union of the future

Edited by Barbara Lawes and Louise Vincer

In 1876 Mary Sumner responded to the needs of local women in the parish of Old Alresford in Hampshire by founding the Mothers' Union. Today 80 per cent of the MU membership lives outside the UK and Ireland, mainly in sub-Saharan Africa, where membership is continuing to grow. They are supported by 240 MU workers and 25 Provincial Trainers, all nationals of the countries in which they work.

Every member promises that prayer, worship and Bible study will be a part of her daily life and increasingly women look to the Church and the

Mothers' Union for support and encouragement in every other aspect of their lives and those of their families.

From different countries and cultures, united by the common bond of their membership of the Mothers' Union and their commitment to all that strengthens family life, five women write about how they believe the Mothers' Union of the future can meet the needs of the women and families with whom they work.

Although each writes from her own perspective, many of their thoughts and suggestions will be valuable to Church and Mothers' Union leaders and workers across all the dioceses and Provinces of the Anglican Communion. They must form part of our joint agenda for the future if we are serious about building the body of Christ and working for the coming of his kingdom.

Mothers' Union and the youth of the future

Rosemary Kinyanjui, Kenya

In Kenya today our youth are in need of help. Parents feel threatened by their children and society is threatened by low moral standards. Parents, the government, the Church and teachers have all recognized the need for youth programmes but none of the parties want to shoulder the problem.

The African culture provided a holistic system of education which met all dimensions of life. For example, education for the children, youths and adults was provided. Through this education religion permeated into their everyday lives. It was taught, lived and experienced. It was a process which started at birth and ended at the time of death.

The present system of education has changed greatly. Education 'experts' make the parents and those outside the system feel inadequate. As a result, the parents' role is replaced by that of teachers and church leaders. Education is too compartmentalized, each subject seen as separate from another. Children find it difficult to relate these bits and pieces in their everyday lives.

Parents are not confident as role models for their children. Christian parents are unable to communicate Christian morals to their children at the right time. Their children are willing to lead Christian lives but lack the proper Christian foundation. They are unable to make proper decisions and like the home built upon the sand, they are not secure enough to resist a fall.

When faced with the outside world the children end up as victims of the following:

1.   Premarital sex: youth are suffering from AIDS and other sexually

transmitted diseases. It also leads to unwanted pregnancies which increase the school drop-out rate and financial restraints which lead to prostitution. Illegal abortions cause untimely deaths, psychological disturbances and permanent disabilities.

2. Polygamous marriages: also, due to the wrong concept of marriage and greed for money, the girls end up getting involved with married men.

3. Drug abuse and alcoholism which causes poor school performances, unproductive careers, and unstable family relationships.

The above factors cause excessive rebellion against the parents, school authorities and the society at large. Due to the various conflicting experiences the youth may also end up under stress or in depression. A lot of efforts are geared towards helping the casualties rather than finding the root causes of these problems.

Is the Mothers' Union, with all its endeavours to strengthen family life, addressing the needs of the mothers and not their children? Do some children feel neglected as they cannot relate to their parents? Are Mothers' Union meetings reflecting an artificial image of life? Can members really feel part of their Church activities when their very real concern for their families is not recognized? Has a lot of effort been to sharpen the sword on one side while the other side is left unattended?

- The Mothers' Union should provide education which will instil confidence in the parenting process. Parents should feel responsible for their children's character formation and the right values.
- Education for girls, aimed at helping them to be responsible for their lives as individuals, should be introduced and encouraged in the Mothers' Union and in the Church at large. Confidence should be instilled early enough and their talents fully utilized.
- Education for boys should be introduced for preparation for responsible adulthood. Misguided ideas instilled in them previously, like being stronger than girls, being less prone to dangers than girls and bearing problems silently as a sign of manhood, should be corrected.
- Forums for both girls and boys should be encouraged for both parties to share experiences, worries and expectations. AIDS-awareness and other sexually-related programmes should be given prominence.

Family sharing where children are not passive listeners but active participants should be encouraged. Parents need to be open to criticism.

Children need to be made part of the decision-making process of their families.

The need to revitalize an ageing and declining membership for effective service
Esla Crawford, Trinidad and Tobago

The Mothers' Union in Trinidad and Tobago was founded 76 years ago by a group of Christian women who felt the need for spiritual guidance in the upbringing of their children. It has become a way of life for many Anglican women.

Family life, once very strong in our society, has encountered severe problems. The major cause is the drug problem. Perched as we are on the north coast of South America, Trinidad and Tobago serves as a major transit point for the drug trade and efforts by the government have not lessened the problem. Crime has escalated as addicts seek to support their habit, resulting in an increase in murders, burglaries, extortion, abduction and physical and sexual abuse of women and children. Incest is on the increase. Unemployed young people are used as drug mules to transport drugs to other countries.

Trinidad and Tobago has become a free society, where marriage is not seen as a priority. Teenage pregnancy is rampant, one-parent families are common and quite often offspring are the ones who suffer. Migration of parents has added to the problem, often leaving children in the care of grandmothers who just cannot cope. Families no longer get together to go to church, to play, to converse or to pray. There is dwindling attendance at Sunday Schools resulting in a decline of moral and spiritual values.

What are we doing and what must be done in the future to meet the needs of these families and help members to face their responsibilities? The ageing and declining membership of the Mothers' Union in these islands, as in some other parts of the world, is an acute problem and has to be addressed if we are to serve in a more meaningful way.

At present the Social Action Committee assists needy families with clothes, food, school books, and transportation among other things. Nearly-new shops are used to provide clothes at a reasonable cost and the proceeds are used to help Samaan House, a drop-in centre for drug addicts, and a soup kitchen for the underprivileged. Through the Nurses' Fellowship care is given to senior citizens, children in nurseries and in hospitals, while the Indoor Members' Prayer Circle visits the sick and shut-ins. The Christian Education Committee provides literature and conducts an annual Sunday School Quiz and Rally. An Anglican Church Training and Employment Mission conducts training and assists in finding employment for those in need of it.

Sadly, this work is insufficient to eradicate the severe problems encountered. The Mothers' Union of the future must broaden its horizons to meet the changing needs of society in Trinidad and Tobago and worldwide. We need to be more vibrant and vigilant, and join with other organizations to agitate for a change in the laws relating to families, for better education, meaningful employment, better rehabilitation for drugs users and protection for women and children. To this end we have embarked on a diocesan-wide training programme.

Members will be trained so that the nearly-new shops can be used as listening centres where anyone in trouble can come for help. At these centres people will receive sympathetic understanding and be referred to other agencies as appropriate. Members need to keep in touch with the newly confirmed and must get involved in helping our young people prepare for marriage and in follow-up after marriage. We must seek out prospective members and conduct short meetings, prayer sessions and Bible studies in homes.

In the secondary schools we have conducted seminars on parenting and will continue with workshops on topical issues including drugs and human sexuality. There is a need to inculcate moral values and help young people to recognize that marriage is a reflection of the Union of Christ and his Church and that the family is the God-given unit of society. Fathers in our nation need to get away from the erroneous notion that the raising of children is the responsibility of mothers alone and must be encouraged to take their proper place in the family. God is not going to change his plan for the human race just because human beings are unwilling to follow it.

The Mothers' Union of Trinidad and Tobago is building a Children's' Home for those who need a place of safety. For children whose parents are drug addicts, those who are victims of incest or sexual or physical abuse and those who have been abandoned. Short-term care of children whose mothers have been hospitalized and children whose parents are in prison will also be available.

Our prayer lives too must be intensified. We have to develop disciplined spiritual lives because as Christian women we have a responsibility for the spiritual condition of our nation. We must become women of faith and prayer, of obedience and service. It is only in so doing that we can forge the course of the Mothers' Union of the future and so help to solve the problem of our ageing and declining membership and set up a spiritual standard, confident and well equipped as we move into the next millennium.

The Mothers' Union role in reconciliation, rebuilding and rehabilitation

Clavéra B. Ntukamazima, Burundi

It's not easy to talk about these concepts separately as they all deal with bringing back something which has been lost. The loss is noticed in the moral, physical, material and spiritual side of people's lives in countries where wars have destroyed people's minds, hearts, and houses. These all need to be rehabilitated, reconciled and rebuilt. As Mothers' Union members, we are called to lead people to achieve this aim, by starting with our own families and going outwards.

- In order to be able to rebuild a country, one has to know who destroyed it and for what reason. Burundi, for example, has been destroyed by its own people who want to have more than they can honestly earn, by taking others' properties or rights by force. The country can also be destroyed by foreigners who want to control it economically. This is also possible when the natives are greedy enough to let foreigners do so.
- Reconciliation is only possible when two groups in conflict *feel* that they are tired of fighting, need to share what their country can provide, need peace and get reconciled. Then they can *sit together* and share about what wrong has been done by each group. Finally, they can *decide* to change their bad thoughts and deeds of killing and get reconciled, rebuild and rehabilitate.

In some provinces in Burundi, on Saturdays everyone has to join his neighbours in making bricks for rebuilding houses. Those who earn money have to pay a fixed amount each month to enable the government to rebuild houses.

Rehabilitation means that people should be able to live in their property; farmers go back and work as before the war and civil servants in government or private offices go back to their jobs.

Every month, people from one village meet and teach one another about new ideas and methods of rebuilding. They are also taught how to raise chickens and new methods of farming so that they can grow as much as possible. They are also taught hygiene and nutrition.

What is the role of the Mothers' Union in the future as far as reconciliation, rebuilding and rehabilitation are concerned? The Mothers' Union members all over the world, and especially in countries where there are or have been conflicts, are aware of their great responsibility in community and family welfare. They are determined to do all in their power so that people can be reconciled and live a better life.

To be able to achieve this MU members have to get together and set up a programme, hold seminars about reconciliation so that people can talk about their problems and be gradually healed. During these seminars, people will also be taught that working in groups is encouraging and drives away barriers set up by tribes or any kind of divisions. Mothers' Union should be a model for this.

This work in groups has a two-fold aim: it not only helps people to run income-generating projects to help themselves live a better life, but it also brings people near to one another. For example, one MU group will run a project on agriculture or farming or raising animals like goats, cows or chickens. Another group of women will grow vegetables and sell them to another group of women where they cannot be grown. Then, contacts between MU groups will be frequent and close. They will go beyond business affairs so that nutrition, parenting skills, etc. can be dealt with. The MU committee has to plan all these activities aiming at the same time at reconciliation, rebuilding and rehabilitation.

The Mothers' Union is determined to be the bridge between the conflicting sides bearing in mind that God has asked us to be peacemakers. We are confident that he will enable us to succeed in this undertaking, since we know that we can do all things in him who strengthens us (Phil 4.13).

Economic literacy and income-generation for future stability
Hellen Wangusa, Uganda

Poverty and indebtedness

The quality of life a family enjoys depends, among other things, on its resources. There is a great chasm between the rich and poor. The level of human subsistence today is so uneven and so unjust that the quality of life a pet enjoys in one place is ten times that of a child in another. One wonders whether it is Christian for a pet to eat a more balanced diet than a human being. Or that whereas it may be important for a family in the North to have all the labour- and time-saving devices, one in the South has to be content with a bunch of firewood.

Poverty is not new; what is new is its magnitude. The global economy has changed now, so dramatically that stagnation, abject poverty and indebtedness characterize some parts of the world. There was indeed a time when donations and handouts would flow towards areas of felt need. Today the language is of loans, interest, profit, and donor fatigue. Indebtedness has cost lives. Its impact literally echoes what is written in Joel 3.3 about

383

the advantaged and the disadvantaged. 'And they cast lots for my people and have given a boy for a harlot, and sold a girl for wine, that they might drink.'

Children have paid for the Third World debt with sacrifices of their normal growth, health and opportunities for education. The Mothers' Union is already involved in discussions of all those issues that are found to be morally inconsistent with God's plans for the stability of family life, and to advocate for an economy that does not justify lifestyles according to location but rather to Christian values.

Women are the most affected and yet the least capable of coping under any economic crisis. Some women's only defence is that they believe they are under a curse. Economic literacy is an alternative that will help create awareness on how economic issues affect women's lives and that of their families. It is an analytical tool that enables one to participate in economic decisions at whatever level. It begins with one's knowledge of the household economy which is then linked with other levels and broader economic concepts without getting lost in economic jargon.

The Mothers' Union has been involved in training in income-generation. Women are being trained in project identification, design, management, research and evaluation. This promotes various income-generating activities for members, ranging from agro-based textile cottage and group projects to animal husbandry and educational centres. The scale and scope of this work must increase.

Beside income-generation, the Mothers' Union is maintaining Christian ethics as the basis for all its activities. This is done through Bible studies, prayer meetings, consultations and counselling. It is developing a woman's resource, by jointly planning and writing with members about the Mothers' Union of the future. The participatory process and consultation also allows the members to shape the Mothers' Union of the future. It is bound to come up with practical, meaningful and relevant ways to meet the needs of women.

Mothers' Union can lead in valuing traditions and culture
Nellie Siba, Ysabel, Melanesia

There were many agents of cultural change in our past history: the arrival of both the first Europeans with their material goods, and the missionaries with their cultural and religious values, schools, hospitals, shops and clothes have had profound effects on our people today.

Schools uproot students from their villages and place them together in a boarding school for six years and some are away for nearly the rest of their lives in different cultural areas. While in schools for six or more years, young boys and girls lose the knowledge of making gardens, houses made of local materials, dances, weaving baskets and mats, and forget customary stories and only remember Western stories. Young people do not dance customary dances but rather use tape recorders to dance Western dances; they no longer use wooden canoes and paddles but fibreglass canoes and outboard motors. There are more broken marriages now because of wealth. Many have freedom to choose their own partners. People change their diets from locally-grown food and fresh fish to food from shops. Some people speak pidgin (broken English) in their villages instead of their own languages.

These are a few examples of effects that have come from the West and which mean that we are now living in a society that is not fully Melanesian. We adopt cultures which are not ours and try to make them become our cultures.

There is a need now and in the future that Mothers' Union members are involved in educating our young women of tomorrow in their cultures and these women, when becoming mothers, will influence their own children. The main role for Mothers' Union now is to become involved with the changes in our culture and enable their children to see the values of their culture and traditions and hopefully begin to respect them as they are part of their lives given to them by God.

If the Mothers' Union is to maintain its important place in women's lives and unique role in the Anglican Communion it must continue to adapt to meet the needs of women and families where they are. This must be done in the holistic, Christ-centred way.

A vision for a Church in jubilee: the Anglican Church and social justice in the next millennium[1]

Njongonkulu Ndungane

Stories of homelessness and hopelessness, of unemployment and under-employment, all bedfellows of poverty, abound in my country. We hear of incredible technological advances that are able to make life easier for the affluent, but little of what is being done for the poor, by either state or

Church. One hears of expensive buildings being constructed for which money has been used that could have been better utilized in launching a massive programme for the poor and those who require the acquisition of skills in order to make them a productive and useful part of our developing country. A congregation and local church leadership that allows the building of a communion rail at the altar that retracts at the push of a button into the basement in a massive multi-million-rand church building complex sounds to me like a Church community that has got its theological priorities mixed up.

In a land where we are attempting to heal the pain caused by so many years of oppression and degradation, poverty remains the scar on humanity's face. In Christ's name we are called to remove the scar. Unless we all act together, we will find that the new South Africa about which we have all become so excited could degenerate into a morass of hopelessness. We can see the effects of poverty in the hills and valleys around Durban: in poor health conditions, in the lack of potable water in a province that is rich in this resource, in shortage of housing, in unemployment and in the resurgence of tuberculosis. The South African Human Sciences Research Council estimated that in 1993 the proportion of households living in poverty was 35.2 per cent, and of individuals was a massive 45.7 per cent.

In the days of whites-only privileges, amazing work was done in the years following the Great Depression to address the problem of the so-called 'poor white'. Thankfully, I hope, we have left behind those myopic days when everything was seen in terms of race: now it is the problem of the poverty of all who claim to be Africans. For humanity is humanity, made in the image of God.

We can point to international programmes against poverty. The Marshall Plan was instituted for the restitution of Europe after the Second World War. In the new Germany resources are drastically redeployed, as that country struggles through the pain of reunification. What is required in such cases is a commitment to improvement and a willingness to share, and this includes commitment from the Church. In the feeding of the five thousand we saw the miraculous effects which sharing can have.

Our people listen to our clergy who are taught to preach about this. The question is: how do they implement it? How do they perform modern miracles? Do they even try? Or is this something that is left to the ecumenical movement to talk about and to a few Church leaders to pontificate about? If that is so then the Church is failing in its calling to be the body of Christ in an age when we are seeking to spend possibly millions of dollars in celebrating the second millennium of Christ. This celebration will be meaningless if around us we continue to see the number of poor and uncared-for increasing.

In 1991 Bishop Stanley Mogoba of the Methodist Church of Southern Africa had the vision to recognize that in the changing South Africa the Church was scared of sharing – nervous of 'the unknown tomorrow'. In a poignant sentence, he told his own Church: 'We fear that we may lose our comfortable homes, wages, environment, security.' All our Churches have continued to illustrate this fear.

Bishop Mogoba went on to note that it was easy to change statutes. We have seen this happen in our land, with its new constitution and new laws. But the poor and their needs are still with us, a blot on our land. When we have had good rains, good weather, better economic growth than for a long time, one would have thought that this would not be so. But it is, and the Church has to recognize that it has to go beyond being just an onlooker.

In 1988 the Anglican report *Faith in the City* stated categorically that poverty is not just about shortage of money, but about rights and relationships, about how people are treated and how they regard themselves; about powerlessness, exclusion and loss of dignity. It is questions of distribution that are at the centre of the problem, how wealth is shared indicating how we measure the value of each person theoretically equal in the sight of God.

Bishop Mogoba added: ' ... an obsession with the value of production, balanced church budgets and wealth for wealth's sake, can blind us to other norms and values of our Christian beliefs. It is this obsession that blocks the lens of our mind and leads to selfishness and greed.'

Poverty and its bedfellows – not least of which, of course, is crime – are issues that require the attention of all of Christendom and of the other faiths with whom we are in dialogue. Let us recall Luke 12.13–15, where we read the story of the rich fool: 'A man in the crowd said to Jesus, "Teacher, tell my brother to divide with me the property our father left us." Jesus answered him, "Man, who gave me the right to judge or to divide the property between you two?" And he went on to say to them all, "Watch out and guard yourselves from every kind of greed; because a person's true life is not made up of the things he owns, no matter how rich he may be." '

In South Africa, an Ecumenical Commission on Poverty has come into being. Church leaders, including those from the Dutch Reformed Churches, called on the country's financial institutions to declare a moratorium on the country's debts and on individuals' debts. They recognized the Pope's call for the year 2000 to be a year of jubilee. Christians, who occupy influential positions in financial institutions throughout the world, should hear this call. Such a moratorium would mean an immediate improvement in the standard of living of many, enabling the provision of services where none exist, and a levelling of the economic playing fields.

In South Africa where most public debt is owed to domestic financial institutions, the solution to the problem is not simply to write off the debt but to find creative ways of dealing with it, thus ensuring that a recipe is found whereby there is a win–win situation. Church leaders have also acknowledged the link with the refugee problem. Refugees are among the most poverty-stricken people of South Africa.

That we have not seen either state, business or Church come up yet with a solid response bodes ill for the future. Yet this call would dovetail admirably with the United Nations Resolution that 1997 to 2006 should be the first UN Decade for the Eradication of Poverty, and state and Church should acknowledge this.

Poverty requires a holistic approach. The poor are not a problem, but an opportunity for us to serve God. The Salvation Army, among others, has much to teach us in this respect, and we should not decry the 'soup kitchen'-style ministry. But that type of mission is necessarily short-term. We need a long-term strategy, both denominationally and ecumenically, at local, national and international level.

Central should be the work of the Ecumenical Commission on Poverty. It should be replicated at every level, ecumenically and denominationally. For the Anglican Church, this means at regional, diocesan and parish level. We should not forget that the poor themselves will have much to contribute. Such partnership may enable the poor, by their inclusion, to minister to those who are materially wealthier, but spiritually poorer.

We must challenge business to confront the need for an adequate response to the call for a year of jubilee. Unless we do so directly, business will continue to ignore us, as they are, by definition, interested primarily in making bigger profits. But business played a positive role in the political changes in South Africa when it realized that that was the way to go, and indeed it was in their interest. And governments need to be challenged as to the stewardship of funds earmarked for development. One hears all too often of funds for reconstruction and development scandalously lying unspent in state coffers.

Any society that continues to allow the re-creation of the poor in its midst without taking action is one that will assume grotesque proportions. Any Church that allows that to happen does not understand the urgent imperative of the Gospel message. The agenda is clear. It can be nerve-racking, to be sure. But, like Mother Teresa as she was confronted with 'the poorest of the poor' in Calcutta, we have no alternative.

Note

1 This chapter is edited from an address initially given to an ecumenical audience in Durban.

The theological and mission task facing Hong Kong Anglicans in the years of reunification with China after 1997

Michael Poon

As from 1 July 1997, Hong Kong is reunited with China. It now exists as a Special Administrative Region (SAR) in the People's Republic of China. For the next 50 years it continues to enjoy a high degree of autonomy as guaranteed by the 'One country, two systems' formula in the Basic Law.

What does this historic event mean for Hong Kong and China? Some interpret this as the final exorcism of the ghost of foreign imperialistic aggression against China which had haunted China in the last two centuries. The reunification is hailed as the triumph of Deng Xiaoping's pragmatic policy, and hence the justification of its continued adoption into mainland China, looking towards the eventual reunification with Taiwan, and the building up of a strong China in the next millennium.

It is not the Church's primary concern to refute or condone such views as propagated by mainland authorities. For the reunification carries a profound significance beyond the rights and wrongs of both China and Britain in the past 150 years. The mainland authorities now face the dilemma: will China be able to limit Hong Kong's influence strictly within the economic order, or will Hong Kong become a Trojan horse which works towards political change with ramifications for the entire country? In any case, Hong Kong people are no longer simply residents. They are Chinese nationals, given eventual citizen rights and a share in shaping the future of the whole nation, beyond the transitional period of the next 50 years. Hong Kong Christians must set their vision on future reunification and integration with the national Christian Church of the mainland. This framework should inform our discussion on the theological and mission task of Hong Kong Anglicans in the post-1997 era.

What are the specific challenges and opportunities open to Hong Kong Anglicans? I believe the underlying issue concerns the character of Christianity in China. Chinese Christianity is involved in two problematic events in the history of the modern China: the Opium War and the Taiping Movement in the last century. The first implicates Christianity as a tool of foreign aggression; the second – a truly agrarian and populist revolution inspired by a heretical form of Christianity – conjures deep-seated fear

389

Michael Poon

among Chinese of anarchy in the country. To this day, the mainland Chinese Church and government officials have as much to fear from the outbreak of unorthodox Christianity in the countryside (which constitutes the majority of the Christian population) as from foreign interference in Chinese affairs. For any form of social disorder in the countryside is difficult to contain, with potential political consequences. The right interpretation of Christianity is therefore a crucial issue for the long-term welfare of the Chinese Church, both as an apologetic task vis-à-vis the secular authorities, and as a pastoral concern vis-à-vis the Christian community as a whole. It is equally of advantage to Chinese authorities that Christianity remains within mainstream traditions. There is thus an urgent need for the formation of theologically articulate pastors in China once the present leaders fade from the scene. The present acute lack of theological books and teachers in China, made worse by the upheavals in the Cultural Revolution, testifies to such need.

What has Sheng Kung Hui (The Anglican Church of China), a small minority Church (of fewer than 30,000 members) within a Christian minority in Hong Kong and greater China, to offer? Anglicans, and therefore Hong Kong Anglicans as well, see themselves as part of the catholic Church rather than a denomination. It takes its origins beyond the confines of the English Reformation. Its theology is catholic in breadth, drinking deep from the springs of all Christian traditions. This basis provides it with a unique contribution to the welfare of its partner Churches in Hong Kong, and of the mainland Churches in the years ahead.

Hong Kong Anglicans may be tempted to retreat from such vision. Theological leadership in Hong Kong is now overtaken by conservative evangelicalism or a social activism. Anglican clergy no longer dominate the intellectual front as before. The paucity of theological works, even in the form of popular theology, published by Hong Kong Anglicans is revealing. Chung Chi College Theological Division in the Hong Kong Chinese University of Hong Kong was the most prestigious theological institution in the territory. It is a truly local institution, co-founded by mainline Churches, and is the only local theological college which exists in a secular university. It has been the main centre of learning for mainline Churches and was instrumental in fostering friendship among theological students from different traditions during their early years of formation. Yet, whether such ecumenical vision can endure remains to be seen. On a wider front, academic research in Christian classics is now conducted, and in a way overtaken, by non-Christian mainland Chinese who approach the subject as an academic discipline. Given such circumstances, the question is asked – if Hong Kong Anglicanism is to keep its catholic roots, is it not better for it to withdraw from the ecumenical forums which it helped to create in the past decades, and venture it alone?

Such withdrawal may seem necessary to allow the Anglican Church to create the much-needed space to foster its own identity. After all, according to this argument, Anglicans must gain confidence in themselves before they are able to engage in fruitful dialogue with other traditions. It also takes pride in its liturgical tradition as distinctive from that of other Churches. Nevertheless, consolidation is not the same as withdrawal. Liturgical life becomes arid ritual if it is detached from its theological moorings. Efforts of consolidation should have in view the eventual strengthening of the wider ecumenical fellowship. The Anglican Church ceases to be true to its calling if it regards itself as a denominational Church, or retreats from making theological contribution to the wider Church. For if the theological battle is lost, then all is lost.

I believe the Anglican Church has much to offer intellectually. It needs to engage its Christian partners in theological discussion on three important areas on the nature of Christianity. In the first place, it should ask: what place should we accord to tradition in our understanding of the Christian faith? Anglicans are committed to apostolicity, the Holy Scriptures, the ecumenical creeds, and Christian classics approached with the spirit of intellectual honesty. This provides the Church the necessary platform for renewal and cultivation of ecumenical fellowship. How seriously is the Hong Kong Church committed to a catholic theology? If it regards the presentation of one-sided evangelicalism or social activism as inadequate, is it able to put forward an alternative, and is it prepared to defend it in public? It is shocking that serious studies in historical theology stopped nearly a generation ago. The translation of Christian classics (published by the Hong Kong Chinese Christian Literature Council), executed one or two generations ago by scholars of stature like Xie Fuya, looks glaringly outdated and inadequate, unable to reflect contemporary scholarship in historical theology. Have we given up the intellectual battle for the right interpretation of Christianity? We may not appreciate the apologetic edge in this concern. The Hong Kong Christian Church is a socially accepted and still a respected community. After all, overseas literature is readily accessible in Hong Kong. The Church is able to remain theologically informed if it chooses to be. Yet, such resources are not readily available in mainland China. And in any case foreign literature is of limited use because not written in Chinese. What resources are open to Chinese government officials and to the local pastors if they want to know about Christianity?

The second issue is on the question of the integrity of the Chinese Church as a national Church. The three-self policy of self-governing, self-propagating, and self-supporting defines the relation of the Chinese Church with its foreign partners. If it is to be a credible Church, it must be able to make its contribution to the wider Church. Yet what does Christianity in

China (with its 5,000 years of culture) have to contribute to the wider world? The neglect is glaring. Theological teachers find themselves without any substantial theological resources written in Chinese. Those which are available are mostly in the form of biblical commentaries rather than in doctrinal studies.

For some, such shortcoming is a non-issue. In economic terms, China is merely a vast market, a dumping-ground for inferior products or a laboratory for testing new ideas. In the same way, theologically, the vast population in China provides various religious groups the opportunity to promote their particular brand of Christianity. Hong Kong is used as a launching pad for such outreach to China. Thus, the primary issue of 1997 for such religious groups is survival. It is content if laws in the SAR and China allow religious groups to continue with their present activities. And in anticipation of possible change of governmental policy in China in the future, perhaps the Chinese Church would one day again allow denominational Churches to build up their power centres in China. It is questionable whether such utilitarian calculation and crystal ball-gazing do more harm than good. At least, it blinds the Church from taking seriously the ecumenical mandate and the cultivation of an integral Chinese Christianity.

Anglicans here can make a positive contribution. We hold a positive evaluation of local culture. Anglicans see their own theological task as not simply the regurgitation of confessional statements in the past. They are committed to seek afresh the fuller implications of the Gospel in its encounter with new cultural contexts. Furthermore, Hong Kong Anglicans as a de facto autonomous entity (whose ambiguous status should rightly be rectified by the creation of a Province of Hong Kong) are an autonomous Church. It is not answerable to any patrons overseas, as many local evangelical Churches are required to be. Further, it cannot be suspected of acting as a mouthpiece for foreign institutions. It is paramount for Hong Kong Anglicans to be radically committed to the good of the Chinese Church, and labour towards the eventual integration of Hong Kong Anglican Church with the national body. It begins to do this by encouraging the clergy and laity to gain a critical understanding of the history and culture of Hong Kong and China, by exploring with its partner Churches new patterns of co-operation and trust-building, by creating opportunities for the Chinese Church to be heard in international forums, and by fostering communication and resource-sharing with the mainland Church.

And lastly we should ask: is there a commitment for the Hong Kong Christian community, and its leaders in particular, to set themselves as a role model in public? An important characteristic of the mainland Chinese Church is in the experience of suffering by Christian leaders, especially in the time of the Cultural Revolution. Such marks of endurance help the present leadership to gain credibility in relation to the public and to the

Christian community alike, and goes a long way in overcoming past denominational squabbles. It now matters less for the Christian community whether leaders are of the YMCA background or of pietistic tradition. All underwent considerable personal loss. It is not an accident that bishops of the mainland Church possess spiritual rather than jurisdictional authority in the Church.

The question is made more urgent because the justification of Hong Kong's status as a Special Administrative Region lies to a great extent in its economic status. The 'get rich' mentality is all too prevalent. The Church has the duty to raise in public the wider questions of justice and compassion, and to speak out for the welfare of Hong Kong, and for the whole nation. It is disturbing that Church leaders are rather silent in this area. The Church may have good reasons to dissociate itself from the present democratic movements in Hong Kong, perhaps in order to maintain a good working relationship with the secular authorities. Nevertheless, the Church must not retreat from the duty to witness for Christ in the public arena. The Gospel remains necessarily controversial. The question is whether we are controversial for the right cause. If the Church has deep reservations about the popular democracy movement providing the right model for young people, it should hold out a different vision. The English Church holds an honoured tradition towards saintliness, not simply in divines like George Herbert, but also in public figures like Thomas Becket, Latimer and William Temple. They never took for granted their office as privileged advisors to the Crown. They did not retreat into a cloistered life and shy away from public glare. They were prepared to confess their faith in the public square.

What vision should Hong Kong Anglicans follow? What dream do Anglican leaders hold before the laity and the rest of the Christian community? Are Christian leaders prepared to provide a true alternative? Or are they content simply to be respectable members of the community? Mission of the Church should not be reduced to a technological project of Church growth, or expressed simply in terms of community service. The Church's existence is defined not simply by utilitarian considerations or numerical strength. The Christian Church is called by Jesus Christ to be the hope of the world, to be the tangible sign of the presence of Jesus Christ. If the ideals of democracy and of justice are intelligible and coherent only in the Incarnation of the Word, then all the more it is the duty of the Church to embody the vision of Christ in its life and mission. Spiritual sanctity, moral courage and personal sacrifice should mark the life of Christian shepherds. Only so would they be able to speak with moral and spiritual conviction, and be able to steer young people from being absorbed with the hourly updates on the stock markets to sit under the tutelage of

Jesus Christ. And perhaps some would hear the call to be another St Anthony, or Mother Teresa, or Bonhoeffer in this generation.

It is not my aim to provide a litany of the urgent tasks which press daily upon the present leadership in the Hong Kong Anglican Church. Many of them are already under severe strain in maintaining the network of schools, social-service centres, and churches of the diocese. My purpose is to clarify the broader horizons which have steered Anglicans in the past. Then perhaps we can approach our daily tasks and make decisions in a more theologically informed manner. We are invited, along the pilgrim way, to set our vision clear, never retreating from controversies which arise from the Gospel, and continue to drink deep from the springs of theological heritage in which we grow up. We should continue in all circumstances to uphold before the world and our partner Churches the vision of an apostolic community, a national Church, and above all, ourselves as lovers of God, to the glory of God.

Revisioning our Church as a community of belonging: a task for all

Peter B. Price

The 1998 Lambeth Conference is not only the last to be held in the second millennium, but also comes at the end of a century which has seen the effective end of Christendom. 'And still nothing new has begun.'[1] In addition to a perceived end of Christendom and the Constantinian era, the twentieth century ends with a questioning of establishments of every kind, ecclesial, political, social and economic. Economically, the collapse of Soviet socialism iconized by the fall of the Berlin Wall in 1989 also marks the end of an era, and the questioning of economic priorities. Of course the ends of eras are not neat and tidy, and, as Douglas John Hall has reflected, 'the social and religious climate which made the establishment possible in the first place, and sustained it for many centuries still pertains'.[2]

Who has the say?

In the minds of many within the Church the Lambeth Conference represents the dominant concerns of those who have the say over against those who have no say. Let two women's voices be symptomatic of those who *have no say*: one Irish woman spoke for many when she said 'As a lay person, I have the impression that the official leaders of the Church often speak for me and sometimes at me, but rarely or never with me ... If the official Church doesn't listen to the feelings of the people of God, it will lose the emotional allegiance of its members.'[3] While a leading lay woman[4] in Korea observed ' "In due course" is the most popular clerical response on a whole range of issues regarding women, including church programmes, synodical structures, as well as the more contentious issue of ordination'.

Revisioning the Church – a task for bishops and people

No one envies the bishops the task of revisioning the Church for the twenty-first century, but this is what they increasingly must do if there is to be a viable future for the Communion. The process of listening to the real questions of people and arriving at answers should provide a basis and environment for revisioning an ecclesiology. It is to rediscover the Church as *home* – a place of *belonging* – an *ecclesia* not *for* the people but *of* the people.

Signs in the wind – 'pushing against the complacent centre'

There are signs in the wind. Lambeth 1988 met against the background of a worldwide burgeoning pentecostal movement exposing a capacity not only to wean away the faithful from mainline traditions such as Anglicans and Roman Catholics, but to successfully evangelize the unchurched. The growth, for example, of independent Churches in Africa, Asia and Latin America can only be described as phenomenal, particularly with their emphasis on the supernatural and miraculous. Much of this energy continues to drive ecclesial movements in the 1990s.

In the 1970s and 1980s the growth of the Latin American *comunidades de base* following both Vatican II (1962–65) and the subsequent Conferences of Latin American Bishops at Medellín (1968), Puebla (1979) and Santo Domingo (1992), with their emphases on a theological preferential option for the poor, are examples within the Roman Catholic tradition. For many, such communities represented the creation of 'households of justice' in situations where people had suffered for the lack of justice.

Alternative movements within Anglicanism

With less formal process but no less significance, alternative movements have sprung up within Anglicanism. Examples are to be found in base communities in the informal townships of South Africa; Houses of Sharing in Korea among the Minjung – the poor or 'ordinary people'; and the effective 'Women Church' movements initially formed around the issue of ordination.

In Rwanda following the holocaust, groups led by *animateurs* skilled in self-empowerment are helping people work towards solving the problems that have so tragically divided the region. Many begin with Bible study, then the group is encouraged to talk over a particular community problem. Initially the reaction is 'The leader must tell us what to do, and take all the decisions'. One *animateur* comments 'We try to show them that community efforts often fail because people will not share in the decision-making. They just wait for someone else.' Speaking of another group, she recalls 'A different group we met last July told us they had no land to grow food, no seeds. We helped them talk over their problems. We visited in November and they were proud to show us their field of potatoes. They have really understood that they are capable of helping themselves and achieving their aims.'[5]

A revisioned Church – as a community of belonging

Listening to such voices from the South, and the concerns they represent, provides important elements to revisioning the Church into the third millennium. Voices from the North need hearing too. One commentator has reflected recently that 'Globalisation is frightening to the non-elite (the vast majority) simply because it is anti-home'.[6] There is an important theological connection between 'home' and 'justice'. 'The heart of justice is participation in God's economy or God's household. Unless the power of God's love creates household, justice will disintegrate into meaninglessness.'[7]

Any attempt to revision the Church of the twenty-first century needs to have due regard for the value of 'belonging' and the creation of a household of justice. My own experience of ministry has frequently brought me into contact with those who have no sense of 'belonging'. I offer three examples. In the early 1970s I helped to create a congregation on an outer-city estate in England. New residents were being housed in a large new building development nearby. Members of the congregation visited, welcoming folk with information about the locality, and frequently with gifts of flowers and cakes. It was a heady time. Over the next few months we noticed that no one came to the church from among the new neighbours. During a parish visit a woman approached me and said 'I am pleased to see you. You are probably wondering why none of us are coming to church. We have felt very welcomed and people have been so kind to us. But, you see, we would not know what to do if we came.'

Towards the end of the 1980s on one of London's many soulless inner-city estates, I worked with a small ecumenical group among people who saw themselves as 'refugees' within institutional religion. Individually, most of the group went to different local churches. Those churches were engaged in many good things, but did not have the pastoral models and agenda to enable people to find hope in situations where the physical environment was frequently both depressing and dangerous.

During a visit to Bangalore, India in 1996 I spent time with a Hindu community of street people during the festival of Deepavali. Some Christian theological students had, at the suggestion of their principal, helped to empower these people by enabling them to obtain basic citizenship rights and health care. The community, after years of dislocation, and infighting, called itself Deenajana, literally meaning 'Now people'. Like the 'foreigners without citizenship' mentioned by 1 Peter, these who were 'once a *non-people*; . . . *now* are a *people*' (1 Peter 2.10; author's emphasis).

A revisioned Church – as a community of economic re-ordering

Economic growth in the world's developed countries during the past 50 years has paradoxically led to the fragmentation of family, of community and of a sense of belonging. The drive for material prosperity with its attendant philosophies of individualism and 'letting the market dictate' has led to a culture that focuses on the needs of the self rather than the other.

The Lambeth Conference is being held against the demise of economic socialism, a heightened awareness of the realities of the limitations of capitalism, and the pressing need for remission of debt for the poorest countries. Movements such as Jubilee 2000 fall within what Ulrich Duchrow has identified as 'the biblical model of prophetic criticism of power and legal regulations'. He believes that such a movement has the capacity to show 'its significance and its power' and 'in practice this approach means that churches and theology today should take part in alliances within civil society and so begin to develop an alternative counter force'.[8]

A Communion such as ours needs an evangel and ecclesiology that

397

creates and nurtures community and social solidarity. If the South is not to fall into the capitalist idolatry of the North, it must learn and teach from its own experience. The African concept of *Ubuntu* offers a philosophy of belonging. *Ubuntu* means 'humanity', and simply stated reflects:

> I am because we are
> I am a person because of other people
> I am a person because of community
> No one is outside of community.

This could be a lesson for us all, which leads to contextual theologies, appropriate ecclesiologies, and what might be called jubilee economics.

A revisioned Church flexible in authority and structure

What is at stake is the continued material viability of the Communion. Few people wish to see an end to the Church, and the idea that ecclesiastical offices can simply be dispensed with in favour of some kind of charismatic structure is fanciful in the extreme. One theologian when asked why she stays in the Church responds by saying 'First of all, I don't stay within. That's not the terminology I would use. I am the church. We are the church. And then, where would one go? Nothing's perfect.'[9] But neither authority, nor loyalty to authority, can be taken for granted any more. 'Authority in the church', argues Hall, 'must always reflect this proviso: for the better realization of its vocation; for the life of the world. For the church does not exist for itself, but to be a *witnessing* community, whose witness is meant for the enhancement of all creaturely existence.'[10] What is required is flexibility both of authority and of structure.

A revisioned Church as the Jesus society

Revisioning is about recognizing our belonging, the discernment of God in the 'ordinary' could lead to a 're-embedding' of the Church as household in the heart of the community. We should not be over anxious to maintain homogeneity, if by so doing we stifle belonging by the disinherited and dispossessed. The witness of the Church must not be impaired by the inflexibility of either its structures or authority. Above all it must bear testimony to Jesus who says 'in his society there is a new way to live:

> you show wisdom, by trusting people;
> you handle leadership, by serving;
> you handle offenders, by forgiving;
> you handle money, by sharing;

you handle enemies, by loving;
and you handle violence, by suffering.

Because this is a Jesus society, and you repent, not by feeling bad, but by *thinking different*.'[11] And then something new will have begun.

Notes

1 Frei Betto, 'Comment: how Frei Betto sees us', *New Blackfriars* (January 1988), pp. 2–3.
2 Douglas John Hall, *Thinking the Faith: Christian Theology in a North American Context* (Chicago: Fortress, 1991), p. 206.
3 An anonymous woman quoted by Sean Fagan, 'The vocation and mission of the laity' in William Jenkinson and Helene O'Sullivan (eds), *Trends in Mission: Towards the Third Millennium* (Maryknoll, NY: Orbis, 1991).
4 In conversation with the author in Seoul in 1993.
5 From the *Newsletter* of E. Honore (December 1996).
6 Larry Elliott, 'Pulling up home roots', *The Guardian* (7 July 1997).
7 Wayne Meeks, *God the Economist: The Doctrine of God and Political Economy* (Chicago: Fortress, 1989), p. 36.
8 Ulrich Duchrow, 'Christianity in the context of globalised capitalistic markets', *Concilium*, 97/2 (Edinburgh: T. & T. Clark, 1997), p. 41.
9 In Winter *Sojourners*, p. 19.
10 Hall, op. cit., p. 445.
11 Rudy Wiebe, *The Blue Mountains of China* (Toronto: McClelland and Stewart), pp. 215–16.

The future of the mission agency

Diana Witts

'Where do you see the mission agencies now and where do you see them going over the next ten years?'

A moment of opportunity

The mission agencies of the Anglican Communion are at a crucial stage of change and development. The traditional sending agencies of the West are making a radical re-assessment of their role in international mission and are exploring fresh ways of working together with partners from around the world. New mission structures are emerging from the Churches of the South, many of which are at a formative stage in shaping their steadily growing response to the challenge of world mission. This is an exciting and creative moment for the Communion as all member Churches seek to be obedient to their calling to participate in the *Missio Dei*. This is a moment when a paradigm shift in patterns of mission is needed in order to respond effectively to challenges of a rapidly changing world.

How is the world changing? It may be helpful to look next at some of the major changes that are happening around the world that most closely affect current and future patterns of mission.

The changing context of mission

In recent years the centre of gravity of the Christian world has been moving steadily from North to South. There are now more Christians in Latin America, sub-Saharan Africa and South and East Asia than in the old strongholds of Christianity in Europe and North America. This demographic shift is reflected in the Anglican Communion, where many of the largest and fastest growing Churches are in Africa and parts of Asia. This means that the greatest people resources for mission are to be found in the Churches of the South.

The economic power-centre of the world is moving from the Atlantic Rim to the Pacific Rim as the tiger economies of East Asia overtake the economies of western Europe. At the same time global economic structures produce an ever-increasing gap between the wealth of industrialized countries and the poverty of debt-burdened countries of the Two-Thirds World. As a result many of the Churches that are richest in people resources have few financial resources, and vice versa.

This mismatch between people and financial resources calls for new initiatives of partnership within the World Church. In the nineteenth century British-based agencies had all the people resources of the Evangelical Awakening *and* the financial resources of the Industrial Revolution. Today we are in a very different position, with the people resources in some of the poorest countries of the world and many of the financial resources still tied up in the post-Christian West and in the minority Christian communities of East Asia. A notable exception comes from the Pacific Rim, where the South Korean Churches are wealthy in both people and finance and are thus able to send out large numbers of people in mission.

There has been dramatic growth in the number of mission agencies from the South over the last 40 years. Countries such as Brazil, India, Congo and Korea are rapidly becoming major sending countries in Christian mission.

There have been some such initiatives from within the Anglican Communion (see below, p. 403), but in general the pattern has not been widely reflected. Does this mean that some Anglicans in the South have inherited a 'pastoral' rather than 'mission' model of being Church?

The greatest Church growth is happening among Pentecostal, Independent and 'New' Churches. The more traditional historic families of Churches – Orthodox, Roman Catholic and Protestant – remain static (as a percentage of the population) or contract. This means that the World Council of Churches is becoming increasingly unrepresentative of the worldwide Christian family.

Rising fundamentalism is affecting at least three of the major world religions: Islam, Christianity and Hinduism. This has important implications for mission, in terms of both how fundamentalism can shape (or distort) mission, and how it can resist mission. A vital concern here is whether mission becomes a force for the building or for the fragmentation of community.

The political shape of the world map has changed dramatically within the last decade. The collapse of communism in many countries has given new freedom to national Churches to worship and minister openly and to be in touch with other parts of the World Church. New partnerships in mission have become possible in many places. In particular the break-up of the USSR has meant that many largely unevangelized areas of Central Asia are now accessible to Christians from neighbouring countries.

Many other factors could be mentioned in this list, such as urbanization (the growth of mega-cities and the fragility of rural economies), the growing proportion of young people within the world community, the rising refugee population, etc. All these, and other factors, affect the mission of the Churches.

The response of the traditional mission agencies

The traditional mission agencies of the 'West' (i.e. those based in Australia, Britain, Canada, Ireland, New Zealand and the USA) are re-evaluating their role in the light of the changing context described above. Many of these agencies belong to Churches that are set in a post-Christian society, which means that their support bases are in decline. It also means that mission *to* the West has been recognized as an urgent priority, and many of these agencies have already played a significant role in enabling their own Churches to receive the gifts of the World Church in mission. In Britain in recent years a significant number of people from around the world (mainly from the Churches of Africa and Asia) have been brought by the mission agencies to Britain to help the British Churches in their own task of

Diana Witts

mission. This is a pattern that is becoming common elsewhere as well and 'South–North mission' has started to become a reality.

Both partner Churches and mission agencies have been trying hard to overcome patterns of paternalism and dependency inherited from the past. Much progress has been made, and relationships are transformed whenever a genuine, two-way sharing of gifts in mission becomes a reality. However, economic imbalances continue to distort many relationships. While mission agencies are trying to ensure that their involvement is focused on mission priorities, some economically dependent Churches still look to their 'parent' agency as the one who will come to their rescue in order to help to maintain the structures of the Church. This is at the root of continuing tension, and represents a dilemma from which all parties long to be freed.

The idea of 'Moratorium' that came from East Africa in the 1960s has largely been dropped in recent years. The theological reality that within the Body of Christ we all have need of one another, and that the gifts of the Spirit are given to all God's people for the building up of the whole body (1 Cor 12.4–13), has been affirmed. Interdependence, not independence, is the Christian ideal.

Mission agencies are being invited to share in the mission of their partner Churches in a wide variety of ways. Training for mission has become a priority in many places, and new centres for such training are being opened in the South. These will be added to the many well-established centres in the North that have already become a major resource for the Communion as a whole.

Other areas of involvement include community development, primary health care, theological education, information technology and advocacy. Agencies can act as a voice for the voiceless in situations of war, persecution and poverty. The need for work among refugees increases all the time as the refugee population around the world grows. Work for reconciliation and peace is urgently needed in the context of continuing divisions within communities. Mission in the context of multi-faith communities is a first priority for many Churches. All this involvement will continue to be needed for the foreseeable future.

Most agencies have a significant programme for the provision of scholarships in order to enhance the education and experience of lay and ordained Church leaders. Mission training centres such as Selly Oak, in Birmingham, though still preparing mission partners from Europe, have now diversified, to become centres of excellence in mission theology and practice, where the South–South encounter is central, as experienced leaders from all over the world learn from each other. These opportunities are now also increasingly balanced by study in centres in the South itself, supported also by the mission agencies.

402

Agencies have sometimes been able to facilitate South–South move-ments in mission by making appropriate links, and then by providing some modest financial support such as the provision of air fares. For instance, in Britain USPG and CMS jointly acted in this way in 1996 in order to enable an Indian Christian from Delhi to go as a mission partner to a parish on the outskirts of Johannesburg, where many of the local people are of Indian origin. The Indian priest has brought with him an understanding of Hinduism and Islam that is greatly needed in this multi-ethnic, multi-cultural, multi-faith community. A similar initiative enabled a young woman social worker from Brazil (a Portuguese-speaker) to go to Maputo in Mozambique to help the Church there in the urgent task of the rebuilding of community following the civil war. These are just two recent examples of South–South movements in mission – a part of mission from Everywhere to Everywhere.

The emergence of mission agencies from the South

The first mission structure to emerge from within the Anglican Churches of the South was the Indian Missionary Society which was founded in the (then Anglican) Church in South India in 1903. Although many local initiatives have been taken within countries since then, the Church of Nigeria has become the next Church in the Communion to set up a national agency for the purpose of local and international mission. The Church of Nigeria Missionary Society (CNMS) was formed in 1996 through a decision of the Provincial Standing Committee. Although introduced through provincial structures, the CNMS has a layman as Chairman of its Council, and is responsible for raising its own support and appointing its own officers and mission personnel. The aim of the CNMS is to send missionaries (lay and ordained) to northern Nigeria and then to elsewhere in Africa – and the rest of the world.

The membership of the Church of Nigeria is an estimated ten million Christians, so the establishing of the CNMS releases potentially a huge resource of people for mission. There are many large Anglican Churches in sub-Saharan Africa, so if some of the other African Provinces were to take a similar step the whole shape of mission in the Anglican Communion could change.

A number of mission structures have come into being in recent years around the Communion. For instance the Anglican Church in Singapore has a Board of Mission which co-ordinates the sending of missionaries who are supported on a congregational basis. In the Diocese of Sabah the Anglican Interior Mission sends missionaries into the unevangelized areas of the country. Within the Church of the Province of Kenya there are

Diana Witts

Diocesan Missionary Associations which support evangelists working in the remoter areas of the country. These are just some examples, and they give a taste of the diversity of mission activity that already exists.

Much involvement in mission is also being undertaken by Churches that have no formally designated structures for mission. In some Provinces the work of mission and evangelism is being carried out faithfully by committed church members, lay and ordained, and in many places, especially in Africa, through the Mothers' Union. A Church that has no organization that is identified as a mission agency can still be active in mission. However, history suggests that where enthusiasts for mission are able to act together and provide a focus for mission for the whole Church, this can release energy for mission in a particularly effective way.

At their 1997 meeting in Kuala Lumpur the Churches of the South expressed a strong commitment to mission and evangelism. It will be very exciting to see how this commitment can lead to a shared movement in mission throughout the Communion.

The future

The challenge of poverty

The United Nations has recognized this as the overwhelming challenge facing its members in the opening decades of the twenty-first century. This reality is experienced by church members on a day-to-day level throughout the world, and this includes a recognition of the great disparities of wealth and poverty there are between Churches, and within Churches. The mission agencies, through their practical experience of poverty within the variety of contexts in which they work, have an economically small, but symbolically important role in the sharing of resources and, in their medical, educational and development work, in providing a contribution at a local level, to alleviating the crippling burdens of so many.

But, perhaps, equally significantly, they can play a part in the kind of advocacy work that involves coalitions such as that of Jubilee 2000. This focuses the attention of governments, financial agencies and multinational companies, to the realities of such problems as international debt, and also to the debilitating effects of such not only for the indebted but also for the donors.

In all such efforts, central will be the theological recognition that the poor and excluded have a special place in God's heart. Promoting justice and sharing of resources is a vital part of the proclaiming of the reconciling work of God in Christ for all, and the furthering of His kingdom. In this, as in other things, they clearly do not act on their own, but as part of the whole Church, which itself is being moved to such action.

A new way of being Church

Because of their worldwide involvement, mission agencies are well placed to discover ways that Christian communities are living and working together in new and sometimes radical ways. Such communities may never become the norm, but can provide alternative ways for being Church that can be an encouragement for all who are willing to learn from them. The same can be said for alternative patterns of ministry and of theological learning. Mission agencies can provide opportunities for people to learn from each other about such initiatives, as they enable people to meet across geographical and cultural boundaries.

New patterns of mission

Would it be possible, within the next ten years, to see a network of mission agencies established across the Anglican Communion that would involve every member Church? Information about needs and opportunities for mission could then be matched with information about resources available. Such a network would enable mission resources to be moved freely across the Communion in multidirectional ways. Thanks to modern technology this could be done without setting up heavy central structures – the Internet functions as a communication network that has no centre. Could Missio help to make this dream a reality? The Anglican Communion, blessed with the diverse riches of a worldwide family of Churches, is in a unique position to be able to bring such a vision into being.

Such a network would enable the movement of people from Everywhere to Everywhere to become a reality. Partnerships could become multilateral as different resources were brought together in any given situation of mission opportunity. For instance the resources for mission in France might come from the Anglican Churches in Congo (people), Britain (finance), Singapore (training), etc.

If such a dream were to become a reality the hope would be that the new mission agencies of the South would develop totally fresh models of mission. Traditional models of sending and receiving people internationally in mission are highly cost-intensive and may no longer be appropriate for the new situation.

Diana Witts

New relationships in mission

Relationships with other Churches are also important as agencies seek that unity with one another which alone will enable the world to believe (John 17.23). Ecumenical partnerships are often the best and most effective way of bringing together the resources needed for mission. Mission agencies relating to the United Churches of India, Pakistan and Bangladesh have already been brought together across denominational divides in a situation where an ecumenical response has been the only possibility. This 'forced' getting-together has been a real gift to the agencies as they have started to discover the richness of working together – a step that they might not otherwise have taken.

In every place the local church is the primary agent of mission. This important principle is fully recognized throughout the Anglican Communion and is honoured by all mission agencies. However, this principle can sometimes be inadequate – what, for instance, do we do when there is no local church? There are still some two billion people in the world, a third of the total population, who have never had any meaningful opportunity to hear the Gospel of Jesus Christ. There are 30 countries in which over half the population are 'unevangelized' in this sense. In many of these countries the small number of local Christians are not free to come together as an organized 'church' group, and in most of these countries there is no Anglican Church. So how do we, as Anglicans, respond to this challenge?

We could avoid the challenge by continuing to be involved in mission only in those situations where there is already an established Anglican Church. However, many Churches within the Communion are starting to become aware of the needs of the wider world; for instance Christians in Pakistan are hearing a call to the newly-accessible countries of Central Asia. Christians in South Asia are aware of the needs of the countries of the Mekong basin, and in Africa Kenyans are becoming aware of the need for the Gospel in the unevangelized countries of the Horn of Africa. The leaders of the Church of Nigeria Missionary Society are aware that across their northern border lies the largely unevangelized country of Niger.

In all these situations the definition of the local Church can be widened to mean the nearest Church, even though it may be in a neighbouring country. This Church can then call for partners to go with them (or to share resources in some other way) in taking fresh initiatives in the unevangelized area. There may be Christians of other traditions already working in the area, in which case ecumenical partnerships may be appropriate. In either case the serving of the *Missio Dei*, rather than the planting of Anglican Churches, will be the primary concern.

406

Further reading

A *Growing Partnership: The Church of England and World Mission* (London: Church House, 1994).

Michael Nazir-Ali, *From Everywhere to Everywhere* (London: Collins, 1991).

Cyril Okorocha, *The Cutting Edge of Mission* (London: ACC, 1996).

Larry Pate, *From Every People: A Handbook of Two-Thirds World Missions* (Monrovia, CA: MARC California, 1989).

P. Price, *Seeds of the Word* (London: Darton, Longman and Todd, 1996).

V. Samuel and C. Sugden, *AD 2000 and Beyond* (Oxford: Regnum, 1991).

A vision for the Anglican contribution in the minority context of Korea over the next decade

Jeremiah Guen Seok Yang

Christianity was first introduced into Korea 200 years ago, at the end of the eighteenth century. It was a result of the voluntary effort of Korean intellectuals, not by the direct intervention of missionaries.[1] As a result the Korean Catholic Church came into being. Protestant mission in Korea began at the end of the nineteenth century, when the last dynasty of Korea was shattered by foreign imperial powers and Korea became a battlefield for the colonial power struggle to dominate North-east Asia, culminating in the Japanese colonial conquest and colonization of Korea in 1910. Protestant missions in Korea, including the Anglican, started in this miserable period of Korean history. When the first Anglican missionary bishop, John Corpe, wrote that 'it is like going to a battlefield with a small ferry boat',[2] he was not simply expressing his feeling as a lonely adventurer, for Korea was truly a battlefield.

Life in this small peninsula has for the last century been in the vortex of all sorts of confrontations and wars – wars among foreign colonial powers, between Koreans and colonial powers, the Second World War, and the Korean war – the Cold War fought on Korean soil. Millions of lives were sacrificed. Since the 1950s, this country has been divided into North and

South in ideological confrontation. In the international scene, the so-called Cold War seems to have passed away. But it is still very vividly alive in this small peninsula.

The division is more than a simple geographical separation but reproduces all sorts of social antagonism, both North and South.[3] Military and civil autocracy, class and sexual discrimination, regional confrontation, religious and cultural exclusivism (including excessive denominationalism within Christianity) have developed and legitimized themselves within this system. Moreover, people have internalized the divisive spirit and ideology. Even religious teachings and the interpretations of their scriptures have been contaminated by the system, legitimizing confrontation and war between North and South.[4] It is a kind of psychological and spiritual disease as well as socio-political-economic confrontation. Although the miracle economic development in the South is admired and propagated as a remedy for all these problems, the individual and collective disease of division needs a more fundamental healing process.

The Christian mission in Korea is now called to this fundamental healing process within which the vision for a new humanity and community has to be found. The Anglican Church of Korea is still a minority Church, having less than 1 per cent of all Christians in Korea. We are still nothing more than a small ferry boat which looks too weak to cope with such a great missionary task. But we can renew our active participation in the Korean struggle to reunite our community, thereby inscribing the work of our Church upon the hearts of the Korean people. We are not alone in this struggle. There are historical religions, other Christians, and competing political groups in this land. They have wasted their energies because of confrontation. We are now called to find the possibilities for repentance and the yearnings for reconciliation. Within this struggle to overcome division, Anglicans have to be reborn as an authentic Korean Church.

The Anglican Church of Korea is a minority not only within Korean religions and Christian Churches, but also within the World Anglican Communion. It is distinguished from other partner Churches in that it has a distinctive historical experience of mission. We are not one of the former British colonies. Of course, this does not mean that the Anglican Church of Korea is absolutely free from the suspicion of cultural colonialism, the so-called 'Anglo-Saxon captivity' of the Anglican Communion.[5]

This fact that we are a minority not only within Korean religious society but also within the World Anglican Communion makes the identity crisis more acute. In the colonial missionary period, the identity of Christian Churches in Asia or Africa was imported as a ready-made form from European home Churches. Now, the identity crisis in Asian and African Churches is not the issue of importation, translation or adaptation, but of forming it from their own peoples' life and struggle. We do not want to be a branch of the European Church in Korea,[6] but an authentic Korean Church which finds its reason to exist in Korea from the Korean people's struggle for the new human community. We believe that this is the way for us to participate as a responsible member in the World Anglican Communion.

We share the Anglican heritage with other Communion members. However, our more important concern is directed to the Anglicans' particular historical experience or process through which they have discovered their historic faith. Gospel and theology are incarnational in their own natures. Therefore, the Gospel can be heard as a living word for peoples in various cultures, and thus theology has to be truly contextualized or localized. The Church also has to be built as the body of Christ truly incarnated into the various peoples' life and struggle. It can never be totalized.

The unity in diversity, as an ecumenical spirit, creates a theological tension: the conflict between those who focus on unity and those who focus on diversity is never settled. One is looking for non-negotiable fixed boundaries, emphasizing the priority of unity; the other is trying to deconstruct the boundaries for the fully incarnated Church and its contextualized theology. But we can never give up both unity and diversity. We have to find the mature way to keep a healthy tension, rather than to give it up. For us, as a minority Church, to see the Korean Church fully incarnated into the Korean soil is surely our primary task. We also want to rediscover the unity in those Churches fully incarnated into the diverse religious, cultural, racial and political settings.

The spirit of the Via Media as an historical heritage of the Anglican Communion is therefore understood as a missionary spirit encouraging us to build an authentic Korean Church and to reflect and rediscover continuously the unity or the catholicity of the Christian Church. It demands of us to renew commitment to our people's life and struggle, to rediscover the truth of Gospel in this commitment, and to work out an authentic Korean Anglican Church, which is faithful to God and responsible for Korean peoples.

This struggle, together with all Korean Christians, will be a new experience of the liberating Christ, present in his word and in the new Christian community. These are our visions and reflections reading out of the Anglican reformation history and the new mission experience in this post-colonial and post-missionary period. Therefore, the basic mission principle for the Anglican Church of Korea is the rebirth of the Church through participation in the struggle of the Korean people.

As I said before, the division is the concrete place in which Korean people now struggle for their future. Diverse religions and ideologies are living together, sometimes conflicting and sometimes co-operating. Class and sexual divisions are also collaborating with this division system.

The primary missionary task for all of us living in this divided land is 'reconciliation'. The reconciliation does not mean just the political settlement of the antagonistic confrontation between the North and the South. Division is a spiritual and physical disease ruling all aspects of our lives on both sides. It works in all dimensions of politics, economics, cultures and religions, and in all sorts of conflicts between groups and individuals. All aspects and dimensions are working as a kind of organic system. The political and territorial division provide the useful bases for the oppression and exploitation of peoples. The oppression and exploitation reproduce conflicts, confrontations and inhumane competition. These further legitimize and perpetuate the political division. Therefore, the reconciliation we have to accomplish is a fundamental destruction of this division system.

For this fundamental reconciliation, first of all, we need a deep theological reflection on the mission carried on during the last half-century. Church, mission and theology in this period have been developed under the division system. They are not only the system's victims but also the system's agents. They have been distorted by the system and also have reproduced the division system within the Church and society. We have to re-examine carefully and critically this ambivalent character of the Korean Church. Moreover, it should reach to the deep spiritual repentance of our sins that we have internalized the division. As I think, the critical reflection of the Church, its mission and theology has to be the beginning point of the theology for peace and reconciliation in this divided land.

A minority can be a very effective catalyst for this critical theological reflection and for working out a theology of true repentance, reconciliation and peace. The minority can more easily overcome the self-distortions made in the period of division. We can be a small ferry boat which can take decisive action before the big ships which cannot give up their vested interests.

Secondly, what we need is a dialogical solidarity for peace and reconciliation. All things in the division system are ambivalent. All are both sufferers and offenders. They have at the same time both hope and frustration. In dialogue, however, the Church can rediscover and strengthen our hope for a new world in the midst of ambivalence. It is a process to read the signs of hope from ourselves and others. Moreover, it is a critical dialogue to invite all participants to a deep self-reflection in the sensitivity of the existence of others. All different religions and ideologies are partners in this dialogue. This is the dialogical solidarity through which all of them are reborn and see a common vision for a new humanity and community. I believe Anglicans can find their own true identity within this process of self-discovery and self-renewal for a common vision. In this sense, the Korean struggle for overcoming the division provides an opportunity for us and others to find a true reason to exist in this divided land and to experience the solidarity for a common cause.

Thirdly, we have to renew our participation in the ecumenical movement within Korea. Confrontational and exclusive denominationalism of Korean Churches is the greatest obstacle to proclaiming the Gospel within this divided land. Such denominational competition originates from colonial mission policies. Even now, each denomination is looking for its continuity as a historical Church from its mission agencies in Europe or America. Their common experiences of colonialism, war and division do not inform the denominations' own self-understandings. This colonialism still works within Korean Churches and keeps them from finding the necessary common ground in the present struggle of Koreans. The unity of Churches is not what should be confirmed only in remote antiquity. We have to listen to the urgent demands coming from the present. There is a strong voice expecting the common efforts of Churches to overcome the division of Korea. This is the real foundation for the unity of Korean Churches.

Fourthly, we need a thorough re-examination of our relationship to Christ in our mission, evangelism and ministry. The Anglican Church of Korea has failed relatively in quantitative growth, when we compare with the enormous growth of other Christian denominations in such a short period. But we need to think seriously about the fact that the collapse of social morality has increased and accelerated in nearly inverse proportion to the numerical growth of Christian Churches in this country! Although Christians are more than 30 per cent of the whole population in Korea, their contribution to this country has never been only positive. Christian Churches also have internalized the cruel competitive system of capitalist society within itself. It is true that, to a certain extent, the numerical growth of Christian Churches has even resulted from the Christians' uncritical compromise with the capitalist principle of competition. Therefore, we don't need to think that our failure is only in size. More fundamentally, our problem is in our blurred relationship with Christ and his Gospel. What we really need to reflect is whether our mission practices are really based on our faithful relationship with Christ, and whether we witness truly good news for this divided and struggling world. The renewal of our mission and ministry should not be an attempt to catch up the numerical growth of other Churches in Korea but a recovery of the faithful relationship with Christ.

Finally, I hope that the Anglican Church of Korea becomes a Church doing all its efforts to show the vision for a new humanity, new human relationship, and new community. For these purposes, Church life and structure should be radically renewed. Worship, liturgy and education within the Church have to be the activities to witness Christ as the King of peace and reconciliation, and to realize an equal and peaceful relationship among all members. All hierarchical and discriminating relationships, between clergy and lay, between male and female, or among generations and classes, have to be reconciled and restructured so that a true fellowship (*koinonia*) has to be realized first within the Church. Expecting a new decade and a new millennium, I hope that this small minority Church, the Anglican Church of Korea, can become a true light for Koreans who struggle to find a new life.

Notes

1 The first Korean Christian community was established by the leadership of a group of young Confucians in the last dynasty. They read books which were written by Jesuit missionaries in China. In their effort to reform their own Confucian society, they adopted and re-interpreted Christianity in their Confucian context and established voluntarily a distinctive Korean-style Christian community. See Guen Seok Yang, 'Korean biblical hermeneutics old and new: a criticism of Korean reading practices' (thesis submitted to the Faculty of Arts of the University of Birmingham for the degree of Doctor of Philosophy, 1997), pp. 1–54.
2 Lee Jae Joung, *The Centenary History of Anglican Church of Korea* (Seoul: The Publishing Board of the Anglican Church of Korea, 1990), p. 32.
3 See Paik Nag-chung, 'South Korea: unification and democratic challenge', *New Left Review* (1993), p. 197. Here, he understands the division as a 'system'.
4 See NCCK, 'Declaration of the Churches of Korea on national reunification and peace' in World Alliance of Reformed Church (ed.), *Testimonies of Faith in Korea*, pp. 291–307.
5 About the efforts to overcome Anglo-Saxon cultural captivity within the world Anglican Communion, see John S. Pobee, 'Newer dioceses of Anglican Communion – movement and prospect' in Stephen Sykes and John Booty (eds), *The Study of Anglicanism* (London: SPCK, 1988), pp. 393–405; Mandy Goedhals, 'From paternalism to partnership? The Church of the Province of South Africa and mission 1848–1988' in Frank England and Torquil Paterson (eds), *Bounty in Bondage* (Johannesburg: Ravan Press, 1989), pp. 104–29; Luke Pato, 'Becoming an African Church' in England and Paterson (eds), *Bounty in Bondage*, pp. 159–76.
6 Aloysius Pieris SJ, *An Asian Theology of Liberation* (New York: Orbis, 1988), pp. 35–6.

Afterword by the
Archbishop of Canterbury

So where are we going? On the threshold of the third millennium, what if anything does Anglicanism have to offer our world? There are, after all, plenty of doom and gloom merchants around who are only too ready to tell us that Anglicanism is a dying tradition, that all mainstream Churches are locked into a *modus operandi* which is doomed in the modern world. On the one hand, there are those who point to the extraordinary progress of humanity over the last century to demonstrate that we have no need of God. On the other, many of the great world faiths are being challenged by powerful movements within themselves which preach extreme forms of fundamentalism allied with political and cultural messages which seem to have blossomed from extreme right-wing philosophies. Their mission, notably aimed at the poorest communities in the world, is often undergirded by offers of material and financial support, and can be seriously disruptive to community life. They are direct, forceful, and have little regard for ecclesiastical politics of structures. They are also very successful.

We must heed these challenges. They are real and they are substantial. But I am concerned by how readily some people within our own Anglican tradition are seduced by one or other of them, or else fall into gloom themselves. I was recently encouraged, however, to read something by a well-known Catholic writer in England, Donald Nicholl, who sadly died a short time ago. He was leading a meditation at the St Theosevia Centre for Christian Spirituality in Oxford a few years ago, and dealing with the problem of the growing abandonment of faith. He was struck by a conversation he had with a young girl about nuclear weapons. She had suggested to him that, given the condition of the human heart, even if such weapons were abandoned, they would soon be reinvented. Donald Nicholl, reflecting on the truth of these words, went on to say:

> Surely it is vital for Christians these days to grasp the truth of what the young girl said, because nowadays, do you not find that so many

413

> Christians are filled with gloom and despondency because they see so
> much contempt for our faith? But what we have got to remember is that
> in spite of all our failings and our wretchedness, it is actually only
> believers who are actively engaged in the one thing necessary, the task of
> redemption, which can only happen if there is a change of heart. . . . And
> that lays an enormous responsibility on us. But with the responsibility
> comes energy. Once we assume responsibility we get tremendous
> energy. We get no energy through gloom and despondency.

That is a very important reflection. We are called to take responsibility.
Whether it is issues over which we are divided within the Church, or the
enormous challenges to work for peace and justice in our world, we have a
responsibility to God and to one another to change human hearts, to offer
all people the opportunity of transformation in the Gospel of redemption.
If we take on that responsibility, we will be given fresh energy with which
to pursue the task.

Now, it is easy to say that our divisions are so wide that there is no point
in expending our energy in transforming them, that we should simply get
on with our own lives, pursuing our own journey of faith, and leaving
others to sort themselves out. But what sort of message of hope is that? And
how does that tie up with the extraordinary array of stories which have been
told in this book? Let me quote again some lines from that remarkable song
with which Marc Nikkel's contribution begins, written in the midst of the
dreadful Sudanese civil war:

> Let us encourage our hearts in the hope of God
> who once breathed the breath of life into the human body . . .
>   Let us be branches of your son.
> Jesus will come with the final word of judgement,
> Bringing glory to the earth, peace and the truth of faith.

That comes out of a Church which has been through the most intense
suffering and persecution for fifteen years and more. Anyone who has been
to visit Sudanese Christians, and I have been privileged to do so twice, will
have been transformed by the experience, by their steadfastness, by their joy
and by their energy. They truly take responsibility for their people. Here
we see true ecumenism in action. Here we see every member ministry really
happening. And as Marc notes:

> Today it is the youth and the women, the widows and children of war,
> who are frequently in the vanguard. Articulate women are amongst the
> most effective evangelists, preachers and church planters. (p. 74)

In many ways the Church in Sudan is structurally weak, but in the face of
disaster, who could deny their Godliness?

Or look at the story told by Edward Saw Marks about the Church in Myanmar. Only occasionally do we hear anything from there, although we have all come to admire the remarkable witness of Aung San Suu Kyi. But how many of know about the growth of the Church there? And how encouraging to hear about the indigenization of its mission, meeting the people where they are and passing the message of the Gospel on through art in a way which is entirely natural to the Burmese tradition. I could pick out so many more stones from every part of the Communion, but it is clear that in all sorts of contexts, Anglicans are engaged with people in their struggles, whether it be oppression, isolation, or injustice, or indeed in a struggle to live and grow in faith.

We do not deny our divisions. Throughout its history, the Church has had to deal with dissent and argument. If, at times, it is hard to see the way forward over a particular issue, we need then to demonstrate the sort of faith in our gracious God which we find in the Sudanese Church, or the Burmese Church. He will lead us forward. Unity is one of his gifts to the Church. It is we who deny his gift. And if we are to lead the world forwards, then we must do so responsibly. We can show the world that differences can be resolved peacefully, that there are ways to build justice for all, and that the Gospel of Jesus Christ is indeed Good News for all humanity. Read again those great words of St Paul in the Second Letter to the Corinthians, which have been placed at the heart of the Lambeth Conference:

> You yourselves are our letter of recommendation, written on your hearts, to be known and read by all men; and you show that you are a letter from Christ delivered by us, written not with ink but with the Spirit of the Living God, not on tablets of stone, but on tablets of human hearts. . . . Since we have such a hope we are very bold. . . . And we all, with unveiled face, beholding the glory of the Lord, are being changed into his likeness from one degree of glory into another; . . . Therefore having this ministry by the mercy of God, we do not lose heart! (2 Cor 3.2–3, 12, 18; 4.1)

The Anglican Communion, I believe, is a wonderful witness to the world. And it is, perhaps, the word 'witness' that should be the final word. At the last Lambeth Conference it was the Third World bishops who challenged the Conference to move from 'maintenance to mission'. This motion was accepted overwhelmingly and became the lynchpin of the Decade of Evangelism. This decade has seen a shift towards dynamic mission in all senses of the word – from exciting methods of evangelism to faithful service, prophetic witness and social action. It is no accident that our word 'martyr' comes from the root meaning to 'bear witness' because honest, faithful and obedient discipleship is often costly – sometimes even to death, as so many Christians know.

I believe that our Communion is in good heart, and I know that, blessed by God, we will advance into the new Millennium confident in the Gospel, humble before God's grace, and energized by the Great Commission, which is our responsibility to 'go out, and make disciples of all nations' in the knowledge that Christ is with us 'always, to the close of the age' (Matthew 28.19, 20).